Personality and
Impersonality

Daniel Albright

Personality and Impersonality

LAWRENCE, WOOLF, AND MANN

THE UNIVERSITY OF CHICAGO PRESS
Chicago and London

DANIEL ALBRIGHT is associate professor of English at the University of Virginia and the author of *The Myth against Myth: A Study of Yeats's Imagination in Old Age.*

THE UNIVERSITY OF CHICAGO PRESS, CHICAGO 60637
THE UNIVERSITY OF CHICAGO PRESS, LTD., LONDON

© 1978 by The University of Chicago
All rights reserved. Published 1978
Printed in the United States of America
82 81 80 79 78   5 4 3 2 1

Autographs of Lawrence, Woolf, and Mann courtesy of the Department of Special Collections, the University of Chicago Library.

LIBRARY OF CONGRESS CATALOGING IN PUBLICATION DATA

Albright, Daniel
  Personality and impersonality.

  Bibliography: p.
  Includes index.
  1. Lawrence, David Herbert, 1885–1930—
Characters.   2. Woolf, Virgina Stephen, 1882–1941
—Characters.   3. Mann, Thomas, 1875–1955—
Characters.   4. Psychology and literature.
I. Title.
PN3411.A4   809.3'3   77–23873
ISBN 0–226–01249–2

Contents

Acknowledgments

I thank the National Endowment for the Humanities, whose fellowship in 1973–74 allowed me to spend an extraordinarily pleasant year in Richmond, Surrey, writing a good deal of this book; and the University of Virginia, for a number of summer research grants beginning in 1970.

Scores, hundreds, of people should appear here, whose names grow indistinct in the brightness of my gratitude; but I record an Anne-Bullen's-handful of colleagues from the University of Virginia, whose intellectual assets I have appropriated and whose friendship will forgive me for mentioning their names: Cecil Lang, Robert Langbaum, Irvin Ehrenpreis, V. A. Kolve, Anthony Winner, Robert Kellogg. And I thank her who remembers and is remembered on every page, coauthor not of this book but of me, Karin Larson.

List of Works

THE NOVELS OF D. H. LAWRENCE
The White Peacock (1911)
The Trespasser (1912)
Sons and Lovers (1913)
The Rainbow (1915)
Women in Love (1920)
The Lost Girl (1920)
Aaron's Rod (1922)
Kangaroo (1923)
St. Mawr (1925)
The Plumed Serpent (1926)
Lady Chatterley's Lover (1928)
The Man Who Died (1929)
The Virgin and the Gipsy (1930)

THE NOVELS OF VIRGINIA WOOLF
The Voyage Out (1915)
Night and Day (1919)
Jacob's Room (1922)
Mrs. Dalloway (1925)
To the Lighthouse (1927)
Orlando (1928)
The Waves (1931)
Flush (1933)
The Years (1937)
Between the Acts (1941)

THE NOVELS OF THOMAS MANN
Buddenbrooks (1901)

Royal Highness (Königliche Hoheit,
  1909)
Death in Venice (Der Tod in Vene-
  dig, 1913)
The Magic Mountain (Der Zauber-
  berg, 1924)
Mario and the Magician (Mario und
  der Zauberer, 1930)
Joseph and his Brothers (Joseph und
  seine Brüder)
  I. The Tales of Jacob (Die Ge-
    schichten Jaacobs, 1933)
  II. Young Joseph (Der Junge
    Joseph, 1934)
  III. Joseph in Egypt (Joseph in
    Ägypten, 1936)
  IV. Joseph the Provider (Joseph,
    der Ernährer, 1943)
Lotte in Weimar (1939)
The Transposed Heads (Die Vertau-
  schten Köpfe, 1940)
The Tables of the Law (Das Gesetz,
  1944)
Doktor Faustus (1947)
The Holy Sinner (Der Erwählte,
  1951)
The Black Swan (Die Betrogene,
  1953)
Confessions of Felix Krull, Confi-
  dence Man (Bekenntnisse des
  Hochstaplers Felix Krull, 1954)

O N E

Introduction

It is hard for us to appreciate the need for Henry James's declaration near the turn of the century that the novel was henceforth to be considered a respectable form of art, for in our age many of the highest achievements of the sentient intellect have been called novels. Indeed, in a brief period during the first quarter of this century,. several authors attempted through the medium of the novel a project that ranks among the most ambitious ever attempted by our race: the complete depiction of the human mind, the creation of the verbal analogue of an entire personality. From 1920 to 1925 appear *Women in Love*, *Ulysses*, *The Magic Mountain*, the latter parts of *Remembrance of Things Past*, *Mrs. Dalloway*, and Yeats's *A Vision*, books which have little in common except the enormousness of the author's sensibility, a certain loosening of the boundaries between character and character so that all thought, emotion, perception, gesture will appear to be the reflex of a single controlling mind. In these books, the first climax of modern literature, the traditional apparatus of the nineteenth-century novel is wholly subverted in order that self-expression may be at last perfected: the author pays little regard to the consistency of behavior, the idiosyncrasy, the distinctness of his characters, for he conceives his characters only as versions of himself, fractured into some fable only because the mind is dynamic and can never conceive itself in its totality. Thus in *Ulysses* Joyce will attribute his thoughts indifferently to Bloom or Dedalus as whim moves him, will delight in the shared dreams, the secret homogeneity of his great protagonists, will conduct in the Ithaca chapter an omniscient author's interrogation of his own omniscience; and in *Mrs. Dalloway* Virginia Woolf's handwriting will be legible in some public sky as her characters indulge in the easy telepathy of those who cohabit in the

1

same brain; and Proust will enclose all he touches in the labyrinth of his hyperesthesia, until the immensity of his experience rises up before his eyes like some luminous field in a painting of Rothko. Lawrence and Mann are more dialectical, prefer to create characters who epitomize, in the manner of Blake's Zoas, the scattered faculties of the fallen mind; but both are obsessed with a vision of the complete man, the single full consciousness, toward whom all their characters aspire, whom Lawrence conceives as the resurrected body or the Man Who Died, whom Mann calls Felix Krull. Yeats's *A Vision* is in some ways the fullest expression of this mighty drive toward the completion of personality, if only because, not pretending to write a novel, he was not bound to outmoded convention; nonetheless *A Vision* is a true romance of the soul, an account of the soul's progress through all possible modes of self-characterization, its exhaustion of all permutations of personality. In one passage Yeats compares his meditation to staring at his own image reflected in a room full of mirrors; that simile will hold, I believe, for the other authors as well. Each major personage in these novels is a partial image of the author, a tentative attempt at self-definition. In the nineteenth century the novelist created personalities; in the twentieth he creates myths of personality.

I have based this study on the works of Lawrence, Woolf, and Mann because they have seemed to me the three most unlike of those authors whose principal concern was the expression of the self's repleteness, that zenith of personality in which the mind discovers in its interstices family, forest, ocean, sun, stars, all, the monism of Bishop Berkeley except that the mind of the individual has replaced Berkeley's God. Indeed these three seem to represent distinct types of writers: Lawrence is the passionate shepherd who breaks into spontaneous song, though more shrike than nightingale; Woolf is the verbal artificer, whose every sentence must bear some distinguishing mark of her sensibility; and Mann is the traditional craftsman, the dignified worker responsible to the public, even though he elaborates the traditional apparatus of the novel to a point inconceivable to tradition. I have omitted Joyce and Proust for, even though they seemed equally great as the three I have discussed, Joyce attempts a smaller number of major subjective characters, is despite his shenanigans less varied in his depiction of personality, and Proust seemed less interesting because of his comparatively direct autobiographical approach, his lack of deflection and obliquity in his self-presentation, although his idolatry of himself is indeed amazing. That such dissimilar types should converge suggests some common crisis, a tendency inherent in the structure of the nineteenth-century novel itself. I will state the crisis in the following formula: realism demands that each character in a novel possess a mind whose power and complexity seem equal to our intuition of the mind's capacity; but the novelist knows no sensibility but his own, so his characters grow increasingly psychological and indistinct, expressive of the single intelligence of the author.

It seems to me likely that an author whose energy is directed toward such monumental forms of self-expression will almost invariably be disappointed in the results; indeed the careers of most of these novelists suggest a certain revulsion against the images of themselves that they discover on the paper, a reaction against the very ideal of self-expression. In Lawrence the word *personal* is pejorative from the beginning, and although almost nothing happened to him that does not appear in his fiction—indeed, his childhood is perhaps the most vivid childhood available to us in literature or history—he is nevertheless contemptuous of all aspects of experience which cannot be resolved into some impersonal and universal force, the gravitation synonymous with sexual desire, the centrifugal energy synonymous with hate. Other aspects of his career also suggest a certain self-dissatisfaction; for instance, he attempted only once in his novels to create a mature character whose features bear much resemblance to his own face, whose mind approaches the range and depth of his own; that character appears before his literary career is half over, and after Birkin in *Women in Love* his characters simplify, stiffen, turn iconic, allegorical, deliberate. Certain authors discover that the burden of self-description is debilitating, for it requires that experience be kept limited, tractable; Joyce's blindness may have been as inevitable as Proust's cork room, and Virginia Woolf excluded most tactile sensation that she might become the finest mistress of the self-regarding eye. It can never be demonstrated that an author committed suicide for literary reasons, but if such a thing is possible one might see Virginia Woolf's suicide as her ultimate recognition of the failure of her works to constitute a proper image of herself. Indeed, as with Lawrence, the last decade of her literary career appears to us as a retreat from the enormous ramification of her identity that she achieved in *The Waves*. If it were not for Thomas Mann, one might think that the self-absorption that these novelists practiced was necessarily self-defeating; in Mann's case, however, life and art alike seem successful, his canon a great self-portrait already, only twenty years after his death, as satisfying, burnished and burgherly as some Rembrandt masterpiece in oil.

Yet even in Mann's success some of the inherent dangers of the method that these novelists employed are visible; if he avoided disaster it was chiefly because he did not use in his novels the profoundest of his experiences—his first sister's suicide, for example—until time and discipline had rendered them anesthetized, palpable. The construction of his verbal self was the slow labor of a lifetime, nothing to be hurried; ripeness would achieve what passionate self-aggrandizement, self-despair, could not. He did worry that he might spoil it through senility or loss of energy—few things in his letters are more moving than his wish that he had died immediately after *Dr. Faustus*, which he thought a more fitting conclusion to his work than his later efforts—but he never admitted the thought that what he crafted with such care might turn out to present a false version of his being.

Of course all verbal analogues of personality will necessarily fail to be congruent with the personality depicted. Even if we imagine the perfect verbal act of self-expression, in which a mind capable of knowing its operations exactly discovered a pattern of words the form of which was identical to the form of the mind's operation, it would doubtless seem to its creator as useless and sterile as any other mode of perpetuating one's image beyond death—the Grecian Urn, a documentary film, a topiary privet cut to resemble one's body. I believe, in addition, that in every real case in which an author has attempted an ambitious self-revelation in words, he has found that the medium of language was itself a contamination of his being. Any attempt to realize one's self verbally must confront the possibility that grammar is alien to the structure of the mind, and the experiments of Woolf and Joyce suggest that radical self-expression requires the abolition of the usual syntactical forms. One may wish to agree with Jacques Lacan's beguiling thesis, or what is popularly thought to be his thesis, that the structure of the unconscious is the structure of language; but in such statements as these we see the resonance and limitedness of the twentieth-century imagination, for the structure of the unconscious may be said with equal justice to correspond with any antique structure, a pyramid, Euclidean geometry, a ziggurat, Babylonian star-charts. Language offers much, but it does not offer an asylum for the identity.

Self-expression is a romantic doctrine; the history of modern literature is the history of the extension of self-expression to its limit, and the consequent revolt. I have tried in this study to tell half, or nearly half, of this story; the revolt, the work of Gide, Forster, Beckett, Auden, of these men who cured literature of hubris if not of pretension, must be described in another book. The reaction against that mode of literature designed to enhance and expand the self takes many forms, all of which suggest the finitude of the ego and the insensitivity of the body: Gide's *Caves du Vatican* is a charade in which the puppets must learn to acknowledge the wires that guide them; in Forster's *Passage to India* the author regards his characters through the diminishing end of a telescope, takes for his image of the mind a small, smooth, empty cave; and Beckett's first novel *Murphy* contains a parody of the solipsistic novels of Joyce and Woolf, a chapter in which the contents of the protagonist's skull are shown to be congruent with the exterior universe, as tedious and chaotic. In Auden's *The Orators*, as well as in the recent fiction of Donald Barthelme and others, human social behavior is explicable through probability theory, particle interaction, Brownian movement; for in the great revulsion against personality, against the value and uniqueness of the individual, the human consciousness must appear only to be another object in a universe of objects, a clatter of hard steel balls. This kind of novel is the result, not of any inevitable process of literary history, but of the need to protect the human mind from the exterior terror impinging on it; the hero of Beckett's later novels is most lavishly protected, hidden in an ashcan, a womb, a casket; too small to be discovered, too hard to be crushed.

I can correlate these discrepant types of sensibility—the one compelled to an endless stream of self-expression, the other hard-lined, mocking and evasive—with certain observations I have made of the nature of self-awareness in contemporary society. Few people seem to feel no anxiety about their identity, but the least anxious are those who have a distinct image of themselves, a catalog of their traits; they consider themselves arrogant or ordinary, trustworthy or prone to cheat, and so on; they in effect carry about with them a little manikin, which they constantly display to their acquaintances, always accompanied by a single all-important question: does this puppet resemble me? They wish to be reassured every day that they conceive themselves correctly, and they will be displeased if empirical evidence forces them to change the outline of the doll's mouth from a smile to a sneer, from a sneer to an expressionless line. If, however, such a person becomes content with a factitious image of himself, presents to the world a puppet deliberately painted to resemble someone else—it is an easy step from basing one's integrity on an accurate public rehearsal of oneself to basing one's integrity on a private vision which must remain forever inviolate, which the false image obscures and protects—then one will be, if a novelist, a master of misleading fable; characters will be erected so that they may be mocked and destroyed; all behavior will be governed by arbitrary rule; what is trivial will become supple, potent, expressive, while what is important will seem frivolous or grotesque. This kind of person, and this kind of novel, seem to me prevalent today.

There is another kind of person, though, who differs from the first in that he never possessed any image of himself at all. When he was young he discovered that no central principle ruled his action; he was gentle and passive in the company of A, aggressive in the company of B, indifferent in the company of C. He perceived himself as a group of unrelated selves rather than as a single person; afterward, as an adult, he may fall into despair about his lack of a core, or he may learn to accept and employ a certain inchoateness and multiplicity inherent in his being. If he becomes a novelist he will understand his characters in the manner that Proteus understands the eel, the horse, the dragon, the frog: as potential selves, as incomplete aspects of his being. Therefore all he writes will be a self-expression without seam or terminus, in which everything must necessarily constitute authentic self-revelation, for no identity is impossible; but in which the aggregate can never constitute self-definition, for all identities are equally valid. Therefore the work of a Lawrence, a Woolf, a Joyce, a Mann, must continue in furious evolution until the death of the writer, while Gide or Forster exhausts his repertoire of interesting masks at a fairly early age, and Beckett constricts his vision toward a point that grows ever dimmer as the shutters of the iris spin shut. The inchoate or multiple writer may, like Joyce, seem vague and passive in his personal life, and will sometimes exhibit a fascination with the androgyne, for he may scarcely understand himself as man or woman at all. Virginia Woolf seems a very pure example; she remarks in her diary, "I'm twenty people," and envied all for whom day-to-day life was simple and effortless; it is clear that being someone was a great chore to her. In a paragraph criticizing Lawrence's work, she admits that the theme of Lawrence's novels and her own is the struggle for self-definition; the reader is continually immersed in a single ego that may prove hateful and choking:

> I am also reading D. H. L. with the usual sense of frustration: and that he and I have too much in common—the same pressure to be ourselves: so that I don't escape when I read him: am suspended: what I want is to be made free of another world. (*A Writer's Diary*, p. 182)

Lawrence too, though one does not usually speak of him and Virginia Woolf in the same breath, evinces the same fascination with the undefined, the labile, the "quick"; indeed those characters of whom he approves are amorphous and uncrystallized, not yet descended into the deadness of fixed form, a set and settled personality. And this taste for the indefinite is equally characteristic of Mann; one thinks of his boy geniuses who are all potentiality anterior to any achievement, the phantoms of unwritten novels teeming ceaselessly in the head of

Tonio Kröger, or of his Goethe, who creates himself Protean and enormous, or of his Felix Krull, galactic, the end point of phylogeny. Mann remarked late in life that like Proust he was wholly unmemorable as a person, no personality at all; and elsewhere that he and Joyce shared a mysterious kinship. It is in all these cases the kinship of those who are forced to create out of a sense of uncreatedness.

II

In writing this book I have made use of the large body of excellent practical criticism written on the modern novel in the last thirty years; indeed without the work of Frank Kermode, Hillis Miller, Wayne Booth, Ralph Freedman, Robert Langbaum, Richard Ellmann, Robert Scholes and Robert Kellogg, Erich Auerbach, to name a few, I would not have known how to begin at all. If I have managed to consolidate or connect the insights of these men, bring them to bear on a few chosen issues, I will have done enough. But the body of modern criticism that I have received is in some respects not well adapted to the study of personality; its tools are better adapted to the study of books than to the study of authors. We have passed through New Criticism and its emphasis on the autonomy, the self-containedness, of the verbal icon, through the revolt against the exclusivity of New Criticism, to a kind of criticism in which the issue of the isolation of a work of art from its author or context seems almost beside the point; and yet in all these stages in the evolution of criticism a certain impersonality is evident in our handling of literature. We have tried to include information about the author's life in criticism; the chief result has been to show that the events in a novel are often derived from the author's experience or from something he heard about—but the satisfactions of these discoveries have been limited. We have tried to make taxonomies, nosologies of the novel, to make a grammar of romance as unassailable as the grammar of the romance languages, to make criticism as respectable as science—but what frees criticism from the personality of the critic also frees criticism from the personalities of the authors it treats. We have drawn diagrams, geometries of the operations of the creative imagination itself, but the critical process that uncovers the deepest structure may overlook what is shallower and more vital; the central charm of the human body is not the skeleton. And even in the case of structuralism, although Geoffrey Hartman has told us that its second law is intersubjectivity, the mediation of the I–thou relationship, it is the mediation that the structuralists usually discuss, not the *I* or the *thou*. The intuitive method of Poulet and his followers has been helpful to me in speaking of the problems of subjectiveness, but it has seemed most helpful when most speculative and disreputable. How, then, is a critic to treat properly, on a large scale, the personality of a novelist?

It is worth looking at these critical difficulties because they are closely analogous to the difficulties of an author in trying to reduce human beings to objects, the objective case: I saw *him*, I wrote about *him*; the *him* is already cold, delimited, conquered, a caricature of a human being, compared with the suppleness, the plasticity, the characterless ease of the *I*. It is natural to write criticism in the objective case; that is, to treat a novelist as a statue, an achieved being, or as a nearly negligible cause of the novels he wrote. To try to describe the novelist as a personality, a working sensibility, a maker of choices, an *I*, may require some of the same techniques that modern novelists—Woolf, Joyce, Mann, and the others—use to present characters as subjects rather than objects, more perceivers than perceived.

The problem for both novelist and critic is simply this: that everyone conceives himself as a creature different *in kind* from the other people he encounters.

> Subjectively, my experience of life is one of having to make a series of choices between given alternatives and it is this experience of doubt, indecision, temptation, that seems more important and memorable than the actions I take. Further, if I make a choice which I consider the wrong one, I can never believe, however strong the temptation to make it, that it was inevitable, that I could not and should not have made the opposite choice. But when I look at others, I cannot see them making choices; I can only see what they actually do and, if I know them well, it is rarely that I am surprised, that I could not have predicted, given his character and upbringing, how so-and-so would behave.
>
> Compared with myself, that is, other people seem at once less free and stronger in character. No man, however tough he appears to his friends, can help portraying himself in his autobiography as a sensitive plant. (W. H. Auden, *The Dyer's Hand*, pp. 97–98)

This unrecognizability, this incommensurability between the subjective perceiver and the rest of the kingdom of the human, is an issue in the literature of all eras, but in the novels of the 1920s, when self-expression becomes overweening, engorged, it leads to remarkable difficulties. In some cases it is almost as if the subjective novelist is in competition for the reader's attention with his own characters; the novel becomes a battleground between the loose pervasive sentience of the novelist and the smaller, more rigid minds of the characters he animates. It is commonly complained that D. H. Lawrence's later novels are more didactic, irritable, less rich in human interaction than his earlier ones; but I believe that, from Lawrence's point of view, he wanted his victory over his characters to be complete. Lawrence wanted the novel to be "impersonal," to demonstrate the basic biophysical principles that govern indifferently the human temperament and the metallurgy of iron. As a practical matter this meant that his novels had to be governed exclusively by the single omniscience, omnisentience, of the author.

Enough is known of Lawrence's manner of composition that one may speculate that at the beginning of his career Lawrence often included certain material in his novels for sheer mimetic pleasure, material without any particular "point." An early reviewer of *Sons and Lovers* singled out for special praise a passage in which Paul unself-consciously holds down his sweetheart's skirt when it is billowed by the wind. Here is fresh, casual, accurate observation of behavior, and it is exactly what is usually missing from the later novels. Birkin remarks to Gerald in *Women in Love* that there is no such thing as accident; and the world of Lawrence's later fiction is a world utterly purged of accident, purged of independent agents, in which each detail presented is relevant, pointed, carefully stage-managed by the author. Observation is replaced by the inventions of the mythopoeic imagination, and the novelist is increasingly willing to hint at his centrality; the chapter of *Kangaroo* called "Harriet and Lovat at Sea in Marriage" shows a narrator who has achieved mastery by the simple means of making his characters his slaves. What is chiefly represented in Lawrence's novels, even at the beginning of his career, is finally not the characters but the vitality hidden in them, its aura, its radiance, its convection; the novel *intends* the author, and the author's mania. In this manner the search for impersonality becomes the expression of an enormous personalness.

Again, in the case of Virginia Woolf, the novel's traditional balance between the subjective author and the objective world of mimesis is greatly skewed in the direction of the subjective. In such mature novels as *Mrs. Dalloway* and *To the Lighthouse* the characters in many ways still retain their traditional dignity—one is impressed by their amplitude, their sensitivity, their richness—but the author's fascination with the act of *looking* threatens to engulf what is looked at by the sheer elaboration of the process of observing. Lily Briscoe *looking* is much more formidable than Lily Briscoe *looked at*; the latter is an ineffectual and ludicrous prune, the former has genius; and when Lily thinks that fifty pairs of eyes would be needed to see Mrs. Ramsay properly, one hears something of the author's will to pursue endless ramifications of subjectivity, multiply the poverties of the real in a wilderness of mirrors. It is interesting to compare *Jacob's Room*, *Mrs. Dalloway*, and *To the Lighthouse* with a later novel, *The Waves*. The first are portrait novels, three long inquiries into an ample and rather static central figure. In each the central figure is a "character" recognizable by the canons of the nineteenth-century novel; Mrs. Ramsay, for example, is so highly individuated that a glove may be known as hers from the twist of its finger; from the pen of Sterne such an observation would parody the conventions of the novel, but Virginia Woolf is perhaps only pushing individuation to an extreme. *The Waves*, however, is a very different kind of book; at its center is the portrait of the least important character, Percival, a mute, insipid ideal. He, too, is a nineteenth-century "character," a congeries of memorable gestures; the subject of the novel, however, is clearly not Percival but rather the six characters who stare at him; if they have unique traits, characteristic gestures, these fingerprints are, in comparison to *To the Lighthouse*, forced and arbitrary, a slight disguising of their sixfold singleness. Virginia Woolf's means of perfecting the subjectivity of her novels is by accretion, the compounding of perceivers: she adds up fifty pairs of eyes, conflates six characters into one enormous protagonist, remarks of herself as a novelist, "I'm twenty people." Lawrence used the opposite means of arriving at subjectivity, subtraction, stripping the accidentals away from his characters until he discovered the stark paradigm of the anatomy chart, the interplay of the forces in the deep nerves of the body, the forces he felt in his own nerves. Both strategies have dangers: Lawrence's a certain thinness and abstraction, Virginia Woolf's the difficulties of sustaining such an agglutinated visual field without headache and fracture—something of which seems to take place in her last two novels, if one thinks of the fragmented mirror erected at the climax of the pageant in *Between the Acts*. As with Lawrence, personality and impersonality seem to converge when pushed to the limit, for the author who subsumes all possible human personalities is herself only a blank luminosity, a glass eye. It would be difficult for a novelist to extend the proliferation of ego and suppression of object much farther than *The Waves*; the book is so saturated with its author that characterization exists only as an aspect of style.

Thomas Mann, the last novelist I have portrayed in this book, has yet a third strategy for rendering subjective the apparatus of characterization he received from the nineteenth-century novel. None of his novels lacks old-fashioned "characters," quirky, idiosyncratic creatures, usually the rigid objects of satire; but from his earliest work he was fascinated by young genius, so clean and quicksilver that it is almost free from character trait. One usualy speaks of *Buddenbrooks* or *Tonio Kröger* as a *Bildungsroman*, yet it is remarkable how little education or development takes place in the characters of Hanno or Tonio, or the Infant Prodigy, or the Felix Krull of 1911. They do not make moral choices, they do not acquire new perspectives, they change very little, they accomplish almost nothing; they are all soft genius anterior to any deed. Imperceptibly, as Mann ages, and his baby geniuses become first adolescent and then mature, they begin to resemble their author in oblique ways; no author of modern times has been cleverer at smuggling himself into the texts he writes. It may be said of an objective character in any novelist's work that it is effective because it is convincingly verisimilar, accurately depicted; and of a subjective character that it is the author's fantasy of his identity; but such characters as Mann's Leverkühn in *Dr. Faustus*, or his Goethe in *Lotte in Weimar*, are so subjective that they may be described as hallucinations of identity, swollen minds distended by their own greatness. Secret clues abound in Mann's writings to suggest what he is too subtle or abashed to say directly, the magical identity he felt between himself and the nearly limitless characters he created. On one page of *The Story of a Novel* he points out his immense feeling of kinship to his protagonist, Leverkühn, on another he says that Serenus Zeitblom, his surrogate narrator, the perceiver, and Leverkühn, the perceived, are magically the same person; and when he speaks in his fine essay "Goethe and Tolstoy" of Tolstoy's delusion that his greatness would make him physically immortal, his tone assumes a peculiar derogatory awestrickenness, as if he too had the same mad wonder; and when he declares that a "mystic union" with Goethe was needed to write the interior monologue chapter of *Lotte in Weimar*, he is near to confessing the truth. I sense a certain desire in Mann, as in Joyce—one thinks of Mann's experiments with Joycean conflation of European languages in *The Holy Sinner*—to blur the division between text and self, character and author, to make language one's personal kingdom, to incorporate the immortality of language into one's own being; when Mann incorporates treatises on philosophy, psychology, medicine, cosmological physics into his novels, he is in effect making himself into an encyclopedia, the British Museum, at last language itself. The author who can say anything, like the character of whom anything can be said, has expanded beyond personality to a state of impersonal revelry, like the cosmic joy of *Felix Krull*. It may be said only of language that it is simultaneously human and impersonal. Language resists all incursion of personalization, although it is the great achievement of the stylists of the eighteenth and nineteenth centuries to impart to language the illusion of personality; the writers of the twentieth century usually accept the irresistible blandness of language and see what can be done. Mann, and Joyce, used the impersonality of language as a vehicle to self-expression.

This intensification of subjectivity—in Mann, Lawrence, Virginia Woolf, and the others—suggests the debt that the novel of the early twentieth century owes to the criticism of the late nineteenth. Novelists have always been critics; but as novel writing and criticism have evolved, both have become twin aspects of the same process. If it has been the purpose of narrative literature to imitate an objective action, and the purpose of criticism to make a bridge between the world of human experience and the world of fiction, then the introduction into the novel of highly enhanced sensibilities, endlessly sifting perceptions and relations, serves to make the novel discriminating, critical, less indicative than subjunctive, tentatively didactic. A novel like *The Waves* may be described as a complicated reconstruction of an act of criticism, a coming-to-terms with an objective reality that exists behind the novel but not in it; and when Thomas Mann dramatizes his surrogate narrators, such as Zeitblom in *Dr. Faustus,* he is in effect introducing a surrogate reader, a critic who will piece together the events of Leverkühn's aesthetic life and relate them to the greater world of the Second World War, a world that exists long after Leverkühn's death. In such ways as these the novel becomes a criticism of itself, and the proper task of academic criticism becomes an imitation of the novel's protagonist. It was also perhaps inevitable that as the novel grew difficult, cryptic, it became necessary to interpolate into the text the code book necessary to solve the text—or, in the case of *Ulysses,* for the author to smuggle the code book to a trusted friend, who published it as his own original critical research. It is a fine parable for the new incestuousness of novelist and critic, and one may also note that one of the greatest novels written by a man who first grew celebrated as a critic, Wilde's *Dorian Gray,* was epitomized by its author in the following manner: "Basil Hallward is what I think I am, Lord Henry what the world thinks me: Dorian what I would like to be—in other ages, perhaps." This is a remarkable anticipation, not only of subjective novels of the next few decades, but of the language later critics would use to describe them, the psychological language that describes characters as avatars of the author, experiments in self-image and ego ideal. Indeed Wilde's essay "The Critic as Artist" is a kind of manifesto permitting the critic to usurp every literary act, and in a certain sense he has done so.

Many of the strangenesses of contemporary academic criticism of literature become more understandable if one recognizes the situation in which the academic critic labors. The academy usually demands that its professors produce research which is valid, replicable, and consistent; but criticism is the relation of the subjective to the objective and will undergo distortion if it is limited to the accusative case. It is no accident that many of the finest works of twentieth-century criticism use some of the techniques of the subjective novel; John Livingston Lowes' *The Road to Xanadu* was published in the same year as *To the Lighthouse*, and its methods, however well or poorly suited to Coleridge, are ideally consonant with Virginia Woolf's musings on the imperceptible origins of phenomena; in fact the tools of modern psychological criticism could easily be turned back on *The Road to Xanadu*, and one could describe its achievement of persona, the reliability of its voice, the intricate qualification of its discoveries. I do not mean that criticism should be written to enhance the critic, for impressionism is as unsatisfactory as formalism; I only mean that the creation of a critic's voice and point of view, the narrative stance of his criticism, must evolve simultaneously with the elucidation of fiction that he provides. The critic cannot connect what he reads to no one's world in particular, the ideally "modern" world, the "twentieth-century sensibility" that is no one's sensibility at all, but only to the world of his own experience. The impressionist critic reads literature to discover a few momentous passages that illuminate what is sacred to him; alas, he did not write the literature himself. The formalist, or mathematical, critic sees literature as a neutral field of elements that can be tabulated, correlated, brought into geometric pattern and orderly evolution, in which each sentence of an author's work from infancy to old age is equally important; alas, Gödel has proved that in any set of axioms there exist theorems that can be neither proved nor disproved. Both extremes, the subjective and the objective, are errors of the critical imagination.

When I study books of criticism I often try to guess what the critic would consider a perfect critical act. In a fine recent book on Yeats a critic apologized in his preface for not having read everything Yeats had ever read, and it was clear that he believed that one could not criticize Yeats properly if Yeats knew anything of which the critic was ignorant. In many ways it is a remarkable notion of the nature of criticism, and one, I think, which many contemporary critics share. I have spoken before of certain magical acts attempted by novelists; here, I believe, is an attempt at critical magic. If a critic attempts to read, to duplicate in his own experience everything that happened to the author he criticizes, then the critic becomes a clone or *Doppelgänger* of his author and possesses an unimpeachable authority in his critical pronouncements. Again, criticism is novel-like; the critic is Proteus, able to transfigure himself into the author he treats, reconstruct with an impossibly austere act of sympathy his author's processes of feeling, refeel it all again on his own nerve ends. It is a chimerical goal, but a goal exactly appropriate for such Protean

13

novelists as Joyce, Lawrence, Virginia Woolf, Thomas Mann—
novelists of such extensive vicariousness that no human being is
outside their range of feeling. Borges' Pierre Menard, the obscure
modern critic who swallows the world of Cervantes with such a
precision of empathy that he can *write* chapters of *Don Quixote* which
he has not read since childhood, shows the final coalescence of critic
and novelist; novelist and critic alike vanish in the perfection of the
subjective imagination, as the personalities of both Cervantes and
Menard refine themselves out of existence.

Thus criticism shapes itself into the right vehicle for what it
criticizes, or, more exactly, literature and literary criticism elaborate
themselves in one continuous motion, inextricable, coterminous.

III

But I have not yet explained how I plan to approach the question
raised earlier, how to treat the personality of the novelist, to respect
and delineate the subjectivity of these intensely subjective writers. To
some extent one may simply adduce the novel's hidden self-criticism,
let the novelist represent himself; indeed when a certain passage in a
novel appears repeatedly in critical studies it is often because that
passage gestures beyond the events ostensibly related or commented
upon, flings its nets to a world outside the world of the novel. But a
psychological critic needs a psychology; and yet he may impose no
theory alien to the author upon the works he discusses. Here is the
principle which seems to me to lie underneath the diverse psychologies
that writers employ, the proper beginning of a theory of subjective
characterization: every literary act is at once self-disclosure and self-
evasion. It is not that an author succeeds an honest statement about
himself with a dishonest one; self-disclosure and self-evasion do not
alternate, for they are indissolubly one; precisely what makes an act a
disclosure also makes it an evasion. In autobiography there is usually
a certain stiffness, a tension, an abashedness that jars the reader;
when an author consciously intends candor or deception in describing
himself, his touch grows less sure; but in subjective fiction disclosure
and evasion twine amiably, confront each other without discomfort,
present the single aspect, the single face that they together comprise.
To adapt Schiller, it is only in our inventions that we are fully human.
One cannot write a sentence in the first person without a momentary
suspension of commonplace identity, whether the putative speaker is
the Pharaoh of Egypt or a cocker spaniel; and the same is true of
third-person statements which are to any extent subjective, percipient,
expressive of the interior. But the word *identity* too much emphasizes
the sameness of our being; and men enjoy writing novels because the

14

mutations of subjectivity that the novel permits, that the modern novel almost demands, conform to the authentic discontinuity of our beings, the feeling of undefinedness and imaginative malleability which all of us possess as subjective *I*'s, none of us possesses as an objective self.

The modern novel treats personality with such torsion and distension because personality, as most of us conceive it, is itself a fiction. I have not seen a refutation of T. S. Eliot's hypothesis in *Knowledge and Experience* that there is no such thing as a science of psychology, but if there is such a thing it is a science intolerable to human dignity. The vision of personality expressed in the journal of the Russian dissident Andrei Sinyavsky, in an excerpt translated by Saul Bellow from a French edition, well accords with the fierce enhancement of the subjective found in many modern novels:

> Human frontiers blur where they touch the infinite. Beyond biography. Man, each man, eludes biography. When you try to support your weight on "personal characteristics" you sink up to the waist. Personality is a ditch covered lightly by a growth of psychological traits, temperaments, habits, ways of doing things. I have no sooner taken a step toward an approaching stranger than I find that I have fallen into a hole. (*New Yorker*, 12 July 1976, p. 57)

It is hard to believe that Sinyavsky has not created the hole into which he has fallen. To such radical humanism, personality is at last ineffable; it may be framed, alluded to, hinted at, but never touched. Secular existentialism has simply substituted "personality" for the theological concept of the soul, but it is still mysterious, unapproachable, numinous. Just as the soul has needed its mythology—genesis, fall, and redemption—the cult of personality has generated its mythographers, of whom the novelists found in this study are among the most important.

I have assumed that almost everything that these subjective novelists have written, especially what was tantalizing or obscure, was at least partly an elucidation of selfhood; and I have tried to comprehend the entire work of each author as a single act, and to describe in a single, long and complicated statement the indivisible meaning, the crescent face, which the author presents from youth to old age. It is commonplace to observe that even the greatest authors seem to repeat the same strategies and structures from work to work; if the apparent diversity of an author's novels consists simply of the varying inflections of a single shape, then the subjectivity, the personality of each novelist lies in both the constant shape underneath and the shimmer and

15

nuance of the evolving surface, both the continuities and discontinuities of identity. The three essays in this book are independent of each other; I have not imposed a similarity on these novelists greater than what I could discover; yet I hope that my readers will see that as each of three faces in this triptych grows keener and more distinct, the faces will nonetheless display more and more features in common, as if the three aspects converge in a single bright presentation of being. This is partly because Lawrence, Virginia Woolf, and Mann share certain typical preoccupations and techniques of their age; and partly because of the tenuousness of personality itself, its charming evanescence; and partly because all authors must ultimately yield to the impersonality of their medium. The sorcerers of Glubbdubdrib in the third book of *Gulliver's Travels* can conjure up the spirits of the dead, who are bound to answer all questions with exact truthfulness because the dead, being dead, have no further pretext for dissimulation. This will serve as a parable for the nature of language, for the collected writings of the dead, though self-contradictory, temporizing, ironic, prevaricating, exaggerating, exist only as language; after the extinction of the author there is no further self to express or evade. And yet, each critic conceives the author he treats differently from every other critic's conception; so either the dead do manage to lie, or there is some genuine elusiveness in the subjective that even the grave cannot efface.

T W O

The distortions of the modern novel arise chiefly from the search for verisimilitude. The older novel, the kind that Defoe began with his astonishing sense of the furniture of one's life and the heft and the texture of that furniture, the fat, organic nineteenth-century novel swollen by popular consumption, could only work through the creation of elaborate systems of convention whereby perceptual detail could be interpreted as the reflex of a personality: spiky hair means a spiky character, blue eyes must be candid or cold, the people are sad because they weep, the configuration of tables and chairs proves one vulgar or tasteful. The novel itself resembles a body, a most comfortable genre, full of banquets and liaisons, and what it presents are the greater bodies, the full reifications, of its rhetorical subjects. The novelist is expected to know what he is talking about; he is judged by the accuracy of his observation; if Homer was the tutor of warfare, the novelist is the tutor of class.

It is questionable, however, whether any heap of concretions is enough to define a personality. As long as character is conceived as a set of quantifiable traits, good or evil, complacent or irritable, celibate or lustful, muscular or asthenic, objective description of such consistencies of behavior will be adequate; but if the novelist conceives personality as something elusive or tricky, a deep structure or consonance, too inclusive or too exclusive, perhaps something to which exterior behavior is nearly irrelevant, then he must search for new strategies. This is why the subject of the modern novel is often less the personages it treats than a theory of personality; and if modern protagonists seem deformed it is often because such extreme measures are necessary to project them. The body in particular undergoes strange mutations in the modern novel; it must be either

17

inhumanly plastic if it is conceived as a full reflex of the self within it, or, if not, it tends to be ignored or treated as a lump of meat.

One kind of stress, the stress of portraying a personality so broad its elements are contradictory, a personality that resists the usual categories, becomes more frequent as the nineteenth-century novel progresses. Cooper's Deerslayer is too many different things, could not possibly fit into a single skin—he can orate like Wordsworth and grunt like a grizzly bear—and when Mark Twain ridicules Cooper for his inconsistencies he is simply assuming, for a moment, an older canon of taste. George Eliot's difficulties with the character of Dorothea in *Middlemarch*—nunlike, sensible, amorous—seem to be, to some extent, of this nature; like her own Casaubon, Eliot wishes to fit greatly divergent elements into a single pattern. These internal, psychological pressures sometimes have odd effects upon the bodies that house such difficult personalities. Kurtz in Conrad's *Heart of Darkness* is seven feet tall, because that demigod or demidevil, placed in a wholly unstructured, responsive environment, has expanded like a balloon *in vacuo*; the body is emaciated, monstrous, because Kurtz has converted Africa into an image of his mind, a projection of his body—Marlow sees the sandbars in the river forming a spine—and therefore Kurtz has nothing left inside him at all. The bodies of James's later characters have often vanished into a semianimate domestic aura without locus or provenance, subtleties of varnish and resin; Poynton despoiled is indeed death; and after James no one dare talk about furniture, for furniture, as in Ionesco's skit *Le Nouveau Locataire*, can multiply so quickly than it can drive away the human entirely.

The yearning to escape the limitations of the body is found in every era, but perhaps it was more prevalent in the nineteenth century than ever before. If this is true, the reason must be the growth of the machine. The physiological body, much contaminated by mechanical analogue, is too crude, too explicable, too predictable a vehicle for the sentient soul. Marx believed that mechanical labor exactly reversed a man's sense of what is animal and what is human, and if a writer believes that the relation of self to body is that of worker to tool he will to some extent distrust the adequacy of the body as an expression of the personality. This alienation puts a strain in the later nineteenth century on the whole mechanism of characterization, on that fidelity to sensuous apparition which is called realism. By staying close to felt experience, the novelist becomes removed from the soul that feels; identity grows more mysterious as the description of texture, emotion, weight, feeling grows more convoluted, exact. I sense sometimes a kind of desperation in Victorian fiction, for the Victorian habit of accreting details until the novel resembles a great heap of homely and beloved minutiae, everything palpable, plausible, congenial, congenially frightening, is a strategy partly born of a hopeless attempt to define a vision of personality that cannot be formulated through a catalog of its buttonhooks, hautboys, waistcoats, pinafores, whiskers, blushes. Dickens, George Eliot, Trollope seem to exercise their ingenuity to create ceaseless contrasts, idiosyncratic gestures, so that each character may seem wholly distinct and unique, but perhaps the vehemence of this effort suggests a fundamental loss of the knowledge of what constitutes human uniqueness, human identity. Virginia Woolf in "Mr. Bennett and Mrs. Brown" says something similar to this about Bennett and Galsworthy, who are orthodox in the late Victorian faith; but the basis of this indictment is presented much earlier in an essay from which many of Virginia Woolf's ideas are derived, Oscar Wilde's "The Decay of Lying," in which he insists on the folly of imitating clothes, local customs, political controversy, in short, life, the whole matter of the Victorian novel. In the same essay Wilde suggests a theme even more destructive of those assumptions which governed the novel of his time:

> It is a humiliating confession, but we are all of us made out of the same stuff. In Falstaff there is something of Hamlet, in Hamlet there is not a little of Falstaff. The fat knight has his moods of melancholy, and the young prince his moments of coarse humour. Where we differ from each other is purely in accidentals: in dress, manner, tone of voice, religious opinions, personal appearance, tricks of habit, and the like. The more one analyses people, the more all reasons for analysis disappear. (*The Artist as Critic*, p. 297)

If this is the case, then those sharply illuminated boundary lines between character and character are unreal, a novelist's artifice, and verisimilitude demands that the convention of human uniqueness be discarded in favor of the convention that there exists a single human nature, homologous in a billion shapes, the allotropic novel of Lawrence, the comprehensive egocentric novel of Woolf and Joyce.

In those novels of the twenties in which the new mode is seen, there is an abolishing of the demarcation between one character and another; distinct personages are replaced by a single matrix, a fluid sentience endlessly sifting through its perceptions and reflections. It is remarkable how the greatest writers of the time independently regard this kind of novel with the same eyes, unconsciously agree upon critical vocabulary:

> Certain typical books—*Ulysses*, Virginia Woolf's *The Waves*, Mr. Ezra Pound's *Draft of XXX Cantos*—suggest a philosophy like that of the *Samkara* school of ancient India, mental and physical

objects alike material, a deluge of experience breaking over us and within us, melting limits whether of line or tint; man no hard bright mirror dawdling by the dry sticks of a hedge, but a swimmer, or rather the waves themselves. (W. B. Yeats, *Explorations*, p. 373)

The characters of Jonson, of Shakespeare, perhaps of all the greatest drama, are drawn in positive and simple outlines. They may be filled in, and by Shakespeare they are filled in, by much detail or many shifting aspects; but a clear and sharp and simple form remains through these . . . . But Frédéric Moreau [in Flaubert's *L'Education Sentimentale*] is not made in that way. He is constructed partly by negative definition, built up by a great number of observations. We cannot isolate him from the environment in which we find him; it may be an environment which is or can be universalized; nevertheless it and the figure in it consist of very many observed particular facts, the actual world. Without this world the figure dissolves. (T. S. Eliot, *Selected Essays*, pp. 131–32)

So there you have the "serious" novel, dying in a very long-drawn-out fourteen-volume death agony, and absorbedly, childishly interested in the phenomenon. "Did I feel a twinge in my little toe, or didn't I?" asks every character of Mr. Joyce or of Miss Richardson or M. Proust. Is my aura a blend of frankincense and orange pekoe and boot-blacking, or is it myrrh and bacon-fat and Shetland tweed? . . . It is self-consciousness picked into such fine bits that the bits are most of them invisible, and you have to go by smell. Through thousands and thousands of pages Mr. Joyce and Miss Richardson tear themselves to pieces, strip their smallest emotions to the finest threads, till you feel you are sewed inside a wool mattress that is being slowly shaken up, and you are turning to wool along with the rest of the wooliness. (D. H. Lawrence, *Phoenix*, pp. 517–18)

Flaubert is not of the same generation, but Eliot often uses him as a "modern" example. It is clear from these three passages how one should talk of the modern novels of that period: as a dissolution, a blurring, an eating away of outline, a loss of the clear division between perceiver, perception, and object perceived. Yeats and Lawrence are somewhat alarmed by a certain encroaching of the inanimate, as the swimmer turns into the wave, the woolgathering mind turns into wool; as if the attempt to transcribe the nebula of sensation, achieve a full reification of identity, means some threatening declension of the mind into the inorganic. Lawrence treats Joyce as if he were a sorcerer trying to engross the reader's soul into some fearful and smothering prison, but Lawrence is correct in his belief that the doctrine of these modern novelists denies the reader's human uniqueness; he is correct also in feeling that this kind of endlessly self-wound self-analysis can have terrible effects upon the author who engages in it. But what Lawrence fails to understand is how close his own kinship is to Joyce, Richardson, Proust, Woolf, and the others. The quarrels of a generation often serve to mask a more profound resemblance; soon I expect that art historians will tell us that Manet and Puvis de Chavannes are nearly fraternal twins, and it is certainly true of Lawrence that he everywhere seeks to obscure his relation to those whom he resembles most. But many literary men are Antigones who desire nothing so much as to give their brothers an honorable burial.

Here, then, is a summary of the new assumptions of the twentieth-century novel: (1) the implicit subject of the novel is not a congeries of characters but the one personality of the author; (2) a personage in a novel is a coordination of attributions to a proper name, something very difficult to separate out of the rest of the text and bearing only an analogical relation to human experience; (3) all narrators are equally reliable, although they may seem to conflict, for truth and lies do not exist in a novel, only discrepant fictions. The novelist of the next century may find these truths useless, but they were necessary to permit the comprehensive egocentric novel which arose in the teens and 1920s as well as the gamier stuff of Nabokov and Borges. Joyce, Lawrence, Woolf were still amorous of their protagonists, but I think their very amorousness was an image of their self-love: the famous indistinguishability of Stephen Dedalus and Bloom in certain episodes of *Ulysses* is only one sign that the novel has been given over to a pervasive mind under which all characterization is tentative. Joyce believed in the doctrine of negative capability, and that supposition about the role of the artist will lead almost by necessity to huge undefined protagonists, Stephen Dedalus abandoning the personality of his youth in favor of an ironic godhead—if the artist is admirable because he embraces disinterestedly all of human experience, presumably an admirable character will also be negative and capable. The novelist who loves his character will attribute all manner of things to him in an attempt to enhance the human, to revel in the plenitude of the self, and if there is a lesson to be learned from modern fiction it is that overexpansion is dangerous, that a radical attempt to save the sentient, the vulnerable, the quick, from a hostile world will usually result in the destruction of the very humanity it tries to protect.

The Union of the Actor and the Acted-upon

The strain of the apparatus of characterization in the novel first comes to a serious crisis in D. H. Lawrence, and his solution produces characters who seem in retrospect the first modern personages of the novel. His characters are engaged in a perpetual struggle of self-defini-tion; their main business is the determination of exactly where they stop. Lawrence is the purest of the twentieth-century romantic poets, equally extreme, as one must be, in his aspiration and his disillusion. Through all of Lawrence's work he flirts with ultimate self-expansion, the hope that one can become the universe:

> I was so weary of the world,
> I was so sick of it,
> everything was tainted with myself,
> skies, trees, flowers, birds, water,
> people, houses, streets, vehicles, machines,
> nations, armies, war, peace-talking,
> work, recreation, governing, anarchy,
> it was all tainted with myself, I knew it all to start with
> because it was all myself.
>
> When I gathered flowers, I knew it was myself plucking my
>   own flowering.
> When I went in a train, I knew it was myself travelling by
>   my own invention.
> When I heard the cannon of the war, I listened with my own
> ears to my own destruction.
> When I saw the torn dead, I knew it was my own torn dead body.
> It was all me, I had done it all in my own flesh.
>
> (*Poems*, pp. 256–57)

This is "New Heaven and Earth," the climax of the long series of poems that Lawrence wrote about his coming-to-terms with his wife, *Look! We Have Come Through!* and it is the culmination of an important strain of romantic poetry. There is a style of rhetoric in this poem which appears in his novels and which was arrived at, usually independently, by several writers of the previous century: *I am the actor and the acted-upon.* This is the formula of radical monism, the chant proper to an oriental God who is subject and object indiffer-ently, agent and environment; in fact Emerson found this rhetoric in the Bhagavad Gita from which he derived "Brahma," which asserts the unity of slayer and slain:

> When they fly, I am the wings;
> I am the doubter and the doubt,
> And I am the hymn the Brahmin sings.

T. S. Eliot, on a scrap of paper published in the *Waste Land* facsimile, translates more directly, and more ironically, the same Hindu pas-sage, and in his earlier poem "The Death of Saint Narcissus," he expresses the same revulsion against a world that is wholly contaminated by the self, in which Narcissus is the fish and the hand that grabs it, the young girl raped and the drunken man who rapes her, ultimately perhaps the arrows that penetrate the body and the saint's much-violated body.

What is so terrifying about this kind of solipsism that it leads such disparate writers as Lawrence and Eliot to identical self-loathing and world-loathing? The expansion of being that seemed so exhilarating to Blake—the end of *Jerusalem* is a long tribute to the joys of including the universe within the human body—is now, it seems, a familiar experience, and it has left ashes and sand in the mouth, eyes dazzled by the brightness of too much starlight; as with so many aspects of twentieth-century experience when compared to the nineteenth, the chiliast has turned preterist, the apocalypse has taken place and it is not so good as we had hoped. First of all, the oceanic experience involved a complete redefinition of the body: when your hand strokes a tree, you feel the hand feeling the tree and you feel the tree feeling the hand; this titillation of a new coenesthesis, which Birkin feels memorably in *Women in Love* when he goes half mad among the textures of primroses and bark and pine needles, becomes after a while disquieting, even painful. Blake, the first systematizer of these experiences, understood perfectly well that the key to this sensation is, first, to annihilate the internal divisions of the body; the Infernal Veil of the female must be ripped away, then embraces will be comminglings from the head to the feet; after this the body can be made coextensive with the universe. The obstacle is clearly the skin; the skin must be wholly permeable, and this is of course sinister, finally sadistic. Baudelaire uses the rhetoric of *I am the actor and the acted-upon* most instructively in "L'Héautontimorouménos":

> Je suis le plaie et le couteau!
> Je suis le soufflet et la joue!
> Je suis les membres et la roue,
> Et la victime et le bourreau.

All radical experience is predicated on the destruction of categories, and the hardest, most tenacious boundary line is that between the inside and the outside of the body, what is *I* and what is Other. The self's attempts to extend itself beyond its frame of six feet end in heady disaster, the collapse of self and environment alike, the world war of "New Heaven and Earth."

The Myth of the Body

For Lawrence, falling in love is the chief temptation to self-diffusion and the only hope for self-definition, simultaneously problem and solution. "New Heaven and Earth" proceeds from Lawrence's weary self-expansion, the disgust of the hand that touches the beloved's body discovering once again that it is touching itself, to ecstatic limitation:

> Cortes, Pissaro, Columbus, Cabot, they are nothing, nothing!
> I am the first comer!
> I am the discoverer!
> I have found the other world!
>
> The unknown, the unknown!
> I am thrown upon the shore.
> I am covering myself with the sand.
> I am filling my mouth with the earth.
> I am burrowing my body into the soil.
> The unknown, the new world!

(*Poems*, p. 259)

A great change has taken place: instead of *I am the world*, we have a new, equally extravagant formula: *you are the world*; the speaker of the poem (there is no harm in calling him Lawrence) is now quite tiny, intense, burrowing into the beachhead of Frieda's body. It is love, or desire, that makes us intuit the unlimited forces, that puts our nerves in touch with the galaxy and the atom; in fact, Siegmund in *The Trespasser* speaks of his beloved Helena as a perceptual nerve connecting him to the cosmos; and it is love that ought to make us aware of the strangeness, the otherness of all that lies outside ourselves. *Psychoanalysis and the Unconscious* (1921), which constitutes, along with *Fantasia of the Unconscious* (1922), the last, rather shriveled attempt of an author to imitate a grand romantic system of metaphors—both books are almost exactly contemporary with Yeats's *A Vision*—is quite insistent on the dual nature of love, based on a bodily metaphor:

> There is a tremendous great joy in exploring and discovering the beloved. For what is the beloved? She is that which I myself am not. Knowing the breach between us, the uncloseable gulf, I in the same breath realize her *features*. In the first mode of the upper consciousness there is a perfect surpassing of all sense of division between the self and the beloved. In the second mode the very discovery of the features of the beloved contains the full realization of the irreparable, or unsurpassable gulf. This is objective knowledge, as distinct from objective emotion. It contains always the element of self-amplification, as if the self were amplified by knowledge in the beloved. It should also contain the knowledge of the *limits* of the self. (*Psychoanalysis*, p. 38)

The "first mode of the upper consciousness" is the activity of the cardiac plexus, an outward-streaming desire which tends to eradicate boundaries; the second mode is the activity of the thoracic ganglion, which attempts to determine the limits of the self and also to articulate the beloved. What counts is the balance: it is fatal to identify oneself with the universe, as we have seen; it is equally fatal to try to exist as a wholly separate, discrete creature. Proper love will preserve in delicate tension the isolate self and the oceanic self.

Surely the twentieth century has shown more interest in gross anatomy than any other age the world has ever known. Modern poetry and prose have disseminated the vocabulary of the inside of the body more effectively than medicine ever has; Joyce showed us how to convert the peristalsis of the bowels and the filtering of the kidneys into narrative processes; Auden in recent years has been engaged in a long, amusing colloquy with his innards; our era understands inspiration entirely as the oxygenation of red corpuscles. This preoccupation is the necessary concomitant of the loss of a comprehensible structure which relates the self and the world. If what is outside is hostile, or, worse, incomprehensible, the body is secure; its basic rules are easy to follow, it is a highly integrated, useful, functioning structure, a much more amiable habitation despite its upsets, its nausea, than the world of Sartre of even of Matthew Arnold. It is easy to observe, and its habits and tendencies offer to the artist insight into himself; it may even be considered identical to himself. Biology is treasured by the modern artist, physics is repudiated; Lawrence, Auden, and others insist that the earth is, for all human purposes, flat.

If the body is the writer's structure of last resort, Lawrence is the great myth maker of the body. *Fantasia of the Unconscious* is the statement of that myth. First, the body *is* the unconscious; the idea of the thinking body cannot be taken farther than Lawrence takes it. What happens in the head does not seem at first to have any particular function in Lawrence's scheme; "this does not mean that man should immediately cut off his head and try to develop a pair of eyes in his breasts (p. 119)," but that is the only concession Lawrence will make. Second, the body evolves from homogeneity into articulation. At the beginning is the embryo, the fertilized egg, which is radical, without any internal boundaries, somewhat like the expanded self of "New Heaven and Earth"; what saves the embryo is its lack of diffusion, its smallness, its diamondlike brilliance, its mindlessness, its huge potentiality. For Lawrence the embryo as a single cell is an admirable state, and his fascination with it is related to his love of the past, of Eden, of mother, as opposed to the uncertainty of the future. The embryo determines its fate, forms out of itself organs and consciousness alike, spins "the nerves and brain as a web for its own motion, like some subtle spider" (*Psychoanalysis*, p. 18). The embryo is therefore a metaphor for the independent self that lives inside the body, the soul. Third, the body is more or less incorporeal. It is fundamentally a nexus of whirling centers of energy, an exact analogue of the complexities of centrifugal and centripetal forces in the cosmos. This is why Lawrence's anatomical attention is focused on nerve clusters; the inside of the body consists of constellated plexuses and ganglia. However, the entire body can also be considered as a single unit, a star, with urges to merge with other bodies (sympathetic) and urges to retain its own private individuality (volitional). Therefore a society is also an exact analogue of the starry cosmos; but these three analogical levels—the body, society, and the universe—must be kept distinct, even though the form and even the motive forces are identical. As to the nature of physical force, Lawrence is firm: it is sexual desire.

> Everything that exists, even a stone, has two sides to its nature. It fiercely maintains its own individuality, its own solidity. And it reaches forth from itself in the subtlest flow of desire.
> It fiercely resists all inroads. At the same time it sinks down in the curious weight, or flow, of that desire which we call gravitation.
> And imperceptibly, through the course of ages, it flows into delicate combination with the air and sun and rain.
> At one time, men worshipped stones: symbolically, no doubt, because of their mysterious durability, their power of hardness, resistance, their strength of remaining unchanged. Yet even then, worshipping man did not rest till he had erected the stone into a pillar, a menhir, symbol of the eternal desire, as the phallus itself is but a symbol. (*Phoenix II*, p. 456)

The inside of a stone is organized like the inside of the human body; gravity and desire are two names for the same thing. Lawrence has created a set of principles for generating analogues that is every bit as inclusive as the physical philosophy of the Renaissance, even if it is more threadbare—threadbare because Lawrence is tainted with alien doctrine, modern science, and must keep telling himself again and again and again that the sun is not just a blazing ball of gas. But the most remarkable aspect of this passage from "... Love Was Once a Little Boy" is the assertion that the phallus is a symbol: the outward fleshy parts of the body, the physician's describable characteristics, are only a metaphor, an expression, of the deeper self. As Ursula says in *Women in Love*, a book which immediately precedes *Psychoanalysis and the Unconscious*, "The body is only one of the manifestations of the spirit." The inside of the body is a better manifestation, but the cardiac plexus and the thoracic ganglion are still only metaphorical; the electrical network in the body is the creation, the language, of something more rarefied, inhuman, shapeless. The body is art.

The organic and the inorganic are both polar expressions of something undifferentiated, and it is the identification of the inorganic with the organic which is central to much of Lawrence's theory and imagery. When Lawrence in his famous letter of 5 June 1914 to Edward Garnett speaks of his interest in "that which is physic—non-human, in humanity" (*Letters I*, p. 281) and equates the laughter of a woman with the heat of a piece of iron, he is necessarily predicating his assertions on this principle, that beneath all physical, observed reality there is a being, living, fluid, homogeneous, wholly unarticulated. The entire universe, according to the *Fantasia*, has evolved out of a single little living creature, and he articulated himself into a solar system by asexual reproduction and death; at his death his body became the earth and his "hotness and brightness" became the sun (p. 64). But as we have seen, life and death are wholly relative, if even a stone is alive; it is just a question of greater vividness.

> Life is more vivid in the dandelion than in the green fern,
>   or than in a palm tree.
> Life is more vivid in a snake than in a butterfly.
> Life is more vivid in a wren than in an alligator.
> Life is more vivid in a cat than in an ostrich.
>
> (*Phoenix*, p. 468)

This is the basis of Lawrence's concept of natural hierarchy, what some would call his fascism; whatever entity has the highest electrical voltage, is the most libidinous, is supreme. But even the low forms, the cabbages, the mineral, do have some vitality. Kate in *The Plumed Serpent* thinks of iron growing like lichen deep in the earth; for her even the sky is articulated into the form of the human body, so pervasive is Lawrence's sense of the structural interchangeability of everything that has vivacity: "A small bird sat facing the sun; he was red as a drop of new blood, from the arteries of the air" (p. 267). The body is Lawrence's metaphor for anything well integrated, from society to the universe; all art, all expression, finally tends toward bodily form.

If stone, iron, and air have bodies, the reciprocal analogy is also true: one can find iron, stone, whole landscapes inside the body. Gudrun in *Women in Love* melts under Gerald's kisses, melts into his limbs and bones "as if he were soft iron becoming surcharged with her electric life"; and a moment later she is described as "sleeping in him as lightning sleeps in a pure, soft stone" (p. 379). In *The Rainbow* Ursula kisses Skrebensky, fastens on him, "cold as the moon and burning as a fierce salt. Till gradually his warm, soft iron yielded, yielded ... " (p. 320). In both instances the inside of the body is implicitly compared to an electric battery, a wet cell; in the first it is charging, in the second discharging, causing the dissolution of the anode, and we are soon told that Skrebensky has been reduced to a shell without a core. Lawrence has in this way adapted his electrical concept of the body to show what happens when the self is destroyed: it is equivalent to a battery running completely down to a condition in which there is no voltage differential, no polarity, no internal distinctions, only pulpy confusion. One can also note from these passages how impalpable and evasive, delicate, the electrical self, the real self, is within the body; in Gudrun's case it contracts into her mouth, then diffuses outside herself entirely into the body of Gerald. *The Rainbow* is particularly rich in this sort of description: Will's soul leaps, veers, and swoops into the upper reaches of the cathedral; and Tom, agonized and transfixed by the ugly-beautiful mouth of Lydia, kisses her and draws away: "Only in his blue eyes was something of himself concentrated" (p. 43).

In *Aaron's Rod*, Aaron and Lilly debate about whether the self is single or plural: Lilly claims that a human being consists of successive selves, changing his identity with each new stage in his life, while Aaron claims that there is a changeless "man in the middle" (p. 98). Similarly, Kate is bedeviled at the beginning of *The Plumed Serpent* by the sulking of a "little person inside her" (p. 3). Clearly the doctrine of the little person inside the body, the man in the middle, accords very well with Lawrence's notion of allotropic character, as expressed in the letter of 5 June 1914: the novelist's true theme is carbon, not coal or diamond, but the "radically unchanged element" which lies underneath the surface moods and instabilities of the ego (*Letters I*, p. 282). This internal self is stable, the wellspring of identity, but it is also electric, volatile, playing through the veins and bones of the body; and when the stress of passion is strongest it can be brought to the surface of the body, usually the lips, and sometimes conducted out of the body entirely; in fact, much later in *The Plumed Serpent*, the unspoiled Mexican Theresa tells Kate that perfect love demands that the soul be outside one's own body (p. 451). One of Lawrence's puzzling expressions is his description, repeated in many novels, of the body fusing, or fusing like a bead, or the veins fusing; I think this description denotes the radical breakdown of the body's articulation that occurs under extreme stress, the return of the body to the primal simplicity of the inner self, the bland tension of the embryo.

There exist, then, three levels of personality for Lawrence: first, the ego, the public self, the fixed shell, a mask which once was a valid self-expression but which, like anything rigid, has become a grotesque deformity. Lawrence inveighs so often and so bitterly against the ego that it is easy to forget that aboriginally everything, even what is hated most, was holy. According to *Kangaroo*, even the Ten Commandments were once the voice of God (p. 111); according to the essay "The Crown" the vulture was once an eagle until it decided to preserve a static form (*Phoenix II*, p. 405). The real, the only evil, is sitting still; it is a fatal condition because it is unresponsive to the urgencies of self-development. The second level of personality is the body, what Paul Morel in *Sons and Lovers* calls protoplasm; Paul must be the first painter, even in fiction, to argue against form: he says, speaking of a sketch of his, "It's more shimmery, as if I had painted the shimmering protoplasm in the leaves and everywhere, and not the stiffness of the shape. That seems dead to me. . . . The shape is dead crust" (p. 152). This is to some extent an overstatement; what Lawrence wants is not precisely shapelessness but tentative shape, fluid shape. Lawrence's favorite image of living corporality is the wave—Anna and Will turn into waves in a wavy world in their first ecstasy in *The Rainbow*; the cock in *The Man Who Died* is the crest of a short, sharp wave of life (p. 171); and in "The Crown" "Matter is a slow, big wave flowing back to the origin" (*Phoenix II*, p. 412)— but waves are not shapeless, only a very urgent, self-propagating sort of form, a dance nearly indistinguishable from the dancer. The third level of personality, the ultimate, original self, is, as we have seen, neither shaped nor shapeless; it can be described with equal validity as diamond or electricity, embryo or the soul after death. In a fairly late essay, "On Being a Man," Lawrence tries to define the relation between this last self and the body which it inhabits.

> The self that lives in my body I can never finally know. It has such strange attractions, and revulsions, and it lets me in for so much irrational suffering, real torment, and occasional frightening delight. The me that is in my body is a strange animal to me, and often a very trying one. My body is like a jungle in which dwells an unseen me, like a black panther in the night, whose two eyes glare green through my dreams, and, if a shadow falls, through my waking day. (*Phoenix II*, p. 616)

Lawrence calls it a panther, but he is approaching a level of internality where all metaphorical description is arbitrary, fails. It is disquieting to the ego, the ordinary external self, how remote the convulsions of the thing that prowls in the jungle are from common stimulus, common response.

If personality fails, it is because of inattentiveness, letting the more highly articulated parts, such as the ego, lag too far behind the less developed but more intense center. Many readers have felt a certain

inchoateness about Lawrence's heroes, while his villains are ago-
nizingly sharp, defined; this is because the hero must largely efface his
social self in his rapt attention to the earthquakes and volcanoes inside
him; it is hard to have exquisite manners when one's inner ear is
straining after the angels and devils of the hypogastrium. The early
heroes, except for Siegmund—I mean Cyril of *The White Peacock*,
Paul Morel, Will and Tom Brangwen, Rupert Birkin—are men who
possess a fair quantity of definable traits, enough so that Lawrence's
early novels can be read with pleasure by the audience whose canon of
taste is the nineteenth-century novel. I can describe Rupert Birkin: he
is violent, witty, didactic, mercurial, neurasthenic; but even in this
short list of traits I am less sure that another critic would agree with
me than if I were describing, say, Rosamund in *Middlemarch*. As
Lawrence grows older his protagonists have much less of this old-
fashioned character; only the corrupt consist of "an amorphous heap
of elements, qualities" (*Phoenix II*, p. 393), and the protagonists have
no elements or qualities at all. Who is Lovat Somers in *Kangaroo*? He
is a volcano, either erupting or in furious quiescence; Lawrence
develops his metaphors—the volcano, the ship of marriage—at such
length that the tenor is swallowed in the vehicle, that is, the metaphor
"Somers is a volcano" nearly collapses into identity, because the
physical forces inside the volcano and inside Somers are identical, and
the real subject of the novel is indifferently the unleashing of Somers'
devil or an upheaval of lava. Adjectives of attribution are super-
fluous; one might call Somers irascible, but to go much further would
be an exercise of critical ingenuity. Even with Aaron Sisson in *Aaron's
Rod* the inchoateness of the protagonist presents difficulties. Aaron's
progress through the novel is a continual struggle to rid himself of
fossilized accretions of personality, self-expression that is no longer
valid, feelings that are no longer felt; Aaron woos apathy more
fervently than any lover, attempts desperate detachment from human
relationship—the structure of the novel is a set of escapes from
increasingly more monied, cultured, attractive, and maimed circles of
acquaintance—and finally a renunciation of himself, the art of his
flute and even the art of his body:

> All his life he has *hated* knowing what he felt. He had wilfully, if
> not consciously, kept a gulf between his passional soul and his
> open mind. In his mind was pinned up a nice description of him-
> self, and a description of Lottie, sort of authentic passports, to be
> used in the conscious world. These authentic passports, self-
> describing: nose short, mouth normal, etc.; he had insisted that
> they should do all the duty of the man himself. This ready-made
> and very banal idea of himself as a really quite nice individual:

eyes blue, nose short, mouth normal, chin normal: this he had insisted was really himself. It was his conscious mask.

Now at last, after years of struggle, he seemed suddenly to have
dropped his mask on the floor, and broken it. His authentic self-
describing passport, his complete and satisfactory idea of himself
suddenly became a rag of paper, ridiculous. What on earth did it
matter if he was nice or not, if his chin was normal or abnormal?

His mask, his idea of himself dropped and was broken to bits.
There he sat now maskless and invisible. That was how he strictly
felt: invisible and undefined, rather like Wells's *Invisible Man*.
(Pp. 159–60)

In addition to this repudiation of the map of his body, Aaron has a
dream of cannibalism at the end of the book, best interpreted, I think,
as Aaron's symbolic devouring of his own body. In Lawrence's earlier
novels the body is generally sufficiently plastic, labile, responsive to
the core of identity that it is almost a suitable metaphor; but if the
crisis of personality becomes too great, if the ego's infection becomes
too widespread, then complete decapitation, disembodiment, the
renunciation of even the most tentative and subtle self-expression,
must be effected; one must learn to regard oneself, not as a "good-
looking man, fair and pleasant" (p. 3), with a coarse mouth—so
Lawrence describes him earlier—but as something unsheathed, naked
to every wind that blows, as insubstantial as a web of nerves, as
receptive, incompetent, and vague, a *passe-muraille*, glabrous.

Lawrence as his career progresses hews increasingly close to the
inmost self, cuts himself increasingly free from the baggage of the flesh
and the impediments of society. But in *The Trespasser*, the most
romantic, that is, the most mythy, flexible, and foreshadowing, of his
early works, there is an event almost unique in Lawrence's canon, a
suicide of a major character; and the state of Siegmund's mind as he
approaches self-destruction is most intriguing: he lies awake in bed,
feeling his throat produce sounds, his nerves thrilling to his sweat
trickling "like the running of a spider over his sensitive, moveless
body"; "his body was a separate thing, a terrible, heavy, hot thing
over which he had slight control" (p. 182). Even from the beginning of
Lawrence's career there is the sense that the body *in extremis* can be
radically alien from the real self, that coenesthesis can contract to
zero, that one's throat, skin, limbs, heart can be remote objects in an
objectified world. The sinuous, flamy, flexible bodies of Paul Morel
and Ursula are highly literary, figured, untrustworthy; when Lawrence scrutinizes the physical body with any precision or care it is
often with a certain loathing.

The Lady of Shalott

To Shelley and Blake, the world of mutability, the world of sense perception, is mostly a dour lie; the truth tends toward stability, a great unison. To Lawrence, who is in some ways the keenest and most devoted of Blake's children, the perceived world is agonizing, a deceit, not because it is subject to decay and vacillation but because it is fixed, supported unbearably on strong, ornate columns. This is of course an early romantic theme too, but no romantic poet ever preferred the dynamic to the mathematical sublime quite as vigorously as Lawrence. The world underneath the perceived world, the inner world, seethes, boils, seethes; it offers to the penetrating soul no respite, no calm sensible elysium, only a complete pasteurization or cleansing, the promise of a better, more lovely and agile body, a metanoia. Indeed the one saving feature of the world of husks, the horror of glass, steel, and skin, is that it decays. All matter is a huge slow wave returning to the Origin via the River of Dissolution, Birkin's mystical river in *Women in Love*, about which Lawrence has ambiguous feelings: it is a sewer populated by vermin, villains such as the Wildean aesthete Loerke who has wholly surrendered his body to the machine; it is a quagmire entangling the footsteps of those who wish to be holy, productive, single, uncontaminate, for it represents the total destruction of identity and integrity; on the other hand, it reduces the awful fixity of the soul, the awkward paralysis of the body, to the condition of the primal seethe, the world that is inside the world, from which productivity and creation can again emerge. We have seen how the embryo evolves into articulation; and through the River of Dissolution articulation devolves back into homogeneity. The mine owner Gerald Crich organizes his mines into amazing efficiency, but the urge to organize eventually becomes fatal, for if every possible subdivision and sub-subdivision is executed, if every capillary must ramify into invisibility, then the whole structure, held together by myriad tenuous strands, collapses into a heap from its own over-articulation. This is what is happening to the mining company in *Women in Love*; it is behind Lawrence's repeated asseverations that mathematical organization is the first and finest state of chaos. It happens to the human body and soul, too; Gerald's mistress Gudrun, bent on exhausting the limits of pure sensational experience, disintegrates "the vital organic body of life" (p. 515). Articulation is, then, a momentary brilliant form achieved between two states of formlessness, a condition of divine suspension like that of the god Quetzalcoatl in *The Plumed Serpent*, hung between the night and day, between the two major polarities. Beautiful form, like all kinds of heaven in Lawrence, must be transient:

> The error of errors is to try to keep heaven fixed and rocking like a
> boat anchored within the flux of time.... We can no more *stay* in
> this heaven than the flower can stay on its stem. We come and go.
> (*Phoenix II*, p. 413)

Whatever has form, from Ursula's voluptuous body to the huge
oppressive rectilinearities of London, is caught in the processes of
decay, whether from natural evolution, from the erosion of the
weather, or from some thwarted inner urge lacking expression that
reduces the inside to pulp; the solid substantial appearance of the
world belies ceaseless turbation, ghostly roils and swirls, the tremor
and tumescence of the inconceivable origin.

One reason for the unearthliness, sometimes even the illegibility, of
Lawrence's later fiction is that his gaze is steadily set on this inside
world, the world below and before. Except for *The Virgin and the
Gipsy*, and the beginning of *Lady Chatterley's Lover*, Lawrence's
fiction is increasingly purged of middle ground, ordinary furniture, in
order to maximize the intensity of a few brilliant figures placed upon
an ethereal tremulous background. But there is a certain pallor,
transparency, even in most of the heroes; the real subject of the later
fiction is heaven. Now there is nothing wrong with this; indeed
Lawrence's fantasies of the supernatural are more potent than those of
many other writers. But by abandoning close perception of the natural
world Lawrence lost what is, I believe, his unique strength as a writer:
the double perspective, the simultaneous perception of the world and
of the world within the world, the origin. Many of Lawrence's most
impressive pages come from this double perception:

> London was all a sort of dark mirage to him. His wide, nervous-
> looking brown eyes, with a smallish brown pupil that showed the
> white all round, seemed to be focused on the far distance, as if he
> could not see things too near. He was watching the pale deserts of
> Arizona shimmer with moving light, the long mirage of a shallow
> lake ripple, the great pallid concave of earth and sky expanding
> with interchanged light. And a horse-shape loom large and
> portentous in the mirage, like some prehistoric beast. (*St. Mawr*,
> p. 20)

This is from a rather late novella, *St. Mawr* (1925); the Indian called
Phoenix, whose eagle eyes can outstare the sun, sees through the false
mirage of London to the real mirage of the Arizona he has imported to
England. It is a choice between phantasm and phantasm; but Arizona
is a satisfactory metaphor for inhuman, alien actuality, interpene-
trated, undifferentiated, the font of formlessness and form, while
London is not satisfactory, for it has been rendered comfortable,
chopped into humanly apprehensible areas, upholstered with easy

corruption. Like so much of Lawrence's work from *Women in Love* on, the plot of *St. Mawr* proceeds from civilization to starkness, in the case to simmering electric New Mexico; but in other works, notoriously *The Man Who Died*, civilization is dispensed with entirely, and the whole fable takes place in afterlife, prelife, or ritual analogue of life, neither old Palestine nor modern, a Palestine only encountered by people whose eyes can rotate 360 degrees and whose noses have not been so distorted that they can only smell straight down.

Irony is a favorite word of Lawrence, though perhaps he is not usually thought an ironic writer; when Lawrence insists that a character is ironic, as with Alvina Houghton in *The Lost Girl* or March in *The Fox*, he often means to imply a certain inborn suspiciousness, an intuition that the world of appearances, of teatime and domestic chores, is not all that life holds. For Lawrence the real irony is the wisdom of incommensurability, the realization of the discrepancy between the point-blank vivacity of things and the external world which makes such a debased counterpoint to it, slow, dissonant, cancrizans. Habitual civilized life is a surrogate, a counterfeit, and Lawrence evolved some remarkable figurations to embody the relation between this deformed world and the inner world it so stutteringly represents. The most interesting of these figurations, and the one whose tracing is the most illuminating, is the Lady of Shalott.

Tennyson's vicarious lady first appears in Lawrence's fiction in the one well-known passage from Lawrence's first novel, *The White Peacock*, celebrated because it is a startling foreshadowing of the theme of his last novel, *Lady Chatterley's Lover*: in the passage the gamekeeper Annable, whom Lawrence has presented as a *genius loci*, a wild belligerent nature-spirit, "something between a bull and a couple of worms stuck together" (p. 157), an orator against civilization, tells Cyril the astonishing news that he used to be a parson, and was moreover married to a titled woman, Lady Crystabel; the marriage, much contaminated by the lady's sexual fantasies derived from French novels, did not prosper:

> Ah . . . You don't know what it is to have the pride of a body like mine. But she wouldn't have children—no, she wouldn't—said she daren't. That was the root of the difference at first. But she cooled down, and if you don't know the pride of my body you'd never know my humiliation. I tried to remonstrate—and she looked simply astounded at my cheek. I never got over that amazement.
>
> She began to get souly. A poet got hold of her, and she began to affect Burne-Jones—or Waterhouse—it was Waterhouse—she was a lot like one of his women—Lady of Shalott, I believe. At any rate, she got souly, and I was her animal—*son animal—son boeuf*. I put up with that for above a year. Then I got some servants' clothes and went. (P. 177)

Annable, whom one would scarcely have expected to have the faculty of speech, can quote French and discuss Pre-Raphaelite art. But the dialectic is clear: Annable is the body, an integrated, muscular being who relishes sexuality, while Lady Crystabel is the soul, affected, visual, vitiated, abstract—even her name, almost uniquely in Lawrence's canon, has attenuated to mere romantic allusion. She is like the Lady of Shalott in that she feels nothing, but her dead affections can be roused to a yearning optic covetousness for what she lacks, a body, the body's robust delight; but for Lawrence, who tends to distort myths in the direction of female malevolence, the Lady of Shalott does not break her mirror, descend toward a more direct human experience with the picturesque encrusted ruination that Waterhouse showed so beautifully, but instead invites her lover to live with her inside the mirror of her consciousness, tries to absorb him into effete phantasmagoria. Thus Annable finds Lady Crystabel's disturbing gaze fixed steadily on him, finds himself being reduced to a statue of Hercules, rendered nearly eviscerate and marmoreal by her aesthetic vision; her refusal to sleep with him is only an ostensible excuse for leaving her —the real danger for Annable is that she threatens his being.

With the wealthy Hermione in *Women in Love*, a rather exact counterpart to Lady Crystabel, it becomes clear that the content of the Lady of Shalott's mirror, the sum total of all the images registered on that dazzling warped surface, is the modern world itself, her house, London, her own body, everything:

> "You are merely making words," he said; "knowledge means everything to you. Even your animalism, you want it in your head. You don't want to *be* an animal, you want to observe your own animal functions, to get a mental thrill out of them. It is all purely secondary—and more decadent than the most hide-bound intellectualism. What is it but the worst and last form of intellectualism, this love of yours for passion and the animal instincts? Passion and the instincts—you want them hard enough, but through your head, in your consciousness. It all takes place in your head, under that skull of yours. Only you won't be conscious of what actually is: you want the lie that will match the rest of your furniture." . . .
>
> "It's all that Lady of Shalott business," he said, in his strong abstract voice. He seemed to be charging her before the unseeing air. "You've got that mirror, your own fixed will, your immortal understanding, your own tight conscious world, and there is nothing beyond it. There, in the mirror, you must have everything. But now you have come to all your conclusions, you want to go back and be like a savage, without knowledge. You want a life of pure sensation and 'passion.'" (P. 45)

Hermione is, to Lawrence's mind, the culmination of all the life-denying aspects of the tradition of nineteenth-century romanticism, as originally perpetrated by Keats and his doctrine of life as pure sensation, then moving through Tennyson to real decadence; the intellectual milieu of Lawrence's formative years was in part shaped by Wilde and his circle, and Lawrence was steeped in it; for instance, George's desire for Lettie, in *The White Peacock*, is inflamed by his study of Beardsley's Salome, which he claims is an exact likeness of his feelings for her (pp. 187–88). Hermoine, who is unhappy that her affair with Birkin is ending, tries to tempt Birkin by throwing his own rhetoric at him, denounces self-consciousness and praises spontaneity as vigorously as the most avid romantic poet; but even the rhetoric of life-assertion can, after a century, crystallize into a shell, crush the vital novelty of life that it ostensibly enhances. Hermione *seems* to be breaking the mirror, repudiating the Lady of Shalott's disinterested, vain, secondhand scrutiny, but, as Birkin sees, her studied primitivism is the last exhausted refinement of mirror vision, a final translation of the watcher herself, body and soul, into her own mirror, the wizard lost in his own labyrinth. In this condition there are no longer any possible grounds for distinguishing the deliberate from the spontaneous, so all sensations are equally pure, equally jejune, and the search for the life of pure sensation becomes a search for the lost body, more and more penetrating titillation, masochism, sadism.

In the subsequent novels the terms of the Lady of Shalott theme are slightly changed; instead of Tennyson we are given the cinema. Lawrence was fascinated by the cinema and, as a metaphor for the mind perceiving the solid-seeming externalities of the modern world, the cinema is every bit as useful as the Lady of Shalott's mirror: the audience is enthralled by illusory images that seem stable, but the real content of which is stroboscopic froth. The cinema is fairly important in *The Lost Girl*, for one of Alvina's jobs is as an accompanist in a theater for silent films; she discusses the attraction of the cinema for the common folk with a small-time impresario, who asks her why the common people are not jealous of the extraordinary feats they see on film:

> "Because they don't see the flesh-and-blood people. I'm sure that's it. The film is only pictures, like pictures in the *Daily Mirror*. And pictures don't have any feelings apart from their own feelings. I mean the feelings of the people who watch them. And that's why they like them. Because they make them feel that they are everything." (P.133)

The cinema is a projection of one's private world, one's private feelings or private anesthesia; it allows to each member of the audience the giddy feeling of self-expansion, loss of boundaries, which renders the world self-contaminate. Just as Lady Crystabel tried to distort Annable into a Greek statue, a character in a novel, *un boeuf*, anything as long as it was reduced and false, submissive, and as Hermione, more subtly, learned how to substitute an image of her body for her body itself, so the experience of the cinema provides endless opportunities for self-falsification:

> When I went to the film, and saw all the black-and-white
>   feelings that nobody felt,
> and heard the audience sighing and sobbing with all the
>   emotions they none of them felt,
> and saw them cuddling with rising passions they none of
>   them for a moment felt,
> and caught them moaning from close-up kisses, black-and-white
>   kisses that could not be felt,
> It was like being in heaven, which I am sure has a white atmos-
>   phere
> upon which shadows of people, pure personalities
> are cast in black and white, and move
> in flat ecstasy, supremely unfelt,
>   and heavenly.
>
> (Poems, pp. 443–44)

Heaven, as expressed in this late poem, is the mind's discarnate elysium, the pettinesses of personality magnified into twitching ecstasy, an appalling diuturnity. In a passage near the end of *St. Mawr*, after Lou has set up her Texas ranch, the themes of the mirror and cinema are used as interchangeable similes:

> Lou and her mother stayed a fortnight on the ranch. It was all so
> queer: so crude, so rough, so easy, so artificially civilized, and so
> meaningless. Lou could not get over the feeling that it all meant
> nothing. There were no roots of reality at all. No consciousness
> below the surface, no meaning in anything save the obvious, the
> blatantly obvious. It was like life enacted in a mirror. Visually,
> it was wildy vital. But there was nothing behind it. Or like a cine-
> matograph: flat shapes, exactly like men, but without any sub-
> stance of reality, rapidly rattling away with talk, emotions, activ-
> ity, all in the flat, nothing behind it. No deeper consciousness at
> all.—So it seemed to her. (P. 130)

Again, the cinema exaggerates, emphasizes, those truths of our pedestrian lives that we try to avoid, the flatness, the chattering squalor, the continual parody of real emotion, real event. Hermione's mirror, the weary modern world of "New Heaven and Earth," even the dismal cinema of the lower classes, all point toward the same truth: the external world, with its filthy cities and rubbery bodies, is a grotesque fantasy of the human consciousness, usurped by mad Urizen; once the mind's mirror is smashed we will see the buzzing underworld for which we now lack concepts, stride through it in rethought bodies.

In most of the work of Lawrence's last years the message is the same: "Let us lose sight of ourselves, and break the mirrors" (*Poems*, p. 477), as he expresses it in a poem, and the settings of his stories become increasingly plastic, emblematized, distended into transparency. Kate in *The Plumed Serpent* attains a society where all things conspire toward the induction of trance, corporeal self-effacement: the Woman Who Rode Away rides into a heaven in which even the angelic furniture, the garden, the town of white houses, is dismissed as mere insubstantial shadow, in which the earth and the sun have shivered away, dissolved in their own music. But at the very end, in *The Virgin and the Gipsy*, the Lady of Shalott returns in triumph—indeed Tennyson's poem constitutes the plot of the book—but the world inside the mirror has attained the upper hand and allows no escape, unlike *The White Peacock* or *Women in Love:*

> At the first landing, she stood as she nearly always did, to gaze
> through the window that looked to the road and the bridge.
> Like the Lady of Shalott, she seemed always to imagine that
> someone would come along singing *Tirra-lirra!* or something
> equally intelligent, by the river. (P. 51)

The Virgin and the Gipsy is perhaps Lawrence's most compelling presentation of the hideousness, the incalculable tenacity, of the mirror world, that is, ordinary England, in which under the smooth, oak-joisted coventionalities of teas and parties, dinners and teas, there lies monstrous prevarication, perversion; when the rector reminds Yvette of her hereditary depravity he threatens to murder her before the conversation is over. Yvette is first compared to the Lady of Shalott just after she has an argument with her tyrant grandmother over a mirror which she *nearly* broke; and that is the correct emblem for the resolution of this little revision of Tennyson's myth, for Yvette rebels, stamps her foot, allows the flood to wash over her—a dam bursts at the climax of the novella, and Lawrence admits "the flood was in her soul" (p. 107) as well as over her house—but she is weak, realizes that it is proper for the gipsy to abandon her, for she cannot break out of her familiar involution, cannot even assign to the gipsy the minimal reality of a proper name. Much pressure, hydraulic pressure, is put upon the mirror, but it finally does not break, although Granny, blissfully, drowns. As in "The Princess," a story which shares many common plot elements with *The Virgin and the*

Gipsy, the heroine has her glimpse of her Lancelot, the body's body—an excellent locution from the poem "Manifesto"—but eventually we are to suppose that the memory of the man is obliterated, or converted wholly to romance, made into a dream within the mirror, a most ironic fate for what is so warm, so real. Yvette's grisly opaque homelife is described minutely and lavishly, but it is still not so firmly established that an eye much exercised by an image of preternatural vividness cannot see through it as if it were so much gauze; at one point Yvette looks at some effeminate dancers and sees something very different:

> And again, since she was one of the people who are conscious in visual images, she saw the dark-green jersey rolled on the black trousers of the gipsy, his fine, quick hips, alert as eyes. They were elegant. The elegance of these dancers seemed so stuffed, hips merely wadded with flesh. Leo the same, thinking himself such a fine dancer! and a fine figure of a fellow!
> Then she saw the gipsy's face; the straight nose, the slender mobile lips, and the level, significant stare of the black eyes, which seemed to shoot her in some vital, undiscovered place, unerring. (P. 62)

Her emotional response is directed toward the vision of the gipsy, not toward any element of the mirror-scene before her; she treasures the acuteness of such images; such sensations, but she knows that becoming a gipsy-wife in a gipsy-caravan would be squalid, intolerable, a kind of death; and Lawrence's Ladies of Shalott never die, only wither away in their mirrors, leave their wild men to their own interior wildernesses. In terms of the physiology of *Fantasia of the Unconscious*, the plane of the mirror intersects the neck, severing the head from the marvels of the spine and the chest; as long as the mirror remains intact, the brain hypertrophies, swallows the world and grinds it into concepts—that much is well-known—but also, which is worse, the torso is much impoverished by the loss of the head, stumbles beautifully through the seething darkness but is disoriented, disspirited. The virgin needs the gipsy, but the gipsy needs the virgin too.

Indeed the pure savage does not exist in Lawrence. Annable was a rector; Mellors was a well-educated lieutenant, more gentlemanly than any gentleman, and his manners improve with each draft of *Lady Chatterley's Lover*. When Lawrence uses his powers of observation upon real illiterates, such as the descendants he saw in Mexico of his extravagantly beloved Aztecs, he typically feels revulsion; *The Plumed Serpent* is full of accounts of their bankruptcy, their inertia, the raging black holes at their centers. The true savage, like one of

39

Halliday's West African statuettes in *Women in Love,* is all swollen body with a shriveled skull contracted to coleopteran ugliness, lapsed as far into the River of Dissolution as the hardest and most abject European; the body that is without a mind has trouble keeping a fixed form, tends toward steatopygy, enormous genitalia, an overde-veloped sympathetic system, finally melts out of all individuality into putrid diffusion. It is for that reason that Lawrence's heroic savages are such literary savages, never really wild, only feral. Lawrence's principal vision of the origin, the lovely pre-world, not antediluvian but all flood, that preceded the intricate corpse of Europe, is a world of whispering naked men among fern trees not much different from themselves, Henri Rousseau's sensitive plants, sensitive jaguars, sensi-tive horses so astonished that acute teeth have been sunk into their acute necks. But when Lawrence considers the origin from the vantage point of the African, the genuinely uncultured, he has a quite different vision: the antecedent of the formless is formal, severe, highly delineated, even educated. The mind searches through its past for the abandoned body, the body searches for the mind.

The First World

The inadequacy of sheer body is a highly submerged truth in Lawrence's work, but it is important, even profound. It is true that *Fantasia of the Unconscious* is largely an attempt to relocate the mind in the torso, to show that most functions usually ascribed to the brain actually occur much lower; but a careful reading shows that even the brain, generally the most venomous of organs in Lawrence's scheme, has its proper uses. For instance, in the parable of the bicycle, a most mechanical fantasy based on Lawrence's favorite story from Plato, the chariot of the *Phaedrus,* the head is the bicycle's steering mechanism, a function not to be belittled (*Fantasia,* p. 96). In a later chapter, Lawrence says a word in favor of the ideal, which is astonishing, since Lawrence's canon usually reads as one long tedious polemic against idealism:

> In the same way, we *know* we cannot live purely by impulse.
> Neither can we live solely by tradition. We must live by all three,
> ideal, impulse, and tradition, each in its hour. But the real guide is
> the pure conscience, the voice of the self in its wholeness, the Holy
> Ghost.
> We have fallen now into the mistake of idealism. Man always
> falls into one of the three mistakes. In China, it is tradition. And in
> the South Seas, it seems to have been impulse. Ours is idealism.
> Each of the three modes is a true life-mode. But any one, alone or
> dominant, brings us to destruction. (P. 166)

Even the ideal is necessary, and heaven is the integration of mind and body together, fourfold, eightfold, sixteenfold, to the inconceivable end of powers of two.

Images of the body in its mindless, unencumbered state are not rare in Lawrence, and reduce finally to the image of the caveman, a creature who exists in two opposite species in Lawrence's imagination. The first kind of caveman is the snuffling anthropoid popularized by anthropologists, a creature for whom Lawrence has nothing but contempt:

> The mill of the mind grinds on, grinds the old grist over and over and over and over again. The blackest savage in Africa is the same, in this respect, as the whitest Member of Parliament in Westminster. His risk of death, his woman, his hunger, his chieftain, his lust, his immeasurable fear, all these are fixed ideas in the mind of the black African savage. They are ideas based on certain sensual reactions in the black breast and bowels, that is true. They are nonetheless ideas, however "primitive." And the difference between a primitive idea and a civilized one is not very great. It is remarkable how little change there is in man's rudimentary ideas. . . .
> Since man became a domesticated, thinking animal, long, long ago, a little lower than the angels, he long, long ago left off being a wild instinctive animal. If he ever was such, which I don't believe. In my own opinion, the most prognathous cave-man was an ideal beast. He ground on his crude, obstinate ideas. He was not more like the wild deer or the jaguar among the mountains than we are. He ground his ideas in the slow ponderous mill of his heavy cranium. (*Phoenix II*, p. 623)

The life of pure instinct is the full corruption of the thinking body, a sort of mental mindlessness. Hunger, lust, and fear are automatic reflexes, and all automatism, from knee-jerk liberalism on down, is a prison. The indiscrimate body is therefore depraved, and to that extent our bodies carry in them a kind of original sin. Lawrence has, however, the contrary vision as well, of a caveman who walks in beauty, whose body is supple, glorious, beastlike:

> "What do you want, Louise? You *do* want the caveman who'll knock you on the head with a club."
> "Don't be silly, mother. That's much more your subconscious line, you admirer of Mind.—I don't consider the caveman is a real human animal at all. He's a brute, a degenerate. A pure animal man would be as lovely as a deer or a leopard, burning like a flame fed straight from underneath. And he'd be a part of the unseen, like a mouse is, even. And he'd never cease to wonder, he'd breathe silence and unseen wonder, as the partridges do, running in

stubble. He'd be all the animals in turn, instead of one fixed, automatic thing, which he is now, grinding on the nerves." (*St. Mawr,* p. 50)

When Lawrence rhapsodizes he often shoots out similes in great bursts: animal man is compared in this one paragraph to a deer, a leopard, a mouse, a partridge, but no attention is paid to these vehicles; a hundred other animals could fit in the slots equally well. The point is not that unfallen man has any of the attributes of these animals, stealth, ferocity, cunning, good flavor, but that he has *all* attributes; man is superior to the other animals insofar as he sums them all up. This protean and ardent body is Lawrence's grandest hope for the body's interior potentialities, for the adequacy of the body as a metaphoric vehicle.

Lawrence's most admired poems, at least as far as his contemporaries were concerned, were his poems on animals; and the observations in these poems are remarkable not only for their precision but for their empathy, Lawrence's ability to respond to the animals with animal-like immediacy. Indeed the structure of most of these poems is based on the degree to which this transference can take place, from "Bibbles," in which every detail of the dog's behavior is easily, minutely, comprehended, to "Fish," in which thought and language are greatly twisted to form some reflex of the fishy world but in which Lawrence admits that the attempt fails utterly. When Lawrence's empathy is nearly complete, a number of bizarre changes often take place in the poet's body:

A Doe at Evening

As I went through the marshes
a doe sprang out of the corn
and flashed up the hill-side
leaving her fawn. . . .

I looked at her
and felt her watching;
I became a strange being.
Still, I had my right to be there with her. . . .

Ah yes, being male, is not my head hard-balanced, antlered?
Are not my haunches light?
Has she not fled on the same wind with me?
Does not my fear cover her fear?

(*Poems,* p. 222)

The buck's body is incipient in a man's, and not only as a metaphor for cuckolding; as always, when the body is in its states of highest vivacity, most flexible responsiveness to the alien interior and alien

42

exterior, its form is tentative, quicksilver, arbitrary. To be male, to be a polar thing, that is unchangeable and absolute; but all males are interchangeable with all other males. In his fine essay "... Love Was Once a Little Boy" Lawrence describes with harrowing intensity his celibate cow Susan and her philanthropy, her flirtings with her owner:

> But in the frail, subtle desirousness of the true male, towards everything female, and the equally frail, indescribable desirability of every female for every male, lies the real clue to the equating, or the *relating*, of things which otherwise are incommensurable.
> And this, this desire, is the reality which is inside love. The ego itself plays a false part in it. The individual is like a deep pool, or tarn, in the mountains, fed from beneath by unseen springs, and having no obvious inlet or outlet. The springs which feed the individual at the depths are sources of power, power from the unknown. But it is not until the stream of desire overflows and goes running downhill into the open world, that the individual has his further, secondary existence. (*Phoenix II*, p. 452)

The body must be malleable only because self-expression, always secondary and nugatory, is necessarily so complex; strands connect us to so much that is outside ourselves that it is never enough merely to contort our faces into grins and grimaces; we must be attentive to every conceivable resource of the body if our external shape is to constitute at all an image of our internal configuration. The caveman's body of modern anthropology, squat, hulking, all too fleshy, can be fit into the schemata of *Fantasia of the Unconscious* without much shoving; but the beautiful caveman of *St. Mawr*, who embraces the traits of all animals in sheerest disregard of the modern human form, the nearly incorporeal Pan visible through the third eye, is a pure construct of Lawrence's myth of the origin, the embryo of the human race, man prior to humanity, distilled protoplasm, an amoeba, Adam.

Just as the eye can always deduce from a perspective drawing the form in the landscape which it represents, so the eye ought to be able to see through evolved natural shapes to the inner world, inarticulate, unarticulatable, of which the landscapes of nature, as well as the bodies of men and animals, are a clumsy representation:

> A child mustn't understand things. He must have them his own way. His vision isn't ours. When a boy of eight sees a horse, he doesn't see the correct biological object we intend him to see. He sees a big living presence of no particular shape with hair dangling from its neck and four legs. If he puts two eyes in the profile, he is quite right. Because he does *not* see with optical, photographic vision. The image on his retina is *not* the image of his consciousness. The image on his retina just does not go into him. His unconscious-

ness is filled with a strong, dark, vague prescience of a powerful presence, a two-eyed, four-legged, long-maned presence looming imminent. (*Fantasia*, pp. 175–76)

The child sees correctly; the retina and the camera lie. Much of Lawrence's genius went into verbal representations of what a man could see if he carved eyes in his breast, the world of original energies that existed before the splitting of the firmament, the separation into the great polarities of male and female, sun and moon, day and night that is the fundamental condition of our present existence:

GRAPES

Ours is the universe of the unfolded rose,
The explicit
The candid revelation.

But long ago, oh, long ago
Before the rose began to simper supreme,
Before the rose of all roses, rose of all the world, was even in bud,
Before the glaciers were gathered up in a bunch out of the
      unsettled seas and winds,
Or else before they had been let down again, in Noah's flood,
There was another world, a dusky, flowerless, tendrilled world
And creatures webbed and marshy,
And on the margin, men soft-footed and pristine,
Still, and sensitive, and active,
Audile, tactile sensitiveness as of a tendril which orientates
      and reaches out.
Reaching out and grasping by an instinct more delicate
      than the moon's as she feels for the tides.

Of which world, the vine was the invisible rose,
Before petals spread, before colour made its disturbance,
      before eyes saw too much.
In a green, muddy, web-foot, unutterably songless world
The vine was rose of all roses.

(*Poems*, pp. 285–86)

First of all, the origin is a world without expression. We have seen how expression always falsifies, how little adequate the body is to the inner self, how quickly polluted the open stream becomes after it is no longer underground. The origin consists of vines that never flower, nor need to, for every creature is interconnected on the great network of vines, wires through which every creature is simultaneously sender and recipient, actor and acted-upon. But if we look more deeply at the language of this poem we see that there are no distinct creatures, no distinct race of men, that all such attribution of subject is verbal convention: the whole world consists of tendriled creatures and tendriled men in tendriled marshes, in short, the world is a sphere, each point of which is linked to every other point, no longer intricate and convoluted, tangled, but black with solid connection, an egg groping with delicate gravity toward its own hatching. The fact that the creatures are webbed, soft, suggests that they are fetal, their limbs still not fully articulated; the creatures, the vines, are wonderfully reticent, inward, and next to them the rose is but blatancy. Yet this vision is immanent in our modern world, just as the student of the rose can easily imagine the bud from which it sprang, can see its analogues among more primitive, vinier plants; indeed the anatomical fact that "apples and strawberries and peaches and pears and blackberries/ Are all Rosaceae" (*Poems*, p. 285) allows Lawrence to derive the multifarious expressions of the modern world from a single uniform source: the grape's pre-world is only a continuation of this infolding tendency, this collapsing of complexity into complex homogeneity. The modern grape is of course a metaphor for the prehistoric vine-world, and intoxication by wine is an analogue of the sensations proper to prehistoric man, the deliriousness, the scrambling of categories, the hyperesthesia; in fact the grape has "the power of invisibility" (*Poems*, p. 286), Aaron's invisibility, the oblivion of the body.

Other avenues besides alcohol lead in the direction of the world of the origin, as in, for instance, the later poem "Swan":

> But he stoops, now
> in the dark
> upon us;
> he is treading our women
> and we men are put out
> as the vast white bird
> furrows our featherless women
> with unknown shocks
> and stamps his black marsh-feet on their white and marshy flesh.
> (*Poems*, p. 436)

As in the cosmogonic myth of *Fantasia of the Unconscious*, there must exist a single finite living being at the core of the universe, prior to the articulation of either time or space; in this poem it is imaged as the swan, "the great swan upon the waters of all endings/the swan within vast chaos, within the electron" (*Poems*, p. 435). We need not search out this original being, deliberately induce the trance-world through stimulus; the millennial bird, the swan, like Quetzalcoatl in *The Plumed Serpent*, is ready to pounce upon us, whether we wish it or not. The image of Zeus raping Leda shows how the creative power latent in the origin can rise up at any moment, shatter our brittle world and inseminate our race in a great discharge of polarity, the male taking the female, night seizing the day; and in the instant of the shock there comes a glimpse of the first world itself, the indiscriminate marshiness of the swan and the woman alike, the homogeneity anterior to any polarity. In a related poem, "Give us Gods," we see that males too can feel their bodies interpenetrate with the swan's vitality: "The father of all things swims in a mist of atoms ... like a wild swan, or a goose, whose honk goes through my bladder" (*Poems*, p. 438). Lawrence's body, all our bodies and our world, are, if seen with properly inarticulate eyes, little more than atomic mist, a bog, the physical corpus of an undifferentiated vitality.

The structure of the poem "Grapes" is predicated on the contrast between the world of roses and the world of vines, that is, the formed and the formless homologues of the same experience. As is usual in Lawrence, the main fascination is the double perspective, the interface between structure and unstructure, the embryo yearning for full development, the mature man yearning for simplicity, annihilating purity. Lawrence likes nothing better than to describe chaos and old night, "sliding whirlwinds, blue-hot weights" (*Poems*, p. 529), the "wild orgasms of chaos" that resemble exactly the "wild orgasms of love" (*Poems*, p. 477); but nothing is more unstable than chaos, more subject to rapid decay. To imagine chaos is to imagine instantly the precipitation into structure, the heaviness contracting into gems (*Poems*, pp. 477, 529), light separating out of darkness, the condensation of gaseous clouds into water droplets:

> And in the great struggle of intangible chaos
> when, at a certain point, a drop of water began to drip downwards
> and a breath of vapour began to wreathe up
> Lo again the shudder of bliss through all the atoms!
> Oh, God is born!
>
> (*Poems*, p. 682)

This is Lawrence's physical metaphor for the splitting of the firmament. He conceives chaos as whirlwinds, a great struggling; and out of these myriad struggles separate the major polarities:

> Throughout the aeons, as the lizard swirls his tail finer than water,
> as the peacock turns to the sun, and could not be more splendid,
> as the leopard smites the small calf with a spangled paw, perfect,
> the universe trembles: God is born! God is here!
>
> (*Poems*, p. 683)

The narcissus and the peacock, vain self-sufficiencies, are among the first to announce God's birth; but God's birth is an ongoing parturition, manifest in increasingly structured entities, and soon the celebration of the divine is a leopard killing a calf, the necessary ferocity of a polar universe.

Once in his poems Lawrence imagines chaos, the original world of "Grapes," as it would be with exactly one division in it, the first, starkest division between the actor and the acted-upon:

HUMMING-BIRD

I can imagine, in some otherworld
Primeval-dumb, far back
In that most awful stillness, that only gasped and hummed,
Humming-birds raced down the avenues.

Before anything had a soul,
While life was a heave of Matter, half inanimate,
This little bit chipped off in brilliance
And went whizzing through the slow, vast, succulent stems.

I believe there were no flowers then,
In the world where the humming-bird flashed ahead of creation.
I believe he pierced the slow vegetable veins with his long beak.

Probably he was big
As mosses, and little lizards, they say, were once big.
Probably he was a jabbing, terrifying monster.

We look at him through the wrong end of the long telescope of
    Time,
Luckily for us.

(Poems, p. 372)

As the poem progresses, the basic confusions do not really resolve— the pre-world is still neither animate nor inanimate—but a line of demarcation finally obtains: the hummingbirds coalesce into one hummingbird, monstrous and unique, as irreducible as the phoenix, the world's one agent, piercing with his beak the vegetable veins, the world's total passivity, as inexpressive and flowerless as the vines in the poem "Grapes." Time constricts, contracts, breaks down, brings to small fruition. This poem is sometimes taken as an example of Lawrence's obsessive phallic consciousness, but he is trying to create a representation of a state for which the apparatus of genitalia would be a cruder metaphor—a brighter, more compelling polarity than anything possible to our modern male and female.

The single animal that evoked the greatest quantity of poetry from Lawrence was the tortoise, and one of the reasons for that was the dorsal cruciform design:

The Cross!
It goes right through him, the sprottling insect,
Through his cross-wise cloven psyche,

Through his five-fold complex-nature.

So turn him over on his toes again;
Four pin-point toes, and a problematical thumb-piece,
Four rowing limbs, and one wedge-balancing head,
Four and one makes five, which is the clue to all mathematics.

The Lord wrote it all down on the little slate
Of the baby tortoise.
Outward and visible indication of the plan within,
The complex, manifold involvedness of an individual creature.

(Poems, p. 356)

The Lord is the eager cartographer of *Fantasia of the Unconscious*, seeking bodily metaphor for the structure of the self; the tortoise, even as a baby, is a highly evolved, figured creature, and as an adolescent, crucified by sexuality—Lawrence speaks of tortoise-desire in a manner remarkably similar to that of Plato's Aristophanes in the *Symposium*—the tortoise is a polar fragment desiring a "consummation beyond himself" (*Poems*, p. 361); he achieves it in coition and emits a peculiar intense shriek:

His scream, and his moment's subsidence,
The moment of eternal silence,
Yet unreleased, and after the moment, the sudden, startling
    jerk of coition, and at once
The inexpressible faint yell—
And so on, till the last plasm of my body was melted back
To the primeval rudiments of life, and the secret.

(Poems, p. 365)

Hidden in the aching polarities of our modern world are noises, *frissons*, visions, in which the unsplit, original world can be felt; for an instant the positive and the negative can cancel each other out, leaving the body melted away into the divine nullity of plasma.

In Lawrence's novels the desire for regression to the origin is much more acute in the later novels than in the earlier. As in many other aspects of his career, Lawrence's novels fall into two fairly well-defined sequences: *The White Peacock* through *Women in Love*, England; *Aaron's Rod* through *Lady Chatterley's Lover*, exile and return. In the earlier sequence there is easy commerce between the ordinary and the inconceivable; at any moment a simple touch may reduce the world and the body to flame; the world of the origin is intimate, impending, scarcely concealed within the corpus of the everyday. In the later sequence, the shell is more rigid, impenetrable, disjunct from the core; to get to the inside, extreme measures must be taken, exile, self-abandonment, finally ritual approach. It is for this reason that the novels of Lawrence's long world-traveling contain the most sustained descriptions of the pre-world; in the earlier novels the origin was never far enough away nor strange enough to require a Baedeker account of its flora, fauna, and customs of the natives; and the local exotica that Lawrence beheld, especially in Australia, gave him a whole new metaphoric apparatus for the clothing of his intuitions of the prehistoric:

> The previous world!—the world of the coal age. The lonely, lonely world that had waited, it seemed, since the coal age. These ancient flat-topped tree-ferns, these towsled palms like mops. What was the good of trying to be an alert conscious man here? You couldn't. Drift, drift into a sort of obscurity, backwards into a nameless past, hoary as the country is hoary. Strange old feelings wake in the soul: old, non-human feelings. And an old, old indifference, like a torpor invades the spirit. An old, saurian torpor. . . . Worlds come, and worlds go: even worlds. And when the old, old influence of the fern-world comes over a man, how can he care? He breathes the fern seed and drifts back, becomes darkly half vegetable, devoid of pre-occupations. Even the never-slumbering urge of sex sinks down into something darker, more monotonous, incapable of caring: like sex in trees. (*Kangaroo*, p. 179)

One puts a fern seed to one's mouth, exactly as at the end of the poem "Grapes," and drifts into vegetable trance, a perfect renunciation of human emotion, human personality, human pettiness. In the earlier novels one could simply wait for the internal lightning to discharge, expect the transfiguration that comes out of intense human relationship; in the later novels, in which personality is older, more encrusted, clotted, there must be a painful cutting-away, cleansing, without familiar people, a solitary self-dismemberment, before human relationship can be attempted once again. In *Kangaroo*, the world within the world loses some of its tension, becomes chiefly diffuse, languid, an image of the apathy that is Somers' desired state and of the fatigue that is pervasive in him; not until *The Plumed Serpent* does it regain its usual fury. In *Kangaroo* the pre-world is invariably slack, a time that precedes not only the major polarities but all struggle, energy, or significance; Australia is a continent the inside of which is sheer vacant space without inner meaning (pp. 22, 36), identical to the terrain of the Australians' consciousness; the emu is a gentle bird "belonging to far past twilight ages, before enemies and iron weapons were perfected" (p. 208). This climate has an effect on Somers' blood, thinning it to transparency, although Somers is too self-willed to attain the invisibility of Aaron Sisson.

Language
Closely related to this downward search for the first world, *n'importe où hors du monde*, is the search for a first language, a purified inward speech as remote from English as the Jurassic is from the modern. In the earlier novels there is a certain distrust of the verbal, but from *Women in Love* on, there is strident mockery of language and its inadequacies. Language, like the body, is a structured attempt at self-expression; and, like the body, it is finally a glassy shell which stifles and crushes the vital center that it ought to express:

> Half-made, like insects that can run fast and be so busy and suddenly grow wings, but which are only winged grubs after all. A world full of half-made creatures on two legs, eating food and degrading the one mystery left to them, sex. Spinning a great lot of words, burying themselves inside the cocoons of words and ideas that they spin round themselves, and inside the cocoons, mostly perishing inert and overwhelmed. (*Plumed Serpent*, p. 116)

What is hateful about language is that its expressions are such a grisly parody of what we really wish to express:

> He said "Your nose is beautiful, your chin is adorable." But it sounded like lies, and she was disappointed, hurt. Even when he said, whispering with truth, "I love you, I love you," it was not the real truth. It was something beyond love, such a gladness of having surpassed oneself, of having transcended the old existence. How could he say "I" when he was something new and unknown, not himself at all? This I, this old formula of the age, was a dead letter. (*Women in Love*, p. 423)

The statement "I love you" is a low deformed analogue of what Birkin wishes to say, the ape-speech of a thick tongue. Pronouns falsify; Birkin is not "I" nor is Ursula "you," for such reference is a defamation, an attribution of the trivialities of the ego to the transcendent impersonal self; and *love* is not the right word either, for it is a word much debased by common usage, lust, impure emotional blurring and confusion, a word rendered unsatisfactory for the binary-star relation which Ursula and Birkin are attempting. The body is repudiated along with language; Ursula's nose and chin are as irrelevant to her stark being as the dead letter of the pronoun "I." This identification of language with the body is even clearer in an earlier chapter:

> She knew, as well as he knew, that words themselves do not convey meaning, that they are but a gesture we make, a dumb show like any other. And she seemed to feel his gesture through her blood, and she drew back, even though her desire sent her forward. (P. 212)

This is the best hope for verbal expression, that it can be a charade, an enactment of the inner self, which the listener, after much perplexity and speculation, and with the help of intuitive sympathy, the vague sonorousness and resonance of the gesture, may be able to solve. But the dangers of such attempts at expression are quite striking: Birkin is much ridiculed for his incomprehensible preachiness, often finds himself tiresome, a Hamletizer, a word-bag (pp. 212–13). Ultimately there is no real speech except silence:

> He stood on the hearth-rug looking at her, at her face that was upturned exactly like a flower, a fresh, luminous flower, glinting faintly golden with the dew of the first light. And he was smiling faintly as if there were no speech in the world, save the silent delight of flowers in each other. Smilingly they delighted in each other's presence, pure presence, not to be thought of, even known. But his eyes had a faintly ironical contraction. (P. 357)

This is the linguistic analogue of Birkin's favorite fantasy, the lovely clean humanless world that is all grass after the perishing of the human race, its supersession: a world swept bare of words; but the irony in Birkin's eyes, as faint as a flower or as speechlessness itself, suggests the double perspective, the simultaneous awareness of the ordinary Ursula and the Ursula who is one of the daughters of men in Genesis, of speechlessness and speech.

In Lawrence's subsequent novels he uses quite frequently a device which never appears in the novels published before 1920: he will take a word or a metaphor and play with it for a paragraph or even longer, twist it, overliteralize it, make a succession of puns, rhymes, jokes. This occurs most notoriously in *Kangaroo*, in which one whole chapter, "Harriet and Lovat at Sea in Marriage," is a long set of variations on a single figure of speech, which is toyed with, pawed, cuffed, squeezed like an accordion, a signal exercise in misguided virtuousity. Usually this kind of event is accompanied by a dismissal of the fiction, Lawrence speaking *in propria persona* to his readers, haranguing them, calling them gentle readers and even worse epithets. Whenever Lawrence does this, he is in effect surrendering to the devil, sleeping with a whore, wallowing in a fallen language. This is his satirical mode; by manipulating corrupt speech, by making it feel even queasier than it usually does, he is trying to provide a verbal image of a corrupt subject. One of Lawrence's first efforts at sustained fiction after *Women in Love* was the abortive satirical novel *Mr. Noon*, and it is there that he developed most of these techniques, in an analysis of the verb *spoon*, a slang expression which Lawrence equates with overrefined modern sexuality, the taming and full domestication of the beast, its aestheticism:

Why bother about spades being spades any more? It isn't the point. Adam no more delves than Eve spins, in our day. *Nous avons changé tout cela.* Call a spoon a spoon, if you like. But don't drag in garden implements. It's almost as bad as the Greeks with their horrid plough metaphor.

Ah, dear reader, you don't need me to tell you how to sip love with a spoon, to get the juice out of it. You know well enough. But you will be obliged to me, I am sure, if I pull down that weary old scarecrow of a dark designing seducer, and the alpaca bogey of lust . . . .

Let us mention that this melting and ripening capacity is one of the first qualities for a good modern daughter of Venus, a perfect sweetness in a love-making girl, the affectionate comradeship of a dear girl deepening to a voluptuous enveloping warmth, a bath for the soft Narcissus, into which he slips with voluptuous inno-cence . . . .

We have risen to great heights, dear reader, and sunk to great depths. Yet we have hardly fathomed the heights and depths of the spoon in the Co-op. entry. Don't you wish you were as good at it as Noon and Emmie! Practise, then; and you too may swing suspended in the heights, or depths, of infinity, like the popular picture we used to see over the railway bookstalls, winged spooners mid-heaven in the blue ether. Ah, we are all so clean, nowadays; fine clean young men, infinitely spoony, and clean young spoony maidens to match. Nothing earthy; not we. All in mid-air, our goings-on. (*Phoenix II*, pp. 125, 128)

Spoon, spoon, spoon; Lawrence repeats the word until it is pure inanition, all meaning vanished in the physical grossness of the rounded lips that pronounce it, of the little metal implement of its homonym; the novel becomes mistuned, miswritten, the descriptions of the caresses a parody both of sentimental convention and of Lawrence's own earlier verbal ecstasies. Having played with a word until it cracked, having perverted the mysteries of his high style, Lawrence seems to have been left with a permanent suspiciousness; certain beauties were expunged from his style forever, Will and Anna will never deliquesce under the haystacks again, nor will Paul Morel walk with Clara with the village lights beneath them, step through a wilderness of stars. The basic trick of Lawrence's new, low style is to play with the physical, external aspects of words, their sounds and rhymes, and to overelaborate the metaphorical vehicles; this latter is one of Swift's favorite habits, and sometimes Lawrence's words attain the weight and heft of the words spewed from the theater in *A Tale of a Tub*, which leave dents on the skulls of those in the audience. Once near the end of his career, Lawrence even looks so far outward that he turns his ridicule toward typographical devices:

> It suits the modern temper better to have its state of mind made up of apparently irrelevant thoughts that scurry in different directions, yet belong to the same nest; each thought trotting down the page like an independent creature, each with its own small head and tail, trotting its own little way, then curling up to sleep. We prefer it, at least the young seem to prefer it to those solid blocks of mental pabulum packed like bales in the pages of a proper heavy book. Even we prefer it to those slightly didactic opinions and slices of wisdom which are laid horizontally across the pages of Pascal's *Pensées* or La Bruyère's *Caractères*, separated only by *pattes de mouches*, like faint sprigs of parsley. Let every pensée trot on its own little paws, not be laid like a cutlet trimmed with a *patte de mouche*. (*Poems*, p. 417)

Those aspects of literary art which are the most physical, the deliberate choice of figures of speech, the sound of words, the setting of pen to paper, the layout of the printed page, are the aspects most like the glossy shell of the physical body or the ego, the most wretched and corrupt. It is interesting that for Lawrence the worst of all languages is English, if Don Ramon in *The Plumed Serpent* is a trustworthy spokesman (p. 390); if this is true then his hatred of language—he says in *Fantasia of the Unconscious* that it is criminal to teach children how to read and write—seems to be a reflex of his self-hatred, for Lawrence recognizes that anyone who desires the annihilation of the word means in part that he wishes himself destroyed.

Lawrence has left us a few hints by which we may construct something of the morphology and syntax of real language, the language inside English, the language spoken by the beautiful caveman and the divine embryo. Clearly real language consists of sounds in the throat anterior to any sort of phonic articulation, a bird's cry or the uninflected breathing of a lover:

> All the while the peewits were screaming in the field. When he came to, he wondered what was near his eyes, curving and strong with life in the dark, and what voice it was speaking. Then he realised it was the grass, and the peewit was calling. The warmth was Clara's breathing heaving. He lifted his head, and looked into her eyes. They were dark and shining and strange, life wild at the source staring into his life, stranger to him, yet meeting him; and he put his face down on her throat, afraid. What was she? (*Sons and Lovers*, p. 353)

Paul Morel, coming to consciousness out of sexual trance, senses for a moment the primal earth that is prior to any mental conceptualization or language, hears the peewit and Clara's breathing without knowing what they are, as if they were the first noises in a newly created world; the sound of the breathing is wild, fascinating, and Paul seems to put his ear near her throat in order to gain closer access to this new-born language. Usually Lawrence recognizes in his narration that intense, molten experience is not adequately conveyed by words; whenever his flautist, Aaron Sisson, is moved by great events Lawrence informs us that the words of the description are the author's attempt to translate it to an alien medium, something that Aaron would never have done; the content of Aaron's mind is pure music:

> He was a musician. And hence even his deepest *ideas* were not word-ideas, his very thoughts were not composed of words and ideal concepts. They too, his thoughts and his ideas, were dark and invisible, as electric vibrations are invisible no matter how many words they may purport. If I, as a word-user, must translate his deep conscious vibrations into finite words, that is my own business. I do but make a translation of the man. He would speak in music. I speak with words.
>
> The inaudible music of his conscious soul conveyed his meaning in him quite as clearly as I convey it in words: probably much more clearly. But in his own mode only: and it was in his own mode only he realised what I must put into words. These words are my own affair. His mind was music. (Pp. 160–61)

One writes novels because real language is private; the public expression in English may be a distortion and falsification, as all highly defined and accessible expressions must be, but it is presumably better than nothing. There is some discussion in *Kangaroo* about the nature of the novelist's calling: the novel ought not to be a "mere record of emotion-adventures," but instead a "thought-adventure," a term that does not denote a list of opinions nor a catalog of pensées, but instead something more like an electroencephalogram, a graph of the tensions and resolutions of the electric interior. In a later chapter Lawrence suggests that the highest calling of the novelist is to be tuned into the Godhead through a wireless set:

> The highest function of *mind* is its function of messenger. The curious throbs and pulses of the God-urge in man would go on for ever ignored, if it were not for some few exquisitely sensitive and fearless souls who struggle with all their might to make that strange translation of the low, dark throbbing into open act or speech. Like a wireless message the new suggestion enters the soul, throb-throb, throb-throb-throb . . . .
>
> Alas, there is no Morse code for interpreting the new life-prompting, the new God-urge. And there never will be. It needs a new term of speech invented each time. A whole new concept of the universe gradually born, shedding the old concept. (Pp. 301, 302)

The divine pulsings constitute a language, but it is always a language for which we have no key to interpretation, which we have never heard before. It is significant that almost the only language for which Lawrence ever showed much enthusiasm was Etruscan, a language which seems an adequate expression of the universe's creative urge simply because the meanings of all its words have been forgotten. Real language is not a system of semaphores and dumb shows but the point-blank manifestation of the alien presences that surround us, names indistinguishable from things, the tangible leafy names that Adam gave to trees, the feathery involuntary names that Adam gave to birds.

It would seem that Lawrence should be rendered almost mute by such radical contempt for his chief expressive instrument, the English language; and it is true that more of his energies went into painting than many believe; however, English was discovered to be a language that could afford a few pleasures and which, through craft and stealth, could render certain warm approximations to inner language, real language. Sometimes Lawrence uses English words as icons, idolatrous representations of reality; Lawrence can even be discovered naming the unnamable attributes of the first world, like awesome Adam in his second week of paradise:

> Come up, thou red thing.
> Come up, and be called a moon. . . .
>
> Rise, thou red thing,
> Unfold slowly upwards, blood-dark!
>
> Burst the night's membrane of tranquil stars
> Finally.
>
> Maculate
> The red Macula.
>
> (*Poems*, p. 302)

Moon is a name that is being invested with the sacred, reserved for holy usage, as the old Latin cognates of $\pi\upsilon\rho$ and $\H{\upsilon}\delta\omega\rho$ became divine names eventually expunged from common speech. The expression "Maculate/The red Macula" suggests that there are certain kinds of rhetoric for which ordinary syntax, divisions into verbs and nouns, is inappropriate, and a study of any of several passages from novels which describe moments of extreme intensity will bear this out:

> And timorously, his hands went over her, over the *salt*, compact *brillance* of her body. If he could but have her, how he would enjoy her! If he could but net her *brilliant*, cold, *salt-burning* body in the soft iron of his own hands, net her, capture her, hold her

55

down, how madly he would enjoy her. He strove subtly, but with all his energy, to enclose her, to have her. And always she was *burning* and *brilliant* and hard as *salt*, and deadly. Yet obstinately, all his flesh *burning* and *corroding*, as if he were invaded by some consuming, scathing poison, still he persisted, thinking at last he might overcome her. Even, in his frenzy, he sought for her mouth with his mouth, though it was like putting his face into some awful death. She yielded to him, and he pressed himself upon her in extremity, his soul groaning over and over.

She took him in the kiss, hard her kiss seized upon him, hard and fierce and *burning corrosive* as the moonlight. (*Rainbow*, pp. 319–20)

The word *salt* keeps shifting, flickering between nominal and adjectival usage, a magnetic verbal unit that attaches itself to compounds and then whirls away; Ursula is salt, a salt-burning body that burns like a fierce salt, a brilliance and brilliant, a corroding corrosive that causes corrosion. Here we have English that is approaching the condition of the real language, homogeneous, in which the interchangeability of all elements is proved by taking simple sentence forms and exhausting the permutations of a few words, in which the absolute uniqueness of the rhetorical subject is proved by the use of that haunting twentieth-century device, the reflexive simile: salt is like salt, Ursula is like Ursula, iron is like iron, Skrebensky is like Skrebensky. The classical apparatus of simile is used for the indication of resemblance, that is, difference; here, no definition of the thing is possible except the thing itself. The structure is attenuating, vanishing, into simple identities, a double nexus. Almost the entire content of this paragraph and the subsequent ones could be expressed as the following:

> Ursula-brilliant-cold-salt-burning-corrosive
> Skrebensky-iron-dissolved-burned-corroded

In the real grammar of the real language, the sole distinction is between present participle and past participle, the actor and the acted-upon; all other structures only represent the recalcitrance of fallen English. The participle is a favorite form of Lawrence's, and we can see its usefulness, straddling between noun and verb, dynamically linking presumed subject and presumed object without requiring close definition of either. Real language is of course highly dynamic, fluctuant, a speech reborn with each experience; as Ezra Pound says, In the beginning was the Verb.

In the novels of Lawrence's later years, as we have noted, this assault on syntax almost disappears, and Lawrence uses language more dourly, gingerly, with a grudging submission to its irrefragability and convention. Nevertheless, in one or two passages some extensions of the old manipulations can be observed:.

> From her doorway, from her porch, she could watch the vast, eagle-like wheeling of the daylight, that turned as the eagles which lived in the near rocks turned overhead in the blue, turning their luminous, dark-edged-patterned bellies and under-wings upon the pure air, like winged orbs. (*St. Mawr*, p. 147)

This is an interesting rhetorical play, a spirallike description of a spiral motion: the daylight is like eagles, and the eagles are like winged orbs. The basic pattern of the simile is: A is like B is like A', for the "winged orbs" suggest both the rotating planets for which "wheeling of the daylight" is a fanciful description, and the impalpable principle of vivacity in the universe, Quetzalcoatl silent and serene between his two wings, the major polarities. Again, all elements of description are interchangeable: as things are above, so are they below. But more remarkable than this passage from *St. Mawr* are two passages, written entirely in standard English, which seek to define soberly, from above, the nature of both the primal world and the primal language. The first is from *Aaron's Rod*:

> As in clairvoyance he perceived it: that our life is only a fragment of the shell of life. That there has been and will be life, human life such as we do not begin to conceive. Much that is life has passed away from men, leaving us all mere bits. In the dark, mindful silence and inflection of the cypress trees, lost races, lost languages, lost human ways of feeling and of knowing. Men have known as we can no more know, have felt as we can no more feel. Great life-realities gone into the darkness. But the cypresses commemorate. In the afternoon, Aaron felt the cypresses rising dark about him, like so many high visitants from an old, lost, lost subtle world, where men had the wonder of demons about them, the aura of demons, such as still clings to the cypresses, in Tuscany. (P. 357)

The cypress trees lead Aaron to contemplate lost languages; but clearly the key to the lost languages is the "inflection of the cypress trees" themselves. The grammar of the real language *is* the real world; the inflected cypress trees are hieroglyphs, self-commemorative, self-signifying, self-sustaining. This language, the language of things uttering themselves, is a major hope in the twentieth century, a language as unwieldy as the bag of objects that the pedants of Lagado carry on their backs but a language in which the work of poetry is perfectible and immediate; "Sepulchral señors ... Should make the intricate Sierra scan" (Stevens, "The Comedian as the Letter C"). In *Kangaroo* it seems that real language, which has escaped into the first world in *Aaron's Rod*, has become elusive beyond the artist's range, at last abandons the province of the human altogether:

> Richard rocking with the radium-urgent passion of the night: the huge, desirous swing, the call clamour, the low hiss of retreat. The call, call! And the answerer. Where was his answerer? There was no living answerer. No dark-bodied, warm-bodied answerer. He knew that when he had spoken a word to the night-half-hidden ponies with their fluffy legs. No animate answer this time. The radium-rocking, wave-knocking night his call and his answer both. This God without feet or knees and face. This sluicing, knocking, urging night, heaving like a woman with unspeakable desire, but no woman, no thighs or breast, no body. The moon, the concave mother-of-pearl of night, the great radium-swinging, and his little self. The call and the answer, without intermediary. Non-human gods, non-human human beings. (P. 348)

The throb of the wireless, real language, is addressed not to the novelist or to anyone else, but goes straight from night to night, Godhead to Godhead, the deity who is at once actor and acted-upon, womanlike but no woman, finally freed from the vain clumsy metaphor of the human body, the human tongue. We fancy that many things, our speech, our bodies, are representations, prefigurations, analogues, expressions, of the creative utterance; but in fact our bodies and our languages have been tested and have failed, radio-active deity stands alone and apart, the *sol niger* was kindled not to light our feet to the underworld but as triumphant self-expression, self-delighting, invisible beyond our eyes, impalpable beyond our hands.

Lawrence intercepts few broadcasts after *Kangaroo*; his attempts to frame the first world through circumlocution do not stop, but real language is neither explored much nor defined. There is some evidence in *Lady Chatterley's Lover* and in *Apropos of Lady Chatterley's Lover* that certain common sexual monosyllables may be the only extant words of the real language: "We shall never free the phallic reality from the 'uplift' taint till we give it its own phallic language, and use the obscene words" (*Phoenix II*, p. 514). But probably even obscenities have only metaphorical value, since the phallus itself, as we know, is itself but a metaphor; probably Lawrence had been brought up in such a way that even as an adult he could feel a slight thrill at vulgar talk, and this thrilling language could provide a low analogue for the profound shock, the stupefaction, which would surely accompany the utterance of a real word. In the introduction to *Pansies* Lawrence suggests that *arse* might have the iconic or idolatrous value which he had sometimes assigned to English words earlier in his career: "The word arse is as much god as the word face" (*Poems*, p. 418). But for the most part Lawrence's attention seems to turn away from the verbal aspect of verbal craft, and he remains alternately oblivious to or exasperated with the fallen language that he is forced to use, eschews grandeur or delicacy in favor of sobriety or flippancy, dashes out words, words, words that alas have nothing to do with what they mean.

Ritual

We have seen that in Lawrence's fiction from about 1920 to 1926 there is retrenchment, abandonment, disillusion with the standard instruments of human expression, language and the body; and to a large extent in these novels and stories what replaces them is ritual. Ritual, on the one hand, is itself a kind of language, in that it is like the gestures and dumb shows to which Lawrence compared language in *Women in Love*; but on the other hand ritual is the opposite of language in that it is the antithesis of self-expression: ritual is the attempt to express something alien to oneself by altering deliberately the configurations of one's body and mind. Ritual is a reduction of the self to a type, a self-stereotyping, almost a self-mortification. Ritual behavior is still ostensibly an attempt to uncover the inmost self, the core; but Lawrence now conceives the core as something wholly incompatible with the comfortable, self-preserving shell, something alien, interstellar; and he has come to wonder whether the shell—that is, the body, the mind, and the ego—can really be dispensed with. He has already spent over a decade investigating the interior, the prime; and he has discovered that Ultima Thule is a country convulsive, invertebrate, ululant, tremendous, no place for the casual tourist or perhaps even for the living.

The antecedents of the peculiarly rigid and defined rituals which are the chief substance of the novels of the 1920s are a long series of fleeting but resonant episodes in the earlier novels. Lawrence's first novel, *The White Peacock* (1910), is probably his most ritualized piece of fiction until "The Woman Who Rode Away" (1924). The whole action of the book is played out against a highly figured, literary tapestry of fairies, nature-sprites, *A Midsummer Night's Dream*, peony-myth, "a giddy little pastoral—fit for old Theocritus" (p. 262). Those who believe Lawrence to be some sort of unspoiled primitive, the nature-child of Nottinghamshire or the Derby Cro-Magnon, would do well to consider the following passage:

> "He'd make old Daphnis there,"—pointing to Leslie—"sing a match with me, Damoetas—contesting the merits of our various shepherdesses—begin Daphnis, sing up for Amaryllis, I mean

Nais, dam 'em, they were for ever getting mixed up with their nymphs."

"I say, Mr. Cresswell, your language! Consider whom you're damning," said Miss Denus, leaning over and tapping his head with her silk glove.

"You say any giddy thing in a pastoral." (P. 262)

Just as the gamekeeper Annable is really a rector, so the rhetoric of pastoral ease and simplicity is imported from Cambridge, adapted from Theocritus and old ballads, and stands in uncomfortable juxtaposition to the fussy ordinariness of those who really live in the country. Lawrence in later life hated the Bloomsbury circle of writers, thought them affected and precious, almost forgot that he was himself a faithful immediate Georgian (*Phoenix*, pp. 304–7), a true brother of Rupert Brooke and a close cousin of E. M. Forster, whose wild men, whose Pan-spirits so closely resemble Lawrence's own. Cyril, the unique first-person narrator in any of Lawrence's novels, is most certainly an embryonic self-projection of Lawrence himself, a Lawrence nearly unknown to us, who greatly enjoys the city despite his nostalgia, whose mother is still alive, a brittle effete young man, the heir of the post-Pre-Raphaelites. A more flippant and posturing narrator than Cyril never told a story in Bloomsbury; Cyril is swoony, sentimental, a scholar, looks when naked like "one of Aubrey Beardsley's long, lean, ugly fellows," manages to inhibit the conversation of the vulgar simply by his funereal presence. The last third of the novel seems to be young Lawrence's fanciful projection of his weary prosperous middle age, a self increasingly involute and moribund, full of whispers of misogyny, in short someone very like Lawrence's later image of all that was bad in contemporary writers. One excoriates chiefly what one sees in oneself.

When in *The White Peacock* the characters crack jokes about a pagan vital past; when picnic guests enact Theocritus or when the girls twine flowers in George's hair and pretend that he is Bottom with the ass's head, we may take it that the characters are making an attempt to express some vague stirring of real awe or rapture, a stirring that is strained, distorted into smart talk and coyness. Sometimes, however, a character will try an expression that is less arch, more honest, for instance in this speech in a discussion of Druidic symbolism of mistletoe and snowdrops:

"Look at all the snowdrops"—they hung in dim, strange flecks among the dusky leaves—" look at them—closed up, retreating, powerless. They belong to some knowledge we have lost, that I have lost and that I need. I feel afraid. They seem like something in fate. Do you think, Cyril, we can lose things off the earth—like

mastodons, and those old monstrosities—but things that matter—
wisdom?"

"It is against my creed," said I. (P. 154)

But Cyril feels it too; all of them in one place or another put
themselves to the trouble and embarrassment of enacting old legends,
making gestures which are a graceless self-conscious imitation of
prehistoric gesture. In fact Cyril's sensibility is more avid for emblems
than any other in Lawrence's early work; when anything moves Cyril
it veers into type and symbol, loses common identity. When he sees his
girlfriend Emily and his sister Lettie studying snowdrops he thinks:
"The girls bent among them, touching them with their fingers, and
symbolizing the yearning which I felt" (p. 153); the girls have turned
into projections of a private vision. Cyril's desired relation to the
country-folk is that of Wordsworth to the leech-gatherer; he wishes to
be a connoisseur, wishes to fit his friends and his countryside into a
systematized romantic set of emblems. This habit is more obvious in a
scene in which Emily is grazed by a dog's bite and then, basking in
Cyril's attentiveness, entwines red berries in her hair while Cyril
makes a coronet of convolvulus; Cyril becomes serious, tells her she is
neither Chloe nor Bacchante but something Pre-Raphaelite:

> "You are like Burne-Jones' damsels. Troublesome shadows are
> always crowding across your eyes, and you cherish them. You
> think the flesh of the apple is nothing, nothing. You only care for
> the eternal pips. Why don't you snatch your apple and eat it, and
> throw the core away?"
> She looked at me sadly, not understanding, but believing that I
> in my wisdom spoke truth, as she always believed when I lost her
> in a maze of words. (P. 86)

The sudden solemnity yields only a highfalutin speech, the sense of
which is that Emily is too idealized, angelic, inhuman, insufficiently
sexual. But Cyril's effacement of Emily has only begun: soon he
laments that Emily is one of those who instead of "bringing with them
clouds of glory, trail clouds of sorrow" (p. 87); and, as if this sad
Wordsworthian moralism were not enough, the lovers, or close
friends, start walking by the old Kennels "which had been the scene of
so much animation in the time of Lord Byron" (p. 87). Emily touches
Cyril's sensibility, and all the plangencies reverberate into the nineteenth century; she becomes indifferently an old painting or poem,
anything as long as it is aesthetic, lacking individuality, and part of
a more tremulous, more sensitive part.

There is a famous scene in *Sons and Lovers*, which is to some extent
a counterpart of this scene, in which Paul pelts Miriam with cherries,
pelts her until she gladly garlands herself with them, in a great

cleansing ritual release of sexual energy. The suggestion of an old *sacre du printemps* in this later, more vigorous episode is unmistakable; it is as romantic and mythy as the scene in the earlier novel, but the figured literary background is suppressed, the action is allowed to generate its own resonance. But the rituals of *The White Peacock*, for all their belabored allusiveness, are true ancestors for all the later rituals, which are equally aesthetic and equally part of the past. The mode of all ritual is the double perspective, the superposition of a modern figure, a modern action against the contours of prehistoric figure and traditional event. The vapid selfless gaze of a woman in a Burne-Jones painting is not a permissible back-figure for ritual description after *The White Peacock*, for the artists who interested Lawrence later in his career were the cave-painters of early southern Europe and the intriguing men of early Britain who erected menhirs and dolmens—although there are mastodons even in *The White Peacock*. All ritual is life struggling to be art, and therefore must have the power and limitation of all other attempts at formality.

After the little rituals of *The White Peacock*, there come, first, an ambitious but quite inept attempt in *The Trespasser* to correlate the two principal characters with various Wagnerian operatic roles; then, some delicately handled use of fertility myth, the paraphernalia of haystacks and fruit festivals, in "Love Among the Haystacks" and *Sons and Lovers*; the generational structure of *The Rainbow*, in which each succeeding pair of lovers reenacts the same rites as the previous pair; and the more sophisticated and arty rituals of *Women in Love*, where the sisters can make little ballets, Naomi and Ruth, or the eurhythmic dance of Gudrun in front of the cattle, in a vague attempt to define certain subliminal relations between the characters or simply to exercise real magic, control the forces of nature. None of this, however, constitutes much more than a premonition of the remarkable rituals of "The Woman Who Rode Away" or *The Plumed Serpent*; the one transitional work, the true indicator of the origin and tendency of ritual evolution in Lawrence's canon, is *The Lost Girl*, completed after *Women in Love* but begun in 1912. Here, the action of the plot centers, astonishingly, on a seedy theatrical troupe that comes to a small English town and contrives to recruit, with varying success, the novel's heroine, Alvina Houghton. Lawrence suggests here and there that the five members of the troupe are competent vaudeville performers, but basically they have only one act, a little drama they keep performing, the White Prisoner, in which some American Indians capture and torture a white man for whom the squaw feels sympathy; one of the braves drags a bear into the wigwam, apparently dead, but the bear revives, attacks and kills the Indian who had tortured the white man. The drama ends with the white man managing to kill the bear, then kneeling with the squaw, holding her hand. This inauspicious sentimental scene is a parable of the history of the human race, a simplified analogue of what the wise young Indian will tell the Woman Who Rode Away:

> "... why aren't you Indians masters of the white men?"
> "Because," he said, "the Indian got weak, and lost his power with the sun, so the white men stole the sun. But they can't keep him—they don't know how. They got him, but they don't know what to do with him, like a boy who catch a big grizzly bear, and can't kill him, and can't run away from him." (*Short Stories II*, p. 571)

Modern Indians, whether the false Hurons of *The Lost Girl* or the incorrupt Chilchui of "The Woman Who Rode Away," are effete, have surrendered their power, their vivacity—that which is called Quetzalcoatl in *The Plumed Serpent*—but the white man has proved a poor custodian, and the Indian will soon arise in triumph, resume his old dominion. This millennial upheaval is stated explicitly in "The Woman Who Rode Away," but in *The Lost Girl* the dénouement, the execution, is worked out within the subtle confines of myth. The original script of the White Prisoner clearly brings us only so far as the white man's usurpation, his conquering of the sun, namely the bear, and of the moon, namely the heart of the squaw Kishwégin; but in a later performance, Ciccio, the hero of the novel, the actor who plays the role of the torturing Indian killed by the bear, has a whim or caprice, and refuses to die on stage, says derisively "Vivo sempre, Madame," to the consternation of the other actors; in this manner history finds its proper parabolic expression, the lucid homeostasis of the world's body sets the allegory aright. "The Woman Who Rode Away," which ends in the sacrificial murder of the heroine, the white prisoner, is largely a literalization of this allegory, deprived of the irony and complexity that the double roles provide in *The Lost Girl*; Lawrence first writes the parody, then attempts the serious expression of ritual, just as T. S. Eliot's career evolves from *Sweeney Agonistes* to *The Family Reunion*. But Lawrence's parody in *the Lost Girl*, like the shamefaced pastoralisms of *The White Peacock*, both manifests and hides the profound tensions that underlie human interaction. The five strolling players travel under the collective name of Natcha-Kee-Tawara, have partly assumed in ordinary life their Indian stage identities; and Alvina, prompted partly by her love for Ciccio, joins the Tawaras in a remarkable initiation ceremony, the first extended ritual scene in Lawrence's novels. Madame Rochard, alias Kishwégin, the leader of the troupe, wishes to bestow upon Alvina the Indian name Vaali, but through inebriate pun this is changed to Viale, then Allée, and finally Allaye; and the Way is the best of possible ritual names, for ritual itself is but a halfway station on the road to the interior, a form which is nothing more than approximation to real form. As Alvina is rechristened, paganed, Ciccio furtively feels her knee, the whole company gets drunker; the scene is no solemn ceremony but all roisterous celebration, gay with self-mockery, in a disreputable but impressive chant: "We are the Hirondelles. We are Kishwégin. We are Mondagua." and, finally, "We are Allaye." Identities are diffused and merged, subsumed into the tribal identity, but no one takes it too seriously; indeed later, when Alvina undergoes ritual marriage with Ciccio, the male members of the Tawaras, after many jovial insults at each other, inform Alvina that she is the bride of the Tawara:

> "I can't be the bride of all four of you," said Alvina, laughing.
> "No—no! No—no! Such a thing does not come into my mind. But you are the Bride of Tawara. You dwell in the tent of Pacohuila. And comes the day, should it ever be so, there is no room for you in the tent of Pacohuila, then the lodge of Wal-gatchka the bear is open for you. Open, yes, wide open—" He spread his arms from his ample chest, at the end of the table. "Open, and when Allaye enters, it is the lodge of Allaye, Walgatchka is the bear that serves Allaye. By the law of the Pale Face, by the law of the Yenghees, by the law of that Fransayes, Walgatchka shall be husband-bear to Allaye, that day she lifts the door-curtain of his tent—"
> He rolled his eyes and looked around. Alvina watched him.
> "But I might be afraid of a husband-bear," she said. (Pp. 255–56)

Pacohuila, of course, is Ciccio's Indian name. The leering polyandry that is suggested here is mostly comical banter, but surely there is an undertone of real sexual desire, an interest in further exploring the ramifications of genuine communality, loss of private identity. Alvina is the real White Prisoner of the novel; and she is to some extent lacking, a disappointment to the Tawaras, partly the undoing of their close-knit tribe, for she is too caught up by her self-will to be able to relinquish her private identity, her personal ego. The ritual union of the Tawaras is for no one, however, a complete self-abnegation. They quarrel perpetually, and accept quotidian strife with fair tolerance; but they believe just enough in the mumbo jumbo to remain a relatively cohesive benevolent group despite the difficulties of travel, work, and excessive closeness. They are strong and successful insofar as they walk the knife-edge between the overritualized and the overordinary, between the Indian roles and their assigned European identities—the best acrobatic act in Lawrence's work. Lawrence did not find the jocular rituals of *The Lost Girl* his definitive expression of the nature of ritual, but perhaps *The Lost Girl* is, more than any other of his works, evocative of the delicate spirit of ritual, the double perspective. In this novel all balances keep shifting, all conclusions are tentative; at one point Alvina tries to reweigh the values of her home town, Woodhouse, against the interior and fantastic world of the Tawaras:

> They sat down to their tea and toast and marmalade, during this harangue. Miss Pinnegar was always like a douche of cold water to Alvina, bringing her back to consciousness after a delicious excitement. In a minute Madame and Ciccio and all seemed to become unreal—the actual unrealities: while the ragged dithering pictures of the film were actual, real as the day. And Alvina was always put out when this happened. She really hated Miss Pinnegar. Yet she had nothing to answer. They *were* unreal, Madame and Ciccio and the rest. Ciccio was just a fantasy blown in on the wind, to blow away again. The real, permanent thing was Woodhouse, the *semper idem* Knarborough Road, and the unchangeable grubby gloom of Manchester House, with the stuffy, padding Miss Pinnegar, and her father, whose very soul seemed dirty with pennies. (Pp. 162–63)

In no other work is the evanescent boundary between the external and the ultimate explored with greater tact and precision; the rituals of "The Woman Who Rode Away" proceed inexorably, with the annihilating simplicity of an avalanche or the rotation of the earth, but in *The Lost Girl* the ritual cohabits easily with the day-to-day, is fluid and responsive to our ordinary complexities, seems a pragmatic solution for the lovelorn and the lowly.

The Lost Girl, Alvina, comes eventually to a real renunciation and self-sacrifice, leaves England and goes to live with Ciccio in an old, ghost-ridden pagan Italy. She does not revert to Indian barbarism—indeed she finds even the illiterate Italian peasants inert, malicious—but instead tries to keep, rather successfully, her British egoism well poised against the brighter impersonal self that she discovered in ritual. She is still, in effect, half in theater and half in common life, has managed to create with Ciccio a simple ongoing ritual *à deux*. In "The Woman Who Rode Away" the heroine's self-sacrifice is not just metaphor but an actual ritual murder. This story is Lawrence's first sustained fantasy of worldlessness, heaven or anteheaven, and in many ways his most impressive and precisely delineated. A nameless American woman in Mexico, married to a mining executive with the usual fumbling *politesse* of marriages between the white-skinned, rides out for no explicable reason except internal necessity in the direction of a remote valley populated by the descendants of the Aztecs, prelapsarian, tantalizing, inaccessible. Through a process of continual dying, self-collapse, self-attenuation, she does arrive among the unique Indians, whose community is not so impermeable that one of them, her interpreter, has not returned from the United States after having worked in Chicago. As it turns out, the world within the world is tiny, agrarian, sharp, sapid:

> They passed the maize, and came to a big wall or earthwork made of earth and adobe bricks. The wooden doors were open. Passing on, they were in a network of small gardens, watered by a tiny ditch of running water. Among each cluster of trees and flowers was a small, glittering white house, windowless, and with closed door. The place was a network of little paths, small streams, and little bridges among square, flowering gardens.
>
> Following the broadest path—a short narrow track between leaves and grass, a path worn smooth by centuries of human feet, no hoof of horse nor any wheel to disfigure it—they came to the little river of swift bright water, and crossed on a log bridge. Everthing was silent—there was not a human being anywhere. (*Short Stories II*, p. 561)

Heaven is an enclosed miniature garden, a scale map of an outer world from the distant past that never knew machine, civil, humanized, a landscape enhanced and productive to the last possible refinement; as is often the case in Lawrence's fiction, a reduction in size is accompanied by a concentration, an intensification. But there is restlessness even in Arcady, an impatience with a world in which the Chilchui valley is only an island amid Caucasian despoliation; the modern era, the Christian era, is only an interregnum, a usurpation of the powers of sun and moon by a race that cannot control them. The Indians await that millennium in which their triumph will become worldwide, when Indian governors will hold the dancing lash over the disintegrated white races. This millennium is absolutely preordained, ineluctable, imminent; the coming of a white woman is mere annunciation, her sacrifice is mere dramatization. As the woman prepares for her execution, as the Indians lead her up the rock-slopes into the rock-cleft, the rock-womb, she understands perfectly well that the ritual is only a celebration, a vivid analogue to real experience: "I am dead already. What difference does it make, the transition from the dead I am to the dead I shall be, very soon" (*Short Stories II*, p. 579). Ritual action never accomplishes anything; it is only a manipulation of comparatively inert materials into the semblance of the movements that actually occur in the nickel core of the earth or in the corona of the sun; it is a cosmic puppet show, in which the actors wear flame-colored, night-colored, wind-colored, death-colored clothes. The Woman Who Rode Away is systematically purged of everything that is not symbol, until she is a counter in a game; she wanders into a fixed play, a company of actors who know but one drama, and she is given costume and mask, carefully coached, taught her role, a role which it is her innermost will to enact to completion, a most satisfying role in which the irresistible pressures of history and the cosmos find expression, fruition, in her humble body, interesting death. The heavenly valley of the Chilchuis is all frigid potentiality:

> They were following a stream-bed: but the stream was dry, like summer, dried up by the frozenness of the lead-waters. There were dark, red-bronze willow bushes with wattles like wild hair, and pallid aspen trees looking cold fresh against the snow. Then jutting dark rocks.
>
> At last she could tell that the dancers were moving forward no more. Nearer and nearer she came upon the drums, as to a lair of mysterious animals. Then through the bushes she emerged into a strange amphitheatre. Facing was a great wall of hollow rock, down the front of which hung a great, dripping, fang-like spoke of ice. The ice came pouring over the rock from the precipice above, and then stood arrested, dripping out of high heaven, almost down to the hollow stones where the stream-pool should be below. But the pool was dry. (*Short Stories II*, p. 579)

Ritual landscape and stage props are like this, mysterious, wild, impending; a place fit for ritual should have a landscape that is suspended, scarcely equilibrated, about to fall or burst, a place in which huge natural forces are about to manifest themselves, in this case the melting of the ice, which will fecundate the world, release the Indians from their enchantment. The ritual execution, insofar as it is an emblematization of the enervation, the slackness, the passing away of the white races, is an enactment of what is already happening; insofar as it represents the Indian takeover of the globe, the Aztec millennium, it is an act of magic, because it attempts to hurry along the forces of the universe by making a symbolic physical expression in anticipation of the actual event. Thus Lawrence's later novels to some extent are themselves magical acts, ceremonies often repeated in public in order to foreshadow and hasten the millennium, through description of the shape of those actions which tend to bring it about.

The theatrical apparatus of *The Lost Girl* returns, in more solemn form, in *The Plumed Serpent*, but instead of shabby troupers we are given a cadre of upper-class Mexicans who wish to stage a political revolution by playing the roles of the old Aztec deities. The ring-leader, Don Ramon, has devised a set of bodily and mental exercises, like yoga, which, through systematic tension and relaxation of the muscles of the arm and chest and the nerves of the spine, affects the consciousness in such a way as to cause blackout, hypnotic trance; this is a deliberate induction of oceanic feeling, sensory expansion, the willed assumption of his divine inner self, Quetzalcoatl, the Plumed Serpent, the conjunction of sky and earth, the spherical wholeness that is on the far side of polarity. This is a small, private indication of the function of ritual in the novel: if you can alter your body into the proper configuration, the archetype will manifest itself, Quetzalcoatl will wear you as his mask. One of the bodily gestures, the salute to God by thrusting the clenched fist high over the head, is also part of the public ceremony of Don Ramon's followers, the men of Quetzal-coatl; and these scenes show us another aspect of mass ritual, the advertising, the publicity, that accompanies the enactment. In crowd ritual, everyone does the same thing; all the men make one kind of gesture, one kind of speech, one kind of dance, and all the women do another. The rituals of *The Plumed Serpent* make all men, except possibly Don Ramon-Quetzalcoatl and his lieutenant, Don Cipriano-Huitzilopochtli, identical and interchangeable. This typing, this pure self-surrender, this tuning of one's core into the ceaseless inaudible strid-ulation of the cosmos, is the highest gift that ritual can offer; it is analo-gous to the potion given to the Woman Who Rode Away that enabled her to hear the sunlight raining down and the mild bark of a dog's embryo in the womb, to summon from the skies the unfallen snow. In the great rit-ual scene of *The Plumed Serpent*, the Opening of the Church, the refur-bishment and paganization of the local Christian church, Don Ramon has unlikely intercourse with a statue of Quetzalcoatl that he has made:

> The drum began to beat, the men of Quetzalcoatl suddenly
> took off their serapes, and Ramon did the same. They were now
> men naked to the waist. The eight men from the altar steps filed up
> to the altar where the fire burned, and one by one kindled tall
> green candles, which burned with a clear light. They ranged
> themselves on either side of the chancel, holding the lights high, so
> that the wooden face of the image glowed as if alive, and the eyes
> of silver and jet flashed most curiously.... Kate looked up in
> consternation at Ramon. He had dropped his arm, and stood with
> his hands against his thighs, like a statue. (Pp. 374, 377)

Don Ramon becomes statuelike, the statue becomes human; man and statue are properly interchangeable, for Don Ramon is trying to turn himself into an icon, aesthetic, impersonal, a spectacle for public awe; and indeed a large portion of the novel is iconographic, a careful description of those banners and flags that will signal the leader's triumphant emergence. Pictures and rituals have almost no intrinsic import; in *The Rainbow* Will and Anna do not see the same stained-glass lamb, because one is a Believer and the other is not; but a picture can be a framework, a scaffolding, which the viewer can charge with his own meaning, thereby making it a representation of what moves him, and giving his vague feelings an approximate form. There is always some tacit sympathy among men that precedes public ritual, that makes the ritual possible, not vice versa.

The chief purpose of the ritual of the Opening of the Church, related to the establishment of Don Ramon's godhead, is the purification of the human body. Four men approach Don Ramon with four bowls, each containing a colored liquid which is touched to a different part of the body; Don Ramon holds a mixing bowl, and while the liquids are mixed he intones:

> For save the Unknown God pours His Spirit over my head and fire into my heart, and sends his power like a fountain of oil into my belly, and His lightning like a hot spring into my loins, I am not. I am nothing. I am a dead gourd. (P. 375)

Spirit, fire, power, lightning—four different modes of the single electricity of the divine being—must flow into the prime centers of the body, an anatomy well known from *Fantasia of the Unconscious*. The cleansed body approaches transparency, incorporeality, an intense simplified state; in fact, the cacique who executes the Woman Who Rode Away has a glassy body, is an "aged man, like a skeleton covered with dark glass" (*Short Stories II*, p. 580), the same stuff as his sacrificial obsidian. When one's body contorts itself to ritual shape, light shines through it, it is sexually irresistible; shortly before Don Cipriano takes for his lover Kate Leslie, the sodden Englishwoman who is the heroine of *The Plumed Serpent*, no Lost Girl but a lost woman forty years old, Kate has a vision of an inner electrical world that is congruent point for point with our more familiar world:

> It was one of those little periods when the rain seems strangled, the air thick with thunder, silent, ponderous thunder latent in the air from day to day, among the thick, heavy sunshine. Kate, in these days in Mexico, felt that between the volcanic violence under the earth, and the electric violence of the air above, men walked dark and incalculable, like demons from another planet.
> The wind on the lake seemed fresh, from the west, but it was a running mass of electricity, that burned her face and her eyes and the roots of her hair. When she had wakened in the night and pushed the sheets, heavy sparks fell from her finger-tips. She felt she could not live.

The lake was like some frail milk of thunder; the dark soldiers
curled under the awning of the boat, motionless. They seemed
dark as lava and sulphur, and full of a dormant, diabolic
electricity. Like salamanders. (P. 348)

Kate can see directly through some stray soldiers, see their insides
turn molten, sublime altogether; this remarkable vision, in which
every detail of the landscape has resolved into electricity, has been
translated into impalpable pools and heaps of scintillae, is not directly
vouchsafed by ritual, but occurs soon after Cipriano and Ramon have
suggested to her that she too could be a goddess, Huitzilopochtli's
bride; and such vague intimations of one's own divinity, which are
the origin of all ritual, suffice to wash away the apparent solidity of the
world, sweep it into apotheosis. Rituals are performed in order to
picture the interior of things by slight dislocations of ordinary objects,
by an assignation of symbols the primary purpose of which is to
persuade that all things material are but symbols. Ritual is the
yearning of a fallen world to assume the candid garments of a defunct
innocence, a whore amorous of painted virginity.

Kate, who feels herself approaching virginity through her novel
liaison with the Indian Don Cipriano, takes no direct part in the ritual
overthrow of the Mexican government, even in her role as the goddess
Malintzi; she is not to be sacrificed, for the major ritual of the book
lies neither in marriage nor death but in the exclusively male-to-male
political bonding previously observed in *Kangaroo*. Yet in a sense the
whole ritual apparatus is mustered for her benefit, for it is only through
the induction of a complete outsider, a civilized European, that the
force of ritual can be tested and perfected. When she leaves for Europe
at the end, it is clear that she has to some extent failed her friends and
lover; but it is also true that they have to some extent failed her, still
need her, just as gipsies, Indians, and gamekeepers always require
some high-toned woman. The ritual union of men is, at best, a form of
high integration, a conjoining into a single human body that moves
with one motion and one purpose, *headed* by Don Ramon, *armed* by
Don Cipriano. This intricate ritual body is created in order to
accomplish male goals, which we know from the *Fantasia* consist of
the building of the external world, the edifying of the human race.
However, integrated structures always seek greater complexity,
greater integrity. The male ritual body of Don Ramon and his gang, as
effective and unanimous as it is, is nevertheless deficient, finally
perhaps incompetent. It is flawed because it is all male, out of balance,
a wild single pole, a free-floating radical. Don Ramon in his depths is
raging and empty until he meets Theresa; Don Cipriano without Kate
is bewildered and fragmentary. "We are all fragments. And at the

best, halves" (p. 426). Kate finds this difficult, bitter wisdom: we wish to be self-contained, individual, but we are each of us Aristophanes mooning after the egg. Without Kate, the ritual union of the Mexicans lacks two faculties important to that fully integrated human body that is Lawrence's best hope for structure: it lacks the female principle, and it lacks European mind, analysis, and sophistication. Barbarism is never enough, despite Lawrence's fascination: "The scientific fair-and-square Europe has to mate once more with the old giants" (p. 456). This marriage, the marriage of the brain and torso, heaven and hell, must be accomplished circumspectly, delicately:

> But the change, Kate felt, must not come on her too soon and too suddenly, or it would rupture her and she would die. The old way has its horror. The heavy-footed *à terre* spirit of aboriginal Mexico would be so horrible to her, as to make her wicked. The slow, indomitable kind of existing and persisting, without hope or elan, which is in the aboriginal American, sometimes made her feel she would go mad. The sullen will persisting over the slow, dark centuries, counting the individual existence a trifle! A tenacity of demons, less than human. And a sudden ferocity, a sudden lust of death rousing incalculable and terrible. (P. 456)

It is into this demonic world, this inertia near death, that Mexican ritual leads without her; the Southern tribe requires ritual marriage or sacrifice of the white goddess from the North, for it is only through symbolic absorption of her faculties that equipoise can be found, the vernier adjustments effected, the final triumph made possible. Kate represents the assertion of individuality, while the tribe chants: "*The blood is one blood. In the blood, you and I are undifferentiated*" (p. 457). These forces always oppose, and their vigorous opposition, according to the *Fantasia*, is health. Lawrence has no great fondness for Kate; the Woman Who Rode Away is timorous, dull, a "white ant"; Alvina Houghton is fairly likable, although often querulous; but they are the necessary angels of the millennium, unwitting redeemers of our race, even if they are but little cerebra who have ambled into a great dormant body, dazed by the solar plexus, made nervous by the spasms of the hypogastrium.

Lawrence wrote, evidently around October 1927, a peculiar essay titled by Edward McDonald "Autobiographical Fragment," in which he indicated exactly the nature of those superhuman ceremonies of which ritual is a poor imitation. It begins simply enough, with an account of a visit to Lawrence's birthplace and a comparison of the inferior present-day town to the town as he knew it as a child; he takes a tour of a quarry he had known well, and finds it in a new rock-cleft leading to a crystalline cavity, a rock-womb. He goes to

71

sleep. A millennium passes; it is the year 2927, Lawrence is awakened, washed, by a man, a "movingness," who speaks words, an "aloudness." Lawrence is in heaven, naked, simultaneously inside and outside of his new body: he has the use of his ordinary sense-apparatus, but he can also perceive his body as if from a distance:

> And I opened my eyes again and blinked with terror, knowing the light of day. I shut them again, and felt sensations out in space, somewhere, and yet upon *me*. Again my eyes were opened, and I even saw objects, great things that were here and were there and then were not there. And the sensations out in space drew nearer, as it were, to me, the middle me.
>
> So consciousness swooped and swerved, returning in great swoops. I realized that I was I, and that this I was also a body that ended abruptly in feet and hands. Feet! yes, feet! I remembered even the word. Feet!
>
> I roused a little, and saw a greyish pale nearness that I recognized was my body, and something terrible moving upon it and making sensations in it. Why was it grey, my own nearness? (*Phoenix*, p. 825)

In heaven one is released from the confines of the sick body, in heaven nouns and verbs and adjectives are one, and the best words are the words that denote the parts of the body. What has happened to Quetzalcoatl and the Man Who Died, the summoning to resurrection, the coalescing of the split self, actor and acted-upon, into a single new body, heavy beyond gravity, terrestrial beyond earth, has happened to the wishful author too. The doctrine of allotropic characters, characters who are carbon rather than diamond or soot, leads, as one might have predicted, to a kind of autobiography; if individuation is explicable through imbalances in nerve centers, then Lawrence can write about no one whose tendencies are not amplifications and projections of aspects of his own being; and in the "Autobiographical Sketch" we see that he can work through the common problems of his fictions under his own name as easily as any other.

This is the first and only heaven in Lawrence's writings in which the landscape does not consist of stylizations, waysigns pointing toward some still superior place, in which social event is not ritual, not emblematic of some more profound integration. Heaven is, simply, Home:

> And at the top of the hill was a town, all yellow in the late afternoon light, with yellow, curved walls rising massive from the yellow-leaved orchards, and above, buildings swerving in a long, oval curve, and round, faintly conical towers rearing up. It had something at once soft and majestical about it, with its soft yet

> powerful curves, and no sharp angles or edges, the whole
> substance seeming soft and golden like the golden flesh of a city.
>   And I knew, even while I looked at it, that it was the place
> where I was born, the ugly colliery townlet of dirty red brick. Even
> as a child, coming home from Moorgreen, I had looked up and seen
> the squares of miner's dwellings, built by the Company, rising from
> the hill-top in the afternoon light like the walls of Jerusalem, and
> I had wished it were a golden city, as in the hymns we sang in the
> Congregational Chapel. (*Phoenix*, p. 829)

It is Lawrence's dirty red hometown translated brick for brick into elysium. What the boy's religious fantasy had adumbrated is the reckless truth: Newthorpe, turned by easy metathesis, a loosening of the vocal chords, into Nethrupp, has become New Jerusalem, purged of rectilinearity, all golden flesh, a human body, in short, Mother. The society of heaven, like all good societies, is hierarchical: the proletariat consists of those who resemble berries, "a whole fruit, body and mind and spirit, without split" (*Phoenix*, p. 830). Those in authority are more like flowers than berries; the supreme leader, though, is neither fruit nor flower, impassive nor radiant, but has "a quavering glimmer like light coming through water" (*Phoenix*, p. 835), a highly evolved variant of the transparent cacique in "The Woman Who Rode Away," a continuation of the earlier tendencies of Lovat Somers toward transparent blood, Aaron Sisson toward invisibility. Whether fruit, flower, or pure light, the bodies of the heavenly residents are wholly integrated; and next to them Lawrence feels immature, "a green apple," a butterfly just out of the chrysalis. Something is still wrong: Lawrence has died into life, transfigured himself into that innocence that is on the far side of experience—into art—but he is yet no angel; he has handed himself halo and harp, so to speak, but is dissatisfied, frustrated, human:

> They were dancing the sun down, and dancing as birds wheel and
> dance, and fishes in shoals, controlled by some strange unanimous
> instinct. It was at once terrifying and magnificent, I wanted to die,
> so as not to see it, and I wanted to rush down, to be one of them.
> To be a drop in that wave of life. (*Phoenix*, p. 832)

Lawrence can image himself as many things, but not as strictly inhuman, strictly purified; the necessity of double perspective haunts him to the end. At the beginning of the sketch he opines that the miners of the 1920s have become weak because they have fulfilled their mothers' fantasies of proper manners and conduct:

> We are, more or less, such stuff as our grandmothers' dreams are
> made on. But the dream changes with every new generation of

grandmothers. Already my mother, while having a definite ideal for her sons, of "humble, adoring, high-minded" men, began to have secret dreams of her own: dreams of some Don Juan sort of person whose influence would make the vine of Dionysus grow and coil over the pulpit of our Congregational Chapel. I myself, her son, could see the dream peeping out, thrusting little tendrils through her paved intention of having "good sons." It was my turn to be the "good son." It would be my son's turn to fulfil the other dream, or dreams: the secret ones.

Thank God I have no son to undertake the onerous burden. Oh, if only every father could say to his boy: Look here, my son! These are your grandmother's dreams of a man. Now you look out!—My dear old grandmother, my mother's mother, I'm sure she dreamed me almost to a *t*, except for a few details. (*Phoenix*, p. 819)

Lawrence accepts not only sardonically but in fact that he exists largely in the image that others have made; in the poem "Image-Making Love" he rails against the attempt of another to fasten an alien form onto him, but as to his mother and grandmother the shaping force is inescapable; he is Bert Lawrence, Lorenzo, and also Paul Morel, Rupert Birkin, a thousand littlenesses, a face whose contours are among the best known of the twentieth century; and even in heaven he carries his old impedimenta, his old inadequacies, must die again out of his death. W. H. Auden and the psychiatrist R. D. Laing agree that the highest form of despair, as we understand it in this century, is the wish to be someone else; and Lawrence felt that wish. Indeed he wished to be no one at all, and at the end of his life he turned the gloom of Arnold's Empedocles on Etna, who was rendered alien from the grandeur of the cosmos because of his spark of mind, his individuation, into limpid ecstasy, a dying man's prayer for death couched in the rhetoric of life-enhancement, life-simplification:

The dead may look after the afterwards. But the magnificent here and now of life in the flesh is ours, and ours alone, and ours only for a time. We ought to dance with rapture that we should be alive and in the flesh, and part of the living, incarnate cosmos. I am part of the sun as my eye is part of me. That I am part of the earth my feet know perfectly, and my blood is part of the sea. My soul knows that I am part of the human race, my soul is an organic part of the great human soul, as my spirit is part of my nation. In my own very self, I am part of my family. There is nothing of me that is alone and absolute except my mind, and we shall find that the mind has no existence by itself, it is only the glitter of the sun on the surface of the waters. (*Apocalypse*, pp. 199–200)

To become an eye, a limb in the body of the cosmos is one of the high goals of all those ritual regenerations that he had designed and set in motion; but the lesson of his own fiction is plain, if he had looked, that he could not be both the immediate dancer in the dance of the sun, orthodox and inconsequent, and D. H. Lawrence, a grandson, an evolved painful thing, disfigured, irreducible, interesting.

Sexuality

The basis of Lawrence's highly structured later rituals is the necessity for finding artificial equivalents to self-expression, since simple self-expression has been made impossible by the fall of the body, its stiffening. The accommodating young labile bodies of Lawrence's early novels have no need for such extravagances of ritual; their ceremonies are more graceful, spontaneous, and economical, though they are never much easier. What Lovat Somers or the Woman Who Rode Away can scarcely manage through world travel, self-abandonment, death, Paul Morel can accomplish in his backyard, in a kiss or caress. The rituals in the later novels are partly or wholly allegories of marriage, for all their millennial politics; but in the early novels young people can get together without special fuss, the gates of heaven open noiselessly without any apparatus of potions, chants, altars, costumes, body-paint, and so forth. As we have seen in *The White Peacock*, the stage props, the scrim screens and scenic back-drops are never completely remote from the most ordinary human love-contact; but the aestheticism is mostly ancillary. In the early novels the real ritual is sexual action; to some extent the late rituals are extensions, sublimations, or even evasions of sexual intercourse; but in his last novel it is to physical sex that Lawrence returns.

The secret of Lawrence's early novels is that sex is art. Kisses are profoundly moving, evoke all forms of nineteenth-century ecstasy, but there is usually something wrong, something sinister or even malevolent. What is wrong is that the body, even if it is all fluid or fire, is still an inadequate expressive instrument, and the artist rages over the obtuseness of his instrument, its possibilities for meaningless virtuosity. *The White Peacock* is a chaste book, although Cyril at one point receives a highly sensual rubdown from his friend George; still, Lawrence had no reason to be surprised that its publisher would dismiss *Sons and Lovers* as the dirtiest book he had ever read. *The Trespasser*, Lawrence's second novel, is not a chaste book; here is Lawrence's first attempt in his career at hot sexual description:

> She was hurt and crushed, but it was pain delicious to her. It was marvellous to her how strong he was, to keep up that grip of her like steel. She swooned in a kind of intense bliss. At length she found herself released, taking a great breath, while Siegmund was

moving his mouth over her throat, something like a dog snuffing her, but with his lips. Her heart leaped away in revulsion. His moustache thrilled her strangely. His lips, brushing and pressing her throat beneath the ear, and his warm breath flying rhythmically upon her, made her vibrate through all her body. Like a violin under the bow, she thrilled beneath his mouth, and shuddered from his moutache. Her heart was like fire in her breast.

Suddenly she strained madly to him, and, drawing back her head, placed her lips on his, close, till at the mouth they seemed to melt and fuse together. It was the long, supreme kiss, in which man and woman have one being, Two-in-one, the only Herma-phrodite.

When Helena drew away her lips, she was exhausted. She belonged to that class of "dreaming women" with whom passion exhausts itself at the mouth. (P. 30)

Women do not like men. Both Miriam and Clara in *Sons and Lovers* are said to hate men; Ursula in *The Rainbow* is no misanthrope but she does burn out her lover's soul with a single kiss. Helena is an early version of Hermione in *Women in Love*, the high priestess of sexual rite, who wishes to worship, to experience minute subtleties of sensual response, to render sex aesthetic; this is only one step above the spooning of Mr. Noon, the conversion of the kiss into a plebeian art form. All these women concentrate on the nerve-experience, the skin-experience, the outward aspects of ritual bodily contact. Men and women come together in order to enact a profound harmony of selves through low analogue, the touching of bodies; but the desire to seize upon the body, exclusive of that profound impersonal communion of which sexual delight is only an allegory, leads to the ossification and degeneration of the ritual. In this sense Lawrence is not nostalgic: ritual sex is born dead, corrupt from the beginning; Helena enjoys the pretense that she is a violin, and instrument of sensation, lusts with her lips for the light touch of a moustache, the useful shudder.

If women are usually connoisseurs of emotion or the body, men are usually deeply disturbed by the failure of the body, the body's coarse complications to human love. Women are happy in the flesh, or, more subtly, in their mental image of the flesh, men are dualists who distrust the body; women swoon away in gross ecstasy, men attempt to isolate themselves, stay out of the whirlpool of feminine sensation. Siegmund in *The Trespasser* is violated in a hundred ways by contacts such as the one above. For one thing, Helena loves not Siegmund but her fantasy of him, a hero from romance or Wagner, not a thirty-eight-year-old musician with a wife and family; and she values him largely for his capacity to induce sensation in her. Siegmund too is expanded, made delirious by their adulterous beach-holiday; he feels he has abandoned the usual squalor of his wife and children to replace them with a larger, more awesome family:

> "Whatever I have or haven't from now, the darkness is a sort of mother, and the moon a sister, and the stars children, and sometimes the sea is a brother: and there's a family in one house, you see."
> "And I, Siegmund?" she said softly, taking him in all seriousness. She looked up at him piteously. He saw the silver of tears among the moonlit ivory of her face. His heart tightened with tenderness, and he laughed, then bent to kiss her.
> "The key of the castle," he said. He put his face against hers, and felt on his cheek the smart of her tears. (P. 37)

Helena leads him onward to rapture of the deep, rapture of the heights; but this self-diffusion, the disease diagnosed in "New Heaven and Earth," has fatal consequences:

> "Surely," he told himself, "I have drunk life too hot, and it has hurt my cup. My soul seems to leak out—I am half here, half gone away. That's why I understand the trees and the night so painfully." (P. 77)

Siegmund tries to find certain truths which permit self-containment, restraint; at one point Siegmund hurts his elbow while swimming in the ocean, and discovers that oceanic exhilaration is not the truth of the human condition, which is more typically a solitary pain. But after such knowledge, such overextensions, human life is impossible for Siegmund, and he kills himself rather than go back to the old insipidities of his family; the perversion of ritual leads to real annihilation, the demonic inverse of that exhilaration and cleansing to which proper ritual leads.

It is not clear in *The Trespasser* that Helena and her oceanic experiences are associated with the body; indeed we are told often that Siegmund is the animal, the sex-lover, while Helena is dainty and refined. Helena differs from Hermione in that Helena loves kisses while Hermione's religion requires more advanced intimacy, sexual intercourse, a sacerdotal mission made especially clear in the deleted first chapter of *Women in Love*. However, Lawrence in his very first novels has a peculiar motivation for dissociating cosmic pathos, starry exaltation, from sexual intercourse:

> Yet as he lay helplessly looking up at her some other consciousness inside him murmured: "Hawwa—Eve—Mother!" She stood compassionate over him. Without touching him she seemed to be yearning over him like a mother. Her compassion, her benignity,

seemed so different from his little Helena. This woman, tall and pale, drooping with the strength of her compassion, seemed stable, immortal, not a fragile human being, but a personification of the great mother-hood of women. (*Trespasser*, p. 74)

Helena in her most archetypal self is maternal; and the vastnesses, the tense impersonality of the whole cosmos, add up to Mother:

"The best sort of women—the most interesting—are the worst for us. . . . By instinct they aim at suppressing the gross and animal in us. Then they are supersensitive—refined a bit beyond humanity. We, who are as little gross as need be, become their instruments. Life is grounded in them, like electricity in the earth; and we take from them their unrealized life, turn it into light or warmth or power for them. The ordinary woman is, alone, a great potential force, an accumulator, if you like, charged from the source of life. In us her force becomes evident.

"She can't live without us, but she destroys us. These deep, interesting women don't want *us*; they want the flowers of the spirit they can gather of us. We, as natural men, are more or less degrading to them and to their love of us; therefore they destroy the natural man in us—that is, us altogether." (P. 84)

I believe that the rhetoric of this passage, perhaps more prefigurative of Lawrence's later style than anything else written before *Sons and Lovers*, is one of Lawrence's attempts to convert his mother into a full-blown romantic myth: mother, along with other women to a lesser extent, is the great battery, the fountain of electricity in our lives, passive but vivifying. Mother is no whore, however, but a woman of decent manners, refined, incorporeal; she discourages our sexuality, tries to "destroy the natural man in us," so the embodiment of ecstasy becomes the kiss, what is permissible between son and mother, no incestuous sexual intercourse. We know enough of Lawrence's childhood to know that his sexual attitudes were genuinely determined in part by old Protestant asceticism; it is no accident in *Sons and Lovers* that Mrs. Morel, whose father's favorite Apostle was Paul (p. 10), so named her best son: Paul, the Moral.

By the time of *Sons and Lovers*, however, Lawrence understood that sexual intercourse was not necessarily a response any more honest to human emotion than the kisses of *The Trespasser*; the only new revelation is that women can destroy the natural man, not only by high romance, teasing and sexual frustration, but also by corruptive sexual surrender. The rivalry between Miriam, Paul's sensitive poetical first love, and Paul's mother for Paul's affection is a struggle between womb and womb, and Paul, whether he wriggles in either direction, veers into blackness, facelessness, immensity, the moonlight, rediscovers the blind excitement of the spermatazoon. In this novel the female sensibility tends to the cosmic; in the first chapter Mrs. Morel, long before Paul's birth, after an argument with her husband in which she was locked out of her home, slides effortlessly into moony trance, melts away into lily-perfume and moonlight, goes blurred and lunatic through her garden; and on the last page of the novel, an extremely celebrated passage, Paul stares into starry night and perceives it as sheer womb, feels the desperate temptation to let go of his constricted small life, join his mother in huge death:

> But yet there was his body, his chest, that leaned against the stile, his hands on the wooden bar. They seemed something. Where was he?—one tiny upright speck of flesh, less than an ear of wheat lost in the field. He could not bear it. On every side the immense dark silence seemed pressing him, so tiny a spark, into extinction, and yet, almost nothing, he could not be extinct. Night, in which everything was lost, went reaching out, beyond stars and sun. Stars and sun, a few bright grains, went spinning round for terror, and holding each other in embrace, there in a darkness that outpassed them all, and left them tiny and daunted. So much, and himself, infinitesimal, at the core a nothingness, and yet not nothing.
> "Mother!" he whimpered—"mother!" (P. 420)

Of course he resists; the whole movement of the novel consists of a single turn: first, his intriguing exploration of womb-consciousness, the state of melting away into the blank night, the howling night; then, renunciation, retrenchment, deliberate self-contraction. One wishes to experience the incomparable expansion of being that sexual ritual, ritual death, can offer, but one dare not fuzz away entirely, lose hold of private identity; it is the usual necessity for balance between the sympathetic and volitional systems. One keeps hold on oneself by staying conscious, even in high ecstasy, of the contours of one's body, its limitation to six feet or less in size, the small intricacies of its limbs and organs. Paul deliberately thinks about his body, his tininess, in order to avoid mother's beckoning from the nocturnal sky at the end of the novel; wakeful coenesthesis amid upheaval constitutes the double perspective of sexual ritual, just as Lawrence in heaven in the "Autobiographical Sketch" simultaneously watches his little body and feels the winds of the upper air.

Paul's first sexual experiences with Miriam define this double perspective quite well. As they initiate sexual intercourse, Paul rejoices in his impersonality, feels that he is rid of individuation, "as if his living were smeared away into the beyond"; but he understands immediately that this wonderful exhilaration, this exploration, this palpating of a soft divinity, leads inevitably to "the sense of failure and death" (p. 287). Surrender to complete self-diffusion is, as always, fatal. It is not hard to understand why their sexual intercourse is such a perverse rite, so morbid: Miriam regards sex as her high sacrifice to Paul's brutishness; she is incapable of orgasm, just relaxes, relaxes, lets Paul ease his pruritus: "She relinquished herself to him" (p. 286); she looks "like a creature awaiting immolation" (pp. 289–90). By this pure passivity, this lack of participation in sex, Miriam becomes the perfect image of the womb, a great yielding mass which offers no resistance anywhere but in which Paul is helplessly smothered. From the very beginning of their sexual relation she criticizes Paul for "fighting away from me" (p. 297); and Paul must indeed try increasingly radical measures to keep himself from being wholly digested by her warm, cetacean body; she is easily capable of sucking away his soul, as his mother, who ought to be a good witness, repeatedly says. Even when they were quite young Paul felt the need for sharp self-definition against her threatening body:

> If Miriam caused his mother suffering, then he hated her— and he easily hated her. Why did she make him feel as if he were uncertain of himself, insecure, an indefinite thing, as if he had not sufficient sheathing to prevent the night and the space breaking into him? How he hated her! And then, what a rush of tenderness and humility! (P. 193)

Paul cannot find the right equilibrium, but he knows that it is crucial to prevent Miriam from erasing the outline of his body, from leaving him unsheathed, an open cylinder of gas thinning into vacuum. Again, the shell, the hateful outer fixity, does have its uses; and the employment of the body for ritual purposes, as in sexual intercourse, must give some respect to the merely physical and aesthetic, while never allowing the body, the representation, to divert attention from the inner truths that it represents.

Bodily sensation and emotion are often insidious, overwhelming; if one succumbs to the temptation of testing the resistance of an infinitely yielding mass, as Walter does with Griselda's patience in "The Clerk's Tale," one tends to be spoiled, abusive, shapeless; and not only is the personality falsified, but one's entire view of the universe becomes distorted, dissolute, self-indulgent:

> The little, interesting diversity of shapes had vanished from the scene; all that remained was a vast, dark matrix of sorrow and tragedy, the same in all the houses and the river-flats and the people and the birds; they were only shapen differently. And now that the forms seemed to have melted away, there remained the mass from which all the landscape was composed, a dark mass of

struggle and pain. The factory, the girls, his mother, the large, uplifted church, the thicket of the town, merged into one atmosphere—dark, brooding, and sorrowful, every bit.

"Is that two o'clock striking?" Mrs. Daws said in surprise.

Paul started, and everything sprang into form, regained its individuality, its forgetfulness, and its cheerfulness. (P. 273)

It is heresy ever to claim that the world is a reflex of one's emotional self, the reductive contamination of the ego; it is a loss of the necessary boundary between what is one's own and what is alien.

Clara's coition with Paul provides an instructive contrast to Miriam's. Miriam is young, a sexual idealist who wishes to devour Paul into a dim consummation, an amber matrix that would capture and hold her prey: "She seems to draw me and draw me, and she wouldn't leave a single hair of me free to fall out and blow away" (p. 277). Clara, on the other hand, is older, married, somewhat disillusioned, an active feminist; and she has no strong desire to violate his being, only a vague wish to trap him into a rather conventional domestic relation. Their sexual intercourse is still imperfect—she, like Miriam, still hopes that maybe Paul will be petty, personal, reflective, ordinary, accuses him of liking *It*, not *me*, when they make love (p. 363)—but it is vastly more satisfactory than his former affair. Clara does not lie still, but participates in their bodily liaison; so the ritual is correct, proper, since the niceties of external form are observed. Even though Clara's soul is refractory, unsatisfied, she goes through the right motions, the exterior prayers, and so the ritual succeeds, the heavens open:

What was she? A strong, strange, wild life, that breathed with his in the darkness through this hour. It was all so much bigger than themselves that he was hushed. They had met, and included in their meeting the thrust of the manifold grass stems, the cry of the peewit, the wheel of the stars. . . .

And after such an evening they both were very still, having known the immensity of passion. They felt small, half-afraid, childish and wondering, like Adam and Eve when they lost their innocence and realised the magnificence of the power which drove them out of Paradise and across the great night and the great day of humanity. It was for each of them an initiation and a satisfaction. To know their own nothingness, to know the tremendous living flood which carried them always, gave them rest within themselves. If so great a magnificent power could overwhelm them, identify them altogether with itself, so that they knew they were only grains in the tremendous heave that lifted every grass blade its little height, and every tree, and living thing, then why fret about themselves? (Pp. 353–54)

Miriam in coition seems undefined, inarticulate, without limits to her physical extension, but Clara has a clear, finite human shape, plays archetypal Eve to Paul's archetypal Adam. Miriam demands fusion, a dissolution of Paul's body into hers; Clara neither sacrifices herself nor demands submission, but simply enacts passionately the ancient rite, responds vigorously to Paul's need. The two lovers become sharp foci of the cosmic forces, the wheeling of the stars; Lawrence's language suggests not dimness, diffusion, but heightened intensity. Lawrence uses the word *identify*, but it seems less an identity than an analogy: to be identified with the macrocosm is death, but to be a brilliant analogue, a map, a concentration and distillation of the astronomical tensions, that is success; it is the same high gift granted by the less casual rituals of Lawrence's later fictions. Paul and Clara are grains, solid points, impelled by a great wave, not things wholly dissolved. Shortly after this first coition with Clara, we see Paul at the beach, struggling with the definition of analogical relationships:

> "What is she, after all?" he said to himself. "Here's the seacoast morning, big and permanent and beautiful; there is she, fretting, always unsatisfied, and temporary as a bubble of foam. What does she mean to me, after all? She represents something, like a bubble of foam represents the sea. But what is *she*? It's not her I care for.". . . When they were drying themselves, panting heavily, he watched her laughing, breathless face, her bright shoulders, her breasts that swayed and made him frightened as she rubbed them, and he thought again:
> "But she is magnificent, and even bigger than the morning and the sea. Is she—? Is she—" (P. 358)

He understands that Clara is a synecdoche, not the ocean itself but a part, a bubble, a representation; but he cannot get a clear conception of relative size, of real value, for the tiny intense point, Clara, makes possible his mediate relation to the cosmos, which must be approached through women, ritual, not with Protestant lack of intercession. The small is better than the large; it is, so to speak, larger than the large. Therefore Paul's will to be a limited, compact being is a necessary part of his strategy of self-illumination; the tongue of fire can settle only upon a clearly defined head, the apocalypse will not come to those, like Miriam, who are too huge, nearly disembodied. Miriam is strangely uncomfortable with the finitude of her body, its obvious inadequacy as an instrument of expression for her foamy all-too-permeable soul: "Her body was not flexible and living. She walked with a swing, rather heavily, her head bowed forward, pondering" (p. 153). Clara's body, on the other hand, is wondrous, an obsession to Paul, charged with sexuality; at one point they attend a

performance of *La Dame aux Camélias,* and Paul has an elaborate
fantasy about her body:

> The drama continued. He saw it all in the distance, going on
> somewhere; he did not know where, but it seemed far away inside
> him. He was Clara's white heavy arms, her throat, her moving
> bosom. That seemed to be himself. Then away somewhere the play
> went on, and he was identified with that also. There was no himself.
> The grey and black eyes of Clara, her bosom coming down on
> him, her arm that he held gripped between his hands, were all that
> existed. Then he felt himself small and helpless, her towering in her
> force above him. (P. 331)

The common transference of love, the volatile soul's entry into the
other's body, is not a diffusion, an incoherency of being, but instead a
playing of electricity upon a finite form; and in another episode, when
Paul and Clara make love, Paul becomes as obsessed with his own
hands as he was before with Clara's:

> His hands were like creatures, living; his limbs, his body, were all
> life and consciousness, subject to no will of his, but living in them-
> selves. Just as he was, so it seemed the vigorous, wintry stars were
> strong also with life. He and they struck with the same pulse of
> fire, and the same joy of strength which held the bracken-frond
> still near his eyes held his own body firm. (Pp. 363–64)

Proper sexuality, sexuality at its best, converts the body into point-
blank expressive form, hands thinking their manual thoughts with no
lag, no stuttering, between the will and its representations; this is
purified representation, as it might be in heaven, expression so perfect
and immediate that it has almost ceased to be ritual. Paul in this
passage comes to utter realization of his newborn body, sustained by
the same forces that sustain the bracken-frond, no blurring away of the
physical into abstract blackness but all transfiguration, preternatural
firmness of outline and shape.

But like all revelation it is transient. The coition of Paul and Clara
starts decaying at this very moment:

> Gradually, some mechanical effort spoilt their loving, or, when
> they had splendid moments, they had them separately, and not so
> satisfactorily. So often he seemed merely to be running on alone;
> often they realised it had been a failure, not what they had wanted.
> He left her, knowing *that* evening had only made a little split
> between them. (P. 364)

The body when not attended to becomes involuntary, automatic; the
tragedy of sex is that one's highest spiritual experiences produce the
most intense physical sensation, and so one tends to reverse the

causality, to manipulate the body into intense sensation in order to try to evoke metanoia, rapturous awareness of the unanimous forces that uphold the living and the dead—an act of ritual magic which more often than not fails to succeed, leads to unholy connoisseurship of the body. And so Paul retreats, explores the converse spiritual bonds of hate with Clara's husband, finds ways to insulate himself from Clara, Miriam, and, ultimately, mother; expelled from Paradise he proceeds to healthy labor, healthy apathy.

In the subsequent pair of novels, *The Rainbow* and *Women in Love*, which constitute, as Lawrence himself realized, his masterwork, we see the major characters groping in a fashion similar to Paul's after a definition of the body's expressive form. Hermione in *Women in Love* is the classic case of the virtuoso of bodily sensation, the high priestess of neuralgia, fibrillation; and it would seem in this novel that Hermione and Ursula form a polar pair, the mind, the ideal—that is, refined sensation—*versus* the body:

> And was not Ursula's way of emotional intimacy, emotional and physical, was it not just as dangerous as Hermione's abstract spiritual intimacy? Fusion, fusion, this horrible fusion of two beings, which every woman and most men insisted on, was it not nauseous and horrible anyhow, whether it was a fusion of the spirit or of the emotional body? Hermione saw herself as the perfect Idea, to which all men must come: And Ursula was the perfect Womb, the bath of birth, to which all men must come! And both were horrible. Why could they not remain individuals, limited by their own limits? (P. 353)

Both of these, as we have seen, are perversions obtained through body: in the case of Hermione, and of Helena in *The Trespasser*, the body is exercised in such a way as to obtain maximum response from minimum stimulus, in almost masturbatory fashion; in the case of Ursula, her body's action during sexual intercourse has misled her about the nature of love. This meditation goes on in the mind of the hero, the school inspector, Rupert Birkin, who is angry at both his present and his past lovers; but his dialectic is largely wrong, for although his description of Hermione is correct—that is, it agrees with Lawrence's—his description of Ursula is a falsification caused by her own improper rhetoric:

> She wanted unspeakable intimacies. She wanted to have him, utterly, finally to have him as her own, oh, so unspeakably, in intimacy. To drink him down—ah, like a life-draught. She made great professions, to herself, of her willingness to warm his foot-soles between her breasts, after the fashion of the nauseous Meredith poem. But only on condition that he, her lover, loved

her absolutely, with complete self-abandon. And subtly enough, she knew he would never abandon himself finally to her. (P. 302)

This is the rhetoric of Miriam as well as Ursula, the amoeba claiming humility while she surrounds and digests her lover. Ursula has noticed that in sexual activity the bodies of the lovers seem at times so attentive, pliant, invisible, that loss of self-definition occurs; this is what happened to her first lover Skrebensky in the great interlunar kiss in *The Rainbow*. She has come to confuse one of the body's tricks, a breathless mingling, vertiginous suspension of self-awareness, with the true nature of the contact between men and women, which as Birkin keeps insisting is like the binary star, not the electric discharge of coition, but the force of gravity between delimited bodies, violating neither identity, tantalizing, remote, supervalent. Ursula has confused the metaphor with the reality, thought that her body's velleities and contaminations were an integral part of human love.

For this reason, Lawrence, and his spokesmen in his fiction before *Lady Chatterley's Lover*, have remarkable distrust of sexual intercourse. Birkin tries with all his might to avoid it: when he and Ursula first make love, after the drowning of Gerald's sister, Ursula has to inflame his lust deliberately while he whimpers, "Not this, not this" (p. 213). In the chapter "Moony" Ursula again tries to rouse him with kisses, but he, more self-possessed and peaceful, persuades her to nestle against him celibate. To Birkin, Ursula's sexuality is sheer aggression, will to master; and the great sexual scenes of the novel are not scenes of coition but of more theatrical, adventurous sexuality, the wrestling of Gerald and Birkin and Ursula's clasping of Birkin's loins in the Inn, both of which are close prefigurations of the sexual rituals of the later novels. Coition is old, formalized, conventional, ordinary; people approach it with set expectations; it is rigid, no longer a valid form of self-expression. If coition is too much governed by the automatic reflexes of the body, too full of misleading orgasmic intensities, it must be replaced by something more novel, an expressive vehicle structured with greater care to accurate representation. The old sexuality is spasmodic, haphazard, a kind of easy treachery; the new sexual act must be respectful, stark, and, most of all, nonorgasmic.

It is quite accurate to say that Lawrence despises the female orgasm; everywhere he perceives it as affronting to the male, a bullying attempt to sacrifice a gullible victim for the sake of the petty feminine ego. The new coition, as it is performed in ritual or in heaven, must at all costs be freed from this plague; here is Kate at the end of *The Plumed Serpent* thinking about the contrast between sex with Cipriano and the old European way:

Her strange seething feminine will and desire subsided in her and swept away, leaving her soft and powerfully potent, like the hot springs of water that gushed up so noiseless, so soft, yet so powerful, with a sort of secret potency.

She realised, almost with wonder, the death in her of the Aphrodite of the foam: the seething, frictional, ecstatic Aphrodite. By a swift dark instinct, Cipriano drew away from this in her. When, in their love, it came back on her, the seething electric female ecstasy, which knows such spasms of delirium, he recoiled from her. It was what she used to call her "satisfaction." She had loved Joachim for this, that again, and again, and again he would give her this orgiastic "satisfaction," in spasms that made her cry aloud. (Pp. 462–63)

In *Lady Chatterley's Lover* Mellors' first wife Bertha chews him up with her beaklike vagina; he declares that her orgasmic pleasure is superficial, thrilling, and extremely destructive to the male; the vagina can talk, for the fallen body has its own language, and what it screams is "Self! Self! Self!" (p. 261). Even the female orgasm, like all rigidities, is only a kind of corrupt self-expression.

In *The Rainbow*, Ursula after her devirgination investigates the limits of sexual intensities, loves Skrebensky in a way that Birkin would have found quite satisfactory, loves him for his "permanent self," "not the young man of the world but the undifferentiated man he was" (p. 452). But despite the general wholesomeness and benevolence of her love, the mere fact of her extraordinary attention to his body has an unsettling effect on Skrebensky:

She enjoyed him, she made much of him. She liked to put her fingers on the soft skin of his sides, or on the softness of his back, when he made the muscles hard underneath, the muscles developed very strong through riding; and she had a great thrill of excitement and passion, because of the unimpressible hardness of his body, that was so soft and smooth under her fingers, that came to her with such absolute service.

She owned his body and enjoyed it with all the delight and carelessness of a possessor. But he had become gradually afraid of her body. He wanted her, he wanted her endlessly. But there had come a tension into his desire, a constraint which prevented his enjoying the delicious approach and the lovable close of the endless embrace. He was afraid. His will was always tense, fixed. (Pp. 459–60)

Such minute doting on the body, exactly parallel to Will's fascination in the preceding generation with Anna's blue veins and his flirtations with cheap girls, always leads to ill consequences, exuberation into stagnation in the case of Will and Anna, utter castration in the case of Skrebensky: "He felt cut off at the knees"; "He felt himself a mere attribution of her" (pp. 461–62). The steady refrain of the protagonists of the later novels, especially the Man Who Died, is *Noli me tangere*; and in an early poem in the *Look! We Have Come Through!* sequence, "'She Said as Well to Me,'" we have a purified conversation between Lawrence and his wife in which Frieda admires his body at length, his chest, his hairy legs, speaks of the tactile blandishment of so much flesh, but Lawrence recoils from her touch, demands respect for his weasel dignity, his serpent dignity. Women dare not make demands for interesting sexual sensation, or the men will tend to lose their identities, blur away into the corpus of the women, like those deep-sea fish in which the small male fastens his body to the rear of the huge female, allows his head to be absorbed into her body, his nervous system to dissipate, until he is vestigial, a mere protuberance from the female, a sexual ancilla. When Lawrence's women talk of fusion, what they really want is this sapping mastery.

Ursula is not a malevolent woman and seems to be partly unaware of the effects that her behavior has on Skrebensky; but in the later stages of their affair it is clear that she is trying to use his body as an analogical vehicle without much concern for Skrebensky's welfare. Her sexual initiation is preceded by a scene in which she stares at a "plant-animal" under a microscope, and understands its fierce intention to be its little self: "Self was a oneness with the infinite" (p. 441), that is, a tiny analogue of the infinite, contracted to brilliance. As her affair progresses, she, like Paul Morel, tries to explore her own potentiality for being a focus of the cosmos, a point of contraction; she stares at the high downs around Arundel castle and thinks of "the intercourse between their great, unabateable body and the changeful body of the sky":

> And she lay face downwards on the downs, that were so strong, that cared only for their intercourse with the over-lasting skies, and she wished she could become a strong mound smooth under the sky, bosom and limbs bared to all winds and clouds and bursts of sunshine. (P. 463)

Skrebensky is highly useful for inducing such sensations; and their coition sublimes into pure impersonality, pure metaphor:

> In the round dew-pond the stars were untroubled. She ventured softly into the water, grasping at the stars with her hands. . . .
> She took him, she clasped him, clenched him close, but her eyes were open looking at the stars, it was as if the stars were lying with her and entering the unfathomable darkness of her womb, fathoming her at last. It was not him. (P. 464)

Ursula is capable of exploring the limits of the body's pleasures and then going beyond the limits of the body to realms of experience for which bodily sensation can constitute only a tenuous metaphor; but her conduit Skrebensky is exposed to currents that are altogether too intense, and he burns himself out. The proper attitude that one should take toward one's body is a certain negligence, for excessive curiosity about one's own physical titillation leads to the terrifying orgasms of Hermione Roddice or Bertha Coutts. New sexuality, redeemed sexuality, is selfless, public, dramatic, figurations of tight pairs into parallel lines, circles, dances, constellations, a star-map; and if there is a single controlling image in Lawrence's fiction for what human society should be it is the field of stars: individuals as similar and absolutely distinct as cut diamonds, sharp points, grains, scintillae, bristling against unconscious black, not calm and astronomical but whirling, vivid, leaving great trails and whorls in the heavens, the paisley heavens of Leibnitz or Van Gogh's starry night.

Ursula has learned a little about new sexuality at the end of *The Rainbow*, that it has superhuman reference, the intercourse of hills and sky, stars reflected in pools; and by the end of *Women in Love* she has begun to learn a great deal more, that the best sexuality is complex and intricate beyond the bounds of the pair relationship, although she resists the knowledge:

> "Having you, I can live all my life without anybody else, any other sheer intimacy. But to make it complete, really happy, I wanted eternal union with a man too: another kind of love," he said.
> "I don't believe it," she said. "It's an obstinacy, a theory, a perversity."
> "Well—" he said.
> "You can't have two kinds of love. Why should you!"
> "It seems as if I can't," he said. "Yet I wanted it."
> "You can't have it, because it's false, impossible," she said.
> "I don't believe that," he answered. (P. 548)

The participants in new sexuality usually investigate other human gravitations beyond the union of one man and one woman; and the pure relation of man to man is necessary to Lawrence's new sexual scheme. Lawrence, in *Fantasia of the Unconscious* and almost every novel, makes elaborate theoretical defense of the notion of male bonding; for one thing, it is the cooperation requisite to the construction of buildings, great works, all deeds of self-glorification. Though Lawrence did not like the word, there is no reason not to call this union homosexuality; as the wrestling in *Women in Love* shows, the relation of man to man can be as sensual as the relation of man to woman, and whenever sensuality becomes an end in itself, whether homosexual or heterosexual, it is annihilating, as the parody homosexuals in Lawrence's novels, like the putrefying couple with whom Aaron Sisson travels in Italy, would testify to. The first principle of new sexuality is to put oneself into relation, sensual relation, with everything sacred in the cosmos, attractive women, attractive men, attractive cows, attractive trees, and so forth. Lawrence is no sexual libertarian, but he does believe in throwing off the shackles of repression, inhibition. Part of the reason for Lawrence's baroque argumentation on the nature of incest in *Psychoanalysis and the Unconscious* is that Lawrence wishes to demonstrate that men have no natural sexual desire for their mothers, and therefore one's failure to commit incest is a good thing, not repression or self-betrayal. It is clear from the deleted first chapter of *Women in Love* that one of Birkin's major problems is his repression of homosexuality:

> So the trouble went on, he became more hollow and deathly, more like a spectre with hollow bones. He knew that he was not very far from dissolution.
> All the time, he recognized that, although he was always drawn to women, feeling more at home with a woman than with a man, yet it was for men that he felt the hot, flushing roused attraction which a man is supposed to feel for the other sex. Although nearly all his living interchange went on with one woman or another, although he was always terribly intimate with at least one woman, and practically never intimate with a man, yet the male physique had a fascination for him, and for the female physique he felt only a fondness, a sort of sacred love, as for a sister. (*Phoenix II*, pp. 103–4)

It is not odd that Birkin should wish to form a supernal friendship with a man, a *Blutbrüderschaft*; the important question of *Women in Love*, though, is, Why Gerald? Gerald is almost Lawrence's Satan, so what does Birkin find attractive about him, the very personification of that destructive *Wille zur Macht* against which Birkin rails, the machine-leader of mechanical men? For one thing, Gerald has a physique for which Birkin feels attraction; we are told in the deleted chapter that Birkin likes two sorts of men, "dark-skinned, supple, night-smelling men" and white-skinned crystalline Northern men whose blood is "acrid, like cranberries" (*Phoenix II*, pp. 105–6). Gerald is the latter sort, muscular, large, arctic, a good polar antithesis to Birkin's physique, which is slight, dark, asthenic. Still, Gerald owns and operates mines, and has become overextended through insufficient self-limitations, his eyes "blue false bubbles" (p. 264), his soul utterly evacuated by projection, like that of Conrad's

Kurtz. Perhaps the reason for Birkin's attraction to him is Lawrence's half-conscious realization that his own scheme for the perfection of humanity, generally congruent with Birkin's, is inadequate without what Gerald represents, the Will. The convergence of the four main characters—Birkin, Ursula, Gerald, and Gudrun—is a myth about the integration of the fallen faculties of the human soul, tentatively identifiable as the Spirit, the Body, the Will, and the Mind; at least Birkin, pale and abstract, is concerned with the fate of the human race, Ursula has earth-mother tendencies, Gerald loves power, mathematical organization, self-aggrandizement, and Gudrun is a remote intelligence, manipulating miniatures in order to gain control over them, so aloof from her body that she is nearly discarnate. The latter faculties are those which Lawrence usually abominates, but, as we have seen before, whenever he fills in the schema with sufficient detail, he discovers the usefulness, even the necessity, of the more cerebral aspects of man; even Blake allows Urizen his proper place among the united, resurrected Zoas. The new sexuality strives always for plenitude, richer organization, for the dance at the end of time where nothing may be omitted; but the myth of *Women in Love* is a frustrated, limited myth, in which Gerald dies, Gudrun flies out of orbit, the apocalypse is weak, private, partial, a *Dies Irae* where the trumpet makes a dim blast and people go about their business as usual.

In the novels that follow, the image at the end of *Women in Love*, two people huddling together for warmth and security while the world rages outside, remains stable; the protagonists all achieve glimpses of more potent and inclusive human relationship, new sexuality, but their real achievement in that direction is small, a partial rejuvenation of the simple one-to-one pair relationship. The Lost Girl flirts with the communal sexuality of the Tawaras before she goes off to huddle alone with Ciccio in Italy; significantly, even this revery is threatened by Ciccio's conscription into the army. Aaron Sisson has an affair with the Marchesa in which he sees an intimation of an impersonal ritual inside ordinary sexuality, archetypal, stark, but finally not very interesting:

> She was absolutely gone in her own incantations. She was abso-
> lutely gone, like a priestess utterly involved in her own terrible
> rites. And he was part of the ritual only, God and victim in one.
> God and victim. All the time, God and victim. When his aloof
> soul realised, amid the incantation, how he was being used—not
> as himself, but as something quite different: God and victim; then
> he dilated with intense surprise, and his remote soul stood up tall
> and knew itself alone. He did not want it—not at all. (Pp. 264–65)

Just as Ursula in *The Rainbow* used Skrebensky as a vehicle toward the greater sexuality of earth and sky, so Aaron finds that he is being employed for services in which his body is largely irrelevant; but he has reached such apathy that he does not even feel indignation, and he simply retreats to a position where his privacy will be more respected. For Aaron all heterosexual contact is hopelessly polluted; his one hope of relation is to a man, Lilly, whose offer of friendship he has spurned once; at the end of the novel Aaron is left trying to decide whether to accept Lilly or not. In *Kangaroo* the new social model is the fascist political cadre, which is a male quasi-sexual organization full of tactile ceremony; the members of the cadre are *mates*, and their relation is understood to be more binding than the love of a man for his wife. Lovat Somers finds much that is intriguing, appealing, about this new mode, but finally he and his wife leave Australia, although it is clear that their marriage is not the hopeful sign for the human race that the cadre is. Similarly in *The Plumed Serpent* Kate leaves the Mexican revolutionaries for Europe, but she leaves alone and has striking relationships in Mexico which may bring her back; each novel in the sequence, except *Aaron's Rod*, explores the new society, the new sexuality, with more and more interest, and the breakaway, the regression to the ego, the old European alternative, is accepted with more and more reluctance and difficulty.

All of this is changed, astonishingly changed, in Lawrence's last full-scale work, *Lady Chatterley's Lover*. As in the "Autobiographical Sketch," he has discovered that the new mode of life is not to be found in an isolated antarctic pocket but is all around us, at home, in Sherwood Forest, fluent, able, viviparous. The millennium will not be achieved by a flutter of tomahawks, painted Indians in loincloths, but by simple Derby miners taking off their overalls and putting on, according to Mellors' fantasy, red trousers, having fun in the streets.

The heart of *Lady Chatterley's Lover* is a sequence of eight sexual episodes between Lady Constance Chatterley and her husband's game-keeper, Oliver Mellors, a highly literate man who has renounced literacy for broad dialect, that is, sought the innocence that lies on the far side of experience; these eight encounters are a step-by-step initiation, really for both of them, into the new sexuality, society after apocalypse. Lawrence's assumptions about the nature of human evolution, human perfection, must have changed importantly around 1925 or so to permit the quite novel myth of *Lady Chatterley's Lover*. Here, the pair relation is enough, or almost enough; Mellors makes one reference to male-to-male relations in his red-trousers fantasies, but from all we see it seems that the simple union of Mellors and Connie is really adequate to their needs, self-sustaining. The bodies of Connie

and Mellors are different from any previous bodies in Lawrence's
fiction. We have seen Lawrence's investigation of the sinuosity of
bodies in his early novels, their contortions, their agonized efforts to
become proper expressive instruments; here, we have bodies that are
at last adequate, even calmly adequate. Connie before her exposure to
Mellors has obviously a fallen body, thick, unripe, opaque:

> Instead of ripening its firm, down-running curves, her body
> was flattening and going a little harsh. It was as if it had not had
> enough sun and warmth; it was a little greyish and sapless.
>
> Disappointed of its real womanhood, it had not succeeded in
> becoming boyish, and unsubstantial, and transparent; instead it
> had gone opaque.
>
> Her breasts were rather small, and dropping pear-shaped. But
> they were unripe, a little bitter, without meaning hanging there.
> (P. 111)

Her first two sexual meetings with Mellors bring her curious peace, a
little resentment, no sensual intensity, but at her third meeting her
body starts to open:

> Then as he began to move, in the sudden helpless orgasm, there
> awoke in her new strange thrills rippling inside her. Rippling,
> rippling, rippling, like a flapping overlapping of soft flames, soft
> as feathers, running to points of brilliance, exquisite, exquisite and
> melting her all molten inside. It was like bells rippling up and up
> to a culmination. (P. 153)

Rippling, rippling, flapping overlapping: Lawrence's language is
approaching linguistic paradise, that country in which all words
rhyme; inside Connie Chatterley's body is a strange landscape,
perhaps something of Chagall's, full of feathers, pools, bells, jumbled
by synesthesia and consonance into an astonishing clamor. The
Second Coming, the millennium is right there, inside her body.

> "For hands she hath none, nor eyes, nor feet, nor golden
> Treasure of hair . . . ."
>
> She was like a forest, like the dark interlacing of the oak-wood,
> humming inaudibly with myriad unfolding buds. Meanwhile the
> birds of desire were asleep in the vast interlaced intricacy of her
> body. (P. 188)

Tommy Dukes, the Moses of the novel, the affable soldier who could
see the Promised Land but not enter, spoke earlier of a chirpy penis;
and the huge interstices of the body are full of birds, not a single
identity but a congeries of independent desires, humorous, eager to be
roused, pullulating. It is because of this internal complexity that
Connie's body can achieve unfallen novelty, almost angelic, an

instrument that can play any tune. Connie's personality is equally complex, ill-defined; she is quickly at home in all worlds, guilefully responsive to her crippled husband, at ease in Mellors' branchy bowers, clean dirt; and Mellors himself is so complex as to be almost schizoid, a standard-English-self and a dialect-self. They need no society but themselves because their bodies together constitute a society, all societies; they can generate out of themselves the high and the low, the primitive and the evolved.

During their third encounter Mellors and Connie attain mutual orgasm, and it is clear that this is good; the female orgasm, to which Lawrence was almost obsessively opposed as late as *The Plumed Serpent*, has been found redeemable. Lawrence no longer seems to regard the female orgasm as necessarily a kind of blank detonation which women inveigle men into provoking, but instead as itself a flexible instrument of sexual expression. *Lady Chatterley's Lover* is justly celebrated for its minute attention to sexual detail, and in providing this detail Lawrence has created two fictive bodies that are at last responsive to the real nuances of human interaction; the wan Lawrence of the late 1920s has been broken into a kind of realist, has accepted a corporality in which the body is not merely a metaphor but the thing itself. The mutual orgasm of the third encounter is described as a whirlpool, the tumescent gradual orgasm of the fourth encounter, achieved after some humiliating failure, is described as sea-tumult, self-parturition, the birth of Venus; the oceanic feeling has become literalized into a real, internal ocean:

> And it seemed she was like the sea, nothing but dark waves rising and heaving, heaving with a great swell, so that slowly her whole darkness was in motion, and she was ocean rolling its dark, dumb mass. Oh, and far down inside her the deeps parted and rolled asunder, in long, far-travelling billows, and ever, at the quick of her, the depths parted and rolled asunder, from the center of soft plunging, as the plunger went deeper and deeper, touching lower, and she was deeper and deeper and deeper disclosed, and heavier the billows of her rolled away to some shore, uncovering her, and closer and closer plunged the palpable unknown, and further and further rolled the waves of herself away from herself, leaving her, till suddenly, in a soft, shuddering convulsion, the quick of all her plasm was touched, she knew herself touched, the consummation was upon her, and she was gone. She was gone, she was not, and she was born: a woman. (P. 229)

This interior self, this newly uncovered plasm, is defined, however, in a manner somewhat different from that of Lawrence's previous novels:

"What is cunt?" she said.

"An' doesn't ter know? Cunt! It's thee down theer; an' what I get when I'm i'side thee; it's a' as it is, all on't."

"All on't," she teased. "Cunt! It's like fuck then."

"Nay, nay! Fuck's only what you do. Animals fuck. But cunt's a lot more than that. It's thee, dost see: an' tha'rt a lot besides an animal, aren't ter? even ter fuck! Cunt! Eh, that's the beauty o' thee, lass." (P. 234)

The vagina is not the road to the origin but the origin itself; the generative organs of the body are the actual, substantial identity of the human body, the core, strange to our cerebral selves, with strange, detached, private will, unfathomable, what Mellors calls John Thomas and Lady Jane.

The later sexual encounters of this curious couple, lashed by subtle braids of pubic hair, differ in emphasis from the ones just described. The actual coition is less prominent; the language by which it is described is cursory, allusive to the earlier episodes, though still suggesting extreme intensity. Instead the lovers dramatize their sexuality, make analogues, divagate; having uncovered their authentic organs they wish to phallicize the natural world, invaginate it. The famous episode of the sixth encounter, in which Connie dances naked in the rain, nothing visible except lucid breasts, buttocks, and loins, and Mellors runs after her and takes her like an animal, concludes with a wonderful flower ceremony, the entwining of myriad flowers in each other's hair, the dewy wedding of the genitals. The marriage of John Thomas and Lady Jane is not wholly analogous to the similar decorations and grimmer ritual of the preceding novels; it is not a prayer or even a confirmation, but ritual as it would be in heaven, without forethought or paradigm, pure play, the delight of self-exhibition. After this Connie and Mellors are supremely easy in their sexuality, neither ecstatic nor squeamish nor fussy but wholly sacred. They commit anal intercourse in sensual exultation; it is simply another happy exploration of the inconceivable complexities of response in the labyrinth of the human body. One of the great romantic fallacies is the belief that the number of permutations of mucous membranes is not extremely limited; and surely no one ever believed that more dogmatically than the Lawrence of *Lady Chatterley's Lover*.

The novel ends, however, not with sexual joy but with chastity, enchanted chastity, the peace on the far side of coition. Most of Lawrence's more personal late works end similarly, with quiet slumber, cessation, other indications of death. Lawrence felt quite optimistic about death, perhaps alone of the great twentieth-century writers; his last great poem, "The Ship of Death," ends with a Lawrence reconceived, re-umbilical; indeed Lawrence believed that men invent myths in order to explain death, their intimations of a return to earth beyond the grave. He sets forth his theory of myth at the beginning of his book on Thomas Hardy; it is quite similar to that of Ezra Pound, who tells a little story of how a man in ancient times saw a tree, felt some strange tree-feelings by a process of transference, was ridiculed when he tried to explain his feelings to his friends, and therefore created the myth of Daphne. Lawrence's ancient man finds himself identifying with poppies:

> . . . the old man watched the last poppy coming out, the red flame licking into sight; watched the blaze at the top clinging around a little tender dust, and he wept, thinking of his youth. Till the red flag fell before him, lay in rags on the earth. Then he did not know whether to pay homage to the void, or to preach.
> So he compromised, and made a story about a phoenix. "Yes, my dears, in the waste desert, I know the green and graceful tree where the phoenix has her nest. And there I have seen the eternal phoenix escape away into flame, leaving life behind in her ashes. Suddenly she went up in to red flame, and was gone, leaving life to rise from her ashes."
> "And did it?"
> "Oh, yes, it rose up."
> "What did it do then?"
> "It grew up, and burst into flame again." (*Phoenix*, p. 399)

The general pattern of the myth of the phoenix, resurrection after dissolution, is of course an implicit hope in every one of his mature novels, and Lawrence explains haltingly in many places that he believes in an undefinable personal resurrection; and perhaps many of his readers respond to these magical elements in his fiction, the enactment of the struggle toward personal immortality through all the lengthy mass of his work. But the evidence for the truth of the vegetable analogy, between poppies and the human, is perhaps not compelling; as Rilke says, women are not like flowers, if only because they remain shut. Our era has not been completely comfortable with millennial vision, which by the latter third of the twentieth century seems more characteristic of the nineteenth, although children in America electrify cow pastures in their search for fields that exist only in the imagination, a generation of fumbling apocalyptists. Lawrence's prophecies do not seem as valuable as his diagnosis; and of D. H. Lawrence transubstantial, or of his best world, unmenaced by Descartes or Copernicus, the authentic hylozoism, I can find now, more than forty years after his death, no sign.

THREE

Virginia Woolf

Who am I? What am I? What is life? These are the incessant questions
that form and disperse throughout Virginia Woolf's work, questions
as evanescent, helpless, and stubborn as the characters who pose them.
The nineteenth century prepares us for many of the characteristic
forms of the twentieth, but not, I think, for this tumult, this agony of
identity, these dubious characters merging into each other or splitting
like amoebas, whose only joy is self-assertion, whose only lament is
that there is no one here to lament. When reading her novels we feel
that her world's dynamics are impossible, exaggerated: one cannot say
that her characters develop, for when they are moving it is with dizzy
speed, swirling into the wind and the waves; when they are still they
are struck dead still, grounded, sunk. Age, face, body, even sex—the
usual marks by which the reader can sort out the actors in a
novel—are as unstable as coat and dress; Orlando, fluctuant, trans-
sexual, three hundred years old, wholly outrageous, is only an
exaggeration of the liberties which Virginia Woolf's characters habitually take. Well might these invisible voices cry Who am I? out of the
dazzling foreground of *Mrs. Dalloway* or *To the Lighthouse* or *The
Waves*; and one must inquire carefully to learn what form a response
might take, to learn what sort of outline, delimitation, or uniqueness
is proper to these British names who seem to implore us from the text
to help them. It is possible that humanity will not turn out to be quite
so abject as it seems; for the chameleon's agony, the rage of Caliban,
the very indefiniteness of character itself, may prove a secret witness
to the impalpable triumphs of the human imagination.

Virginia Woolf attempts in several places the rudiments of a theory
of personality, and if this theory is hesitant, partial, even contradictory, it may only be an example of one of her strengths as writer,
empiricism. She admires Roger Fry in her biography for his fecundity

of theories, always testing them against facts, always letting facts spawn new theories, so that the theories themselves have the spontaneous vivid patterns that any tentative crystallization of the real ought to have; and her own theories occur principally in novels, are themselves art. These theories of human development are to a large extent epistemological, just as her realism as novelist is primarily ocular, perceptual, like the realism of those nineteenth-century impressionists who regarded their paintings as the finest representation of retinal truth. Her fullest statement about the origin of human personality occurs in a passage which is perhaps her single most impressive achievement, surely her most painful, the final soliloquy of *The Waves*:

> Then a wood-pigeon flew out of the trees. And being in love for the first time, I made a phrase—a poem about a wood-pigeon—a single phrase, for a hole had been knocked in my mind, one of those sudden transparences through which one sees everything. Then more bread and butter and more flies droning round the nursery ceiling on which quivered islands of light, ruffled, opalescent, while the pointed fingers of the lustre dripped blue pools on the corner of the mantlepiece. Day after day as we sat at tea we observed these sights. (P. 343)
>
> But we were all different. The wax—the virginal wax that coats the spine melted in different patches for each of us. The growl of the boot-boy making love to the tweeny among the gooseberry bushes; the clothes blown out hard on the line; the dead man in the gutter; the apple tree, stark in the moonlight; the rat swarming with maggots; the lustre dripping blue—our white wax was streaked and stained by each of these differently. Louis was disgusted by the nature of human flesh; Rhoda by our cruelty; Susan could not share; Neville wanted order; Jinny love; and so on. We suffered terribly as we became separate bodies. (P. 344)

In the beginning there is neither body nor mind, only a nerve and its waxy insulation. This myth of the origin of the self is the culmination of a set of images that had been growing in Virginia Woolf's mind since the beginning of her career as a writer of fiction: in the early story "Kew Gardens" she speaks of heavy waxen bodies, candles whose flames are their voices. The use of wax as an image which defines the relation of the self to the environment makes certain obvious assumptions: we are born without features, without individuation, just lumps, passive, waiting for impression, quiet, dumb, incompetent. This passivity seems identical to that of the helpless mind menaced by perception that appears in an essay of 1919:

The mind receives a myriad impressions—trivial, fantastic,

evanescent, or engraved with the sharpness of steel. From
all sides they come, an incessant shower of innumerable atoms;
and as they fall, as they shape themselves into the life of
Monday or Tuesday, the accent falls differently from of old.
(*Essays II*, p. 106)

The wax is surrounded by a storm of sharp points; but somehow,
miraculously, the needles score the wax into a precise pattern—a nose,
a face, articulate limbs—as if a magnet were guiding the iron filings
into a predictable form. The wax, then, is perhaps not purely passive,
no simple three-dimensional analogue of Locke's *tabula rasa*; there is
something inside, and the substance, the form of this core is the basis
of identity, although not the determinant of it. The six characters of
The Waves are identical, Bernard implies, at birth; but different
experiences—and experience is always red-hot—destroy different
patches of our insulation, leave us mottled, figured, articulated,
regrettably human. The quick is half-enclosed, half-revealed; the
sense of touch, quickened, leaves Louis permanently disgusted by
flesh but permanently susceptible to it, for the waxy sheath, once
violated, cannot be repaired: perfume, paprika, the sun, hot water are
all dangerous and inevitable, make us increasingly battered, sodden,
until the core itself begins to fail with age. It seems from Bernard's
monologue that most perception is revulsion, that one person differs
from another chiefly in shifting permutations of exposure and disgust;
as Bernard remarks of his own sensory awakening, which occurred
in a hot bath when he was very young, "Sometimes indeed, when I
pass a cottage with a light in the window when a child has been born, I
could implore them not to squeeze the sponge over that new body."
So San Sebastian pleads that others not be martyred; it would seem
that one is best advised to be left a fetus in a womb, a blanket, a bed, a
glass jar filled with alcohol, anywhere unmolested and safe.

In Virginia Woolf all such feelings are half-truths to be debated.
Sometimes we wish to be closed; other times we wish to be open. The
nerve inside the spinal sheath is for the most part tranquil; when
agitated it has but one desire, an extremely powerful one: it requires
the existence of an external world. It is this urgency that makes womb
an impossible climate, that drives us toward self-actualization; one
can confirm one's own existence only through that which one most
dreads, sensation. Bernard himself is far from immune from this
feeling: he speaks often of the lovely palpability, objectivity, of things
in themselves, seen unclogged, uncontaminated, with newborn eyes,
and *The Waves* ends joyously in the confirmation of existence of
things in themselves, cup, knife, fork, that are not Bernard, and *I*,
who am Bernard, "worn out with all this rubbing of my nose along the

surface of things." The compelling appetite for a real world is again a very ancient theme in Virginia Woolf; in "The Mark on the Wall," for example, she speaks of awakening from nightmare, the terrifying dark of the mind shut in itself, and "worshipping reality, worshipping the impersonal world which is proof of some existence other than ours. That is what one waits to be sure of . . . " (*Haunted House*, p. 45). But of course at best our relation to an objective world is love and hate commingled; our evolution is a process of maiming and abrasion; but we can be shocked, if only for a moment, out of bad dreams.

Sometimes perception can be a source of delight, although if it is intense enough it is a scary delight; when Bernard sees the wood-pigeon, when a pigeon-shaped hole is knocked out of his waxy insulation, letting in the radical light, he feels a kind of exultation. But to explain this rapture we must, perhaps, look beyond the model of wax and spinal nerve. There is another class of myth of the origin of personality in Virginia Woolf's writing, never stated as explicitly as the previous one, but at least as important: the model of skull and eye.

> But when the door shuts on us, all that vanishes. The shell-like covering which our souls have excreted to house themselves, to make for themselves a shape distinct from others, is broken, and there is left of all these wrinkles and roughness a central oyster of perceptiveness, an enormous eye. (*Essays IV*, p. 156)

The whole brain, the whole inside of the body, is, according to this essay, written at the same time as *The Waves*, equivalent to an eye; and in her essay on Walter Sickert one of the speakers mentions South American insects in which the eye is so developed that they are all eye: "Were we once insects like that, too . . . all eye? . . . Ages ago we left the forest and went into the world, and the eye shrivelled and the heart grew, and the liver and the intestines and the tongue and the hands and the feet" (*Essays II*, pp. 234–35). This myth of human evolution, which is equivalent to a myth of the birth of mind, has its epistemological ramifications. Here the quick interior does not recoil from perception—the eye has instead a desperate need to see; and the mind's concepts, its abstract knowledge of the outer world, are metaphorically identical to retinal images. Openness to experience, the melting of the wax sheath, is in this class of myth a felicitous event, the enriching of the mind's eye with perception, the populating of the internal kingdom. In this manner the two classes of myth are diametrically opposed in value, even though their forms are so similar; I would attribute this disparity to Virginia Woolf's basic hatred of sexuality, the sexual body, about which Quentin Bell has recently enlightened us—the myth of the waxy spine is fundamentally a myth of touch—as opposed to her fascination with the act of vision. The eye that constitutes the whole self is not at all passive or reticent; it changes form, shuts its lids, clouds itself with tears, hallucinates and storms; the eye has all the possibilities for aperture and closure, the stippledness of personality, of the wax around the spine.

In fact the eye's own motility throws into doubt the whole solidity and objectivity of the real world. Usually Virginia Woolf behaves, as has been suggested, like a good dualist; but she makes no final affirmations, and it is possible that what the eye sees takes place, not in any external world, but inside the eye itself. Bernard's wood-pigeon seems to be, originally, outside, alien, in the forest; then to fly into Bernard's field of vision, into his eye; then to meet in there something congruent to itself, a poem about a wood-pigeon, an abstract constructed wood-pigeon that is part of the contents of Bernard's brain; and in the exact congruence, the identity, between the real wood-pigeon and the wood-pigeon-poem lies the source of much of Bernard's delight. In fact Bernard's career as a writer consists of making an A to Z catalog of the entire universe, reducing methodically the totality of things and events to phrases, data of the consciousness, his own objective, huge, but nevertheless private interior world. In other places, however, this same congruence between the inner and the outer does not exist; if someone is too open or too closed, and both are clearly insane states, one cannot effect a balance; often a kind of disturbing monism results. In a peculiar rhapsody in *Orlando*, an artificial verbal analogue to Orlando's unmentionable experiences in giving birth to a son, there is a kingfisher that flies around, intensely blue, "like a match struck right in the ball of the innermost eye" (p. 295). Perhaps the kingfisher itself, the whole terrestrial orbit, is imprisoned in the glassy ball of that interior eye, like the intricate nest of eels Orlando saw entrapped in the frozen Thames. In earlier novels one can point to a certain number of hallucinations, momentary and adventitious, the eye's sturdy volition to see what seems not to exist; and sometimes one finds passages in which the external world produces phenomena which fit into the mind's wandering fancies in an extraordinarily obliging manner. For instance, in *Jacob's Room*, Jacob Flanders, amusing himself during his boat trip with Timothy Durrant, sings monotonously, as if to himself, the hymn "Rock of Ages," and a great brown rock rises out of the waters; it is as if the song conjured the rock out of the ocean, the form of a rock, the memory of a rock, seen in Cornwall many years ago, superimposed on his field of perception. In *Orlando* a somewhat similar event occurs, which has more radical consequences: Orlando is just returning to England after her century's interlude, her liberation in a Turkish green world from the ordinary shackles of gender and role:

> Among the hurry of these thoughts, however, there now rose, like a dome of smooth, white marble, something which, whether fact or fancy, was so impressive to her fevered imagination that she settled upon it as one has seen a swarm of vibrant dragon-flies alight, with apparent satisfaction, upon the glass bell which shelters some tender vegetable. The form of it, by the hazard of fancy, recalled that earliest, most persistent memory—the man with the big forehead in Twitchett's sitting-room, the man who had sat writing. . . . The distraction of sex, which hers was, and what it meant, subsided; she thought now only of the glory of poetry, and the great lines of Marlowe, Shakespeare, Ben Jonson, Milton began booming and reverberating, as if a golden clapper beat against a golden bell in the cathedral tower which was her mind. The truth was that the image of the marble dome which her eyes had first discovered so faintly that it suggested a poet's forehead and thus started a flock of irrelevant ideas, was no figment, but a reality; and as the ship advanced down the Thames before a favouring gale, the image with all its associations gave place to the truth, and revealed itself as nothing more and nothing less than the dome of a vast cathedral rising among the fretwork of white spires. (Pp. 163–64)

It is St. Paul's, evidently half engendered by a strange form in Orlando's mind, as if a mind teeming with poems can throw out an image of itself with miraculous solidity, a cathedral, itself shaped like a skull, a triumphant impression of the internal form upon a malleable world. The skull is the proper shape for buildings: we should live inside our own heads, literally, or inside the head of the human race, like the British Museum of *Jacob's Room*: "Stone lies solid over the British Museum, as bone lies cool over the visions and heat of the brain. Only here the brain is Plato's brain and Shakespeare's" (p. 109). The human skull is expansive, accommodating; and sometimes it seems as if the growth of the mind is simply a long illumination of dark shapes inherent in it, congenital, our knowledge remembrance all.

There are two passages in Virginia Woolf's fiction that explore the structure of the chamber of maiden thought, the nature of the infant's head prior to experience; one of them is in *Between the Acts*, and is almost the last example in her work of the ophthalmic style so well known from the novels of the 1920s:

> George grubbed. The flower blazed between the angles of the roots. Membrane after membrane was torn. It blazed a soft

101

yellow, a lambent light under a film of velvet; it filled the caverns
behind the eyes with light. All that inner darkness became a hall,
leaf smelling, earth smelling, of yellow light. And the tree was
beyond the flower; the grass, the flower and the tree were entire.
Down on his knees grubbing he held the flower complete. (P. 11)

The child's mind is originally a black cavern; perception renders it
civilized, structured, a hall, a garden, as if an explorer, lighting a torch
at the mouth of a cave sealed since the origin of the world, discovered
velvet chairs, a dining room, the formal hedges of an estate, shock and
delight. But of course the more famous example of the birth of
consciousness is the second page of *The Waves*, a set of little sentences
which, after forty years of increasingly strident and complex verbal
experimentation, have lost none of their power to startle and tan-
talize:

> "I see a ring," said Bernard, "hanging above me. It quivers and
> hangs in a loop of light."
> "I see a slab of pale yellow," said Susan, "spreading away until
> it meets a purple stripe."
> "I hear a sound," said Rhoda, "cheep, chirp; cheep, chirp;
> going up and down."
> "I see a globe," said Neville, "hanging down in a drop against
> the enormous flanks of some hill."
> "I see a crimson tassel," said Jinny, "twisted with gold threads."
> "I hear something stamping," said Louis. "A great beast's foot is
> chained. It stamps, and stamps, and stamps."
> "Look at the spider's web on the corner of the balcony," said
> Bernard. "It has beads of water on it, drops of white light." (P. 180)

And the children go on, learning names, defining their perceptions
more exactly, giving substance and texture to what exists originally as
immediate experience, blank form, without scale, size, relation, or
meaning. This is what is first: real kinesthetic sight, kinesthetic sound;
a simple shape and a simple principle of motion. The shapes are the
ring, the slab, the strip, the concert pitch of A, the globe, the cylinder;
the principles of motion are vibration, diffusion, oscillation, distension, torsion, and concussion. The painter can build up any complex
form out of such elementary forms as are described here; and through
permutations of such elementary motions any event can be generated
once the forms are established. Do the children just perceive simply,
pick out for seeing what is most easily apprehensible, so that their
minds become stocked with a supply of basic forms? Or are the simple
forms of structure and motion the inborn contents of the human
brain, against which the complex forms of nature are to be compared
and judged? It is impossible to say. The ring hanging above Bernard,

quivering, may be no more than an ignorant description of the spider's web to which he refers when he next speaks, or of the gold loop made by the brass handle of a cupboard (pp. 342, 379); or it may be something more like the divine wheels of Ezekiel, romantic revelation, a ring embedded inside the brain, the small, bright, newly waked pupil of Bernard's eye. It may be stated that Virginia Woolf always believes that the general, the abstract, is more fundamental than the particular—her essays are full of such allegations; the plots of her novels are based on preordained principles of motion, and the most intense eye is the painter's analytical, knifelike eye. But as to whether the world is fundamentally objective or subjective, exterior or interior, she vacillates, and, since she has no set opinions or philosophy, it is not surprising that her novels do not gel in our minds, remain evasive and penetrating, a crisscross of interpellation.

The World outside Us

We cannot solve the problem of the isolated individual's relation to the world; and, even worse, the individual never exists in isolation, but insists on the contamination of parents, friends, wives, and reader. In the sentences at the beginning of the *The Waves*, the children instantly turn away from the purity of their private perception to look at those things which interest the others: Neville finds Rhoda's bird, soon Jinny issues a command, "Look at the house." In this way the perceptual world of the six children becomes common at a very early age, and for this reason Bernard can call them all a six-sided flower, six homologues of the same person, for they are more intimate than biological sextuplets, pairs of eyes each of which has opened to find five pairs of eyes staring at him. Yet even in the opening sentences there are clues of individuation, signs that the eye chooses, whether or not it creates: the tassel shows Jinny's love of ornamentation, the spider web Bernard's interest in the shimmering surface, the stamping of the beast the dim fear, the early paranoia, that seizes Louis. Much of this can be shared, but much cannot: no one can readily hear in the beat of the waves Louis' beast, which is not surprising, for in this case metaphor has dawned into consciousness far more expressive of purely private anxiety than of the external stimulus that it represents. The structure of *The Waves* is based on perhaps the single most important principle of motion in Virginia Woolf's fiction, unity and dispersal: the characters are always separating and coming together, running off into random privacy, clustering for a moment into satellite groups, such as the affair of Louis and Rhoda, finally all concentrating in Bernard's mind. What sets this apart from the general habits of novelists manipulating characters is, first of all, the technique of the soliloquy, which permits distinctness, pointedness of internal characterization beyond the previous usage of novelists; and the theory of interdefinition, which permits merging of characters far beyond any previous usage. This latter theory reaches a climax in a passage perhaps as moving as any in fiction:

> Here on the nape of my neck is the kiss Jinny gave Louis. My eyes fill with Susan's tears. I see far away, quivering like a gold thread, the pillar Rhoda saw, and feel the rush of the wind of her flight when she leapt. (P. 377)

But all through the novel the characters have been busy defining each other, through gossip, through the discovery of those habitual tendencies of mind which, as in the opening sentences, constitute individuation. One scene is especially helpful in the analysis of the relation between characters themselves, and their relations to the world of nature. Neville is lounging by a riverbank on a beautiful day, trying to write a poem about, among other things, trees; he is feeling dissatisfied with his poetical talent, and is cross too that Bernard, walking up to greet him, is about to violate his privacy:

> "How strange," said Bernard, "the willow looks seen together. I was Byron, and the tree was Byron's tree, lachrymose, down-showering, lamenting. Now that we look at the tree together, it has a combed look, each branch distinct, and I will tell you what I feel, under the compulsion of your clarity." (P. 232)

Bernard has a willow tree absorbed into his private fantasy, and so has Neville; but this subverted tree, mangled by Byron, tossed off as a detail in Neville's artificial poem, suddenly becomes vivid, stereoscopic, as the two images coalesce into an actual tree. If two people can see the same thing, the objective world is ratified, confirmed; the coming-together of two friends is not only mutually fructifying—Bernard says, "Let me then create you. (You have done as much for me.)"—but an important act of honor to the precision, the distinctness of the real world. But the old problems still beset us. There exists an objective world that Bernard and Neville share, congruent branch to branch and drooping leaf to drooping leaf; but we cannot be certain that it is exterior to both of them. It is not strictly necessary to assume that the willow tree exists independently of the two friends; their brains are similar, according to the physiology of the final chapter, and their cerebra may be fluted into the same dendritic pattern, willow-shaped, weeping, its bark running effortlessly into the same cerebral cortex.

The objective interior and the objective exterior seem interchangeable. In *Night and Day* there is an important episode which shows that what seems the most private musing can also be closely shared and objective. The stylish romantical hero, Ralph, tortured to the point of exasperation by his long inconclusive relation with the beautiful Katharine, starts to draw little figures on a sheet of paper, one of which is a blot fringed with flames "meant to represent—perhaps the entire universe"; soon, through the benignity of Katharine's mother, he is brought into the beloved's presence—they make inarticulate noises—they show each other their private papers, their innermost thoughts, in Katharine's case a shameful secret indeed, her antigenteel excursions into higher mathematics. Katharine sees the flame-fringed blot, and approves. Ralph is transported to the limits of shame and despair:

> He was convinced that it could mean nothing to another, although somehow to him it conveyed not only Katharine herself but all those states of mind which had clustered round hers since he first saw her pouring out tea on a Sunday afternoon. It represented by its circumference of smudges surrounding a central blot all that encircling glow which for him surrounded, inexplicably, so many of the objects of life, softening their sharp outline, so that he could see certain streets, books, and situations wearing a halo almost perceptible to the physical eye. . . .
> "Yes, the world looks something like that to me too." (P. 493)

Nothing now can prevent the long-awaited marriage: the schematic representation of the universe, in effect the form of Ralph's mind, is ratified, shared by another; the two skulls enclose the same eye; the flaming blot exists as stoutly, as verifiably, as the willow tree of Bernard and Neville. This is what high love is in Virginia Woolf: the confirmation of the reality of oneself and of the world in which one lives, and the superimposition and absolute congruence of the labyrinths of the two minds.

If this confirmation is lacking, the results are devastating; and much of Virginia Woolf's later fiction shows a populace etiolated, laid waste, by the failure of public vision. At one point, in *To the Lighthouse*, there is a celebrated chapter in which the narrator takes a single setting, a house in the Hebrides and its immediate environs, and systematically destroys every possible perceiver, until no eye is left to interpret it; what remains then is the external world, the real world of Locke, described by blind narration groping in outer night, outer day:

> Night after night, summer and winter, the torment of storms, the arrow-like stillness of fine weather, held their court without interference. Listening (had there been any one to listen) from the upper rooms of the empty house only gigantic chaos streaked with lightning could have been heard tumbling and tossing, as

the winds and waves disported themselves like the amorphous
bulks of leviathans whose brows are pierced by no light of reason,
and mounted one on top of another, and lunged and plunged
in the darkness or the daylight (for night and day, month and
year ran shapelessly together) in idiot games, until it seemed as
if the universe were battling and tumbling, in brute confusion
and wanton lust aimlessly by itself. (Pp. 202–3)

This is the world without categories, prior to any demarcation of
time, prior to the splitting of the firmament; it is the world inside the
egg, waiting to be hatched, and if it is born its birth will be
simultaneous to that of the human mind. The world devoid of the
human race is animate, theriomorphic, in fact all body; these elemental leviathans are, like Lawrence's felicitous whales, enormous
magnifications of the human body, irrational, spasmodic, grossly
sexual, uncontrolled; I believe that this passage is probably a transcription of certain feelings about herself which Virginia Woolf felt to
be insane. The world without a perceiver is the extreme case of the
loss of relation between one's self and the world, and its proper
metaphor is the loss of relation between one's mind and one's body.
Sanity is the suppression of appetite, the body's submissive, accurate
reflection of the soul within; and sanity is also the convergence of
nature and man, nature as serene and marmoreal as a landscape
designed by human architecture. However, it has been observed that
the body is recalcitrant, refuses to be a "sheet of plain glass through
which the soul looks straight and clear":

> All day, all night the body intervenes; blunts or sharpens, colours
> or discolours, turns to wax in the warmth of June, hardens to
> tallow in the murk of February. The creature within can only
> gaze through the pane—smudged or rosy; it cannot separate off
> from the body like the sheath of a knife or the pod of a pea for
> a single instant. (*Essays IV*, p. 193)

Our bodies clog us, according to this essay of 1930, prevent our art
from attaining realism; if one is to present the plain truth of the human
mind, how can one accomplish it if facial expression distorts our
emotion, our mouths sneer at laughter, our eyes weep because they
fail to be sad? And what if nature is not what we see? According to the
"Time Passes" chapter of *To the Lighthouse*, no human eye has ever
seen what is *really* out there. Here is a simple spring day *in re*:

> In spring the garden urns, casually filled with windblown plants,
> were gay as ever. Violets came and daffodils. But the stillness and
> the brightness of the day were as strange as the chaos and tumult of
> night, with the trees standing there, and the flowers standing

> there, looking before them, looking up, yet beholding nothing,
> eyeless, and so terrible. (P. 203)

The key word is *eyeless*:

> Yesterday I finished the first part of *To the Lighthouse*, and
> today began the second. I cannot make it out—here is the most
> difficult abstract piece of writing—I have to give an empty
> house, no people's characters, the passage of time, all eyeless and
> featureless with nothing to cling to. (*A Writer's Diary*, p. 87)

In the comfortable world, the world of Bernard and Neville, the
willow tree magically "looks seen together," like the roses of *Burnt
Norton*, which have the look of flowers that are looked at. Nature
responds, subtly and elegantly, to the impalpable pressures of our
own vision, configures itself to our demand for harmony, preens at
our attention, casts sidelong glances back at us. How can such a
commodious tree be alien from us? It is part of a consciousness itself,
like the cliffs that Lily Briscoe sees later in *To the Lighthouse*: "The
cliffs looked as if they were conscious of the ships, and the ships
looked as if they were conscious of the cliffs." We are flattered that
Nature is so thoughtful—but it is all a lie. Nature appears so
humanized only because our vision distorts it into that pattern; it is
ourselves that are conscious, ourselves that we compliment. If any
structure exists it is in the human mind, and if nature appears
articulate it is only because we stare into a mirror that we have
constructed and admire the features of our own faces.

> At that season those who had gone down to pace the beach and
> ask of the sea and sky what message they reported or what vision
> they affirmed had to consider among the usual tokens of divine
> bounty . . . something out of harmony with this jocundity and
> this serenity. There was the silent apparition of an ashen-coloured
> ship for instance, come, gone; there was a purplish stain upon
> the bland surface of the sea as if something had boiled and bled,
> invisibly, beneath. (P. 201)

We try to imbue nature with a discrete human body, but our effort
fails; the huge corpse spills blood, the tellurian form disperses into
sexual frenzy, a storm of metamorphosis. We try to imbue nature with
our eyes, but the tree's bark remains scaly and blind, and the branches
flail us until we shut our own.

Sanity and Insanity

The doctrine that sanity itself is unreasonable, that the exterior night
is all around us and resists our blandishments, makes art nearly

impossible; and in the next two books, *Orlando* and *The Waves*, not one beam of darkness from the alien outside is allowed to penetrate the compelling closed fantasy of the human consciousness. If the imagination and the mind itself lack support, degenerate into idle fancy, if all the romantic ability of the individual to create or alter his world is denied and mocked, then the careful myths which underpin Virginia Woolf's fiction must collapse. Indeed much of the interest of part 3 of *To the Lighthouse* depends on the reader's fascination with the author's tightrope act, her hairsbreadth extrication of herself from a situation in which continued narration is rendered nearly impossible; like much twentieth-century literature, the novel treads the line beneath a world of myths and a world which renders myth impossible. The great myth of personality which evolves in *The Waves* could be extinguished in an instant by one breath of the insidious drafts of "Time Passes"; such myths depend, as Spenser's myths do, upon a human body and a physical universe which are, metaphorically, accurate projections of those processes of the mind which they reify and elaborate. One can feel Virginia Woolf's methodological kinship with Spenser very strongly in her essay on the *Faerie Queene*, in which the whole work is seen as the "great bubble blown from the poet's brain," just as Rhoda in *The Waves* speaks of the great mental bubble in which the sun rises and sets. Bernard could not trace the development of personality so unerringly if evidence were adduced which belied the stylized waxen bodies of his figure of speech; those opaque lumpish random bodies, which Virginia Woolf complains are absent from fiction in her essay "On Being Ill," are absent from *The Waves* too; Rhoda is clumsy but her clumsiness is purposive, expressive. Death and other immutable enemies exist in *The Waves*, but one can do allegorical combat with them; there is no depiction of a world that is intrinsically beyond human cognition, in which personality in fact does not exist. *The Years* and more daringly *Between the Acts* investigate the problems raised in *To the Lighthouse*, the problem of the possible frailty and folly of any imaginative attempt to come to understanding, the uselessness of the human mind itself; but certain aspects of this theme twist their worrisome course through much of the earlier fiction.

The first appearance of the supersensible reality of "Time Passes," the world that is incommensurable with the human, outside the mind's bubble, is in the South America of *The Voyage Out*. As everyone has seen since its publication in 1915, this South America has nothing to do with any actual continent on the face of the earth; it does not even seem inspired by the accounts of travel writers, for its fauna is as much African as South American. It is bright but often indistinct, uncreated, as if the narrator as well as all the characters averts her gaze from the inconceivable forest, the implausible Amazon. The colors are disturbingly vivid: "The earth, instead of being brown, was red, purple, green ... there is no color like it in England" (p. 96). The landscape is a great ocean of land, deep, wholly lacking boundary lines, British partitions, indeed structure itself: "Why, even the earth sometimes seemed to him very deep, not carved into hills and cities and fields, but heaped in great masses" (p. 79). A small European settlement exists on the edge, a city in miniature; but beyond the chalk line at the circumference one steps out into a world that has never known the feel of the hand, the plastic force of the eye: "One could see the red of the stones at the bottom of it. So it had been at the birth of the world" (pp. 210–11); "The view was one of infinite, sun-dried earth, earth pointed in pinnacles, heaped in vast barriers, earth widening and spreading away and away like the immense floor of the sea" (p. 210). South America is anonymous, impenetrable, and nearly divine:

> So she might have walked until she had lost all knowledge of her way, had it not been for the interruption of a tree, which, although it did not grow across her path, stopped her as effectively as if the branches had struck her in the face. It was an ordinary tree, but to her it appeared so strange that it might have been the only tree in the world. Dark was the trunk in the middle, and the branches sprang here and there, leaving jagged intervals of light between them as distinctly as if it had but that second risen from the ground. Having seen a sight that would last her for a lifetime, and for a lifetime would preserve that second, the tree once more sank into the ordinary ranks of trees. (P. 174)

This tree bears more resemblance to the eyeless tree in the virgin spring of "Time Passes" than to the timid willow of *The Waves*; it is real, the most real entity that the ingenuous heroine Rachel has ever seen, and though it does not exclude Rachel from its world, it is clearly superhuman, supreme.

The American land does serve some romantic functions: it is the green world of comedy, like the Turkey of *Orlando*, and the lovers Hewet and Rachel wander into the forest in order to rid themselves of British emotional stricture; and the Amazonian forest is full of beautiful naked savages, as if the unconscious, in the fashion of the early nineteenth century, were the source of human salvation. But at last South America is not humanly approachable; it drives one to pravity, illness, insanity. Even on the voyage out Rachel caught a glimpse of the kind of transformation that South America imposes upon men: a vile sexual advance was committed upon her innocence by, of all people in the world, Richard Dalloway, the exterior Richard Dalloway, so far removed from the affable obtuse interior man of *Mrs. Dalloway*; this event caused Rachel to have a nightmare:

> At length the tunnel opened and became a vault; she found herself trapped in it, bricks meeting her wherever she turned, alone with a little deformed man who squatted on the floor gibbering, with long nails. His face was pitted and like the face of an animal. The wall behind him oozed with damp, which collected into drops and slid down. (P. 77)

This gibbering little man is but the first specimen in a long series of ape-creatures in Virginia Woolf's fiction, an undistinguished but thriving line which stretches all the way to the last page of *Between the Acts*. South America is that region of the world which is all physical, all body; the hippopotamuses, tigers, and monkeys which populate it are exactly analogous to the tumbling leviathans of "Time Passes"; and in South America human beings tend to decay into shapeless grotesques, for it is only conventional stricture that holds down the gibberer within. If one could see the human body raw, as the narrator in "Time Passes" sees the eyeless tree, if one could see the body without the elaborate apparatus of sympathy, preconception, and telepathy that marks all ordinary human interaction, each one of us would appear the same way: an ape. There is a character in *The Voyage Out*, a scrawny intellectual called St. John Hirst, whose vision is almost sufficiently clean, uninflected, *sec*, that he can perform this nearly impossible feat; here is what he sees as he watches a group of dull Englishmen after dinner:

> As every other person, practically, had received two or three plump letters from England, which they were now engaged in reading, this seemed hard, and prompted Hirst to make the caustic remark that the animals had been fed. Their silence, he said, reminded him of the silence in the lion-house when each beast holds a lump of raw meat in its paws. He went on, stimulated by this comparison, to liken some to hippopotamuses, some to canary birds, some to swine, some to parrots, and some to loathsome reptiles curled round the half-decayed bodies of sheep. (P. 177)

England is clearly "South America" too; in fact often a character will look out at the South American landscape and superimpose an ordinary British scene upon his perception for comparison and contrast. Indeed there is no reason at all why the novel needs to take place outside the environs of London. The world of "South America," the supersensible endless reality, tantalizing and forever new, lies all around us, the intimate matrix that encloses us everywhere: "It was this sea that flowed up to the mouth of the Thames; and the Thames washed the roots of the city of London" (p. 210). It is a region of freedom, danger, the thick appetites of the body; it is a region that Virginia Woolf knew well during the seven years of the novel's composition, for "South America" is that synaptic country where broken nerves seek connection in vain, that cold country which vision broken of its usual habits sees in a trance of clarity.

These two lands, South America and the Hebrides of "Time Passes," are not properly said to be correlative to any mental condition, for they are presumably exterior to all consciousness; but since everything that the human mind describes has reference to itself, we need not seek far to find the source of Virginia Woolf's imagery for this country: it is simply the dead interior everted. It is as if a mind much troubled by corrupt appetite decided to freeze itself to absolute zero, impoverish itself utterly, keep itself incontaminate behind stone walls, and then imagine that the inconceivable world beyond those walls was as black and tumultuous as itself. This is the model that we can derive from Bernard's model of the waxy spine, though it is a model for a situation that never appears in *The Waves*: if no wax ever melted from the sheath, or if the vulnerable spine could rewrap itself in an impervious shell, then the world would consist of a finite number of round hard balls, in no relation whatsoever to each other, unconscious of night or day, bald, blind. This perfectly closed world is not far from the "Time Passes" chapter of *To the Lighthouse*; it is also a model quite suitable for the short story "Solid Objects." In this story a young man with political ambition, John, finds at the beach a large irregular lump in the sand, useful as a paperweight; this stone becomes obsessive, like Borges' Zahir; John spends all his time searching for interesting casual stones and shards, ruins his political career by neglect, abandons his friends entirely for the sake of the secret joys of contemplating pretty fragments. This story is an allegory of the human appetite for the real. The thing in itself is immeasurably concrete, gravid, existent; the rest of the world, the content of human interaction, is spindrift and scum by comparison; the best hope is to become a solid object oneself, an easy seductive declension. "The only thing that moved upon the vast semicircle of the beach was one small black spot. As it came nearer ... it became apparent from a certain tenuity in its blackness that this spot possessed four legs" (*Haunted House*, p. 79); one need not retreat very far from people before they are reduced, like John and his friend Charles, to solid objects themselves. The original lump that Charles

111

finds in the sand is a lump of glass, "so thick as to be almost opaque" (*Haunted House*, p. 80); so we can see that things in themselves are, like human beings themselves, intrinsically neither opaque nor transparent, but a mixture of the open and the closed. The opacity is almost a matter of choice, even as John chooses radical involution over a life of sustained human contact; the lump of glass is both a paradigm of the condition of the inhuman universe and an emblem of certain possibilities which John sees latent in himself. The lump has been scraped and smoothed by the molar ocean, and it is smoothed still further by the action of John's mind:

> Looked at again and again half consciously by a mind thinking of something else, any object mixes itself so profoundly with the stuff of thought that it loses its actual form and recomposes itself a little differently in an ideal shape which haunts the brain when we least expect it. (*Haunted House*, p. 82)

John's mind and the stone deform each other, work in secret toward a hidden *rapprochement*: the stone turns formal, round, like those shapes that seem inherent in the mind in the opening sentences of *The Waves*; John's mind becomes increasingly cold, impermeable, stiff, mineral. Soon John finds a piece of iron identical in shape to the lump of glass but meteorite in origin, a piece of a dead star or a "cinder of a moon" (*Haunted House*, p. 84); "it radiated cold." Just as the South America in *The Voyage Out* represented, among other things, the Ultima Thule of the mind, so this token of the interstellar makes John conscious that we breathe not air but circumambient vacuum, that urges of flesh and bone are only a single variant of the general metallic thrust of the universe; John is ready to turn traitor to the human race, for his brain has been transfixed by the cold of iron, the fatigue of glass, and the leviathan requires from his disciples no fever of campaigning but only lunar calm, a slow rust.

This, then, is the final form of the closed personality: the rock. We cannot know exactly what it is that the rock thinks, and we assume that the fully enclosed brain will become impoverished to the point of suicide; but some of the strangest characters in Virginia Woolf's later fiction are produced by her attempts to depict characters whose skulls are nearly sealed earproof and eyetight. These closed characters, principally Sara Pargiter in *The Years* and Isa in *Between the Acts*, can easily be distinguished from characters that are classically insane, like Septimus Smith in *Mrs. Dalloway*: they do not hallucinate, they menace no one, they shock no one; the texture of their lives contains neither abyss nor abrasion, but consists of an intermittent incomprehensible dialogue inside their heads, as if in the absence of real external auditors the single mind has to become both speaker and listener. Both Sara and Isa seem, at least in the beginning, to be perfectly ordinary, conventional characters; but for no clear reason they are blighted in their external life and begin increasingly to rotate their eyeballs toward the inside. Sara Pargiter is introduced very young, before this quirkiness has set in; and when Sara enters onto the field of *The Years* she is accompanied, astonishingly, by Bishop Berkeley, whose bloodless lips have kissed, weightless arms embraced, so much of the literature of the last two centuries. Sara experiments with that tar-water that we all have drunk so gratefully, the water which can take away all human care:

> "And he says," she murmured, "the world is nothing but . . ."
> She paused. What did he say? Nothing but thought, was it? she asked herself as if she had already forgotten. Well, since it was impossible to read and impossible to sleep, she would let herself *be* thought. It was easier to act things than to think them. Legs, body, hands, the whole of her must be laid out passively to take part in this universal process of thinking which the man said was the world living. She stretched herself out. Where did thought begin?
> In the feet? she asked. There they were, jutting out under the single sheet. They seemed separated, very far away. She closed her eyes. Then against her will something in her hardened. It was impossible to act thought. She became something; a root; lying sunk in the earth; veins seemed to thread the cold mass; the tree put forth branches; the branches had leaves.
> "—the sun shines through the leaves," she said, waggling her finger. She opened her eyes in order to verify the sun on the leaves and saw the actual tree standing out there in the garden. Far from being dappled with sunlight, it had no leaves at all. She felt for a moment as if she had been contradicted. For the tree was black, dead black. (Pp. 132–33)

Berkeley is in fact the bishop who presides over *To the Lighthouse* and *The Waves*, where *esse est percipi*: the trick at which Sara fails, willed perception, is child's play to Lily Briscoe, who can actually see the form of a table in any outlandish place she chooses; although the "Time Passes" chapter routs Berkeley's enchantment utterly, shows the scraps and offal that persist beyond consciousness. In *The Waves* there is very little that exists outside the consciousness; we know from Virginia Woolf's diary that the origin of the book was an attempt to get at what is mysteriously beyond the human, the fin piercing the water, but the world of the interchapters is a reasonably humane place, ruled by a woman whose arm lifts up the sun at dawn. The one place in *The Waves* most comparable to "Time Passes," that curious passage at the end of Bernard's monologue in which Bernard loses his identity and fades out spectre-thin from the kingdom of the living, is an illustration of Berkelean orthodoxy: the world without a perceiver becomes a world without a world, eclipsed, ghostly, desultory, transparent. *The Years* is a book wholly disenchanted: the locus of human circumstance is rigid, murderous, grotesque, in no way malleable to the human consciousness. The image which persists so strongly through the novel, the clash of artificial and natural light, suggests a world that is only made more ghastly by the incursions of the human; and another powerful image, dust and scraps of paper whirling in the wind, suggests, as it does in T. S. Eliot's "Preludes," a universe which derides any attempt to find or impose order. It is not the world of Bishop Berkeley; it is the world whose death Newton diagnosed, whose rigor mortis has decomposed into atomic dust:

> Then the stars. Inscrutable, eternal, indifferent—those were the words; the right words. But I don't feel it, she said, looking at the stars. So why pretend to? What they're really like, she thought, screwing up her eyes to look at them, is little bits of frosty steel. And the moon—there it was—is a polished dish-cover. But she·felt nothing, even when she had reduced the moon and stars to that. (P. 360)

That is the apathy of the scientific temper, the stolid normality of Peggy; but that too is only a subtle way of being blind, shielding oneself from the intensity of the eye. Sara's method of self-protection is to attend to the private noises of her mind, for if one's body cannot configure itself to the shape of God's thought, if the world does not give evidence that there exists a unitary sensibility that binds every detail, then at least the principles of Berkelean cognition can operate, somewhat sinisterly, in the narrow world of Sara's skull, which has few themes but themes that make some internal sense. Our first feeling about the stream of irrelevancies that her lips utter is that it is a highfalutin kind of poetry:

> "Stood on the bridge and looked into the water," she hummed, in time to the music. "Running water; flowing water. May my bones turn to coral; and fish light their lanthorns; fish light their green lanthorns in my eyes." (P. 186)

This seems to be a refracted and ornamental version of Ariel's song in *The Tempest*. The language always suggests this muttering extravagance, inchoate rhythms half-embodied in a vague resonance of diction; she hums sentimental songs nearly forgotten, without realizing that she is humming in order to keep herself rapt in unbreakable trance.

Sometimes a little light filters in and she sings about what she sees;

when she does it is easy to understand why she has renounced vision:

> "In time to come," she said, looking at her sister, "people, looking
> into this room—this cave, this little antre, scooped out of mud
> and dung, will hold their fingers to their noses"—she held her
> fingers to her nose—"and say, 'Pah! They stink!'"
> She fell down into a chair.
> Maggie looked at her. Curled round, with her hair falling over
> her face and her hands screwed together she looked like some
> great ape, crouching there in a little cave of mud and dung. "Pah!"
> Maggie repeated to herself, "They stink" . . . She drove her
> needle through the stuff in a spasm of disgust. It was true, she
> thought; they were nasty little creatures, driven by uncontrol-
> lable lusts. (P. 189)

As in *The Voyage Out*, when loss of sympathy reaches a certain point, human bodies look like apes: Sara sees our race as apes and in turn appears to her sister an ape herself; it is the rock's way of asserting the universal insentience of man and nature. The other characters of *The Years* confirm the accuracy of Sara's vision again and again: Hugh and Milly Gibbs make "the half-inarticulate munchings of animals in a stall. . . . they wallowed in the primeval swamp" (p. 357); they are interchangeably described as hippopotamuses or elephants, or a kind of monster paramecium with "long white tentacles that amorphous bodies leave floating so that they can catch their food" (p. 377). The ape is only the first stage of the human declension into the formless appetites of the profound organic. Those characters who seem most humane, sentient, are not exempt from the universal deformity; the novel's heroine, Eleanor, snoring at a party, reminds the sensitive North that even her gentle and sympathetic hands could rip open one's belly, her teeth sink into one's throat; "We are all deformed" (p. 380).

When North remarks at the begininng of this meditation that "There was an obscenity in unconsciousness" (p. 378), he perhaps suggests to us a general rule of Virginia Woolf's fiction, that her significant experiments in the verbal representation of the mind principally explore the conscious mind, the foreground, the surface. She rarely records dreams, never records any bodily function except eating—although her brilliance in her description of food, as discussed in *A Room of One's Own*, her banquet scenes, may suggest that hunger is a subtle enough, various enough appetite that sexuality itself may be limited in human complexity beside it. She is the aptest student of the eye, in her famous novels of the 1920s, but "We are in danger of digging deeper than the eye approves . . . Let us dally a little longer, be content still with surfaces" (*Essays IV*, p. 157); those words, written in 1930, begin to signal that the old mode is at an end.

The Years and *Between the Acts* attempt to include a far greater range of experience than the earlier novels; if these later novels are bestiaries instead of herbariums, it is because human suffering is more vivid to her than beauty; if the style is kept plain it is because neither the dignity of mourning nor the asperities of human conduct accord well with rhapsody.

In the world of *The Years*, insanity itself would be a luxury, an indulgence; in a peculiar way, the insanity found in *Mrs. Dalloway* or *The Waves* belongs to what in any other novelist would be the comic mode. If any character were insane in *The Years* it would be Sara, but she is not hounded by society, like Septimus Smith, nor does she suffer from extremes of emotion or perceptual dislocation, like Rhoda; although what she says is elliptic, idiosyncratic, almost meaningless, many of the characters regard her as a seer, blessed with some special sensitivity, special understanding of their problems; her young friend North will often try to paraphrase her cryptic remarks, ask her if he has got it right, try to discover what illumination she is attempting with such difficulty to convey. She is exasperating, thorny, unpredictable; but she is not insane; she is if anything too sane, insofar as she deals honestly with the full bleakness of whatever she admits into the depths of her skull. When North revisits her after a long absence, he finds she lives on a street that is an emblem of the cacophony of incommensurable private universes clashing with each other:

> For now a trombone player had struck up in the street below, and as the voice of the woman practising her scales continued, they sounded like two people trying to express completely different views of the world in general at one and the same time. The voice ascended; the trombone wailed. They laughed.
> (P. 316)

Some of us speak in drawing rooms, others blow trombones, but the only difference is volume; we all are black spheres emitting private noise but not receiving anyone else's, voices lacking ears. Sara, by this time in life, is fairly serene; and her unique gift, her sanity, is that she tries to synthesize these discordant vibrations in her head into a consistent totality; at one point she starts to imitate the tune of the trombone, speaking her little words to its melody. Sara is never unconscious that she lives in a world of fragments, jangling versions of the universe, where human identity is itself wholly discontinuous; when she greets North for the first time in years, she has trouble "trying to put two different versions of him together" (p. 313), the present North and her old knowledge of him. But she has light, high-spirited moments too; here is a sample of a story she tells, which suggests that she has the true spirit of the author of *Orlando*:

> "But I had a talisman, a glowing gem, a lucent emerald"—she
> picked up an envelope that lay on the floor—"a letter of intro-
> duction. And I said to the flunkey in peach-blossom trousers,
> 'Admit me, sirrah,' and he led me along corridors piled with
> purple till I came to a door, a mahogany door, and knocked; and
> a voice said, 'Enter.' And what did I find?" She paused. "A stout
> man with red cheeks. On his table three orchids in a vase. Pressed
> into your hand, I thought, as the car crunches the gravel by your
> wife at parting. And over the fireplace the usual picture—"
> "Stop!" North interrupted her. "You have come to an office."
> He tapped the table. "You are presenting a letter of introduc-
> tion—but to whom?" (P. 341)

She can effortlessly translate her simple experience into private
fantasy, high romance; by living in such privacy she has almost
attained a world of Berkelean fluidity of object and event, although
she has done so only on a small scale, and by sacrificing almost
everything. Nevertheless her achievement is great; she has chosen a
style of living which, if restricted, allows her to sustain a fantasy
which corresponds point for point with whatever interjects from
the objective exterior; and that is, I believe, the final criterion of
success in a character from Virginia Woolf.

If Sara is successful, she has had to become nearly incapacitated,
vegetal, to attain it. Isa Oliver in *Between the Acts*, Virginia Woolf's
other major mutterer, is by contrast an efficient domestic manager, an
apt wife in society, by most appearances normal, not at all vatic; but
this superficial ease is only a symptom of a fictive universe radically
darker even than that of *The Years*. Isa's two lives, interior and
exterior, are almost perfectly disjunct; she can blithely act the part of a
British lady because the part has nothing to do with her real identity:

> "The moor is dark beneath the moon, rapid clouds have drunk
> the last pale beams of even. . . . I have ordered the fish," she said
> aloud, turning, "though whether it'll be fresh or not I can't
> promise." (P. 18)

The breadth of "Time Passes" is woven inextricably throughout Isa's
interior dialogue, a wind that becomes the black matrix of her
emotional life. On the surface she is a good and useful wife, quite
competent with cooks; on the surface she feels perfunctory love for
her husband; a little lower she is distressed by her husband's infidelities and contemplates her own; at the core there wells the
irreconcilable night. The poeticisms are clumsy, overfigured and
ornate; sometimes they suggest French decadence with their silvery
lunar metaphors:

117

> Isa dragged her chair across the gravel, muttering: "To what
> dark antre of the unvisited earth, or wind-brushed forest, shall
> we go now? Or spin from star to star and dance in the maze of
> the moon? Or...." (P. 51)

The very artificiality, however, is sinister; the inexpressibility of that
longing for the interstellar, for the center of the earth, for insulation so
thick that not one thin arrow can work its way through, takes the
form of poor expression, the absent mind retreating from the abyss
into offhand half-conventional usage. Isa makes a few small attempts
to connect her stream of reverie to the ordinary world: once she sees
William Dodge holding a knife and has a suicidal fantasy based on the
knife theme; and she does experiment, tentatively and with embarrassment, with allowing others to listen to her musings. But for the
most part she moves through a phenomenal world in which she
attends mechanically to commonplace unreal functions, staring with
fixed eyes right through it to a world freed from the pang of
mutability, the distemper of emotion:

> "Where do I wander?" she mused. "Down what draughty tun-
> nels? Where the eyeless wind blows? And there grows nothing
> for the eye. No rose. To issue where? In some harvestless dim
> field where no evening lets fall her mantle; nor the sun rises. All's
> equal there. Unblowing, ungrowing are the roses there. Change
> is not; nor the mutable and lovable; nor greetings nor partings;
> nor furtive findings and feelings, where hand seeks hand and eye
> seeks shelter from the eye." (P. 154)

Again the crucial word *eyeless*: the real world must be rid of subject
and object, all connection from one entity to another; heaven consists
of sheer separation, crystalline, superb. Eyes must shut; hands must be
retracted; the burial cloth must be wound securely, tightly around the
shivering body; the smiling closed head awaits the lunatic embrace of
things, things in themselves, themselves.

The cause of this schizoid reaction is of course self-revulsion. With
Sara Pargiter the human race is excrement excited by prurient affinity;
the body is wholly despised. With Isa the revulsion extends further;
she repudiates her birth, her memories, in effect everything:

> "How am I burdened with what they drew from the earth;
> memories; possessions...." "That was the burden," she mused,
> "laid on me in the cradle; murmured by waves; breathed by rest-
> less elm trees; crooned by singing women; what we must remem-
> ber: what we would forget." (P. 155)

People, trees, the ocean all conspire to weigh her down with ceaseless
abject gravity; and she finishes her meditation with a prayer for

lightning to free her from the toils of the body. *Between the Acts* is Virginia Woolf's most profound exploration of the body, of physical reality; the tumbling leviathans of "Time Passes" outfit themselves with pants and dress, learn polite and gentle speech—like the ape dressed in a top hat whom Bernard becomes at the end of *The Waves*, in a small attempt to reconcile his volatile soul with his dumb flesh— but the costumes fool no one. Underlying Pointz Hall, the whole novel, there is a strict foundation of mammoth tusks and saber teeth, as Lucy Swithin dictates from her book on evolution, Lucy Swithin who confuses the monster with her maid. People barely can contain themselves to human form; the horns are retracted with difficulty into the head, it is only a weekly manicure that blunts the claws; the narrator everywhere superimposes her vision of animal combat onto the simple plot; and the novel ends with the equivocal love of Isa and Giles itself reduced to the slashings of dog fox and vixen, the plot of a beast fable, an insect fable; the distorting mirror of Miss La Trobe's theater reveals the truest contours of the audience. One surrenders to one's body, in a fever of overt vulgarity, like Mrs. Manresa, a she-ape with one paw demurely placed in front of her, a nervous parody of Botticelli's Venus; or one withdraws into the cool interior, like Isa; or one retreats from sexual identity altogether, like William Dodge, homosexual or eunuch, a man agonized by his own blandness, Isa's only real confidant, somewhat analogous in his neutrality to the homosexual Nicholas of *The Years* whom Sara Pargiter says she loves. The perpetual fighting, the anguish of these armadillos, may be compared to elastic collision in the Newtonian universe; these characters so lacerated by bodily desire discover that the body can be used most effectively as armor, insulation:

> Isabella felt prisoned. Through the bars of the prison, through the sleep haze that deflected them, blunt arrows bruised her; of love, then of hate. Through other people's bodies she felt neither love nor hate distinctly. (P. 66)

The body is a massive buffer, obtuse, accommodating, and inert; we should be grateful to have a skin that so effectively prevents us from feeling; and if gravity weighs on us so ponderously that we are forever earthbound, our legs buckling under the material crush, our faces pulled into unrecognizability from sheer downward stress, we can at least rejoice that all the strings that tether the mind to the body are now nearly cut.

As late as *The Waves*, the body was flexible, lively, and its harrowing development could be employed as metaphor for the evolution of the mind; but in the strident world of the 1930s the voice of Mrs. Woolf, controlled, livid, must take into greater account the exigencies of the inhuman world, dispirited, gravid. In a peculiar broadcast talk that she gave in 1937 she states as universal truths some of the doctrines implicit in *Between the Acts*: the world is dual, consisting of interior meditation and a Newtonian outside, two separate hostile kingdoms, mutually unrecognizable; a sentient mind wandering on a hard floor, bumping into hard walls. Certain odd qualities of tone are common to all of Virginia Woolf's public speeches: she habitually begins, as in *A Room of One's Own* or "Mr. Bennett and Mrs. Brown," with a little episode from her life, her private reveries; but she approaches these personal matters most gingerly, elaborately framing them, qualifying them, deprecating them, holding them out on the end of a pole for public inspection, reducing them to lesson and figure of speech, A Room of One's Own, The Leaning Tower. Clearly she is a woman who thinks twice about baring her soul in public; yet we may assume, I believe, that the experiences recorded in these speeches may be of unusual import; if they were not radioactive they could be handled with more facility. In the broadcast called "Craftsmanship" her point is that words are useless, useless that is in the rectilinear inhuman world of walls and underground railroad cars; what is interesting is that we see a glimpse in her mind of a mutterer, a Sara Pargiter or Isa Oliver:

> Written opposite us in the railway carriage are the words: 'Do not lean out of the window.' At the first reading the useful meaning, the surface meaning, is conveyed; but soon, as we sit looking at the words, they shuffle, they change; and we begin saying, 'Windows, yes windows— casements opening on the foam of perilous seas in faery lands forlorn.' And before we know what we are doing, we have leant out of the window; we are looking for Ruth in tears amid the alien corn. The penalty for that is twenty pounds or a broken neck. (*Essays II*, p. 246)

The fact that there is language everywhere tends only to bring us back to our bumbling interior, the realm of our incompetent fantasy; everything on the outside is, like Isa's knife, a mere stimulus which alters the random flow of our interior, our real, life. She goes on to say that "We are beginning to invent another language—a language perfectly and beautifully adapted to express useful statements, a language of signs":

> But this suggests that in time to come writers will have two languages at their service; one for fact, one for fiction. When the biographer has to convey a useful and necessary fact, as, for

> example, that Oliver Smith went to college and took a third in
> the year 1892, he will say so with a hollow 0 on top of the
> figure five. (*Essays II*, p. 246)

This semiology is satirical, but it gives us a clue about her own new
style of the 1930s: in both *The Years* and *The Waves* there are in
fact two languages, or a continuum between two extremes of language, a muttering fictive language for Sara and Isa, and a much
sparer, more conventional, if not algebraic, language, which is
characteristic of the narrator's achromatic voice. *Mrs. Dalloway*, by
contrast, is written almost exclusively in the associative fictive style of
which language itself is avid, next to which aridity and algebra are
betrayal; but if one must give warning—"Do not lean out of the
window"; "Do be careful when airplanes are dropping bombs on
you"—one must force oneself to speak in that impoverished language
in which such warnings can be understood. Still, Virginia Woolf must
have wished to continue the experiments into real language, the
interior language: To adapt the formula of Lacan, the structure of
language is the consciousness itself.

Large Minds

In Virginia Woolf's middle novels, the novels from 1922 to 1931,
novels which along with *Ulysses* have illuminated the paths of all
subsequent writers in English into the heart of the language, yet have
represented an achievement so high that those who would be followers find themselves imitators—*Jacob's Room, Mrs. Dalloway, To
the Lighthouse, Orlando, The Waves*—we find ourselves blinking in a
world in which characters who resemble no characters in any previous
fiction attempt to reach definition through a language so elusive and
attenuated, volatile and pervasive, that one might as easily attempt to
sculpt one's portrait on a cloud. Traces of personality inhere everywhere—Jacob's shoes that lament his death in the war, the glove the
finger of which Mrs. Ramsay twists so unforgettably that no one
could ever suspect the glove belonged to anyone else—but as for the
full person, who would allege that any of the characters ever presents a face, a full-length figure, a unique personality to the reader?
It is not just that their speaking voices are all identical, and identical to
Virginia Woolf's, as the monologues of *The Waves* show vividly; it is
something deeper. E. M. Forster in his well-known lecture on Virginia
Woolf thought that the character of Jacob Flanders was solid,
substantial, indeed that *Jacob's Room* represented a great advance
over her earlier experimental prose because of her newfound strength
of characterization:

121

The style and sensitiveness of *Kew Gardens* remained, but they were applied to human relationships, and to the structure of society. The blobs of colour continue to drift past, but in their midst, interrupting their course like a closely sealed jar, stands the solid figure of a young man. The improbable has occurred; a method essentially poetic and apparently trifling has been applied to fiction. (*Two Cheers for Democracy*, p. 247)

One might compare this with what Leonard Woolf thought about *Jacob's Room* when he read it for the first time:

> On Sunday L. read through *Jacob's Room*. He thinks it my best work. But his first remark was that it was amazingly well written. We argued about it. He calls it a work of genius; he thinks it un-like any other novel; he says that the people are ghosts; he says it is very strange: I have no philosophy of life, he says; my people are puppets, moved hither and thither by fate. He doesn't agree that fate works in this way. (*A Writer's Diary*, pp. 45–46)

This is perhaps not the first time that two brilliant men, each perhaps more inclined to praise than to damn, have had opposite opinions; but who is right? Mrs. Woolf herself, who intrudes into this novel more significantly than into any other novel, even *Orlando*, and complains that a female novelist ten years older than her male protagonist must have considerable lapses in her understanding of him, certainly gives some sanction for Forster's belief, in the very instant when Jacob best fits Leonard Woolf's description, seems most ghostly; she musters together all the characters who know Jacob and discovers that they believe many contradictory things about him; he is unworldly but loves a dirty joke; no one can begin to say who he is:

> Captain Barfoot liked him best of the boys; but as for saying why . . .
> It seems then that men and women are equally at fault. It seems that a profound, impartial, and absolutely just opinion of our fellow-creatures is utterly unknown. Either we are men, or we are women. Either we are cold, or we are sentimental. Either we are young, or growing old. In any case life is but a procession of shadows, and God knows why it is that we embrace them so eagerly, and see them depart with such anguish, being shadows. And why, if this and much more than this is true, why are we yet surprised in the window corner by a sudden vision that the young man in the chair is of all things in the world the most real, the most solid, the best known to us—why indeed? For the moment after we know nothing about him. (Pp. 71–72)

Surely Forster's description is not quite accurate; one almost suspects he has fallen into a trap that Virginia Woolf has set. The only thing that Jacob's friends and lovers can agree on is that they do not know him; Bonamy, much infatuated with him, says he is undefinable; the only thing the narrator is sure of is that she cannot convey him. A few traits in the form of weak adjectives—"awkward but distinguished" (p. 61)—are regularly applied to him, but they tell us very little; indeed they tend to confuse us because they are to some extent oxymorons—"savage but pedantic" (p. 107). The narrator, we may suspect, presents us a ghost and asks us to believe on faith, without a shred of evidence, that this ghost is the most solid character in the world. Jacob is fleshless, a raw unsubstantiated charisma; strange women approach him from nowhere to say he is "the most beautiful man we have ever seen" (p. 75); those who love him are simply left with their mouths hanging open, stupefied with empty superlatives, "barbaric," "sublime" (p. 164). The phantom has weight; he leaves impressions of mass behind him in his collisions with others; but I think it is fair to say that he is not a character, only the form of a character. Such traits as are evinced as tentative description provide only the loosest, draftiest frame for his personality; the center, the real Jacob, is forever untouched, tantalizing. Finally, there seems to be something ludicrous about the ascription of traits to other human beings, "character-mongering," the assumption of the intelligibility of others:

> But how far was he a mere bumpkin? How far was Jacob Flan-
> ders at the age of twenty-six a stupid fellow? It is no use trying
> to sum people up. One must follow hints, not exactly what is
> said, nor yet entirely what is done. Some, it is true, take inef-
> faceable impressions of character at once. Others dally, loiter,
> and get blown this way and that. Kind old ladies assure us that
> cats are often the best judges of character. A cat will always go to
> a good man, they say; but then, Mrs. Whitehorn, Jacob's land-
> lady, loathed cats.
> There is also the highly respectable opinion that character-
> mongering is much overdone nowadays. After all, what does
> it matter—that Fanny Elmer was all sentiment and sensation,
> and Mrs. Durrant hard as iron? (P. 154)

In both *Jacob's Room* and *Mrs. Dalloway* we are given to understand that the whole novel adds up to the central character: "What do
we seek through millions of pages? Still hopefully turning the pages—
oh, here is Jacob's room" (p. 97). The romantic motto "I become what
I behold"—the motto of the prophetic Blake, the third canto of *Childe
Harold*, the cancelled stanzas of Tennyson's "The Palace of Art"—is

stretched and stretched, the bubble is inflated to the limit of the horizon. The solid Susan, the sanest, earthiest character of *The Waves*, is not so mudbound that she cannot say:

> At this hour, this still early hour, I think I am the field, I am the barn, I am the trees; mine are the flocks of birds, and this young hare who leaps, at the last moment when I step almost on him. (P. 242)

After *The Waves*, such experiences are rarer, but even Eleanor Pargiter can speak similarly about her expansion of perception in city traffic: "The uproar, the confusion, the space of the Strand came upon her with a shock of relief. She felt herself expand" (*Years*, p. 112). Clarissa Dalloway's theory of personality suggests that these feelings are not just momentary delusions, vagrant states of mind, but an intimation of the true nature of human identity itself, whose locus is not the interior of the skull nor the confines of the skin, but the enormous totality of a whole lifetime's perceptual experience:

> It was unsatisfactory, they agreed, how little one knew people. But she said, sitting on the bus going up Shaftesbury Avenue, she felt herself everywhere; not "here, here, here"; and she tapped the back of the seat; but everywhere. She waved her hand, going up Shaftesbury Avenue. She was all that. So that to know her, or any one, one must seek out the people who completed them; even the places. Odd affinities she had with people she had never spoken to, some woman in the street, some man behind a counter—even trees, or barns. It ended in a transcendental theory which, with her horror of death, allowed her to believe, or say that she believed (for all her scepticism), that since our apparitions, the part of us which appears, are so momentary compared with the other, the unseen part of us, which spreads wide, the unseen might survive, be recovered somehow attached to this person or that, or even haunting certain places after death . . . perhaps—perhaps. (Pp. 231–32)

Her use of the word *apparition* is revelatory: it is the body that is apparition, ghost, and the huge tenuous network, suprahuman, secret, is finally real beyond death. The theoretical basis of *Jacob's Room* is the same, but what is emphasized is not the global luminosity of the whole Jacob but the wooliness, the turbidity of identity in a world where a person is not a finite center:

> There remains over something which can never be conveyed to a second person save by Jacob himself. Moreover, part of this is not Jacob but Richard Bonamy—the room; the market carts;

the hour; the very moment of history. Then consider the effect of
sex—how between man and woman it hangs wavy, tremulous,
so that here's a valley, there's a peak, when in truth, perhaps, all's
as flat as my hand. Even the exact words get the wrong accent
on them. (Pp. 72–73)

There are certain indications that Virginia Woolf herself accepted provisionally this theory of identity: she says in an essay on Horace
Walpole:

> The only way to read letters is to read them thus stereoscopically.
> Horace is partly Cole; Cole is partly Horace; Cole's cook is partly
> Cole; therefore Horace Walpole is partly Cole's cook's sister.
> Horace, the whole Horace, is made up of innumerable facts and
> reflections of facts. (*Essays III*, p. 111)

The novelist might wish to feel triumph and despair: nothing is insignificant, irrelevant; every detail of table, acquaintance, speech is
necessary and illuminating; but not even millions of pages will ever be
enough. Jacob can populate his room with "ten or eleven" brand new
acquaintances whenever he enters it; he can become the affective
center of London, a blank magnet with boundless visual thirst; but he
is forever an enigma, his face blurred by its own beauty, his mind
grown shapeless with study and vision.

It is easy to see how effortlessly such swollen personalities as Jacob
Flanders or Clarissa Dalloway can turn insane; Rhoda and Septimus
Smith represent only a slight evolution toward self-awareness. Jacob
is never conscious of how much he embraces; Clarissa has some
insight into her real size but expends most of her attention not upon
her private sensation but upon quotidian conduct; but Septimus is
lunatic from self-consciousness. Septimus could never have been born
into the world of *The Years* or *Between the Acts*, for the world of the
1930s is too highly articulated, indeed, if a fascinating diary entry of
18 November 1935 is the key, it is four-dimensional:

> It struck me, though, that I have now reached a further stage
> in my writer's advance. I see that there are four? dimensions:
> all to be produced, in human life: and that leads to a far richer
> grouping and proportion. I mean: I, and the not I; and the
> outer and the inner—no, I'm too tired to say: but I see it.
> (*A Writer's Diary*, p. 250)

This casual jotting is as close as Virginia Woolf gets to philosophical
organization, those wonderful romantic diagrams so useful and
misleading from Blake to Yeats; this is a puny thing next to *A Vision*'s
thumbscrews, but here it is:

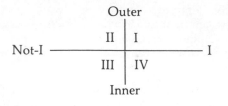

This is the fourfold organization of the bleak sane world of her last two novels. The first quadrant is the body, the ape-self, the self as it appears to others; the second quadrant is the dead exterior, howling with wind; the fourth quadrant is the ego, the nerve locked inside its shell; and the third quadrant is the world of muttering, the outside translated into fantasy in the case of Sara Pargiter, or the objective interior in the case of *The Waves*. This fourfold schema is an adequate diagram for *The Years, Between the Acts,* and to a lesser extent *To the Lighthouse*, in which there are occasional intrusions from the outer black; and this schema is also adequate for the earliest novels, *The Voyage Out* and *Night and Day*—indeed, the central struggle of *Night and Day* is the difficult coalescing of one's ideal beloved with all-too-human reality, Madeline's hard reconciliation of sad blanched Porphyro with the man of her dreams. But in *Jacob's Room, Mrs. Dalloway, Orlando,* and *The Waves* there is no interplay between the outer and the inner, but only the spidery cross-connection of the *I* with the inseparable *not-I* that is everywhere a reflex and talisman of the ego.

From *The Voyage Out* to *The Waves* the tendency is unification, abolition of categories, until the ego and its environment are the yolk and white of one shell; after *The Waves* the tendency is dispersal, until the world is held together by nothing except the rickety historical myth of Miss La Trobe's pageant in *Between the Acts*, a banner held at one end by an idiot, and at the other by a cow. One cannot underestimate the importance of the rise of fascism in the 1930s to this fragmentation; but there are compelling internal reasons for this collapse that can be traced through the novels of the 1920s. The discovery that Virginia Woolf makes in these novels is that in order to banish utterly the world that is outside, the tumbling leviathans, one must be completely open; and too much openness is suicide. The leviathans are gruesome beasts and cannot be trained to fetch newspapers, but they are still much less inimical to the human than the condition of total permeability; thus one chooses one's destruction, for either one is too large and explodes from within or one is too small and is squashed by a predator—it is not accidental that the topos of birds eating snails or worms is omnipresent in *The Waves* and *Between the Acts*. Bernard's nostalgia for the wax casing around the spine, for things in themselves, for the tame ape within him, is a sign of what will become the predominant appetite in the 1930s: the iron necessity of living in an inhuman world, even if it destroys you. Self-expansion, that most giddy experience, reaches its triumphant climax in the six-sided flower in *The Waves* that is Bernard and Jinny and Neville and Susan and Louis and Rhoda and day and night; but even in its greatest achievement it pines after restriction, boundary lines, the safety of the alien. Already in *To the Lighthouse* and *The Waves* the assertion of *Jacob's Room* and *Mrs. Dalloway* has failed, the assertion that the sum of all events might add up to the contours of a single face; in both the banquet scene of *To the Lighthouse*, in which all partitions break down between the characters, and in the six-sided flower of *The Waves*, there is a recognition that humanity is plural and not singular, even if the hope persists that the community will still comprise a single ideal world. But just as the earlier doctrine *I am the world* tends too quickly to schizophrenia, so the doctrine *we are the world* becomes a kind of *folie à six*. If Bernard can feel every wound in his five friends, they are all six as indistinct as the featureless Rhoda who buried her face in the ground; they have come so close that they lose relation with one another; in fact each is much handicapped by the loss of terra firma, a solid extrinsic world. The open and the closed have this much in common: for them there is no order possible. Either there exists no frame on which to find locations, neither abscissa nor ordinate, or there is nothing but rigid night and the clatter of steel balls. The world may be transparent and its bare bones may be visible, but that is no guarantee that the internal structure will constitute pattern, harmonious design, as the narrator of *Between the Acts* remarks when William and Isa speak of death:

> The future shadowed their present, like the sun coming through
> the many-veined transparent vine leaf; a criss-cross of lines
> making no pattern. (P. 114)

Transparency and opacity fail equally in Virginia Woolf's later fiction, for transparency does not reveal, nor opacity protect.

Yet in the 1920s one had every reason to believe that the eye could evolve without measure, become some super-eye before whose X-ray vision walls and flesh would turn transparent, reveal aesthetic structure that was simultaneously pattern and ideogram; that the world and the human body would be finally shown to be no clog of iron and sweating arms but sheer limpid mental construct, confect of light itself. Has not the human race become less gross, more thoughtful and stylish with every passing generation? Even as early as 1915 Helen Ambrose in *The Voyage Out* envisages "a race of men becoming more and more like Hirst" (p. 205), brain unadulterated by body; and this new man whose body is withering away, St. John Hirst, can do marvellous things with his intellect: "My brain . . . is in a condition of abnormal activity . . . I see through everything—absolutely every-thing. Life has no more mysteries for me" (p. 169). Before the naked brain the cosmos gleams with meaning. The fact that for most of us the eye is too enfeebled even to see that there is fog in front of us, much less what lies within, the ear is befuddled with wax, is perhaps due merely to lugubrious self-absorption with our own sufferings; like Wordsworth, like Blake, we were born into mundane glory, have for a moment become encrusted, morbid, and into glory we shall pass away:

> The mainland, not so very far off—you could see clefts
> in the cliffs, white cottages, smoke going up—wore an extra-
> ordinary look of calm, of sunny peace, as if wisdom and piety
> had descended upon the dwellers there. Now a cry sounded, as
> of a man calling pilchards in a main street. It wore an extraordin-
> ary look of piety and peace, as if old men smoked by the door,
> and girls stood, hands on hips, at the well, and horses stood;
> as if the end of the world had come, and cabbage fields and stone
> walls, and coast-guard stations, and, above all, the white sand
> bays with the waves breaking unseen by any one, rose to heaven
> in a kind of ecstasy.
> But imperceptibly the cottage smoke droops, has the look of a
> mourning emblem, a flag floating its caress over a grave. The
> gulls, making their broad flight and then riding at peace, seem
> to mark the grave. . . . Yes, the chimneys and the coast-guard
> stations and the little bays with the waves breaking unseen by
> any one make one remember the overpowering sorrow. And
> what can this sorrow be?
>
> It is brewed by the earth itself. It comes from the houses on the
> coast. We start transparent, and then the cloud thickens. All
> history backs our pane of glass. To escape is vain. (*Jacob's Room*,
> pp. 48–49)

This passage, written in Virginia Woolf's highest style, in fact provides a myth nearly identical to that of "Tintern Abbey": our native state is transparency, and children live in perpetual vividness and exhilaration. Jacob's perception of Cornwall from Timothy's boat is immediate experience, as if Jacob were that day born and Cornwall were a region unvisited by human pain; and so the whole townscape rises into heaven, for the real world is everywhere, for those whose vision is piercing enough, heaven; and the town lowers back to the ground as Jacob sinks back into personality, history, and Cornwall resumes its Cornish context. As in Bernard's myth of the waxy spine, individuation is deformity, but Virginia Woolf's progress from 1922 to 1931 is illustrated by the fact that the two myths are diametrically opposed, for in the first myth human beings are fundamentally transparent, in the second fundamentally opaque. In *The Waves* corporality serves as a metaphor; in the earlier novels corporality is, more simply, evil; it is a principle in the universe that is hostile to the eye, that hinders the development and expansion of the self, that tricks us into doubting the power of the imagination. Extreme joy is almost always accompanied by a feeling of disembodiment, for instance when, in *Jacob's Room*, the narrator opines that it is good that exaltation cannot last long, for if it did "The stars would shine through us" (p. 120). Sometimes the chilling effects of corporality quite definitely manage to quash any sort of visionary or oceanic feeling, as in this remarkable and rather prefigurative passage from *Night and Day*:

> And yet, after gazing for another second, the stars did their usual work upon the mind, froze to cinders the whole of our short human history, and reduced the human body to an ape-like, furry form, crouching amid the brushwood of a barbarous clod of mud. This stage was soon succeeded by another, in which there was nothing in the universe save stars and the light of stars; as she looked up the pupils of her eyes so dilated with starlight that the whole of her seemed dissolved in silver and spilt over the ledges of the stars for ever and ever indefinitely through space. Somehow simultaneously, though incongruously, she was riding with the magnanimous hero upon the shore or under forest trees, and so might have continued were it not for the rebuke forcibly administered by the body, which, content with the normal conditions of life, in no way furthers any attempt on the part of the mind to alter them. She grew cold, shook herself, rose, and walked towards the house. (Pp. 196–97)

The succession of feelings recorded here is nearly a thematic index of those preternatural sensations which all of Virginia Woolf's later novels develop and clarify. Katharine stares at the night sky and feels, first, a sense of personal puniness amid the immensity of the heavens; her body dwindles to ape size, her mind becomes closed tight; it is the freezing world of "Time Passes," *The Years*, the exterior blackness flecked with lumps. Then from this position of utter closure, nearly self-loathing, a metamorphosis begins: the pupil of the eye dilates, becomes huge, the starlight spills in and her being spills out; and this oceanic perception, this monist ecstasy, becomes identified with her early romantic fantasy of prince charming, sublimated sexual transport. Working against this rapture is her own body, that stolid dualist; and this ugly corporality persists in Virginia Woolf's fiction, this suspicion that the body is basically conservative, inert.

Therefore the visionary, the open seeker for the open universe, must be the enemy of the body; and what this entails for the sane visionary is a somewhat bizarre phenomenon of characterization, the fissure of the body into two bodies. Perhaps the first character to announce that she has two bodies is Katharine Hilbery in *Night and Day*:

> All the times she was in fancy looking up through a telescope at white shadow-cleft disks which were other worlds, until she felt herself possessed of two bodies, one walking by the river with Denham, the other concentrated to a silver globe aloft in the fine blue space above the scum of vapours that was covering the visible world. . . . There was no reason, she assured herself, for this feeling of happiness; she was not free; she was not alone; she was still bound to earth by a million fibres; every step took her nearer home. (Pp. 300–301)

One body is airy geometrical form, as globular and felicitous as the eye itself, billowing on the incorporeal sky; the other body is mere obtuse flesh, a participant in life rather than the vertiginous spectator. The relation between the two bodies is complex; in this passage it seems that the globe is almost a metaphor for the brain itself, floating isolated and detached, possessing two methods of perception, the direct vivid eye, and the blunt connections of the other senses which must travel thousands of miles up through the "million fibres" of the body's nerves, as if, were Ralph to brush her elbow, the globe humming through the stratosphere would be eventually informed of the rash deed by some botched, weak, and intermittent telegraphy. But the body that is the globe, the real body of which the reddish flesh is only a simian replica, also can manifest itself on earth as an ideal body complete with arms and legs, astral, luminous; in this same passage Ralph looks at the happy Katharine, and sees her "not so much a real person, as the very woman he dreamt of" (p. 301). In later novels this kind of rapture, in which sexual joy is refined out of the organic entirely, in which the stale body bubbles away into a creature made of light, is much more developed: the young Clarissa Dalloway, at the height of her infatuation for Sally Seton, sees her lover resolve out of pink gauze into luminous fuzz, sublime out of the strictures of gravity: "She *seemed* anyhow, all light, glowing, like some bird or air ball that has flown in, attached itself for a moment to a bramble." By the time of *Orlando* this process of the replacement of one body by another is so well understood by the narrator that she can present

Orlando's two bodies contending for Orlando's spirit, as if a human being were by nature a Siamese twin:

> For Love, to which we may now return, has two faces; one
> white, the other black; two bodies; one smooth, the other hairy.
> It has two hands, two feet, two tails, two, indeed of every
> member and each one is the exact opposite of the other. Yet, so
> strictly are they joined together that you cannot separate them.
> In this case, Orlando's love began her flight towards him with
> her white face turned, and her smooth and lovely body outwards.
> Nearer and nearer she came, wafting before her airs of pure
> delight. All of a sudden (at the sight of the Archduchess pre-
> sumably) she wheeled about, turned the other way round; showed
> herself black, hairy, brutish; and it was Lust the Vulture, not
> Love, the Bird of Paradise that flopped, foully and disgustingly,
> upon his shoulders. (Pp. 117–18)

This memorable passage, which is incidentally the source of Quentin Bell's celebrated description of Virginia Woolf's childhood molestation by her half-brother, shows how far the doctrine of the two bodies has evolved from 1919 to 1928. In *Night and Day* Katharine spends most of her time in her habitual physical body, tending her parents, reading prosaically, doing the common chores of the rich; and there is only occasionally the emergence of the other body, the exaltation that accompanies young love, meditations upon the stars, the solution of mathematical problems. Orlando, however, lives in a world that is close to perpetual fantasy, and finds this rare intrusion of the corporeal, the lower body, most distressing. Orlando may have learned how to survive in a body that is nearly pure ectoplasm, the most quicksilver and obliging body ever seen, given to sudden fits of sexual reversal; yet even in Arcadia there is a second, excrementitious body congruent to one's romantic body hair by hair and toe by toe which asserts itself at the least twinge of low sexual arousal, asserts itself in all its hideous opacity.

These tendencies pushed a little too far result in Septimus Smith. It is he who hates the physical body most intensely of any character in Virginia Woolf; and it is he who is the final proof of the impossibility of openness as a way of life. No character elsewhere is ever so devastated by the dilation of the pupil, the loss of the boundary between the *I* and the *not-I*; it is as if a hole had been cut in his skull, by the ancient operation of trephination mentioned in *Between the Acts*, and the light poured in steadily, uncontrollably. Like most insane characters, he is driven raving by his own transparency, his body so hopelessly transpierced by the sun, and he therefore attempts to close himself utterly, shelter his head from the light. Thus he is brought back to his hateful body, his dog's body, his paranoid self-revulsion; he is isolated from humanity and is hunted down like a dog by "Human Nature;" a pack of doctors; and delirium is his only escape. He oscillates wildly between the closed state and the open, neither of which offers any relief, only a change from one sort of pain to its equally intense opposite. Half the time he declares that nothing has meaning, half the time that everything has meaning; these statements are equally sinister, equally insane. For the insane character, the pellucid meaning inherent in the universe—which Septimus wishes to declare a new religion—is not a pleasant immanence of exterior order, but something thrilling, peculiar:

> There is a God. (He noted such revelations on the backs of envelopes.) Change the world. No one kills from hatred. Make it known (he wrote it down). He waited. He listened. A sparrow perched on the railing opposite chirped Septimus, Septimus, four or five times over and went on, drawing its notes out, to sing freshly and piercingly in Greek words how there is no crime and, joined by another sparrow, they sang in voices prolonged and piercing in Greek words, from trees in the meadow of life beyond a river where the dead walk, how there is no death.
> (*Mrs. Dalloway*, p. 35)

Here is an earlier, more concise version of this theme from the short story "An Unwritten Novel," in which the narrator decides to attribute insanity to an unknown woman sitting across from him in a railroad carriage:

> ... everything has meaning—placards leaning against doorways—names above shop-windows—red fruit in baskets—women's heads in the hairdresser's—all say "Minnie Marsh!" But here's a jerk. "Eggs are cheaper!" That's what always happens! I was heading her over the waterfall, straight for madness.
> (*Haunted House*, p. 14)

This, then, is what everything means if everything has meaning: the whole world utters your name. It is not accusation, but acknowledgment, worship; it is Berkeley's universe paying homage to the mind that informs it, sustains it. We see that the theory of identity of Jacob Flanders and Mrs. Dalloway—that the configurations of the world are a set of cues and indexes toward a single personality—has its demonic extremes: the universe can become the thin penetrating reflex of a single mind. While Septimus can feel ecstasy that all things can resolve themselves into the uniform melody of his name, the liquid justice of his soul, nevertheless the inspiration for this upheaval, this revolt

132

against the established order of things is hatred of the body, revulsion against the physical.

> She threw herself from a window, which, however, was not high
> enough from the ground to cause her serious harm. It was here
> too that she lay in bed, listening to the birds singing in Greek
> and imagining that King Edward VII lurked in the azaleas using
> the foulest possible language. (*Biography I*, p. 90)

This is Quentin Bell's account of Virginia Woolf's breakdown in 1904 following the death of her father; it suggests that even while the wondrous birds sing Greek, the obscene muttering of the body forms a counter-refrain of its own; and in Quentin Bell's description of another episode, in 1913, we learn that she felt her belly, mouth, and excretion tainted, monstrous.

Septimus finds sexuality unbearable, renounces copulation, declares that emotions do not exist, only various forms of lust; indeed there is every reason to believe that in heaven there is neither lust nor emotions, only the one brain, the labyrinth of whose cortex enfolds garden and town, sun and sky. For Septimus the body is forever depraved and deranged, just as Rachel Vinrace in *The Voyage Out*, in the insanity of her final illness, imagines her body growing until her knees are mountains, her toes wholly separated from her body, her mind flitting discarnate around the corners of her sickroom. In Septimus this alienation from his body takes the form of treating his body as a mechanical instrument, as if he were in fact a little man inside his skull, manipulating muscles, staring through the windows of his eyes; he hears his wife sobbing like a "piston thumping," for she must be considered a machine, and makes a deliberate, false gesture, in order to pretend an emotion he does not feel:

> His wife was crying, and he felt nothing; only each time she
> sobbed in this profound, this silent, this hopeless way, he des-
> cended another step into the pit.
> At last, with a melodramatic gesture which he assumed mechan-
> ically and with complete consciousness of its insincerity, he
> dropped his head on his hands. (*Mrs. Dalloway*, p. 136)

This would impress anyone acquainted with the writings of the psychiatrist R. D. Laing as a state identical to what he calls the adoption of a false-self system; indeed much of the progress of Septimus' insanity seems quite similar to our contemporary notions of schizophrenia. Septimus has in effect willed the loss of his identity at the moment when he repudiates the natural ease of his body; and so in *Mrs. Dalloway*, for almost the first time in Virginia Woolf's fiction, we begin to suspect that the physical body, the humble lower self, has its uses, even its advantages, over the rarefied ecstasies of the higher body. Septimus has expunged every trace of human sympathy; indeed he is occasionally disturbed that he cannot feel, is numb even over the death of his beloved, Evans; Septimus at his most transcendent is all brain:

> But what was the scientific explanation (for one must be scientific above all things)? Why could he see through bodies, see into the future, when dogs will become men? It was the heat wave presumably, operating upon a brain made sensitive by eons of evolution. Scientifically speaking, the flesh was melted off the world. His body was macerated until only the nerve fibers were left. It was spread like a veil upon a rock.
> He lay back in his chair, exhausted but upheld. He lay resting, waiting, before he again interpreted, with effort, with agony, to mankind. He lay very high, on the back of the world. The earth thrilled beneath him. Red flowers grew through his flesh; their stiff leaves rustled by his head. (Pp. 102–3)

Virginia Woolf occasionally discusses the condition of the world without flesh, the skeleton of things. There is a fascinating passage near the end of *Jacob's Room*, in which night falls, a breath of exterior wind blows off the flesh of Flanders; but there, as here, what remains when the world is unclothed is no rattling articulation of bone but a network of nerves, as if the absolute core of the body or the world were the optic nerve and the minute reticulation of the tactile nerves, tendrils which creep out of the skin and curl themselves around distant objects; it is the brain's skeleton, the eye's skeleton, the body grown so huge and porous that flowers grow, birds fly, through its interstices. Like Blake, Septimus can see nothing that is not human; so drenched is the world in Septimus' massive single humanity that dogs turn into men as they approach him, a tree vibrates in exact empathy with his spine, he can see another world extending into the depths of printed wallpaper, find Evans inside a painted screen, for his field of existence is interchangeably flat or round, past or present, simply himself.

The brain, unable to bear the lusts of the body, retaliates by annihilating the whole physical world. Sometimes in Virginia Woolf's writing it seems that every act of the eye is a minute aggression against the solidity of the real, against the inductility, the illiteracy, of the body, against death. The great hope of opening one's eyes and pores to their uttermost is that the world, once translated entire into the brain, will conform to one's personal requirements; but instead the world imposes on the open psyche an image of its own fragmentation, tumult; it is the whale swallowed by Jonah. It is much safer to live in the intransigencies of the physical, to admit the otherness of the

Other; and even Septimus is willing to attempt at last to rid his eye of hallucination, to return to a kind of sanity. It is an unusual perceptual experiment for Septimus: he opens his eyes just slightly, for sanity is clearly a middle condition, neither fully open nor fully closed:

> He began, very cautiously, to open his eyes, to see whether
> a gramophone was really there. But real things—real things were
> too exciting. He must be cautious. He would not go mad. First
> he looked at the fashion papers on the lower shelf, then, gradually
> at the gramophone with the green trumpet. Nothing could be
> more exact. And so, gathering courage, he looked at the side-
> board; the plate of bananas; the engraving of Queen Victoria and
> the Prince Consort; at the mantlepiece, with the jar of roses. None
> of these thing moved. All were still; all were real. (*Mrs. Dalloway*,
> p. 215)

The sane world has an amazing inertia; instead of the fluctuance and the lability of hallucination, everything stays still—his wife's face is surprisingly undeformed, just normal; he can achieve real communication, make a little joke; it is, like all things real, very exciting. This passage has in it the seed of all of Virginia Woolf's later retreat from the figured ebullition of the novels of the 1920s; to present the expansive, molten consciousness is a perhaps considerable achievement, she seems to feel, but the vision of reality which it entails is finally wrong. The excitement, the intensity, of Septimus' solipsism is at last somewhat factitious; the brilliance of the external, of plain English is more compelling. Septimus insane is, in effect, unsatisfying; Virginia Woolf wondered even when she was writing *Mrs. Dalloway* if the novel would not be better without him. Since Septimus represents the autonomy of the eye, the brain evolved to the end point of the human, Virginia Woolf's repudiation of him suggests the possibility for a new accommodation with the finitude of the physical world. The body is not always merely apish; it is in *Mrs. Dalloway* the seat of human sympathy, human community. Poised against Septimus' cerebral rapture is Clarissa Dalloway's party:

> "What does the brain matter," said Lady Rosseter, getting up,
> "compared with the heart?"
> "I will come," said Peter, but he sat on for a moment. What is
> this terror? what is this ecstasy? he thought to himself. What is it
> that fills me with extraordinary excitement?
> It is Clarissa, he said.
> For there she was. (P. 296)

The brain is only one organ, just as Septimus exists in a sense for Clarissa's sake, to define one of her problems, and if the brain hypertrophies it leads to a falsification of the self and the world. Clarissa's body, in its physiological totality, is a remarkably full, empathic structure; when she hears of Septimus' death, she feels the rusty spikes pierce her body. Septimus' mode of death is a parody of the openness of his nervous system during his life; but it seems that his life and death signify as much for Clarissa as for himself, her body's intuition, her body's telepathy. The life of the eye and the brain, with its sham fascination, its illusory triumph over the perceived world, seems increasingly insipid next to real human interaction; and two subsequent novels, *To the Lighthouse* and *The Waves*, will be needed in the attempt to mediate between the eye's blandishments and the substantial demands of friends and lovers. The weariness of Septimus' model of himself as a brain stretched out on a rock, with fibers connecting it to all creation, can be observed in an analogous passage from a story which remained unpublished in Virginia Woolf's lifetime, "Together and Apart," in which a vapid middle-aged woman encounters a man who succeeds for an instant in twitching the extinct nerve of her real passion:

> Fibres of her were floated capriciously this way and that, like the tentacles of a sea anemone, now thrilled, now snubbed, and her brain, miles away, cool and distant, up in the air, received messages which it would sum up in time. (*Haunted House*, pp. 139–40)

The nerve fibers do not link the brain to the world so much as hold it at a distance; and in this manner the overextended brain becomes mushy, languid, incompetent. After the oversophistications and dangerous assertions of the brain, it is beguiling to clasp one's body to oneself and rejoice in its delightful simplicities; in a little sketch called "Evening over Sussex: Reflections in a Motor-car," which is almost an alternate version of the last pages of *Orlando*, Virginia Woolf summons her scattered selves, her eager ocular self, her philosophical self, the self that bides aloof from experience, and they meditate on the landscape, affirm in high-toned style the model of it they have made:

> And then the body who had been silent up to now began its song, almost at first as low as the rush of the wheels; 'Eggs and bacon; toast and tea; fire and a bath—fire and a bath—jugged hare,' it went on, 'and red-currant jelly; a glass of wine—with coffee to follow, with coffee to follow— and then to bed; and then to bed.'
> 'Off with you, 'I said to my assembled selves. 'Your work is done. I dismiss you. Good-night.'
> And the rest of the journey was performed in the delicious society of my own body. (*Essays II*, p. 292)

The body here intrudes upon the flights of the mind, just as it does for stargazing Katharine in *Night and Day*; but here the body is not an idiot but a valued if monotonous friend. This redemption of the body is a major development in the novels of the 1920s; *Orlando* suggests uniquely that even sexual desire may be lucid, approachable, even if it is so only in devious romance, the body's elysium. And Bernard is not distressed at the ape that is inside; indeed he cherishes that ape, woos it in a voice he believes less eloquent than the ape's own. The body darkens in the 1930s, but it is never simply corpulent and embarrassing as it was at times in the earliest novels; it has force, even if that force is malevolent.

The insanity found in *The Waves* suggests certain modifications of Virginia Woolf's premises about mental dysfunction. Septimus is almost heroic; his insanity is a violent attempt to wrench an intolerable world into tolerable configurations; his insanity is the result of certain well-defined events in the war, and it is maintained chiefly by the practice of his physicians; he has known human love, and has glimpses of the world undistorted by madness. Septimus, because his insanity was a radical attempt at adjustment, could have been cured; but Rhoda sane is inconceivable; Rhoda *is* her insanity. According to the peculiar physiological determinates so pervasive in *The Waves*, Rhoda was born without a body, without a face, her spine and its wax covering as loose and yielding as jelly:

> "Month by month things are losing their hardness; even my body now lets the light through; my spine is soft like wax near the flame of the candle. I dream; I dream." (P. 205)

In *Mrs. Dalloway* Septimus tries to force the world to conform to his own shape; in *The Waves* Rhoda asks very little of the world or circumstance, certainly not that it change its shape. She wishes only for a handle to grasp as she falls through her bed into the abyss, as she sinks into the quicksand of a sidewalk; her world is all too plastic, drifts aimlessly into random blotches, just as her head is too weak to support eye sockets or the prominence of a nose. In *Mrs. Dalloway* there exists a calm, stable, well-modulated world, a London of parades, traffic jams, and the absolute chronology of Big Ben, a world upon which everyone but Septimus tacitly agrees, and in which Septimus himself can occasionally join in the universal applause; but one is much more hesitant to assert this about *The Waves*, in which Rhoda's version of reality has neither more nor less authority than anyone else's. Who can say then that Rhoda is insane, that her world in which objects pullulate or contract into queasy insubstantiality, a

137

world for which Claes Oldenburg has given us pneumatic representation, is not valid? Jinny and the incomparable Bernard agree that life is volatile, inexhaustible, a swirl of evanescences, and Jinny turns herself into flame in order to become as subtle and rapid as the burning world; and if Neville and Louis turn resolutely toward order, the center of the earth, it is principally because they too are presented with the spectacle of massive chaos. It is arguable that Rhoda, unlike Septimus, is lunatic from the sheer accuracy of her eye, a realist strict and uncompromising. But that is not quite the case; she can see the leviathan's world and loathe it, and like a sane person, she can rebel against it, assert a personal vision. What makes her insane is that, lacking fixed form herself, she must ask the world to define her; and her friends cannot agree on a shape for her, while the leviathan is only too happy to sculpt her in his own unbeautiful image.

It is from beginning to end Rhoda's plasticity that is her undoing: Septimus by contrast is overdefined, too sharp and angular to fit into society. Rhoda's softness is, on one level, a way of saying that she is clumsy, ugly, and that ugly women are persecuted by society as relentlessly as any paranoid by his delusions; and it is physical emblem for a state of inborn lack of identity, which is, in the writings of Virginia Woolf and many subsequent authors, the twentieth-century equivalent of original sin. Being no one, Rhoda lives in a no-world, an environment as malleable and abnegated as Rhoda herself. One becomes timorous in the null world, where one can drown in the treacherous waters of a department store, where the least mudpuddle is as incalculable and urgent as the ocean itself; and one hides behind one's friends, stays in one's room, withers one's lifetime away. Of course the formless ego develops an insatiable longing for form, the clod's nostalgia for the pebble; but all form will be extrinsic, artificial, closely resembling Septimus' false selves:

> The leaves might have hidden me still. But I did not hide behind them. I walked straight up to you instead of circling round to avoid the shock of sensation as I used. But it is only that I have taught my body to do a certain trick. Inwardly I am not taught; I fear, I hate, I love, I envy and despise you, but I never join you happily. (P. 330)

The body-mask is the best kind of self that Rhoda can hope to attain: the semblance of social pose, respectability. Behind the mask of gesture, behind the set of random grimaces whose imprints she has stolen from her friend's faces, will always be that emptiness without provenance or expression, which even despair would falsify. She is pitiable, but no one would hazard to pity her; her face would ape even that tentative sympathy. She hates mirrors precisely because the mirror is her father, mother, lover; and when she deliberately bangs her hand against a door it is an attempt to discover through the sensation of pain an independent, decisive existence, instead of the smooth silver of her specular soul.

> "That is my face," said Rhoda, "in the looking-glass behind
> Susan's shoulder—that face is my face. But I will duck behind
> her to hide it, for I am not here. I have no face. Other people have
> faces; Susan and Jinny have faces; they are here. Their world is
> the real world. The things they lift are heavy. They say Yes, they
> say No; whereas I shift and change and am seen through in a
> second." (Pp. 203–4)

She hates her face, which she says is hideous; she hates her body, which she calls a slab of raw meat. Yet her most typical asseveration is, I have no face; I have no body. It is easy to see, then, what is really unbearable to her: she hates nonexistence.

What Rhoda really needs is, first of all, an intrinsic body, a body that can sustain an impression permanently, instead of the basketful of stray masks which she carries about with her, hoping she will be able to dig out, when necessity arises, one that will give a satisfactory account; and then she needs a strongly organized, solid, palpable world to uphold her new substantiality. And therefore Rhoda dreams throughout the novel of a "world immune from change" (p. 249), a world from which tiger and leviathan are banished:

> I am thrust back to stand burning in this clumsy, this ill-fitting
> body, to receive the shafts of his indifference, and his scorn,
> I who long for marble columns and pools on the other side of the
> world where the swallow dips her wings. (P. 248)

The world of marble columns and pools is not far from Katharine Hilbery's girlish dream in *Night and Day* of a world grown simple with old romance, a medieval walled garden, something antique and impossible; and yet Rhoda's best hope is that England and steel will turn out to be depraved fantasy, and that the inner truth of things will be as stately and precise as stark columns and the intersection of swallows. Like Katharine Hilbery and most other sentient characters in Virginia Woolf, Rhoda has two bodies: "I am the foam that sweeps and fills the uttermost runs of the rocks with whiteness; I am also a girl, here in this room" (p. 249). It is perhaps significant that Rhoda, instead of having an ordinary body and an exalted body, has only the low body of a girl, and an even lower body, all ephemeral flux; to be able to cling to a solid girl's-body would be a remarkable achievement for Rhoda, who can profit from whatever definition she can find.

However, she also knows what a body would look like if it could participate in the world that has gelled into tranquil form:

> "She looks far away over our heads, beyond India."
> "Yes, between your shoulders, over your heads, to a landscape,"
> said Rhoda, "to a hollow where the many-backed steep hills come
> down like birds' wings folded. There, on the short, firm turf,
> are bushes, dark leaved, and against their darkness I see a shape,
> white, but not of stone, moving, perhaps alive. But it is not you,
> it is not you, it is not you; not Percival, Susan, Jinny, Neville
> or Louis. When the white arm rests upon the knee it is a triangle;
> now it is upright—a column; now a fountain, falling. It makes
> no sign, it does not beckon, it does not see us. Behind it roars the
> sea. It is beyond our reach." (P. 271)

This white shape is the body, translated into heaven: it is marble but living; the angles of its limbs and torso are clear and pleasing, simple for the eye; the body is in fact identical to the columnar edifice, the apotheosis of Vitruvian architecture. This is how our friends and our buildings should look to us if we could see with the proper eye; all is lucent, orderly, alive. It is Rhoda's gift to be able to see through the grisly murderous world of mutability to this formal strength that underlies it somewhere on the other side of the world.

It seems for a moment as if this vision of Aurelian calm is almost valid. Bernard, when he gathers Rhoda into the sixfold single character of the last monologue, says, "I see far away, quivering like a gold thread, the pillar Rhoda saw"(p. 377); as if the pillar were ratified, like the willow of Bernard and Neville, by its appearance to another character; and we notice, tantalizingly, the similarity of Rhoda's vision of simple cylinders, triangles, and circles set in a delicate land to the inherent forms of the mind, geometrical and luminous, that the children perceive in the opening sentences of the novel. But, although orientation in *The Waves* is difficult, we may be sure that Rhoda's vision is more fantastic than real. Septimus felt himself damned because he could not feel; and Rhoda, though she experiments with feeling, takes Louis for a lover, is even more lacking in sympathy than Septimus; Rhoda's island of columns and swallows is an evasion of human contact, and finally both the world of tigerish night and the geometrical fantasy seem to be versions of her emptiness turned inside out. Septimus can locate his beloved Evans in his insanity, but Rhoda's fantasy is wholly depopulated except for that white shape that is indifferently body or column or fountain. There is one point in the novel where Rhoda comes near to real human intercourse, when she is granted the insight for one instant, hesitatingly, that the six friends comprise one being:

"I shall fall alone through this thin sheet into gulfs of fire. And
you will not help me. More cruel than the old torturers you will
let me fall, and will tear me to pieces when I am fallen. Yet
there are moments when the walls of the mind grow thin; when
nothing is unabsorbed and I could fancy that we might blow
so vast a bubble that the sun might set and rise in it and we might
take the blue of midday and the black of midnight and be cast
off and escape from here and now." (P. 331)

For a moment she wishes to sail out of the world with her friends, safe
in the balloon of their six minds; but for the rest she wishes to escape
as much from her five friends as with them. When Rhoda speaks of the
world of foam and night and tigers she means, as much as anything,
the world of human emotion, which is soft, pervasive, detestable; the
geometrical fantasy, somewhat like Katharine Hilbery's study of
mathematics, is an attempt to cut down to inhuman rock. There is real
wisdom to be possessed through geometry; if formal structure can be
discovered in experience it can represent salvation, a net of parallel
bars which save one from the abyss of blind matter, but there is
something disturbing as well.

"Then the beetle-shaped men come with their violins; wait;
count; nod; down come their bows. And there is ripple and laughter like the dance of olive trees and their myriad-tongued grey
leaves when a seafarer, biting a twig between his lips where the
many-backed steep hills come down, leaps on shore.
" 'Like' and 'like' and 'like'—but what is the thing that lies
beneath the semblance of the thing? Now that lightning has gashed
the tree and the flowering branch has fallen and Percival, by his
death, has made me this gift, let me see the thing. There is a
square; there is an oblong. The players take the square and place
it upon the oblong. They place it very accurately; they make a
perfect dwelling-place. Very little is left outside. The structure is
now visible; what is inchoate is here stated; we are not so various
or so mean; we have made oblongs and stood them upon squares.
This is our triumph; this is our consolation." (P. 288)

Her first description of the quartet is the human joy of the seafarer
returned to shore; but that is more simile, and the thing itself is the
form, the building constructed by the music, an old conceit vivid to
modern students of literature from Browning's "Abt Vogler," employed at length also in *The Voyage Out* in reference to Beethoven's
opus 111 sonata. The consolations of the aesthetic are of course exceedingly important, and it is to Rhoda's credit that she can employ
them; but the doctrine that emotion, the world of human interaction,
exists for the sake of simile, a hazy frame to the more mordant and

durable truths of form, is not one which Virginia Woolf ever espouses wholly; it is not accidental that aesthetic consolation in *The Waves* is entwined neatly with insanity.

Aestheticism

Much has been made of Virginia Woolf's aestheticism, yet in no work of hers is an aesthetic solution to human problems anything more than tentative and dubious. It is true, however, that the doctrines of Oscar Wilde and other writers of the 1880s and 1890s exerted great and lasting influence over her, and indeed over the whole Bloomsbury movement. Wilde's heyday antedates by scarcely more than ten years the founding of the Stephen household near the British Museum; and I am not sure that the public posture of the circle of writers who gathered there would not have been applauded by Wilde himself. Their ways of courting publicity while seeming to reject it were subtler than Wilde's, and their outrages more impalpable to public scrutiny, and therefore more titillating; the road down which the Bloomsbury writers stroll is nevertheless that same delightful road that Pater designed, that Wilde strewed with saffron and pollen. If there is one crucial and inseminating Victorian writer who prepares the way for the era of Yeats, Joyce, Virginia Woolf, Forster, even Lawrence, it is Oscar Wilde; yet not only his importance but even the basic nature of his thought has only recently begun to be understood. Wilde is not a writer who holds a fiery vision of reality and absorbs a recalcitrant world of politics and habitude indifferently into the compass of his imagination. Shelley, or any writer who sees all phenomena of human life as the multiple phantoms of some primary visionary power, is his exact opposite; indeed the century from Blake to Wilde is a completed curve. For Wilde, reality is dingy, lax, and interesting; he can greet the locomotive, the factory, Queen Victoria, with the mildest complaint, or with what is even less than a complaint, an epigram. Shelley excludes nothing from the great circle of his vitality; Wilde excludes everything, accepts everything. The more Wilde speaks of delectable phantasmagoria, the more affectedly he croons about mythical beasts and green flowers, the stronger is his tacit approval, secret consent with the real; by utterly divorcing art from the natural he shows the highest possible respect for the power of nature, shapeless, excrementitious, overwhelming. Wilde is scientific in his method, skeptical, scrupulous; his contemporaries were outraged chiefly because his distinctions were so much nicer than those of the historians and critics of his time. Wilde rejects life, nature, and nine-tenths of art, but he has been intimate with them all.

What is it then that Wilde includes, finds worthy of his attention and talent? It is, of course, the human; but almost everything must be pared away from our ordinary sense of human nature. The body is not human; the body is only a natural lump, for, as Wilde says in "The Decay of Lying," nature is pernicious in that we feel our individuality taken away from us in forest glen or open air; the body is inert, raw clay to be molded into the least disgusting mask. In addition, our character traits are as haphazard and extrinsic as our bodies; Hamlet could easily have been Falstaff, Falstaff Hamlet. What is uniquely our own, what constitutes individuality? A nerve; a sensitive nerve that shudders with revulsion at the ugly, shudders with joy at the beautiful; a discriminatory nerve; for the rest we simply do mechanically what we are told to do, lead a prosperous life or commit suicide depending on what we have read in magazine serials or *The Sorrows of Young Werther.* As far as I know, the myth of the origin of human personality sketched in "The Critic as Artist" and "The Decay of Lying" is, except for *Marius the Epicurean*, the first example in English literature of what becomes in the twentieth century a standard form for the human. Even Bernard in *The Waves* depends ultimately on Pater and Wilde for his sense of the creation of his friends, and when Virginia Woolf states the premises for her novels of the 1920s in her 1919 essay "Modern Fiction," speaking of life as a luminous halo, the mind drenched with myriad impressions, "an incessant shower of innumerable atoms," she is echoing the ideas and even the language of the "Conclusion" to Pater's *The Renaissance* without major alteration.

Virginia Woolf, like D. H. Lawrence, wrote her first novel considerably under Wilde's enchantment. Mrs. Dalloway, the threadbare Mrs. Dalloway of *The Voyage Out*, looks at the receding shore as the *Euphrosyne* sails out toward South America, and exclaims, "It's so like Whistler!" suggesting, for the first time in Virginia Woolf's fiction, the ceaseless effort of nature to accommodate itself to the painterly eye; but the true Wildean quality of the novel is not in smart talk but in the character of the intellectual, St. John Hirst. Here he is, shortly after Rachel's party arrives in South America:

> Hirst, who had been eating and drinking without interruption, now lit a cigarette, and observed, "Oh, but we're all agreed by this time that nature's a mistake. She's either very ugly, appallingly uncomfortable, or absolutely terrifying. I don't know which alarms me most—a cow or a tree. I once met a cow in a field by night. The creature looked at me. I assure you it turned my hair grey. It's a disgrace that the animals should be allowed to go at large." (P. 121)

He has all the opinions of Wilde, and the cadence of his voice has the friable softness associated with decadence in the popular imagination;

143

but, even though the human race is evolving in his cerebral direction, he is an unlovely character, a deformed neurasthenic, timorous, an intellectual bully, hostile to the human affection of Terence and Rachel. Hirst seems in fact a textbook case of early twentieth-century opinion and prejudice about decadence, and there is some evidence that Strachey's circle at Cambridge embodied every excess here described; as soon as he delivers his little speech about cows, the scholar Hughling Elliot immediately hears its ultimate source, asks him, "Wasn't it Wilde who discovered the fact that nature makes no allowances for hip-bones?" (p. 122). He is a parody homosexual, like his mentor; at one point he claims that what he abhors most of all is the female breast; and he attributes massive insensitivity, lack of tactile feeling, to heterosexuals generally. More significantly, Terence opines, with full authority, that Hirst has lived in a mirror, in the manner of Tennyson's Lady of Shalott, or perhaps Dorian Gray:

> "You see, Miss Vinrace, you must make allowances for Hirst. He's lived all his life in front of a looking-glass, in a beautiful panelled room, hung with Japanese prints and lovely old chairs and tables, just one splash of color, you know, in the right place,—between the windows I think it is,—and there he sits hour after hour with his toes on the fender, talking about philosophy and God and his liver and his heart and the hearts of his friends." (P.156)

This is the aesthetic life; one insulates oneself with cunning beauty, perhaps with some velvet to muffle sound, becomes wrapped in exquisite involution, aesthetic safety. But Virginia Woolf has presented this refuge through a sufficiently unattractive character that the reader does not find the aesthetic life seductive; Hirst is not only ugly, but desperately unhappy, nearly lunatic from self-consciousness. He is a damned academic, a *professor maudit* in the distinguished lineage of Casaubon, forever eunuch and alien, and indeed the novel ends with his brain tortured by the apparitions of the living and the dead, equally black, indistinguishable.

Yet the habits of aesthetic thought are not solely Hirst's, and *The Voyage Out* presents a few signs of a more formidable, credible aestheticism. The theme of the two bodies, the physical and the aesthetic, what Kenneth Clark might call the vegetable and the crystalline, appears in this novel in embryonic form. Rachel Vinrace, the romantic heroine, is a young woman given to flights of fancy very similar to those of Katharine Hilbery in *Night and Day*; in one of the first of these her mind flies out of her body and becomes as round and airy as Katharine's globular self:

> Inextricably mixed in dreamy confusion, her mind seemed to enter into communion, to be delightfully expanded and combined, with

the spirit of the whitish boards on deck, with the spirit of the sea,
with the spirit of Beethoven Op. III, even with the spirit of poor
William Cowper there at Olney. Like a ball of thistledown it kissed
the sea, rose, kissed it again, and thus rising and kissing passed
finally out of sight. (P. 37)

This reduction of the self to a balloon, a bare ball, a bubble, is part of
the common metaphoric apparatus of the novel; a few pages later
Rachel stirs her tea; "the bubbles which swam and clustered in the cup
seemed to her like the union of their minds" (p. 56). And later her
lover Terence Hewet develops independently the theory of the bubbles, in a conversation with Hirst which the intellectual approves:

"The truth of it is that one never is alone, and one never is in
company," he concluded.
"Meaning?" said Hirst.
"Meaning? Oh, something about bubbles—auras—what d'you
call 'em? You can't see my bubble; I can't see yours; all we see of
each other is a speck, like the wick in the middle of that flame. The
flame goes about with us everywhere; it's not ourselves exactly,
but what we feel . . ." (Pp. 108–9)

Here is the original form of many of the later speculations of Virginia
Woolf's novels, the interconnecting caves to which she compares in
her diary the characters of *Mrs. Dalloway*, the six-sided flower of *The
Waves*, the private world-balls of *The Years* which can collide but not
intersect. The aesthetic body, if it can be seen through the physical
body, tends to appear either too hard and shiny, lacking individuation, a subject itself for pictorial composition, or too fuzzy with the
ethereal mass of the internal universe; it is difficult for two people to
relate in their aesthetic bodies, just as all aesthetic philosophy makes
human relation difficult.

"A nice streaky bubble yours must be!" said Hirst.
"And supposing my bubble could run into some one else's
bubble—"
"And they both burst?" put in Hirst.
"Then—then—then—" pondered Hewet, as if to himself, "it
would be an e—nor—mous world," he said, stretching his arms to
their full width, as though even so they could hardly clasp the
billowy universe, for when he was with Hirst he always felt
unusually sanguine and vague. (*Voyage Out*, p. 109)

This is a somewhat jocular version of the intense perils involved in real
fusion of two aesthetic selves, the commingling of souls, romantic
heterosexual love, a condition that Virginia Woolf never again found
credible after *A Voyage Out* and *Night and Day*.
Rachel herself is an unrealized character, the first of many in

145

Virginia Woolf's novels. Clive Bell in 1909, before even the first draft of the novel had been finished, found Rachel "mysterious and remote" (*Biography I*, p. 210), her head full of "better things" than the common run of humanity; and one feels in the final form of the novel too that Rachel is undefined, ideal, lighter than air, thistledown or a patch of light:

> "Does it ever seem to you, Terence, that the world is composed entirely of vast blocks of matter, and that we're nothing but patches of light—" she looked at the soft spots of sun wavering over the carpet and up the wall—"like that?"
> "No," said Terence, "I feel solid; immensely solid; the legs of my chair might be rooted in the bowels of the earth." (Pp. 292–93)

There is little that can be said about her character except that it is vague, elusive, distracted, melodic; when she is at last granted a physical body in addition to an aesthetic one, it is the monstrous corpse that she finds so alarming in her fatal insanity. Katharine Hilbery, on the other hand, oscillates more rapidly between her two bodies; and *Night and Day* ends in health, perhaps more so than any other of Virginia Woolf's novels, with the possibility for real reconciliation between the aesthetic and the physical, one's image of one's beloved become identical with the factual actual, the long-promised merging of two halos, sexual intercourse. By *Jacob's Room* a considerable darkening has occurred; all the characters have turned shadow, even, as we have seen, Jacob; in this novel everyone is left unrealized, quizzically aesthetic, and romantic love has degenerated into heterosexual spasm. The narrator is content to record gesture without being able to make the gesture into the reflex of a personality; Jacob idly arranges date-stones while an acquaintance digs his penknife into the table to mark a point in an argument that is beyond the range of the narrator's hearing (p. 44); Jacob pronounces the word *urbane* (p. 164) so strikingly that Bonamy falls into the rapture of love; but the center of Jacob, where he thinks and feels, is forever unrecorded, unknown. In *Mrs. Dalloway* the narrator's ear can pick up the slightest twitter of her characters' brains, her eye registers the most minute distortion of wish and fear; she sifts through the body nerve by glistening nerve, in the unyielding hope that the sum of all these concretions will constitute the real self, the aesthetic body. But for aesthetic vision all this is prelude to the depiction of the most aesthetic of known characters, an eye unprecedented in ferocity, Lily Briscoe in *To the Lighthouse*.

What constitutes that most evasive and ineluctable of all things, human identity? Who am I? The method of Bernard in *The Waves* is to trace himself and his friends back to the origin, extreme infancy;

and his conclusion is that we are wax figures etched by sensation into complex patterns. The method of Lily Briscoe is to strip away all that is accident, mere mortality, in the manner of Plotinus' dematerializing of object into idea; her hope is that a woman flayed alive in this fashion will be much for the better, not for the worse. Bernard claims that identity is predicated upon early vulnerability to stimulus, patches of openness; therefore a study of personal predilections and revulsions will develop an accurate model of personality; a sentence, a brief description, can sum up the essence, and Bernard produces such sentences with the spattering fecundity of a wet dog shaking himself dry. With Lily the terms are changed. Day-to-day observation of habits provides, if anything, only the obscurest key; most of Mrs. Ramsay's life is devoted to activities which have nothing to do with her innermost self; but the most patient observer—and Lily is nothing if not patient—can eventually discover a momentary scene in which identity is suddenly, dizzyingly, manifest. Mrs. Ramsay knows nothing of it, reads to her little boy unawares; yet on the other side of the window her husband, Lily Briscoe, even the most casual passerby, can see Mrs. Ramsay, the woman-in-herself, perfected, diuturnal. For Lily, the chief variable of characterization is not, as for Bernard, one's affinities and repulsions, but the strength of the ideal buried self. Most of the human race seem as unreal as dew; some are rescued from effacement through a single mnemonic, like the parents of Minta, the Owl and the Poker; a few have the internal fixed form which sustains identity beyond the grave, the charisma of Jacob Flanders, the achieved tranquillity of Clarissa Dalloway and Mrs. Ramsay. In the case of Mrs. Ramsay we know the absolute configuration of the authentic body: it is not a globe, like Katharine Hilbery's, nor is it simply indescribable blackness, like Jacob's; it is a triangular wedge, the Madonna's face and body abstracted out of the insinuations of time and exterior space, "reduced to a shadow without irreverence" (*To the Lighthouse*, pp. 81–82). So she appears on Lily's canvas; and so she feels herself to be during a remarkable meditation in solitude; as she knits she shrinks out of the turmoil of common activity into a "wedge-shaped core of darkness, something invisible to others":

> Her horizon seemed to her limitless. There were all the places she had not seen; the Indian plains; she felt herself pushing aside the thick leather curtain of a church in Rome. This core of darkness could go anywhere, for no one saw it. They could not stop it, she thought, exulting. There was freedom, there was peace, there was, most welcome of all, a summoning together, a resting on a platform of stability. Not as oneself did one find rest ever, in her experience (she accomplished here something dexterous with her needles) but as a wedge of darkness. Losing personality, one lost

> the fret, the hurry, the stir; and there rose to her lips always some
> exclamation of triumph over life when things came together in this
> peace, this rest, this eternity; and pausing there she looked out to
> meet that stroke of the Lighthouse, the long steady stroke, the last
> of the three, which was her stroke, for watching them in this mood
> always at this hour one could not help attaching oneself to one
> thing especially of the things one saw; and this thing, the long
> steady stroke, was her stroke. Often she found herself sitting and
> looking, sitting and looking, with her work in her hands until
> she became the thing she looked at—that light, for example. And it
> would lift up on it some little phrase or other which had been lying
> in her mind like that—"Children don't forget, children don't
> forget"—which she would repeat and begin adding to it, It will
> end, it will end, she said. It will come, it will come, when suddenly
> she added, We are in the hands of the Lord. (Pp. 96–97)

She has discovered through the self-abandonment of trance the
ultimate Mrs. Ramsay, uncontingent, immediate, devoid of all trait
and substance, a free-floating eye; underneath everything she is not
ordinarily beautiful nor charming nor sympathetic nor indulgent; she
is orthodox form in a formal world of lighthouse and plain. And yet,
for all this antarctic purity, something of her beauty, her human
sympathy even, is translated, inherent, in the wedge: "She praised
herself in praising the light . . . she was beautiful like that light." More
strikingly, it is as a real Madonna-image, clasping her son James on
her lap, that Lily depicts her, for in this novel Virginia Woolf makes
her one serious attempt to claim for the aesthetic body and the
aesthetic world the virtues of both humanity and the inanimate; there
is unbroken romantic continuity between Keats's Grecian Urn and
Lily's painting. If critics have confused the lighthouse of this novel,
surely one of the least sexy lighthouses in all literature, with a phallic
symbol, it must be because of the remarkable interdependence of the
human and the inanimate, the organic and the structural; and Mrs.
Ramsay's ecstatic merging of herself and the lighthouse, her metamorphosis into what she beholds, testifies to an aesthetic emotion which is
as strong and complex as the full range of quotidian emotions:

> She looked at the steady light, the pitiless, the remorseless, which
> was so much her, yet so little her . . . as if it were stroking with its
> silver fingers some sealed vessel in her brain whose bursting would
> flood her with delight, she had known happiness, exquisite happi-
> ness, intense happiness, and it silvered the rough waves a little
> more brightly, as daylight faded, and the blue went out of the sea
> and it rolled in waves of pure lemon. (P. 99)

The closed form of the wedge can become open, a direct electrical
circuit between thing and self; it is not sexual intercourse but the

aesthetic equivalent of intercourse, retinal sex, the desperate love of the human for formal inanimation. The lighthouse is dead, but in its vertical stability, its upward sweep, it offers the promise of an ordered external world, a vantage point which will resolve even the chaos of the waves into structure; as Lily notes, the waves that drown the swimmer appear linear and symmetrical from above. With its irradiating eye, the lighthouse seems to vivify and focus the island, Mrs. Ramsay herself; it is the metonymy, the guardian, of the aesthetic world, the world in which aesthetic emotion is valid, just. Mrs. Ramsay is alive, but in her extreme passivity and resignation, her infolding of herself into a solid block, too irreducible ever to be broken, she has imbued herself with the stability of the dead. The mutual rapture of the lighthouse and Mrs. Ramsay suggests that the interface between the quick and the dead, feminine emotion and masculine structure, constitutes salvation from time and the leviathans.

Yet it is not certain that aesthetic salvation is not an illusion of distance, a deceit of the eye. For one thing, the lighthouse itself will not bear close inspecton; as James approaches it, he sees that the lighthouse is no bright sentinel, no axis around which Cartesian order can radiate and converge, but a human habitation, its paint peeling, its massive rocky core used principally as a vehicle for drying clothes. For another thing, everything in *To the Lighthouse*, even Lily's theory of personality, is based on the model of frame and center; and while the frames are extensive, ornate, minutely precise, the centers are mostly blank or arbitrary. The dark wedge that is Mrs. Ramsay's truest core is exactly analogous to that gaping white space in the center of Lily's painting in the final part of the novel; they are both framed by Mrs. Ramsay's house, that is, her domestic self, the personal self that maintains the household, flatters her husband, gives dinners, worries about the greenhouse. The core is so encrusted with frame that it is nearly invisible, and we must ask ourselves how successfully Mrs. Ramsay's identity inheres in the wedge, persists after her death. Lily's eye, at the end, is so engrossed in the triangular shadow that her memory has spun that it can see Mrs. Ramsay, as if alive, immediate, immanent in the window of her house; and this, along with the central line which completes her painting, constitutes a considerable achievement. But the scale of this achievement is extremely limited; it is no accident that Virginia Woolf has made Lily a bad artist, whose painting will be stuffed away and forgotten, whose filled-in center will never express anything of Mrs. Ramsay to another observer. The form of the triangular wedge is too simple to bear the inconceivable intricacies of the human personality. Too much of Mrs. Ramsay must be sacrificed, abandoned to the leviathans; what is left on the canvas is a private hieroglyph, accessible to no one but Lily herself. It is not just Lily that is incompetent, it is the aesthetic mode itself; no painter can hope to make an honest transcription:

> I look at a fresco by Perugino. I conceive that he saw things grouped, contained in certain and invariable forms; expressed in faces, actions—[?which] did not exist; all beauty was contained in the momentary appearance of human beings. He saw it sealed as it were; all its worth in it; not a hint of fear or future. His fresco seems to me infinitely silent; as though beauty had swum up to the top and stayed there, above everything else, speech, paths leading on, relation of brain to brain, don't exist. (*Biography I*, p. 138)

This is an early sample of Virginia Woolf's art criticism, written in 1908. She goes on to say that she desires to make a beauty not of inhuman form but of "infinite discords, showing all the traces of the mind's passage through the world"; by the 1920s, however, she had learned that novels were not necessarily more verisimilar than the visual arts to the development of the soul. Not only do we yearn to record and perpetuate the labyrinth of discords that comprises the human, we unconsciously yearn, like Mrs. Ramsay knitting, to be aesthetic entities ourselves, capable of easy record and perpetuation. But such orderliness, if achieved, is at the expense of everything. The aesthetic mode not only falsifies its subjects but destroys its adherents, for Lily not only fails to resuscitate Mrs. Ramsay fully, either by her painting or by screaming on the beach, but she sacrifices her own life to achieve even failure. St. John Hirst grows skeleton-hard and skeleton-thin by feeding himself on the bones of argumentation; Lily shrivels into funereal Chinese futility; Miss La Trobe turns drunkard, virago, lesbian—all for the sake of aesthetic consolation, cold consolation, the embrace of Polyclitus.

Nothing is less comprehensible to Virginia Woolf than art for art's sake; literature and painting always exist for the sake of emotion. In her essay "On Re-Reading Novels," she examines Percy Lubbock's book *The Craft of Fiction*, and his axiom that the form of the book is the book itself. She is much vexed by such formalism: "The 'book itself' is not form which you see, but emotion which you feel" (*Essays II*, p. 126). And yet she recognizes that form is omnipresent, necessary; she reconciles the formality of all art with its emotional content in this way: "Is there not something beyond emotion, something which though it is inspired by emotion, tranquillizes it, orders it, composes it?" (*Essays II*, p. 127). Emotion itself struggles toward composition, formal expression, art. Of course she knew that she herself was the priestess of form, that no brow was higher than hers; in the company of formalists she will claim her art has direct human reference, while in the company of those who want simple representation of emotion she will defend formality. Forster's *Aspects of the Novel* pleased her little more than Lubbock's book, and her review of it, written at the same time as *To the Lighthouse*, is instructive. Forster's view is "the humane as opposed to the aesthetic view of fiction," and when Forster criticizes Henry James, claiming that he will perish for neglecting life in favor of pattern, Virginia Woolf responds with the following devastating obliquity:

> But at this point the pertinacious pupil may demand: 'What is this "Life" that keeps on cropping up so mysteriously and so complacently in books about fiction? Why is it absent in a pattern and present in a tea party? Why is the pleasure that we get from the pattern in *The Golden Bowl* less valuable than the emotion which Trollope gives us when he describes a lady drinking tea in a parsonage? Surely the definition of life is too arbitrary, and requires to be expanded.' (*Essays II*, p. 53)

There is vitality, "life," in the abstract pattern as well as in the tea party, and all of *To the Lighthouse* depends from the golden necklace of this premise. Mrs. Ramsay's banquet, the idleness of her random life, all secretly work themselves into pattern, a pattern charged with emotion; and when the narrator presents us with the structure of the banquet, the hidden obstacles and rushes of human intercourse, rather than the actual talk, we are to feel truth and beauty together in a dazzling catenation.

There is surely much that is attractive in this theory, much that is true to our experience in reading the novel; and sometimes Virginia Woolf will claim that a certain painting does in fact succeed in presenting a complex human emotion through form, as in Walter Sickert's picture of a music hall:

> At first it suggests the husky voice of Marie Lloyd singing a song about the ruins that Cromwell knocked about a bit; then the song dies away, and we see a scooped-out space filled curiously with the curves of fiddles, bowler hats, and shirt fronts converging into a pattern with a lemon-coloured splash in the centre. It is extraordinarily satisfying. Yet the description is so formal, so superficial, that we can hardly force our lips to frame it; while the emotion is distinct, powerful, and satisfactory. (*Essays II*, pp. 242–43)

This is Lily's painting as it wants to be, the "splash in the centre" perfectly filled in, expressive, revelatory, beautiful. Yet there are powerful forces working against this miraculous equivalence of the human and the aesthetic. The first is the obvious discrepancy between the two versions, that painted Mrs. Ramsay and the physical woman; the

151

ideal Mrs. Ramsay, the wedge, preserves so little of what we know of her. Mrs. Ramsay at her moments of greatest intensity feels herself to be a wedge, a ruby, but Lily desires a fuller, more accessible version of her, a woman who can still scream for her hat when it is seized by the neuter wind. It is devastating to compare the end of Mrs. Dalloway—"It is Clarissa, he said. There she was."—in which the apparition of Clarrisa seems nearly complete, triumphant, a justification of all the author's hopes for the aesthetic mode, with Lily's cry near the end of *To the Lighthouse*, " 'Mrs. Ramsay! Mrs. Ramsay!' . . . There she sat."—a cry at once heroic, painful, and pathetic, for it is pure assertion of artistic success against all evidence, an example, like the kitchen table in the pear tree, of the creation of the unreal.

But even more telling against the power of art to recreate human emotion, human presence, is the nature of the aesthetic emotion itself. If patterns are as vivid as tea parties, then the enormous plenitude of human emotions should be capable of point-for-point translation into aesthetic emotion. In *To the Lighthouse* more different kinds of aesthetic emotion are adduced than ever before; even sexual intercourse has its aesthetic equivalent, and the aesthetic threatens to break out everywhere, even in the middle of a children's game in which the ball freezes in midair, Mr. and Mrs. Ramsay suddenly stiffen into symbols of marriage; but this instantaneous petrification thaws immediately, the game goes on, the aesthetic and the ordinary cohabit with easy luxury. In addition to this hopeful sign, there is much evidence that one can live one's entire life strictly on the aesthetic level, with only occasional excursions into the real; Lily shares an odd habit with Susan in *The Waves*, a habit also practiced to a much lesser extent by Clarissa Dalloway, of taking any intense experience, wrapping it until it is sealed away, burying it in her mind, only exhuming it after time has rendered it safe, aesthetic. For instance, her weak and muffled sexual instincts are stirred when she hears of Paul's hunt for his fiancée's brooch; she regards him as a foolish young man, but is so dazzled by his beauty, his aura of romance, that she impulsively volunteers to go to the beach, look for the brooch herself. Her unaccustomed impulsiveness has no direct consequences whatever in her psyche; but eleven years later this stifled feeling about Paul Rayley erupts in the following manner:

> Suddenly, as suddenly as a star slides in the sky, a reddish light seemed to burn in her mind, covering Paul Rayley, issuing from him. It rose like a fire sent up in token of some celebration by savages on a distant beach. She heard the roar and the crackle. The whole sea for miles round ran red and gold. Some winey smell mixed with it and intoxicated her, for she felt again her own head-

> long desire to throw herself off the cliff and be drowned looking
> for a pearl brooch on a beach. And the roar and the crackle
> repelled her with fear and disgust, as if while she saw its splendour
> and power she saw too how it fed on the treasure of the house,
> greedily, disgustingly, and she loathed it. (P. 261)

What was difficult, jagged, in real life has been smoothed away into fluent picture, allegory; it is true that something loathesome, a memory of real sexuality, remains even in the *son et lumière*, but, since all human context has vanished, Paul Rayley attenuated to rumor, the insupportable desire and insupportable loathing trouble no more.

Yet for all this tentative hope in the aesthetic life, the congruence of the aesthetic to the human, Virginia Woolf has a secret suspicion which the reader can often hear underneath the main narrative flow: the aesthetic is worthless. If the aesthetic is to be valid it must be predicated directly upon the real, and is therefore as unstable as the physical world itself. The aesthetic is a mode which requires the most careful balance to achieve: if the eye gets too close, the symbol decays into cracked reality; if the eye gets too far away, the aesthetic representation becomes tenuous, phantom, illegible; the same wind that murders Mrs. Ramsay and shakes apart the house can blast the diamond, efface Lily's painting. Indeed Virginia Woolf, as her diary explains, never felt that she had solved the problem of part 3 of *To the Lighthouse* satisfactorily, and the problems are perhaps insoluble, for the aesthetic mode is at the limit of its endurance when the representation is eleven years removed from its subject; the triangular wedge grows more difficult to recapture, more puzzling in its meaning as Mrs. Ramsay recedes from sight. The doctrine that the aesthetic requires the real, importunately, abjectly, is of course of great antiquity, but was presented to Virginia Woolf in her language by G. E. Moore; and given the prestige of that philosopher, his intimate intellectual relation with Leonard Woolf and Lytton Strachey, men whose powers she sometimes believed to exceed her own, it would have been surprising if Moore's aesthetics were not an influence upon her own. Quentin Bell has told us that she read *Principia Ethica* with care and enthusiasm in 1908, when writing *A Voyage Out*, and certain features of Moore's belief seem to affect her writing at all stages of her career. The aesthetic occupies an extremely peculiar place in Moore's philosophy, a place which any creative artist would find equivocal. On one hand, he believes that, of all things known to human experience, there are only two which seem greatly good in themselves: aesthetic enjoyments and personal affection. Of these two, he seems to find the former to have more profound ramifications in his philosophical system; so it seems as if aesthetic enjoyment is nearly the cornerstone of human experience. On the other hand, he states, again and again, with severe emphasis, that the aesthetic emotion by itself is worthless. He demands that the perception of a beautiful object be accompanied, not just with mere abstract appreciation, but with enthusiasm, affection, what he calls aesthetic emotion; but that emotion *in vacuo*, isolated, is nugatory:

> . . . it seems to be the case that if we distinguish the emotional element, in any aesthetic appreciation, from the cognitive element, which accompanies it and is, in fact, commonly thought of as a part of the emotion; and if we consider what value this emotional element would have, *existing by itself*, we can hardly think that it has any great value, even if it has any at all. Whereas, if the same emotion be directed to a different object, if, for instance, it is felt towards an object that is positively ugly, the whole state of consciousness is certainly often positively bad in a high degree. (*Principia Ethica*, p. 190)

Moore is most dubious, almost afraid, about this best of all emotions; aesthetic emotion seems pervertible, suspect, and must be watched carefully; it is sinister to feel the emotion associated with beauty in the absence of a beautiful thing. Aesthetic emotion is an absolute good, insofar as we can intuit anything to be good; but this emotion must be accompanied by cognition, honest and accurate knowledge of the object of contemplation, or the whole structure of virtue itself must collapse. This is the artist's shame, for he can never make his art as secure as its subject, or even as beautiful—Moore says that a real landscape arouses better aesthetic emotion than a painted landscape, and yet Moore's theory suggests, obliquely, a kind of glory that is properly the artist's, an astonishing consolation. Moore loves the human—after all, personal affection is the other thing that is greatly good—but he has a curious affection, nostalgia, for the inhuman, an objective world that exists without man. Long before he discusses aesthetics in *Principia Ethica* he decides to prove the proposition that it is "rational to aim at the production of beauty in external nature, apart from any possible contemplation of it by human beings" (p. 83); he demonstrates this by the following sophism: let us imagine a world exceedingly beautiful, exquisitely proportioned, without discord; let us imagine another world that is a heap of filth; even though no human being could ever live on or ever see either world it is better to prefer the existence of the beautiful to the ugly. Not only is beauty not in the eye of the beholder, it even exists in the total absence of the human race. Moore is, like all post-Cartesian philosophers, a skeptic; and, like almost all post-Cartesian philosophers, he thinks he has found a way out. Moore desires the existence of objective reality, and he needs, above all things, beauty, "that of which the admiring contemplation is good in itself" (p. 201). He knows that he feels something he calls aesthetic emotion, and from that slender illumination he derives the entire panoply of the objective world, the world without man. If our aesthetic emotion were not based on palpable reality, we are all madmen wound in the felicity of the unreal; and that is unthinkable. In order to give our aesthetic emotions weight, validity, there *must* be an external world out there, some of which is beautiful; therefore—Moore is quite certain of this—we value cognition only because the aesthetic everywhere justifies it. In this unusual manner the august earth and everything it contains are contingent upon aesthetic emotion; the artist, the sentient man, keeps in his custody the wand which gives substance to an otherwise lean, spectral world, a world sober and insipid beyond human tolerance.

Moore is, then, a conservative influence on Virginia Woolf's aestheticism, but one who magnifies and exalts the aesthetic even while making sure that no contamination of unreality enters in. It is easy to see from *Principia Ethica* what his opinion of Septimus Smith would have been:

> We can imagine the case of a single person, enjoying throughout eternity the contemplation of scenery as beautiful, and intercourse with persons as admirable, as can be imagined; while yet the whole of the objects of his cognition are absolutely unreal. I think we should definitely pronounce the existence of a universe, which consisted solely of such a person, to be *greatly* inferior in value to one in which the objects, in the existence of which he believes, did really exist just as he believes them to do; and that it would be thus inferior *not only* because it would lack the goods which consist in the existence of the objects in question, but *also* merely because his belief would be false. (P. 197)

This same indictment eventually tells against any character whose interest in the aesthetic supersedes his interest in the real; the aesthetic must never be a refuge from reality, only a safeguard and illumination of it. The hope for aesthetic refuge, never very secure, is increasingly dispelled in the fiction which follows *To the Lighthouse*; indeed the whole direction of the aesthetic theme after 1927 is an increasing alienation of the aesthetic from the human. In *Orlando*, it is true, there is no overt discrepancy between the two; but *Orlando* is a novel utterly loosed from the burdens of the real, a novel which so rigorously excludes human pain and physical chaos that it is in a sense entirely aesthetic. A sketch written in 1929, "Three Pictures," shows the tendency of Virginia Woolf's aesthetic imagination more clearly, especially because the story is in outline a miniature version of *To the Lighthouse*, with the ending skewed and darkened, as if she wished two years after the novel to undo something in it that she no longer felt was right. It begins with a general statement of the pervasiveness, almost the obsessiveness, of the aesthetic eye:

> It is impossible that one should not see pictures; because if my father was a blacksmith and yours was a peer of the realm, we must needs be pictures to each other. We cannot possibly break out of the frame of the picture by speaking natural words. You see me leaning against the door of the smithy with a horseshoe in my hand and you think as you go by: 'How picturesque!' I, seeing you sitting so much at your ease in the car, almost as if you were going to bow to the populace, think what a picture of old luxurious aristocratical England! We are both quite wrong in our judgments no doubt, but that is inevitable. (*Essays IV*, p. 151)

In *To the Lighthouse* there is some tentative belief that the pictorial version of someone will be faithful to the ultimate soul of the subject; here the picture is frankly admitted to be wholly wrong, an idle distortion. The eye does not lay bare the inmost self, it merely makes picture postcards; the aesthetic mode is hostile to the human, although the usual alienation between one man and another, whether the result of class difference or not, makes the aesthetic mode, invalid as it is, the only possible one. In *To the Lighthouse* the most intimate moments, Mrs. Ramsay's solitary ecstasy, the breakdown of isolation and communal rush that occurred in the banquet, all tend toward aesthetic revelation; in "Three Pictures" the aesthetic representation is superficial, casual, the opposite of insight. After this introduction, the narrator sees a sailor and creates a picture called "The Sailor's Homecoming," a sweet cheerful scene in which the young sailor and his fruitful wife reunite after long absence, the sort of ruddy picture that has populated scores of Victorian galleries. The narrator's imagination embroiders the picture more and more, makes a complete imaginary life for the pair, ever sweeter and more unreal. Then there is a cry in the night, "made by some extremity of feeling almost sexless, almost expressionless. It was as if human nature had cried out against some iniquity, some inexpressible horror" (*Essays IV*, p. 152). This is point-blank agony, and its inexpressibility defies the pictorial imagination; but finally a picture is created: "an obscure human form, almost without shape, raising a gigantic arm in vain against some overwhelming iniquity." This picture shows the aesthetic imagination pushed to its utmost in its attempt to reconcile the conflict between the aesthetic and the human. Against this intolerable pain we are nearly helpless; it cannot be contemplated, it cannot be given aesthetic relief or distance. Yet, that figure of the shapeless human form protesting against the boot that crushes it nevertheless arises, uniform, invariant, in the depths of the eye; without some such figure the agony would be so unapprehensibly immediate that it would scarcely exist at all. The other analogues in Virginia Woolf's fiction to the figure of the raised gigantic arm suggest some of the resonances which give the figure its potency: in *Mrs. Dalloway* Septimus Smith raises his hand "like some colossal figure who has lamented the fate of man for ages in the desert alone" (pp. 105–6); and in the short story "A Summing Up" there arises "in some back street or public house, the usual terrible sexless, inarticulate voice" (*Haunted House*, p. 148), which so startles the heroine that her soul flies out of her body and into the sky. Thus the figure is linked on one hand with Septimus' insanity, the archetypal lament of the human race for the meaning of experience, and on the other with the inability of man to come to terms with the usual human condition. The figure is related to the triangular wedge in *To the Lighthouse* in that they are both an attempt to find the innermost aesthetic representation possible, the human stripped clean of the accidents of flesh and history to naked identity; but Lily hopes that Mrs. Ramsay will be displayed uniquely, vividly, whereas the image in "Three Pictures" has been generalized to a hieroglyph of oppression, impersonal, sexless, the hurt nerve that is central to the human. The gigantic arm brings no consolation; it preserves no one from the leviathans; indeed the leviathans are intimately represented in the tableau. The middle of "Three Pictures" is exactly equivalent to the "Time Passes" chapter of *To the Lighthouse*; indeed some of the language at the beginning of the third episode is reminiscent of the well-known passage in "Time Passes," in which a purple stain boils up like blood to mar the immaculate surface of the sea:

> The butterflies gambolled over the gorse. All was as quiet, as safe as could be. Yet, one kept thinking, a cry had rent it; all this beauty had been an accomplice that night; had consented; to remain calm, to be still beautiful; at any moment it might be sundered again. This goodness, this safety were only on the surface. (*Essays IV*, p. 153)

The narrator hopes to cheer herself by her picture of the sailor's homecoming, and in her stroll she comes upon some villagers digging a grave:

> Death is cheerful here, one felt. Indeed, look at that picture! A man was digging a grave, and children were picnicking at the side of it while he worked. . . . Who was going to be buried, I asked. Had old Mr. Dodson died at last? 'Oh! no. It's for young Rogers,

the sailor,' the woman answered, staring at me. 'He died two nights ago, of some foreign fever. Didn't you hear his wife? She rushed into the road and cried out . . . Here, Tommy, you're all covered with earth!' (*Essays IV*, pp. 153–54)

She has had her vision; and in 1929 it is not Lily's complex affirmation that her painting of Mrs. Ramsay, unsatisfactory as it is, is finished, an effective effigy, a simulacrum fully realized in her head if not on canvas; instead we have the picture of "The Sailor's Homecoming" left mangled and destroyed by another version of the one real emblem, a memento mori, the earth which smothers equally corpse and grave-digger. The simple geometrical form of the wedge, the Madonna of the shadows, is increasingly blurred out, generalized, as the night overwhelms human attempts at self-representation; and in the 1930s all conventional aesthetic representation, that is, all pictures except Munch's "The Scream," become more and more delapidated and threadbare, are scorned, abandoned.

In *The Waves* Bernard can speak of his intimacy with his friends in the terms of the old aesthetic metaphors—the circle that is formed at the party with Percival, the image of the six- or seven-sided flower—but no great significance is put upon the aesthetic simplification of these vehicles. His aesthetic metaphors are fairly transient phenomena, as indeed all of Bernard's art is, unlike the radical stability and permanence of Mrs. Ramsay's wedge. Rhoda is a true aesthete, the last seeker in Virginia Woolf's fiction for aesthetic refuge; but the structures which bring her so much comfort are not simplifications of human relations or even simplifications of her physical environment, but the revealed pattern of a string quartet, in which the lack of chaos is perhaps unsurprising. She hopes that the house she has found in the music will be a warm habitation for herself and her friends, and she also hopes that the structure revealed there will constitute a general assertion of structure in the universe—she in fact does discover that Wren's palace consists of square and oblong too. But the real burden of her gaze is fixed beyond the realm of the human and its indeterminate structures, toward that region of marble pools and swallows in which she will be at last able to present her bouquet to Percival, the land of the dead. In this way the aesthetic theme grows morbid; what began as an attempt to perpetuate life beyond the grave becomes a glorification of death.

The contrast between Rhoda and Bernard in *The Waves* is the strongest statement of one of Virginia Woolf's prime antinomies: *l'art pour l'art* vs. realism; and one of the reasons for the great achievement of the novel is that the late 1920s was a period of major transition in her life from aestheticism to realism. The terms of course are only relative: the hieratic aestheticism of *To the Lighthouse* is nevertheless an attempt to seize the real, an interior verisimilitude; and in *The Years* the comparative spareness of the style would still seem ornate, full of all manner of virtuosic figuration if compared with Zola; yet a great change does take place. From the beginning Virginia Woolf knew that there exist two kinds of stories; even in *The Voyage Out* the genial Terence Hewet plans to write two novels, one called "Silence, or the Things People Don't Say"—which could be the title of any of Virginia Woolf's aesthetic novels—and the other to be the story of a poor young man obsessed with the idea of being a gentleman, with no money and only one increasingly shabby coat, a study of the corruption of the soul, presumably in the manner of Russian or French realism, with a bow perhaps to Oscar Wilde, for the theme of the story is like that of *Dorian Gray* in that it proves that an inhuman pose cannot forever be sustained, that a gentleman's finery must be supported by an honest gentlemanly character. The aggrandizement of silence is the direction that Virginia Woolf takes after *Night and Day*, for dialogue becomes increasingly rare; the narrator of *Jacob's Room* cannot hear half of what Jacob says, must content herself with representing the form of argumentation; Mrs. Dalloway's spoken language is effusive, nonchalant, predictable, compared with the thrilling current of silent language within. It is refreshing, when we come at last to *The Waves*, to hear Bernard, a chatterer, a blatherer, endlessly fertile and fluent, a great bran pie; although even in *The Waves* we never quite hear human dialogue but only submarine currents of thought fished like transatlantic cables out of the sea, ranged and picked clean into a semblance of formal speech, literary epistles, lucid, adorned, even pompous, but so eerily dissimilar to any known human verbalization that one wonders whether during those episodes in which the characters respond to each other's voices, it is due to the usual mechanisms of larynx and ear or some sort of telepathy masquerading as regular dialogue. So we cannot say that we hear Bernard's garrulous voice; we have only a handful from that encyclopedia of little phrases, which, bound together, constitute a verbal equivalent of the universe; but we do have a lengthy representation of his subvocal muttering, as if the inhibitory mechanisms which prevent the brain from uttering its stray perceptions had been circumvented, and "Butterfly powder" (p. 199) and a tree's "green fingers" and all the other little whorls of feeling or convention which generate like eels from horsehairs in the idle brain come spilling out, helplessly, gratefully, from the "lake of his mind." This is what realism is to Virginia Woolf: not an uninflected recitation of the things in front of one's face but a huge accretion of minute poeticisms,

159

common turns of phrase, a translation of the objective world into the fluency and antique order of speech. To be a realist simply means that one's task is primarily descriptive, objective; but the realist and the aesthete are equally concerned with self-projection, and when Bernard says, "I am a story" (p. 200) he means that the locus, the referent of all his stories is himself. The world of *The Waves*, as is proper in a transitional novel, is well balanced between aestheticism and realism; it is clear that each literary style has its successes and compensating failures. Bernard has elaborated the superficies of life with such plenitude of imagination that he has lost his center; his images of himself have so multiplied over the enormous surface of his human intercourse that he has no notion that there is a solid consistent inner Bernard which can reconcile his furious spawn of self-images. As he attempts to imagine this most central fiction, the bottom Bernard, so remote, so necessary, he is appalled by what he finds:

> "When I say to myself, 'Bernard,' who comes? A faithful, sardonic
> man, disillusioned, but not embittered. A man of no particular age
> or calling. Myself, merely. It is he who now takes the poker and
> rattles the cinders so that they fall in showers through the grate.
> 'Lord,' he says to himself, watching them fall, 'what a pother!' and
> then he adds, lugubriously, but with some sense of consolation,
> 'Mrs. Moffat will come and sweep it all up—' I fancy I shall
> often repeat to myself that phrase, as I rattle and bang through life,
> hitting first this side of the carriage then the other, 'Oh, yes, Mrs.
> Moffat will come and sweep it all up.' And so to bed." (Pp. 230–31)

This is what passes for a core identity in Bernard, what would be the triangular wedge in Mrs. Ramsay; but inside Bernard is no stable geometrical form capable of flotation, rapture, but this blurred ageless figure, incompetent, slack, wretched; "Mrs. Moffat will come and sweep it all up" is almost a parody of Mrs. Ramsay's "We are in the hands of the Lord," her ecstasy of passivity degenerated into dead resignation. In Rhoda's world of naked essences, Bernard would evaporate without a trace; he has put all of himself into ephemeralities, the play of light upon the textures of skin and leaf; on Rhoda's interior level he is dull and perfunctory. And of course Rhoda is equally inept, implausible in the shimmering world in which Bernard is at ease, the world of manners and wit. Bernard is a pointillist, while Rhoda makes dark statues in the conservatories of middle earth; and the contrast between the centrifugal tendencies of Bernard and Jinny, and the centripetal tendencies of Rhoda and Louis is a major structural principle in *The Waves*. *The Waves*, like Lawrence's transitional novel *Women in Love*, is a study of the dispersal of the various faculties of the human character into several unstable personages; the six friends are all amputees, the blind carrying the lame on their shoulders, who attempt through empathy to constitute a single full human being, a creature who possesses at once core and skin, learning and grace.

If the characters of *The Waves* have holes in them they are at least highly elaborate, individuated, memorable, like some drawing of Michelangelo in which the legs and torso are drawn with the most painstaking vividness while the head and one arm exist in mere outline, nearly blank. The characters of the later novels are increasingly sketchy, deformed, unintelligible or overintelligible; as Virginia Woolf abandoned the aesthetic theme, the representation of the full interior, the representation of the diamond at the center of the self, her characters increasingly lose identity, the generations of the Pargiters collapse into a monotonous procession of nervous aggravations and sexual failure, the afflictions of the Olivers reduce to the little morality play in which Giles kicks a stone with three symbolic kicks, neatly explained as Manresa (lust), Dodge (perversion), himself (coward). Identity is lost when the characters are helpless among the twisted forces that govern human conduct; kicked stones and pieces of paper whirling in the wind have no need for such extravagances as despair or acquiescence, feeling or perception. All through her life Virginia Woolf, when asked to explain the modern sensibility, felt apologetic that she could offer no more original answer than fragmentation; and the fragmentation of the full human character, for instance that of Mrs. Ramsay, who is equally core and surface, spectator and participant, artist and subject of art, begun in *The Waves*, reaches its final development in the two last novels, in which inchoate characters, Sara Pargiter, Isa Oliver, contend with brittle masks, Peggy the scientist, Mrs. Manresa the venereal, Colonel Pargiter the claw, the nameless and the misnamed spun in the anonymous wind.

Yet the fragmentation that Virginia Woolf lamented in our century was, as she perhaps failed to recognize, a part of her strength. The profound yearning of the lost fragment for its whole—the male's unrequitable need for the female in Aristophanes' parable in the *Symposium*, the ache that Birkin feels at Gerald's death in *Women in Love*, the exfoliation of Bernard into his five friends that is the triumph of *The Waves*—has provided for several artists of the twentieth century a source of formal tension as strong and complex as the more usual rhythms of art. In any case, what we think of as characterization, the creation of a satisfying artistic version of the individual man, certainly requires some fragmentation of the ideally human. Blake's Albion is not a character; Boswell's Johnson is, as much because he detests Scotsmen as because of his manifold virtue. Fragmentation that is too extensive produces vacant characters, or tiny pieces of single traits, the punctual man, the spendthrift, the glutton, and in this case, the artist's business is in the intricacies of interplay, that kind of tessellation which in literature is called plot. Fragmentation that is insufficient produces monsters, those hopelessly large characters who try to hold in one bag too many irreconcilable qualities. The study of characters in the novel is for the most part an examination of such trinkets and chimeras; and such study, especially in the twentieth century, leads one to suspect a condition which may be generally valid for the world as we know it, the precariousness of identity.

Incomparably the most chimerical of Virginia Woolf's characters is Orlando. We have not yet been told all that we would like to know about the personal sources of her novels, but she indicates in her published diary that *Mrs. Dalloway* is based on Kitty Maxse, the Ramsays on her parents; and these three characters are arguably the most potently identified, developed, *durchkomponiert*, of any characters outside *The Waves*. From those examples we would assume that the definition of identity, for Virginia Woolf, is partially contingent upon ·exterior reference. Now it has always been known that the character of Orlando is intimately drawn from Vita Sackville-West; but whereas Virginia Woolf's parents were remote, stylized, long dead by the time of *To the Lighthouse*, and Kitty Maxse was so roundly disliked that Mrs. Woolf felt anxiety that *Mrs. Dalloway* was flawed by the author's contempt for her character, there is a distinct lack of aesthetic distance in *Orlando*. The exterior reference is not to a sharp image but to an aura, not to a discrete woman but to a palpitant haze that embraces both lovers in a flush of indistinctness. What survives of Vita Sackville-West in *Orlando* is little more, as far as I can tell, than a penchant for the fantastic, Turkish trousers, a few incidents that Quentin Bell describes, the form of the private jokes of lovers in the absence of real communication; and we may be certain that much of the character of Orlando is derived from Virginia Woolf herself, her old penchant for cheroots, her summoning of her multiple selves as recorded in "Evening over Sussex: Reflections in a Motor-car," and the novel takes on the tenor of an intimate, spectral autobiography. *Orlando* is a novel without stricture, in which anything can take place; and in such a milieu it is not surprising that the character of Orlando balloons monstrously, enchantingly, floats off into the literary sky. A catalog of the traits of Orlando's character is nearly impossible, for her character is too ample, inexhaustible, a nearly random compendium of glamorous magnanimity; and yet the author makes sure that not a single reader could miss this distressing amplitude by making several catalogs:

For though these are not matters on which a biographer can profitably enlarge it is plain enough to those who have done a reader's part in making up from bare hints dropped here and there the whole boundary and circumference of a living person; can hear in what we only whisper a living voice; can see, often when we say nothing about it, exactly what he looked like, and know without a word to guide them precisely what he thought and felt and it is for readers such as these alone that we write—it is plain then to such a reader that Orlando was strangely compounded of many humours —of melancholy, of indolence, of passion, of love of solitude, to say nothing of all those contortions and subtleties of temper which were indicated on the first page. (P. 73)

No other novel of Virginia Woolf's is so archly cognizant of the artificiality of personality and the artifice of literary creation—she asserts, exactly as in *Jacob's Room*, that the encyclopedia of traits ascribed to Orlando frame an inexpressible core; but here she disclaims her own responsibility, tells the bewildered reader that he is expected to accomplish that act of characterization for which the stolid author lacks requisite imagination. When Orlando's inability to fall into sexual category is discussed, Virginia Woolf is so eager to indicate her ambiguity that she comes close to a welter of oxymorons: Orlando is "bold and active as a man" (p. 190), but would "burst into tears at the slightest provocation," a fearless but excessively tender-hearted duelist and hostess. There is even a hint that Orlando, in the throes of this sweet androgyny, approaches the most radical of all the expanded forms of the human personality, the coalescence of the actor and the acted-upon, the passive and active principles; when she feels for the first time the delights of coquetry, she notes and asks, thinking of her former masculinity, "Then she had pursued, now she fled. Which is the greater ecstasy?" (p. 155). But the greatest ecstasy, the highest gift of undefinition, is to be pursuer and fleer at once, to chase the endless reflections of oneself through the soft hollows of a world identical to one's own body.

Orlando's lack of definition is a sort of joke, but it is a high joke, a serious joke; for Orlando is Virginia Woolf's chief test case on the nature of human personality. Orlando shows exactly what kind of self-development occurs when a human being is placed in unstructured time, unstructured space, a universe as chameleon and obliging, labile, as the human personality itself. The only principle seems to be vacillation; all the minor characters are at least as undefined as Orlando, and if they gel into shape for a moment they will turn themselves inside out the next. The neurasthenic bilious scrawny Nicholas Greene turns his back, and effortlessly, instantly, after two centuries that pass in that second when one's attention was diverted by a ruse, he is fat and prosperous, changed utterly. In *Orlando* the mask is truth. "There is much to support the view that it is clothes that wear us and not we them" (p. 188); for here there is no gap between intention and realization, desire and fulfillment; one's appearance reflects with perfect tact and economy exactly what one is. In the previous novels the characters sometimes approached this perfectly liquid state—Mrs. Dalloway, for instance, fantasizes that her personality is rather hypothetical too, imagines it is only a chance throw of dice that determined that she hates Miss Kilman instead of loving her—but nothing approaches this subtle responsiveness of the whole being to the lightest velleities.

All the characters in *Orlando* partake of this plasticity, but there is evidence that this condition of expansiveness is especially associated with artists. When we first see Greene we are told that "there was something about him that belonged neither to servant, squire, nor noble" (p. 85); there is unsavory innuendo to this, for there is also something about Greene that compels dogs to bite him, but this vagueness, this unclassifiability, suggests that artists lack definition even more than others. Later the narrator remarks of Swift, "He is so coarse and yet so clear; so brutal, yet so kind; scorns the whole world, yet talks baby language to a girl" (p. 211). This is a facile attempt to imitate the antithetical judiciousness of the eighteenth century, but it forces us to come to terms with a character that can be defined only by a series of contradictions. What sort of artists are these protean characters? The answer is the usual one: realists and aesthetes; with the difference that, by the author's fiat, in the world of *Orlando* beyond any other known the aesthetic is as valid as the real; the structure, the human apprehensibility, is assured; the earth may be diaphanous, shimmering, but it is terra firma nonetheless.

Orlando's role as an artist is as equivocal as his gender; the narrator presents him—the male Orlando of the early chapters—as a ceaseless experimenter in all known literary genres, a poetaster of such awesome prolixity that it seems that his imagination is as huge and blurred as his own personality. We can see in this colossal burden of paper that Orlando treasures in secret something of the literary secretiveness and anxiety that Virginia Woolf manifests in her diary; and we can see in the slender but genuine achievement of his one real poem "The Oak Tree" the author's hope that possibly there exists somewhere in her own extensive corpus a work of lasting merit; but of course all of this is refracted through a medium which heightens colors, conflates, projects, bestows the radiance peculiar to that sort of immediate fantasy that cuts to the quick. It is an oversimplification to say that

Orlando is realist when young and male, aesthete when older and female, but there does remain some of this sexual dialectic, left behind from *To the Lighthouse*: Mr. Ramsay's analytical scimitar opposed to Mrs. Ramsay's healing fountain of emotional sensitivity, William Bankes' botanical exactitude opposed to Lily Briscoe's patches of formal color. The technical means of literary art and the postures of the artist are everywhere the subject of fun in *Orlando*, but, exactly as with the nature of identity, the humor conceals a serious purpose, for the world of *Orlando* is in many ways a laboratory for the study of important matters, a floating island abstracted and sealed from the contaminations of accident and gravity. Orlando's first halting attempts at realism become a test case for the conventionality of Elizabethan art:

> He was describing, as all young poets are for ever describing, nature, and in order to match the shade of green precisely he looked (and here he showed more audacity than most) at the thing itself, which happened to be a laurel bush growing beneath the window. After that, of course, he could write no more. Green in nature is one thing, green in literature another. Nature and letters seem to have a natural antipathy; bring them together and they tear each other to pieces. The shade of green Orlando now saw spoilt his rhyme and split his metre. (Pp. 16–17)

Art has its own rules, its own shades of green, and the laurel bushes of literature have never been observed in an honest forest; and yet the best part of Orlando's young career is this attempt to compare these irreconcilable colors, to bridge the gap. The difficult combination of antipathy and interdependence which marks the relation between nature and art is a serious joke that has large resonances; for instance, this antinomy neatly sums up the reader's problem in trying to define Orlando's character, a task to which Virginia Woolf sets him very early in the novel, for *Orlando* is fantasy written according to private rules, but nevertheless translates an obscure referent in the world of gossips and effete authors, Bloomsbury.

Orlando's one valuable piece of writing, a poem called "The Oak Tree," is just such an attempt to translate reality into words; it is clear from the beginning that the oak tree itself is a synecdoche for Orlando's whole physical environment:

> He sighed profoundly, and flung himself—there was a passion in his movements which deserves the word—on the earth at the foot of the oak tree. He loved, beneath all this summer transiency, to feel the earth's spine beneath him; for such he took the hard root of the oak tree to be; or, for image followed image, it was the back of

a great horse that he was riding; or the deck of a tumbling ship—it was anything indeed, so long as it was hard, for he felt the need of something which he could attach his floating heart to. (P. 19)

The oak tree is the world, and this form of play is only slightly more fantastic than Orlando's subsequent adventures; it is the world beloved, apprehensible, rendered valuable to man, a most pleasant cathexis. The actual making of the oak tree into a poem is arduous, tortured, and involves Orlando in labor for much of three centuries. One would not wish to allege that the attempt ever succeeds entirely, but "The Oak Tree" receives its share of praise and eventually attains a kind of apotheosis. Nicholas Greene—the portly gourmand of the nineteenth century—is most vociferous in his encomium, and singles out for special praise the poem's truth to nature; his suspect eulogy is confirmed in a surprising way by Orlando herself at the end of the book. She flings herself onto the roots of the ancient tree, roots that run out "like ribs from a spine" (p. 324)—the tree is approximating human form, becoming Orlando-like—and decides to bury her little "Oak Tree" underneath the actual oak. She quickly renounces this symbolical gesture as an extravagance, but the intent is clear: the two versions of reality, one dressed in words, the other in bark, must merge into identity. And the incident ends with a defense of the realistic mode which is, I believe, an important formulation in Virginia Woolf's career:

> Was not writing poetry a secret transaction, a voice answering a voice? So that all this chatter and praise, and blame and meeting people who did not admire one was as ill suited as could be to the thing itself—a voice answering a voice. What could have been more secret, she thought, more slow, and like the intercourse of lovers than the stammering answer she had made all these years to the old crooning song of the woods, and the farms and the brown horses standing at the gate, neck to neck, and the smithy and the kitchen and the fields, so laboriously bearing wheat, turnips, grass, and the gardens blowing irises and fritillaries? (P. 325)

The entire perceived world resolves, if the ear is keen enough, into a song, wordless, a persistent thread of revelation, the self-expression of the fields through the flowers; and the literary act is a private response to this secret voice, a duplicate of its articulation in the articulation of words, a celebration of the real, an homage; just as the novel itself is response, celebration, homage.

Yet the novel does not testify with an unmixed voice to the virtue of realism in literature. In the eighteenth century Pope is presented as a realist so savage that the narrator must delete his remarks lest a breath of exterior night destroy the fragile fictions of *Orlando*; and here is the narrator's comment on Orlando's decision to take a ride in a carriage with Mr. Pope:

> For if it is rash to walk into a lion's den unarmed, rash to navigate the Atlantic in a rowing boat, rash to stand on one foot on the top of St. Paul's, it is still more rash to go home alone with a poet. A poet is Atlantic and lion in one. While one drowns us the other gnaws us. If we survive the teeth, we succumb to the waves. A man who can destroy illusions is both beast and flood. Illusions are to the soul what atmosphere is to the earth. Roll up that tender air and the plant dies, the color fades. The earth we walk on is a parched cinder. It is marl we tread and fiery cobbles scorch our feet. By the truth we are undone. Life is a dream. 'Tis waking that kills us. He who robs us of our dreams robs us of our life—(and so on for six pages if you will, but the style is tedious and may well be dropped). (P. 203)

Never were the ferocities of the realistic approach to life couched in more insipid conventionalities of phrase, flaccid rhythms; the theme of the starkness of poetry is embroidered into inanition. It is hard to know whether the joke is that bad writers should not try to emulate the style of Pope or whether the tenacity of illusion defies even Pope's powers; in either case the aggressive ugliness of the narrator's writing does not present the case for the realistic method very favorably. Orlando's "realism" is by no means as severe and imposing as this poetry of cinders and ash; indeed the whole fine glamor of the book is tacit repudiation of such asperities, and Orlando is everywhere complicit with illusion, from his early trust of Sasha's fidelity to his, that is, her final embrace with Shelmerdine on the last page of the book. The point of this satire on Pope is that either extreme is excessive, the overrealistic or the overaesthetic; human life does not consist entirely of cinders, nor is it entirely confect of dreams and emotive illusion, as this passage shows:

> "Ecstasy!" she cried. "Ecstasy! Where's the post office?" she wondered. "For I must wire at once to Shel and tell him . . . ." And repeating "A toy boat on the Serpentine," and "Ecstasy," alternately, for the thoughts were interchangeable and meant exactly the same thing, she hurried towards Park Lane.
> "A toy boat, a toy boat, a toy boat," she repeated, thus enforcing upon herself the fact that it is not articles by Nick Greene on John Donne nor eight-hour bills nor covenants nor factory acts that matter; it's something useless, sudden, violent; something that costs a life; red, blue, purple; a spirit; a splash; like those hyacinths (she was passing a fine bed of them); free from taint, dependence,

167

soilure of humanity or care for one's kind; something rash,
ridiculous, "like my hyacinth, husband I mean, Bonthrop: that's
what it is—a toy boat on the Serpentine, it's ecstasy—ecstasy."
Thus she spoke aloud, waiting for the carriages to pass at Stanhope
Gate, for the consequence of not living with one's husband, except
when the wind is sunk, is that one talks nonsense aloud in Park
Lane. (Pp. 287–88)

This is that rarest mode in Virginia Woolf's writings, self-parody, a
debunking of the painterly, breathless, emblematic and much-semi-
coloned style upon which the previous novels on occasion rely, the
luminous halo with a half-watt bulb. By this glimpse of the aesthetic
style at its worst, carried too far, we can see what Virginia Woolf
considered to be its defects: extreme vagueness, a dismissal of the
known and real in favor of the inconceivable; a formality in which the
reader is bewildered by complete ignorance of the signification; a
certain habit of letting a tiny object or event, in this case a toy boat, a
diminished replica of the boat in *To the Lighthouse*, become so
freighted with emotional content that it sinks, literally, under the
sheer weight of the author's frenzied emoting. It is noteworthy that
both the strict realist and aesthete are inhuman; one writes of a
shriveled earth swept clean of men, the other writes of arbitrary forms
free from the "soilure of humanity"; Orlando's tempered manner of
realism is the only mode of perception sensitive and plastic enough to
capture both the human and the inanimate. Indeed the best art
requires a certain mixture of styles; one thinks of Lily Briscoe as a
truly formidable aesthete, but even she recognizes that in her painting
the feathery evanescence of color must be "clamped together with
bolts of iron" (p. 255), as if Mr. Ramsay's logical mind is a necessary
complement to feminine delicacy if good or even passable art is to
occur. Both Orlando and Lily Briscoe are to some extent ambiguous
creatures who cling to the middle ground; but, although her fond hope
that man and nature carry out an intimate dialogue through poetry is
certainly venturesome, perhaps illusory, Orlando is more of a realist
than Lily; and Orlando's fidelity to her oak, her great declaration that
literature is partly a reflex of inhuman nature, carries some of the
acorns of the style of *The Years* and *Between the Acts*, the unflinching
and somewhat numb realism of the later novels, the screams recorded
with such measured sobriety.

In the laboratory of *Orlando* it is not surprising that art is
discovered to be valid; in a fictive world mounted on gimbals and
submerged in a watertight case for three hundred odd pages the
marriage of the human mind and its environment can take place,
triumphantly, without a murmur of protest; Orlando can hug her

most preposterous fiction Marmaduke Bonthrop Shelmerdine and live with him happily for the rest of her implausible life. The same principles, however, applied to a model of the world that includes more of human experience than *Orlando* will produce much darker results. This is easily demonstrated by comparing *Orlando* with a novel so similar that it is almost its twin, *Between the Acts*. Both novels are myths of history, and by the time of *Between the Acts* history, that great gelid egg, has shattered, and the jagged remains lacerate the hands and feet. *Orlando* is a comedy, one of the greatest of this era, and the inimicality of the twentieth century to the comic spirit is nowhere better demonstrated than by the extreme distortions and rarefications that had to take place in order that it may all cohere —but cohere it does, and nowhere in Virginia Woolf's writings does a novel attain a more compact, globular form. History is cunningly squeezed and pruned until the shape of the last 350 years has all the virtues of the well-made plot—contrast, suspense, drama, dénouement; but of course this is history internalized, brought forcibly within the confines of a single psyche, phylogeny bent into a recapitulation of ontogeny. It has long been fashionable to argue that history and fiction are interchangeable; "D'avisés critiques ont considéré le roman comme de l'histoire qui aurait pu être, l'histoire comme un roman qui avait eu lieu" (*Les Caves du Vatican*, p. 96), as Gide says, stating a useful commonplace. Virginia Woolf might well have acquiesced—the resemblance between her own Orlando and the young Robert Devereux of Lytton Strachey's *Elizabeth and Essex* cannot be coincidence—but she did not. She upbraids Lytton Strachey for confusing the two genres in that very biography:

> . . . fact and fiction refused to mix. Elizabeth never became real in the sense that Queen Victoria had been real, yet she never became fictitious in the sense that Cleopatra or Falstaff is fictitious. The reason would seem to be that very little was known—he was urged to invent; yet something was known—his invention was checked. The Queen thus moves in an ambiguous world, between fact and fiction. (*Essays IV*, pp. 224–25)

According to Virginia Woolf, when writing serious history, one must be faithful to facts, objective knowledge; she believed, at least in the 1930s, that historical truth, impersonal, resistant to art, was ascertainable. So *Orlando* is fictitious without availing itself of the artist's higher claim to truth, and it is easy to see that, insofar as the novel constitutes a vision of history, that vision is wrong. Sometimes in Mrs. Woolf's essays she allows herself the delicious pretense that history did take place roughly as recorded in *Orlando*; for instance, in an essay on Horace Walpole she speaks of the stately delight of Walpole's letters, and goes on to recall the wonderful passage in *Orlando* in which the nineteenth century, suddenly at the stroke of midnight, engulfs the lucid eighteenth-century sky in roiling darkness:

> The first solemn chimes of the nineteenth century, which mean that Horace Walpole must retire, are as vexatious to us as the clock that strikes and sends a child complaining up to bed. (*Essays III*, p. 105)

But this too is a joke; when she is moved to give her honest impression of the nature of the transitions from one century to the next, she can be scornful of the old-fashioned opinions expressed in *Orlando*; she advises her friend the young poet to beware of those facile critics who exaggerate the neatness of their literary categories:

> A pistol shot rings out. "The age of romance was over. The age of realism had begun"—you know the sort of thing. Now of course writers themselves know very well that there is not a word of truth in all this—there are no battles, and no murders and no defeats and no victories. But as it is of the utmost importance that readers should be amused, writers acquiesce. They dress themselves up. They act their parts. (*Essays II*, p. 184)

Abrupt transitions do not exist, but writers conspire to allow this pleasing delusion.

Since Orlando is herself a writer, and not wholly unlike Virginia Woolf, perhaps this passage from the "Letter to a Young Poet" can indicate something of the nature of history in *Orlando*. The novel provides us, not with an honest account of literary and social mores, but with a tinselly, titivated version cooked up to flatter the prejudices of contemporary tastes; it has been observed that the historical views of *Orlando* are little more than a compendium of historical opinions popular in the early twentieth century; and surely the rickety artificiality is part of the grand joke. But more importantly, *Orlando* is also the attempt of a learned and sophisticated mind to come to terms with its own historical erudition. Virginia Woolf, as must be true of all literary figures of a certain rank, spent a great deal of her life in the intimacy of books; and, since her favorite theory is that the reader is complicit in the writing of a book, she must have felt herself profoundly involved in exactly that sort of stylized literary history, refined to specious clarity by generations of critics, through which Orlando slowly floats in her long journey to the present. Orlando sees Samuel Johnson as a silhouette in a window, meets Pope at a party in which his exact witticism cannot quite be captured, feels fairly comfortable in the company of a stylish minor literary figure—

Nicholas Greene—while Shakespeare eludes her entirely. This constitutes in miniature, I believe, what the literary past signified to Virginia Woolf when she searched her mind for images. The impressions one gets from the vast body of her essays are quite similar; she writes unforgettably about, say, William Cowper, but refuses to come to terms with Shakespeare at all; she has a keen eye for the single sharp anecdote, Samuel Johnson at Dr. Burney's party, the ghost of Sterne making noises in the night, but never expands her biography much beyond outline and caricature. Above all her major contemporaries she has the grace of modesty; in her letter to *The Nation* of 12 September 1925 she says that she would "cheerfully become Shakespeare's cat, Scott's pig, or Keats's canary, if by so doing I could share the society of these great men" (*Essays I*, p. 195), and, in a sense, that was exactly what she was shortly to accomplish in her novel *Orlando*.

When Orlando attains the present, the tone of the book changes; whereas Orlando's incredible childhood and interminable youth take place in delightful cliches—the rotund theatricality of some old historical painting, its colors mingled and made rich by time—the loss of aesthetic distance renders her blinded by the velocity and vividness of the year 1928:

> Here the shadows of the plants were miraculously distinct. She noticed the separate grains of earth in the flower beds as if she had a microscope stuck to her eye. She saw the intricacy of the twigs of every tree. Each blade of grass was distinct and the markings of veins and petals. (Pp. 320–21)

She has just summoned her multifarious selves, and the central self that unites them all, and is prepared with her full internal equipment for this confrontation with the immediate; and the relation of history and identity is at last becoming clear. Orlando had always been conscious that she remained "fundamentally the same" (p. 237) despite her dazzling shifts of role and gender; and, as the clamor of the present moment dispels the spectres of history, we understand that a historical era, like a mood or a suit of clothes, is nothing more than a projection from the mottled interior, an environment designed to fit a transitory mood. One had thought that Orlando's finger trembled for a wedding ring because it was the nineteenth century, but it is more accurate to say that it was the nineteenth century because Orlando on some level wanted to be married. Each historical era is partial, a suitable dwelling place for one splinter of Orlando, the glamorous youth, the realist, the romantic; and only in the present is the summation possible, the union of oak tree and poem, the confluence of the realized Orlando and her phantom lover Shelmerdine. In the nineteenth century Shelmerdine was, in a sense, part of Orlando's pathology—in fact a crucial symptom of Septimus's insanity in *Mrs. Dalloway* is attributed to Shelmerdine when a jay shrieks his name from a tree—but in the twentieth century the marriage of sanity and insanity, the real and the fantastic, is effortless, desirable, even healthy. Of course the amount of twentieth-century pain allowed to filter in is limited; it is chiefly the aesthetic pain of Orlando's hyperesthesia, a symptom that occurs as early as *The Voyage Out*, made into philosophy by Bernard's dread in *The Waves* of the arrows of sensation, a difficult loss of padding between the *I* and the *not-I*. At the end of *Orlando* the hyperesthesia reaches its crisis when Orlando feels faint at the sight of her gardener's missing fingernail; she recoils from sensation into the depths of her brain:

> For the shadow of faintness which the thumb without a nail had cast had deepened now, as the back of her brain (which is the part furthest from sight) into a pool where things dwell in darkness so deep that what they are we scarcely know. She now reflected— and, indeed, some say that all our most violent passions, and art and religion are the reflections which we see in the dark hollow at the back of the head when the visible world is obscured for the time. She looked there now, long, deeply, profoundly, and immediately the ferny path up the hill along which she was walking became not entirely a path, but partly the Serpentine; the hawthorn bushes were partly ladies and gentlemen sitting with card cases and gold-mounted canes; the sheep were partly tall Mayfair houses; everything was partly something else, and each gained an odd moving power from this union of itself and some- thing not itself so that with this mixture of truth and falsehood her mind became like a forest in which things moved; lights and shadows changed, and one thing became another. (Pp. 322–23)

This is the value of history: resonance. Immediate sensation, that is, sensation without historical time, is a flat wall that crushes eye and skin; history renders the field of sensation three-dimensional, orderly, a scenic perspective in which interior values mute and shade, impose themselves upon the murderous truth of the real. History is the kingdom of falsehoods, of human experience that objective fact cannot deny; history is memory. Mrs. Ramsay found in the bottom of her brain the strict geometry of a triangular wedge; but Orlando's core, the black pool, is inflected, complex, a great totality of manifold experience in art and life, as intricate as humanity itself.

Orlando is the zenith of the historical myth: every historical event is made triumphantly meaningful, a stage in the development of the human personality; *Between the Acts*, by contrast, represents the absolute repudiation of history. Orlando gladly incorporates into herself all the gifts that time offers; the characters of *Between the Acts* live, as the title suggests, without history, in a brief hiatus or trough in history, oblivious of the bombs that fall. The development of England here is isolated from any human context; the spectators of the skit are simply bored, until the immediacy of the present prevents them from missing the point any longer. Miss La Trobe, who is as much a debasement of Virginia Woolf as Orlando is an idealization, has contrived her play to be a painful representation of humanity; but for the most part the audience is obtuse beyond pain. The play is of course preposterous, much more parodic and inflated than anything in *Orlando*; and yet it can be judged, according to certain terms found in *Orlando*, a work of realistic intent. The narrator of *Orlando* informs us, in connection with eighteenth-century satire, that the purpose of poetry is to dispel illusion, to make us feel the intolerable poverty of human existence; and that is the intent of Miss La Trobe's play. The play itself is chiefly an anthology of typical literary plots from the various centuries, exploded and distorted to reveal the substantial gore that the author finds underneath them. The center of the Elizabethan romance is the torture of an old woman; the center of the Restoration comedy is the prying-off of flattering conventional masks to reveal the gristle and stringy meat that is the true locus of the human; and the center of the nineteenth-century novel-dialogue is a pair of fossilized young lovers, one of whose fathers is searching, appropriately enough, for fossils. The play overall has a structural myth not found in *Orlando*, a novel governed not by evolution so much as vacillation: the development of the human race from its apish childhood—rhinoceroses are among the fauna of England in the first scene—to increasingly clattering articulation, arthritic maturity; but the basic ape keeps a continual howl in the undertone.

The pleasing assumptions of *Orlando* are everywhere demolished. Orlando's allegation that her historical selves add up to one harmonious totality is put into the mouth of the Reverend G. W. Streatfield, a stock clerical fool, who gives an exactly wrong account of the meaning of the drama:

> Am I treading, like angels, where as a fool I should absent myself?
> To me at least it was indicated that we are members one of
> another. Each is part of the whole. Yes, that occurred to me, sitting
> among you in the audience. Did I not perceive Mr. Hardcastle
> here . . . (he pointed) . . . at one time a Viking? And in Lady
> Harridan—excuse me, if I get the names wrong—a Canterbury
> pilgrim? We act different parts; but are the same. (*Between the
> Acts*, p. 192)

173

Orlando too felt that she remained fundamentally the same through-out her historical disguises, and Orlando too found that her world was given resonance by her historical memories; but Orlando's great outpouring of self-acceptance, self-redemption, is obliterated by the menace of war just as Streatfield's voice is drowned out by the airplanes. This is a world without memory, whose only archetypes are ape and insect; the continuity of experience upon which Streatfield so complacently expatiates is a lie, for human life divagates at the slightest sexual stirring, runs intermittently, between the acts. An ancient supernumerary, Mrs. Lynn Jones, suggests in her musing the sheer absurdity of a continuous, integrated life:

> Time went one and on like the hands of the kitchen clock. . . . If they had met with no resistance, she mused, nothing wrong, they'd still be going round and round and round. The Home would have remained; and Papa's beard, she thought, would have grown and grown; and Mama's knitting—what did she do with all her knitting?—Change had to come, she said to herself, or there'd have been yards and yards of Papa's beard, of Mama's knitting. (P. 174)

The intervals of time are discrete, like the ticks of a clock, or the isolated skits which comprise Miss La Trobe's play; and between one second and the next the characters run randomly, incoherently. In *The Waves*, and sometimes in earlier novels, one can prove the community of human minds by comparing the structures of the brain; two people whose brains work similarly, are shaped similarly, can attain real empathy. In *Between the Acts* Bart Oliver wonders that his sister is theist but he is not: "In Lucy's skull, shaped so much like his own, there existed a prayable being" (p. 25). Similarity is only superficial; brother and sister are incomprehensible to each other, community is even more ridiculous.

If anyone is sensitive to the pageant of history, it should be Isa Oliver, the most sentient character in the novel; yet it is she to whom the drama is least meaningful:

> "How am I burdened with what they drew from the earth; memories; possessions. This is the burden that the past laid on me, last little donkey in the long caravanserai crossing the desert. 'Kneel down,' said the past. 'Fill your pannier from our tree. Rise up, donkey. Go your way till your heels blister and your hoofs crack.'" (P. 155)

Orlando wishes to integrate his memories, enrich, plump out his world with history; Isa wishes to be rid forever of the cumbrance of memory, the straitjacket of the body; and she prays for lightning to burn away corporeal history in one flash. The final discontinuity of history is apocalypse, and it is war that will efface the record of useless suffering. History is Orlando's subtlest servant, but the master of the characters of *Between the Acts*; it is true that they reject the message of the pageant, reject the distorted mirror image of themselves that is faithful depiction of inner truth, ape-truth, but it is more important that history is soon to reject them. These timeless souls, caught in a backwater of England, Pointz Hall, are irrelevant to chronology, and the motions of history are divorced from them; by 1941 the aesthetic and the real are irreconcilable, incommensurable, and the inconsequent painting next to the image of the Olivers' ancestor stares facile and bland out of the heart of silence, a green glade where human feet will never tread, a field of vision as inane and tantalizing as history or love.

Language

The fall of language is parallel to the decay of vision. The lens of the eye, an image-making organ of razor clarity in *To the Lighthouse*, thickens, turns brittle, obdurate, and painting and landscape alike recede into the hazy depths of the mirror; and the voice becomes trapped in the volute of the inner ear, grows hopelessly resonant and ambiguous with echoes. The two last novels of Virginia Woolf are both remarkable achievements, but I feel, as many others do, that the fundamental course of the development of her style was checked, routed into a new, more traditional path; and this abdication of style can be partly attributed to a single, terrible paradox which she discovered about the nature of language. Language cannot imitate the workings of the mind unless the content of the conscious mind is fundamentally verbal, which is dubious; and language cannot be an analogue to the structure of the exterior world if that world consists of chaos and the leviathan; therefore the loosing of the ligaments and tendons of grammar is unwarranted, vaguely foolish. On the other hand, the only alternative, the construction of sober, grammatically precise sentences, does not work either, because then the author is supplying the reader with an endless supply of false analogues, puny assertions of structure in a world where structure either does not exist or is inconceivable to man, the structure of mud or the icecap. In this sense Miss La Trobe's play in *Between the Acts* is a metaphor for the essential falseness of art. Auden has his Caliban say in *The Sea and the Mirror*, almost contemporary with *Between the Acts*, that the metaphor of the failed theater, failed grand opera, is the proper metaphor for the human condition, and in the tenor's wobble, the soprano's oblivious screech, lie intimations of authentic redemption; Virginia

Woolf accepts Auden's metaphor as the valid one, but reverses its value to an emblem of damnation. This is why the language of *The Years* and *Between the Acts* is so flat yet so tightly controlled, spare yet laborious; it is damned. Sanity is an inadequate response, yet, in the absence of real order, one might as well obey the old strictures.

In the 1920s, and before, when it seemed that language and the world were twin, amorous, when it seemed as if even intuition and dreams were compounded of subject and predicate, English words, the exhilaration is manifest on every page. As early as *Night and Day* it is perfectly clear that the human brain is a bag of words, a great skein of sentences, a folio of printed pages: when Katharine decides in an early encounter with Ralph that he is not such a vulgar fellow as she first thought, she corrects herself in the following way:

> She hastily recalled her first view of him, in the little room where the relics were kept, and ran a bar through half her impressions, as one cancels a badly written sentence, having found the right one. (P. 96)

Katharine's memory seems to consist of a vast scroll on which she writes her feelings; and therefore one's inner experience can be amended, expunged, italicized, published; it is convenient for a novelist to have such literary characters, just as an opera writer might be interested in characters who know how to sing. Later in *Night and Day* Katharine's fiancé William reads aloud his execrable verse play, and Katharine feels that his monotonous inflection seems to "nail each line firmly on to the same spot in the hearer's brain" (p. 140); soon thereafter Ralph sees Katharine, his sober seraph, a miracle, and rejoices that "the real Katharine could speak the words which seemed to crowd behind the forehead and in the depths of the eye" (p. 147); everywhere in the novel the brain teems with words, swoons with verbal nuance. It is not surprising that the characters like to utter little phrases all the time, write elliptic formulas on the flyleaves of books, speak gnomic sentences while crossing the street; one cannot say that they verbalize their feelings, for their feelings have no existence except as words.

The immense technical advance that occurs between *Night and Day* and *Jacob's Room* shows itself in the daring verbalization of the outer world. Not only do sentences writhe ceaselessly in the nest of the brain, but words and objects are now of equivalent status. In Swift's *Tale of a Tub* words harden into solid balls spewed from the theater, balls of such density that they leave dents upon the skulls of the audience; and since Swift's time these metaphors and locutions in which words have metamorphosed into thick palpability have usually been satirical symptoms of the corruption of language. It is not so in *Jacob's Room*; instead the objectification of words is a sign of the adequate resolution of the world into language; the English and human environment are coterminous, of equal gravity. Some of this verbal dignity can be found in the experimental stories which precede *Jacob's Room*; for instance in "Kew Gardens" an old woman looks at the flowers "through the pattern of falling words" (*Haunted House*, p. 32), and the young and inarticulate lovers manage to make insignificant words successful:

> ... these short insignificant words also expressed something, words with short wings for their heavy body of meaning, inadequate to carry them far and thus alighting awkwardly upon the very common objects that surrounded them, and were to their inexperienced touch so massive; but who knows (so they thought as they pressed the parasol into the earth) what precipices aren't concealed in them, or what slopes of ice don't shine in the sun on the other side? Who knows? Who has ever seen this before? Even when she wondered what sort of tea they gave you at Kew, he felt that something loomed up behind her words, and stood vast and solid behind them. (*Haunted House*, p. 34)

The words scatter and thud with ridiculous overweight, bees loaded with buckshot; and yet, in a preview of Rhoda's stark landscapes, they convey the image of something that exists on the far side of language, a correlative world as vivid and real as Kew Gardens. This passage, like many in the early stories, is a mixture of two modes kept distinct in the later works; and what is developed in *Jacob's Room* is this loving oral fascination with the stream of words issuing from the mouth, as if speech consisted of a balloon of birds, insects, nuggets, fastened to the tongue. When the withered invalid Ellen Barfoot speaks, the words issue "from her lips like crumbs of dry bread" (p. 25); when Professor Sopwith talks to his undergraduates, "the soul itself skipped through the lips in thin silver disks which dissolve in young men's minds like silver, like moonlight" (p. 40); and when the undergraduates respond to him he twines "stiff fibres of awkward speech ... plaiting them round his own smooth garland, making the bright side show, the vivid greens, the sharp thorns, manliness" (p. 41). The human spirit leaves its discreet spoor everywhere, is effortlessly disgorged and ingested; this is a world in which sight and communication are nearly equivalent, for objects have direct human significance, and, like Jacob's lonely shoes, frame and embody mankind at every turn; a world that is candid, subtly responsive. Jacob pronounces the word *urbane* so magnificently that Bonamy is enraptured; the physical sensuous aspect of language is triumphant. It scarely seems unreasonable to us that Jacob's mother's letter would contain his mother's sensibility in miniature, that its graphic heart would be torn by Jacob's sexual transgression in the bedroom. The human and the objective interpenetrate breathlessly; and language is the sacrament that sanctifies and humanizes the physical world.

Men kiss, not by touching lips, but by this bright intercourse of verbal biscuits, disks, and coins. Yet it should not be imagined that the tracks of human speech are limited to this mild rubble of words; there broods over the physical world a much more compelling, all-encompassing blanket of language. Already in *Jacob's Room* we have intimations of this verbal ubiquity: "These pinkish and greenish newspapers are thin sheets of gelatine pressed nightly over the brain and heart of the world" (p. 98). Words are doubly real: they are not only objects in themselves, the tonal qualities of which can be savored, admired, but they are also a transparent covering over their referents. In fact the relation between words and their denotations is the same as that between an author's sensibility and the world he represents in his works. In Virginia Woolf's critical essays she admires those writers, like Ruskin, whose "words lie like a transparent veil upon his meaning" (*Essays I*, p. 207); or Proust, who is "so porous, so pliable, so perfectly receptive that we realize him only as an envelope, thin but elastic, which stretches wider and wider and serves not to enforce a view but to enclose a world" (*Essays II*, p. 83). Virginia Woolf is conscious that she is writing a novel, that everything she describes on paper is not only an object but a noun, not only a sensibility but a phrase; so the transparent verbal universe of this lady of language is an emblem of the internal harmony, vouchsafed by words that do not resist their own verbality.

After *Jacob's Room*, Virginia Woolf's verbal art keeps growing in breadth and glory; in *Mrs. Dalloway* the very sky is vaulted with more or less legible letters, written by an airplane, seen by everyone below, an enormous token of the communality, almost the divinity of language. The high point of language, though, is *To the Lighthouse*, in which the very geraniums are gaily festooned with human speech:

> He slipped, seeing before him that hedge which had over and over again rounded some pause, signified some conclusion, seeing his wife and child, seeing again the urns with the trailing red geraniums which had so often decorated processes of thought, and bore, written up among their leaves, as if they were scraps of paper on which one scribbles notes in the rush of reading. (P. 66)

No longer is the presence of language limited to crumbs and coins;

great trails and banners of speech curl everywhere; and if the geraniums bear legible writing, the mind of Mr. Ramsay returns the compliment by imprinting upon his ratiocinations the image of geraniums. Mrs. Ramsay is almost as discursive in nature as her husband; at one point Lily Briscoe imagines that inside the chambers of Mrs. Ramsay's mind are "tablets, bearing sacred inscriptions, which if one could spell them out, would teach one everything" (p. 79). Man and nature alike reduce to script; the writer's task is merely the transcription of difficult orthography. Virginia Woolf recorded in her diary that the first part of *To the Lighthouse* came to her with unprecedented ease and fluency; and never before or after is her style more vivacious, long-limbed, frisky, full of sudden splashes of rare pigments, extravagant clauses dashed off with no perceptible syntactic relation, parallel constructions flaunted and flogged in great nets that attempt to heave out of the mind's ocean what cannot be defined, much less coherently chained to logical sequence, these outrageous metaphors that skitter and slip into one another as the helpless eye rereads what has just appeared, and all the while the sentence is running off into its last tangent, often a baroque simile, as if a magician, not content with mystifying us by pulling a rabbit out of a hat, had to cook and eat the rabbit before our very eyes. It is all demure; it may verge on catachresis, but real indiscretion is unthinkable, and grammatical amenities are preserved; yet sudden violence, like the knife that the infant James wishes to plunge into his father's breast, is unmistakably in the air. Language has become plastic almost to the point of dissolution; it is a soft matrix in which no convolution of branch or brain is too fine to receive perfect impression, a verbal field as clear and insinuating as air. Grammar is distended until the form of a sentence can imitate the motions of mind and reason; and when the sentence settles into complex order, that order is an affirmation of a world apprehensible to man, in which houses stand as upright as an independent clause. It is a fond hope, a poignant hope, that the world may be as friendly and plausible as language; traces of this belief can be discovered much later, for instance in 1933, when Virginia Woolf wrote in her diary, "The view was like a line of poetry that makes itself; the shaped hill, all flushed with reds and greens; the elongated lines, cultivated every inch" (*A Writer's Diary*, p. 195)—a landscape that has flowed into the outline of cursive script; but it is all delusion and idleness.

Suspicions that language is inadequate occur even before the experiments with a verbalized world begin. *The Voyage Out* manifests everywhere a profound distrust of words; although Rachel Vinrace is eventually driven nearly to ecstasy by the sonorities of Gibbon, what human speech signifies to her is the pervasive empty chatter of the Victorian household:

> Let these odd men and women—her aunts, the Hunts, Ridley, Helen, Mr. Pepper, and the rest—be symbols,—featureless but dignified, symbols of age, of youth, of motherhood, of learning, and beautiful often as people upon the stage are beautiful. It appeared that nobody ever said a thing they meant, or ever talked of a feeling they felt, but that was what music was for. Reality dwelling in what one saw and felt, but did not talk about. (P. 137)

On one side is the stiff world of stale symbols and the calculated irrelevance of words; on the other side is the fascinating interior world of inexpressible perception and feeling. On one level this is what her entrance into South America is: her initiation into the unappeasable, the unthinkable reality. In the heart of South America, as she goes up the Amazon with Hewet, she is conscious that she is entering a region in which language is invalid, annihilated: Hewet attempts to read a poem, "but the number of moving things entirely vanquished his words" (p. 267); and as their wild hearts are further bewildered by new love, "the words of the others seemed to curl up and vanish as the ashes of burnt paper, and left them sitting perfectly silent at the bottom of the world" (p. 276). Mr. Flushing—another featureless symbol—has just found the Amazon a lunatic river peopled by apes and alligators, the creation of an insane God; but to the young lovers this massive derangement of experience is a necessary prelude to self-expression, the loosing of powerful and wordless emotion. This supersession of language is so thorough that Hewet's declaration of love in the innermost reaches of the rain forest is necessarily strained and awkward:

> "You love me?" Terence asked at length, breaking the silence painfully. To speak or to be silent was equally an effort, for when they were silent they were keenly conscious of each other's presence, and yet words were either too trivial or too large.
> She murmured inarticulately, ending, "And you?" (P. 280)

The narrator cannot quite catch Rachel's murmur, so devastated is all speech but the simple word *love* by the overpowering Amazon. The language abolished by this novel is not a very formidable one, mostly the ossified sentiments of the nineteenth-century middle class; but it is an indication *ab ovo* of a major current of Virginia Woolf's sensibility.

In *Jacob's Room* it seems the language has overwhelmed and conquered the whole province of the real, but even in that technically optimistic novel there are disturbing signs that the hold of language is more precarious than it first appears:

> Masters of language, poets of long ages, have turned from the sheet that endures to the sheet that perishes, pushing aside the tea-tray, drawing close to the fire (for letters are written when the dark presses round a bright red cave), and addressed themselves to the task of reaching, touching, penetrating the individual heart. Were it possible! But words have been used too often; touched and turned, and left exposed to the dust of the street. The words we seek hang close to the tree. We come at dawn and find them sweet beneath the leaf. (P. 93)

The greater part of human vocabulary is dead; the experiments of the novels of the 1920s are designed to revive a language that has become desiccated and slack, to distort speech into its lost ideality. English must be somewhat strident and obscure if it is to be listened to at all, but everywhere in her diary Mrs. Woolf reveals anxiety about this style that is so artifically stressed and mutated. And in several places we are permitted a glimpse of an ideal language in which Virginia Woolf, however remotely, believes. Just after she completed *Jacob's Room*, in 1922, she began her essay, "On Not Knowing Greek"; and her description of the Greek language reveals, more tellingly than any other passage she ever wrote, the ultimate potentialities of language:

> Does not the whole of Greece heap itself behind every line of its literature? They admit us to a vision of the earth unravaged, the sea unpolluted, the maturity, tried but unbroken, of mankind. Every word is reinforced by a vigour which pours out of olive-tree and temple and the bodies of the young. The nightingale has only to be named by Sophocles and she sings; the grove has only to be called ἄβατον, 'untrodden', and we imagine the twisted branches and the purple violets. Back and back we are drawn to steep ourselves in what, perhaps, is only an image of the reality, not the reality itself, a summer's day imagined in the heart of a northern winter. (*Essays I*, p. 11)

In ancient Greece things uttered themselves; tree and temple poured their concrete vigor, their thingly vigor, into the very words; men can speak potently when the olive and the sea have tongues. Perfect language is onomatopoeia, words that sing the nightingale's song, identical phrases grown instinct and elaborate with the shape of trees and flowers; the word θάλασσα is itself salty, the word ἀστήρ itself bright and remote. We use these words to express our emotions, Virginia Woolf says, but they are intense and hard beyond the

181

resonance of connotation. This ideal language is a manifestation of her appetite for objective reality, for the quick; the artist wants to write not the noun but the actual presence.

In an ideal Greek the sound and the referent of a given word are the same; therefore, according to this remarkable doctrine, one can understand a passage in Greek if it is correctly declaimed, even if one is wholly ignorant of the language. This partly accounts for the remarkable persistence of Greek in the novels: in *The Voyage Out* Rachel has a dream in which magnified Greek letters stalk about; Jacob Flanders, at dawn, in an ecstasy of friendship, declaims Greek; birds sing to Septimus Smith in joyful Greek; even as late as *The Years* Edward Pargiter will stop a gathering of friends cold by uttering a fairly long passage of Greek, thereby putting a solemn marble backdrop against the ordinary inanities of conversation. In short, Greek is dawn language, the language of the seraph and the bright youth, a nexus of words as intricate, abundant, and palpable as the cosmos. One can notice that, whenever English is approaching the condition of ideal language, it becomes increasingly empty of denotation, conveys substance and emotion solely by sonorities and measure.

> In health meaning has encroached upon sound. Our intelligence domineers over our senses. But in illness, with the police off duty, we creep beneath some obscure poem by Mallarmé or Donne, some phrase in Latin or Greek, and the words give out their scent and distil their flavour, and then, if at last we grasp the meaning, it is all the richer for having come to us sensually first, by way of the palate and the nostrils, like some queer odour. Foreigners, to whom the tongue is strange, have us at a disadvantage. The Chinese must know the sound of *Antony and Cleopatra* better than we do. (*Essays IV*, p. 200)

We could understand English better if it were meaningless to us; the double nature of words, their split into the sensuous and the referential, is a kind of schism in our experience. Similarly Orlando in his youth sees a performance of *Othello* in which the words are spoken so fast that he cannot understand them; nevertheless "the astonishing, sinuous melody of the words stirred Orlando like music" (p. 57). That is the key to ideal language: it is music, thrilling and pure beyond meaning. However, there is something in this yearning, this legacy from Pater and the aesthetes that is inimical to the novelist's art; why should one bother with the burden of character and scene if the best language is so strictly independent, translunar? But Virginia Woolf was a novelist and faithful to the exigencies of the novel; in the 1930s scarcely a breath of music stirs in her fiction; she toils without complaint in the mire of the objective; she abandons her search for unfallen language. It is somewhat sad; but she never overestimated her abilities. She always recognized that the sign that English was approaching vivification, its long-awaited return to Elizabethan greatness, would be the reappearance of the neologism; and that, she says again and again, is a task beyond her generation; and one will not, I think, find a neologism, scarcely an arcane word, on any page she ever wrote. Her failure, as she understood it, was that she was not a poet; when she writes of poets she is wistful, envious; and in her last works she abandons the semblance of poetic diction, the breathless polysyndeton that she employed when excited, her delightful fantasies of hypotaxis in swollen knots, multiple protasis, Greek grammar.

Greek—not the actual language but what Virginia Woolf in her rhapsodies of partial ignorance took it to be—is not the only ideal language which she ever intuited or conceived, but it is incomparably the most developed. The other alternatives to ideal language are either useful only in special cases or are beyond the realm of literature. One of them has already been discussed, the sign language developed in her 1937 broadcast "Craftsmanship," her fantasy of language reduced to algebraic notation, in which a capital H on top of the figure 3 stands for "Mrs. Jones is not at home" (*Essays II*, p. 47), a language about which she meditated for over a decade. This represents in a sense her recognition that language cannot be ideal, if ideal language consists of these parched symbols out of which all life has been squeezed; indeed it is the demonic antithesis of Greek, for instead of rich words which are self-sufficient, self-defining, self-propagating, by their very sound, we have these unpronounceable shards of typography, all reference, refined entirely out of physical presence. In 1937 real language must necessarily be somewhat soiled, unstable, in the midst of an ugly spawning; and it is not to her discredit that she believed that:

> Royal words mate with commoners. English words marry French words, German words, Indian words, Negro words, if they have a fancy. Indeed, the less we inquire into the past of our dear Mother English the better it will be for that lady's reputation. For she has gone a-roving, a-roving fair maid.
> Thus to lay down any laws for such irreclaimable vagabonds is worse than useless. A few trifling rules of grammar and spelling are all the constraint we can put on them. (*Essays II*, p. 250)

This miscegenation, though it is not moving toward the marmoreal ideality of Greek, is clearly healthy; though the verbal energy expressed here, words scarcely restrainable by grammar, seems more descriptive of the novels she had written ten years ago. Two years later, in 1939, the sign language reappears in the essay "Reviewing," in which critics are directed to affix asterisks and daggers, indicating a positive or negative opinion, instead of endeavouring to explain the reasons for their feelings; again, the sign language is evidence of abnegation of reason, the loss of literacy and humanity alike. Curiously, when she begins to describe her little system she makes a sentence in which a poem is concealed.

> Now the public though crass is not such an ass as to invest seven and sixpence on the advice of a reviewer writing under such conditions; and the public though dull is not such a gull as to believe in the great poets, great novelists, and epoch-making works that are weekly discovered under such conditions. (*Essays II*, p. 209)

It is as if she added a secret grimace, a mockery and example of literary style, a protest against the loss of humane values in essay writing.

Another kind of alternative to ideal language is the cinema. Virginia Woolf's one extended description of the cinema occurs in an essay written in 1926, the very time she was working on *To the Lighthouse*; and, like certain parts of the novel, the essay brims with aesthetic enthusiasm, optimism. She rather disliked the realistic cinema of "Anna Karenina," which she thought a sad attempt to respell the novel in "words of one syllable" (*Essays II*, p. 270), an oversimplified symbolic language in which "A kiss is love. A broken cup is jealousy. A grin is happiness. Death is a hearse." This belief that a language is reprehensible for gross conventionality is redolent of her later contempt for sign language, and a fixed part of her literary sensibility; but insofar as she believes that the realistic cinema is defective for its simplicity, those "words of one syllable," she is merely manifesting the aesthetic sanguinity she felt in the middle of the 1920s, and in five years she will repudiate it entirely. In 1926 everything must be complex, it seems, and intricacy is a measure of quality. What seemed vastly exciting in the cinema was the experimental work, like "The Cabinet of Dr. Caligari":

> At a performance of *Dr. Caligari* the other day a shadow shaped like a tadpole suddenly appeared at one corner of the screen. It swelled to an immense size, quivered, bulged, and sank back again into nonentity. For a moment it seemed to embody some monstrous diseased imagination of the lunatic's brain. For a moment it seemed as if thought could be conveyed by shape more effectively than by words. The monstrous quivering tadpole seemed to be fear itself, and not the statement 'I am afraid'. In fact, the shadow was accidental and the effect unintentional. (*Essays II*, p. 270)

This happy demonstration that blind chance itself is a German expressionist led her to augment the possible vocabulary of this new language:

> Terror has besides its ordinary forms the shape of a tadpole; it burgeons, bulges, quivers, disappears. Anger is not merely rant and rhetoric, red faces and clenched fists. It is perhaps a black line wriggling upon a white sheet. Anna and Vronsky need no longer scowl and grimace. They have at their command—but what? Is there, we ask, some secret language which we feel and see, but never speak, and, if so, could this be made visible to the eye? (*Essays II*, pp. 270–71)

The cinema—it is curiously appropriate that Virginia Woolf's fantasy would be realized in twenty years by Walt Disney—has in its province ideality, that almost unimaginable artistry that achieves the direct transcription of emotion; not the image of emotion, that substitute stuff with which writers content themselves, but emotion brain-vivid, an electroencephalogram. Even Greek was merely sensuous, worldly; here is a language which the eye can apprehend, freed from the rigor and ponderousness of all that is not light.

Yet in some ways all three of these versions of the ideal language are unhelpful and misleading in one's attempts to write novels. It is not good for a writer to feel too acutely the poverty of voice and ear; cinema, like painting, cannot be transcribed unmodified into literature, and offers few clues about the solutions to literary problems. As for sign language, it is the death of literature; and yet formulas somewhat resembling the capital H on top of the figure 3 do exist in the novels; Rhoda's square on the oblong is certainly reminiscent. It seems as if sign language has a genuine ideality before 1937 and the "Craftsmanship" broadcast; it is an extrapolation of certain tendencies, the necessity of schematizing experience, anesthetizing it, making it icy and pure. The sign language of 1937 then is the whole aesthetic theme reduced to grinning skeleton; the aesthetic can go so far that ideogram stiffens into bleached Hs and Os. In *Orlando* there is a remarkable passage, faintly echoing certain parts of book 3 of *Gulliver's Travels*, in which the whole aesthetic and symbolist preoccupation with the reduction of human experience to vivid formulas, much indulged in the previous novels and in *The Waves*, is effectively mocked; this is a fevered telegram that Orlando sends to her hazy lover Shelmerdine:

> "My God Shel," she wired; "life literature Greene toady—" here she dropped into a cypher language which they had invented between them so that a whole spiritual state of the utmost complexity might be conveyed in a word or two without the telegraph

clerk being any the wiser, and added the words "Rattigan Glumphoboo," which summed it up precisely. For not only had the events of the morning made a deep impression on her, but it cannot have escaped the reader's attention that Orlando was growing up—which is not necessarily growing better—and "Rattigan Glumphoboo" described a very complicated spiritual state—which if the reader puts all his intelligence at our service he may discover for himself. (Pp. 282–83)

So much for the distortion of language into expressive form; *life* is the favorite vague word of Virginia Woolf's early career, and its appearance in the telegram is deliberate self-parody. It is much better to use soiled common language than to become absurd; *Orlando* is the first major work after the linguistic bravura of *To the Lighthouse*, and it signals the beginning of the new style. There is another passage in *Orlando*, which is in effect a renunciation of onomatopoeic language, after which Greek ideality will never be sought again:

At last, however, she drew up at Marshall & Snelgrove's and went into the shop. Shade and scent enveloped her. The present fell from her like drops of scalding water. Light swayed up and down like thin stuffs puffed out by a summer breeze. She took a list from her bag and began reading in a curious still voice at first as if she were holding the words—boy's boots, bath salts, sardines —under a tap of many-coloured water. She watched them change as the light fell on them. Bath and boots became blunt, obtuse; sardines serrated itself like a saw. (Pp. 299–300)

The ideality of Greek could only be supported in a world in which objects themselves are beautiful; Sophocles' work is an entwining of nightingales, olive trees, stars, and ocean, things as lyrical and dramatic in themselves as they are when uttered. But if English approaches the uncanny vivacity of Greek, it only makes English all the more loathsome, for the modern world consists of sardines and boots. When the word *boot* turns boot-shaped it kicks you in the teeth; the scales of the word *sardine* grate your skin before the fish swims away. Between 1922, when the essay on Greek was written, and 1928, the year of *Orlando*, a great revulsion against the corporeal world has begun, of which the whole of *Orlando* is a symptom; and that stench, sexual acridity, infects the ideal and the real alike. Up to *To the Lighthouse* language is joyous, detergent, purifying; but in the later works, why should the corpse of the twentieth century be wound in language less angular and pustulant than itself?

The problem of language after 1928, though, is not that English words have ugly sounds, or even that they refer to ugly things, but that they refer to unknowable things. The author of *Jacob's Room*, like the author of *Orlando*, informed the reader that she was complicit in a scheme wherein the huge iridescent film of language would surround an unknown core, the character of Jacob; and in the later novels the elaborately painted surface is increasingly weather-beaten and peeled. In *To the Lighthouse* the grammatically inflected world of part 1, so fluent and ornate, is juxtaposed against the speechless night of part 2; and in *The Waves* the characters each must confront the poverty of their orderly and articulated visions against the abjectness and heavy clamor of the solid world below. As the universe of Virginia Woolf's discourse becomes increasingly splendid and chryselephantine, it becomes increasingly irrelevant to the world of primary appetites; the great novels are highly fissured between the world that is all language and the substantial world in which language and civilization are invalid. Language ascends into heaven but Virginia Woolf remains below, mourning the absence of beauty. *The Waves* is a magnificent cry from a woman who has discovered she is consummate mistress of illusion, who can make words obey her every command even though words can neither describe, communicate, nor sound alone. Everywhere is plainsong and lament for human speech. Characters who would gladly talk to each other must instead turn to the audience and soliloquize; characters who would cling to language for structure and support find that language impels them all the faster toward the cataract. The six personages of *The Waves* fall into three pairs, each of which has similar needs and similar speech. The first pair, Louis and Rhoda, have found the world most intolerable and have defended a small perimeter with all conceivable forms of armor; they are creatures of the core for whom language offers little or no succor, its ability to impose grammar onto reality being clearly too weak. When Rhoda says " 'Like' and 'like' and 'like'—but what is the thing that lies beneath the semblance of the thing?" she is recognizing that all language is necessarily simile, a remote and awkward analogue to the real, offering neither illumination nor foothold. The second pair, Susan and Neville, also find experience far too immediate, chaotic, disturbing, and devise elaborate ritual by which sexual pain can be distanced from the self, emotion anesthetized. In the case of Neville, he retreats into language, even as a small boy:

> "Each tense," said Neville, "means differently. There is an order in this world; there are distinctions, there are differences in this world, upon whose verge I step. For this is only a beginning."
> (P. 188)

It is unlikely that his hope is realized; despite Latin declension, the world remains undeclined; despite Latin conjugation, Neville's remarkable will to be faithful seems thwarted. Neville is the least distinct of the six, possibly because his homosexuality necessitated discretion, but even so he lacks most of the apparatus of *leitmotif* by which the others are characterized; his typical phrase has an opening door and the entrance of the beloved, but this figure is also used for Jinny, and more noticeably for Louis, who is like Neville scholarly, poetical, intolerant of ambiguity. But if Neville and Louis still show vestiges of the indeterminate rock out of which both are hewn, it is only a presage of the ultimate unity of the six characters, a trace of the root out of which the six flower. With Jinny and Bernard we come to a world much more tolerable and enchantable than the worlds of the previous pairs; their environment is apt and responsive to their needs, and can be bewitched by Jinny's flickering body, the very opposite of Rhoda's, and by the phrases of Bernard, for whom language is less inadequate than for any other artist in Virginia Woolf's fiction.

The case of Bernard is the last great test of verbal artifice. Here is language given every opportunity to succeed, in the hands of a master for whom language can accomplish whatever it is asked. As an infant Bernard is clever enough that his phrases allow him to escape the oppressive and possibly painful intimacy of Susan's nascent femininity. The world is rendered point for point into Bernard's unobtrusive prose, a set of covering abstractions that bring the world under the human control of Bernard's knuckle.

> Now the awful portals of the station gape; 'the moon-faced clock regards me.' I must make phrases and phrases and so interpose something hard between myself and the stare of housemaids, the stare of clocks, staring faces, indifferent faces, or I shall cry.
> (P. 195)

What more could anyone ask of language? But it is not enough; there is something undesirable about this insulation from parlous reality; language has given us what we asked, but we did not want its gifts after all. Bernard old has discovered the aridity, the rarefaction, of that kind of human life which takes place in stories, itself a story. It is better to venture, even if gingerly, into that world in which tea can burn the tongue, hard seats hurt the back, without the cushion of phrase and story. So at the end of the novel he hunts out things in themselves, though they be common and innocuous, and, like old Prospero, or old George Herbert, or old Yeats, he casts away his book of phrases:

> My book, stuffed with phrases, has dropped to the floor. It lies under the table to be swept up by the charwoman when she comes wearily at dawn looking for scraps of paper, old tram tickets, and

here and there a note screwed into a ball and left with the litter to be swept up. What is the phrase for the moon? And the phrase for love? By what name are we to call death? I do not know. I need a little language such as lovers use, words of one syllable such as children speak when they come into the room and find their mother sewing and pick up some scrap of bright wool, a feather, or a shred of chintz. I need a howl; a cry. (P. 381)

This is the last form of ideal language, what Bernard calls "little language"; and, with a few additions of vocabulary and grammar, the speech of the books after *The Waves* tries to approximate this language at the moments of intensity, just as the earlier novels tried to approximate Greek. There is nothing limpid or transparent about little language; it does not try to mime or project a world; it lacks human reference too, and it is wholly impersonal; it is the racial cry, sexless, unappeasable, without object or intent, like the cry in "Three Pictures," a generalized response to the general and concrete pain of existence. The intricate phantoms of the working mind, and the poetical phrases which try to seize and control experience, are dismissed; what is real is the howl, the uninflected release of tension. Little language is the speech of the body, hideous but inevitable, as is shown by a light essay written at the same time as *The Waves*, "On Being Ill":

Finally, to hinder the description of illness in literature, there is the poverty of the language. English, which can express the thoughts of Hamlet and the tragedy of Lear, has no words for the shiver and the headache. It has all grown one way. The merest schoolgirl, when she falls in love, has Shakespeare or Keats to speak her mind for her—but let a sufferer try to describe a pain in his head to a doctor and language at once runs dry. There is nothing ready made for him. He is forced to coin words himself, and, taking his pain in one hand, and a lump of pure sound in the other (as perhaps the people of Babel did in the beginning), so to crush them together that a brand new work in the end drops out. Probably it will be something laughable. For who of English birth can take liberties with the language? To us it is a sacred thing and therefore doomed to die, unless the Americans, whose genius is so much happier in the making of new words than in the disposition of the old, will come to our help and set the springs aflow. Yet it is not only a new language that we need, more primitive, more sensual, more obscene, but a new hierarchy of the passions; love must be deposed in favour of a temperature of 104; jealousy give place to the pangs of sciatica. (*Essays IV*, pp. 194–95)

There is even in this passage a hint of a myth about the origin of language; at the beginning of language is the naked vowel, a lump of inarticulate sound, a point-blank expression of pain; and presumably our modern tongues are therefore howls grown feeble with notation and cracked by grammar, but still howls. The body, according to this essay, is as subtle as the soul, and one can translate love into fever, emotion into the body's diseased language; the themes are treated deftly and with humor, but the new primacy of body and brute instead of the phantasmagoria of emotion forecasts the whole direction of her imagination.

The language of the later novels is not especially primitive or vigorous, although she does applaud meaty language in other people's fiction; an early example of this is in an essay on American fiction, written in 1925, in which she implores American novelists to use "little American words" (*Essays II*, p. 113), to talk to men in Chicago barrooms. Yet it is clear in the later novels that standard scholarly English is effete, as in Edward Pargiter of *The Years*:

> The past and poetry, he said to himself, that's what I want to talk about, he thought. He wanted to say it aloud. But Edward was too formed and idiosyncratic—too black and white and linear, with his head tilted up on the back of his chair, to ask him questions easily. (P. 408)

Edward is himself all words, a printed page set in some difficult-to-read typeface. To be so verbalized, by the 1930s, is sinister, an emblem of Edward's regressive unreality; to live in words is to live in clouds, like the unfortunate Dr. Burney of the essay "Dr. Burney's Evening Party," who "seems to melt away at last in a cloud of words" (*Essays III*, p. 134). Near the climax of *The Years* the younger generation, the brave new world in infancy, breaks out into song:

> Fanno to par, etto to mar,
> Timin tudo, tido,
> Foll to gar in, mitno to par,
> Eido, tedo, meido—

They sang the second verse more fiercely than the first. The rhythm seemed to rock and the unintelligible words ran themselves together almost into a shriek. The grown-up people did not know whether to laugh or to cry. Their voices were so harsh; the accent was so hideous. (P. 438)

This is presumably a school song, the tutoring of the old bankrupt race; but the instinctive children have converted it into little language, syllables too simple to be English or Italian or Japanese, a private cacophony. This, like the contest of the trombone and soprano on Sara Pargiter's street, is the future; the wordless shriek. An old woman sings an old sentimental song rendered into toothless and tongueless nonsense in the middle of *Mrs. Dalloway*, but that is optimistic by comparison, a shining-forth of a blank forgotten spring through anile incompetence, the world of mutability. In *The Years* we can barely guess what reign of terror or enforced peace will be imposed by that chorus when it reaches maturity; but we may be sure that the old human values, the difficult wisdom of the race, the British Museum, will perish utterly along with the language in which they were conceived. In *Between the Acts* some of the old habits of language from the 1920s are resurrected for a moment, but that novel too, when it reaches certain moments of heightened perception, abandons language entirely in favor of random expressive noises, the howl. Here the old devices which used to glorify language are turned into mockery; for instance, the stream of solid words that issue from the mouth reappears, not as in *Jacob's Room* but with the exact satirical intent of *A Tale of a Tub*: "Her words peppered the audience as with a shower of hard little stones" (p. 78). And there appears, for one last moment, a hint of the landscape blazoned and drenched with human speech that we remember from *To the Lighthouse*:

> The nurses after breakfast were trundling the perambulator up and down the terrace; and as they trundled they were talking—not shaping pellets of information or handing ideas from one to another, but rolling words, like sweets on their tongues; which, as they thinned to transparency, gave off pink, green, and sweetness. (P. 10)

But there is a new tone of something akin to self-parody, an impressive, luminous but finally trivial comparison, words reduced to cellophane unreality. The true attitude toward words is simply stated by the narrator when the Rev. Streatfield begins his pontification:

> He opened his mouth. O Lord, protect and preserve us from words the defilers, from words the impure! What need have we of words to remind us? Must I be Thomas, you Jane? (P. 190)

Words are not only inadequate; they are corruptive. Must you falsify me by giving me a name? It is an affront to the dignity of our pain that it is bent and smoothed into literature. Surely the whole drama of Miss La Trobe is nothing but dim outrage and jest; and counterpointed to its rickety and inexpressive articulation is the eloquence of the cows. When Queen Elizabeth boasts that Shakespeare sang for her, a cow moos at the mention of that sanctified name. When the landscape at sunset seems to say, like the eighteenth-century skit in the foreground, that reason prevails, the cows step forward, "saying the same thing to perfection" (p. 134). And when the story of Sir Lilyliver and Lady Harraden is interrupted by a technical breakdown, dispelling the theatrical illusion, the cows chime in with the most sincere, affecting, one might even say human, emotion expressed in the entire pageant:

> Then suddenly, as the illusion petered out, the cows took up the burden. One had lost her calf. In the very nick of time she lifted her great moon-eyed head and bellowed. All the great moon-eyed heads laid themselves back. From cow after cow came the same yearning bellow. The whole world was filled with dumb yearning. It was the primeval voice sounding loud in the ear of the present moment. Then the whole herd caught the infection. Lashing their tails, blobbed like pokers, they tossed their heads high, plunged and bellowed, as if Eros had planted his dart in their flanks and goaded them to fury. The cows annihilated the gap; bridged the distance; filled the emptiness and continued the emotion.
> (Pp. 140–41)

This is the littlest possible language, this dumb bellow; it is compelling, absolute, ineluctable; and if it too is illusion, like the sad rain that weeps for human suffering, like the giant ear that hears human prayer, it is because our race is so exhausted that there is nothing left to express. The voice on the loudspeaker that gives the true explanation of the pageant, the final laceration, claims to speak, like Bernard, in "words of one syllable" (p. 189); but this attempt at impersonal language, little language, breaks down through mechanical failure too. If *The Years* bequeathes the future to the puzzling and monstrous children who gladly destroy our language, *Between the Acts* lets the future fall by default to cow, swallow, grasshopper, whatever can lurch through or crawl around or fly above the heaps of broken metal, whose howls and stridulations are so much more potent than our own.

And yet, Virginia Woolf is not helpless, bereft of power, even in the hooting and chirping world that will remain in the postliterate era; her first work after *The Waves* has at its affective center a dog, Flush. The theoretical constructions of *Flush* are identical to those of *The Years*, or *Between the Acts*, or the last pages of *The Waves*, but the tone is opposite to that of the later novels, suggesting that, even in the world in which eyes glow, throats clatter, in exterior night, one can find an inkling of joy. For Virginia Woolf in the 1930s, as for Matthew Arnold in "Empedocles on Etna," the human mind is a preposterous fiction, a spectral labyrinth of thought and emotion effaced by the first breath of air:

> Hot, I repeat; and doubt if I'm a poet. *H. P.* hard labour. Brain w—no, I can't think of the word—yes, wilts. An idea. All writers are unhappy. The picture of the world in books is thus too dark.

> The wordless are the happy; women in cottage gardens. (*A Writer's Diary*, p. 332)

This is from the black diary of 1940; I assume that *H.P.* is a fatigued transposition of *P.H.*, *Pointz Hall*, the first title of *Between the Acts*. It seems as if her brain is burning out from stress before our eyes; and yet, as long as illiteracy is possible, human happiness is not excluded. That Virginia Woolf could not enter this promised land, this blessed wordlessness, is clear; her explanation of her suicide was that it was a defense against inevitable insanity, and so she died rather than receive the embrace of the irrational, the oversimple. And yet, *Flush* is proof that real illiteracy was not beyond her imaginative sympathy; and she explored this strict mindlessness with something akin to delight. Flush is, above all her other protagonists, happy; and, what is more astonishing, Flush is a character whose integrity, old-fashioned definition, surpasses that of any other she describes. Like the body shown in the essay "On Being Ill," the dog is nearly as subtle, flexible, and responsive as the intricate human mind; and the dog has many advantages over the human. Flush's brain is incapable of ratiocination, but his affection, like his nose, is far keener than any man's; the delicate situation of Robert Browning's courtship of Elizabeth, its fever pitch restrained and stiffened into trembling household formality, is perfectly lucid to Flush's sensibility; and he is the affective center of the book. Something of the heart-brain split, developed on the last page of *Mrs. Dalloway* to explain the contrast between Clarissa and Septimus, is to be found in *Flush*; Flush is the sane heart, Elizabeth Barrett is the ghostly and somewhat depraved intelligence, floating into unhealthy spiritualism as the book ends. On the last page of *Flush* it is explained that dog and woman are complementary: "each, perhaps, completed what was dormant in the other" (p. 108); Bernard has an ape inside him, Isa Oliver a vixen, but Elizabeth Barrett has Flush, a more independent projection of her physical being. Elizabeth is prudish, Flush is a father while scarcely out of puppyhood; Elizabeth is restrained, Flush spontaneous; Elizabeth can write and speak, Flush is illiterate. But this inability is his great strength; since his brain is not smothered in cerebral cortex Flush can see the real light, touch his paws to an earth that is moister, more tangible, than any ever felt by human foot.

> . . . there are no more than two words and perhaps one-half for what we smell. The human nose is practically non-existent. The greatest poets in the world have smelt nothing but roses on the one hand, and dung on the other. The infinite gradations that lie between are unrecorded. Yet it was in the world of smell that Flush

mostly lived. Love was chiefly smell; form and colour were smell; music and architecture, law, politics and science were smell. (P. 88)

The human mind and the human nose are alike gross and incompetent in their categorization; the mindless animal perceives the plenitude of things, the rainbow from infrared past ultraviolet; its science is the immediacy of its own perception.

> Upon the infinitely sensitive pads of his feet he took the clear stamp of proud Latin inscriptions. In short, he knew Florence as no human being has ever known it; as Ruskin never knew it or George Eliot either. He knew it as only the dumb know. Not a single one of his myriad sensations ever submitted itself to the deformity of words. (P. 89)

The dialectic of the aesthete and the realist here reaches its point of maximum spread: while Elizabeth Barrett explores the most delicate refinements of unreality, Flush is the unconceiving and inconceivable realist. Words would only annihilate the perfection of his vision. When his coat is clipped to rid him of fleas he feels for a moment "emasculated, diminished, ashamed" (p. 91); but finally he rejoices to be free from this minimal encumbrance of the aesthetic—the coat by which he was prized by human connoisseurs. Flush's proper estate is this extremity of nakedness, objectivity; his nakedness and his spontaneity are the badges of his integrity, an integrity far more compact and well-defined than any possible to human beings, who are necessarily mixed and blurred.

Flush, however, has not attained a condition of utter happiness; if his mistress and the reader might well look upon him with envy, he, according to an irresistible reciprocity, must feel envy in return for the human:

> But though it would be pleasant for the biographer to infer that Flush's life in late middle age was an orgy of pleasure transcending all description; to maintain that while the baby day by day picked up a new word and thus removed sensation a little further beyond reach, Flush was fated to remain for ever in a Paradise where essences exist in their utmost purity, and the naked soul of things presses on the naked nerve—it would not be true.... But Flush had lain upon human knees and heard men's voices. His flesh was veined with human passions; he knew all grades of jealousy, anger and despair. (Pp. 89–90)

Flush has been fully educated in human habits; human emotions, refined away from the health of the primary appetites, are more corrosive than fleas. When Flush returns to London, he hears some ominous doggy gossip—for dogs have their own telepathic language

—that Carlyle's dog Nero has committed suicide by jumping out the window; and the dry perfume of human emotion seems to be attractive and corruptive beyond any bounds to the kingdom of dogs. Not only can dogs emulate human despair, but they are susceptible to envy for their master's literacy:

> When he saw Miss Barrett's thin hands delicately lifting some
> silver box or pearl ornament from the ringed table, his own furry
> paws seemed to contract and he longed that they should fine
> themselves to ten separate fingers. When he heard her low voice
> syllabling innumerable sounds, he longed for the day when his
> own rough roar would issue like hers in the little simple sounds
> that had such mysterious meaning. And when he watched the same
> fingers for ever crossing a white page with a straight stick, he
> longed for the time when he too should blacken paper as she did.
> (P. 26)

Language has despoiled the world and laid human experience to waste; yet from the dog's perspective this kind of language is mysterious, glamorous. The human race may have evolved into nothing but needles and boils, but nevertheless Flush envies those ten long, prehensile fingers. Dogs know their small territory better than any man will ever know anything, but the kingdom of the human, insipid and cloudy though it may be, is vastly extensive in space and time, through the febrile linkups of letter and telegram, through the compelling documentation that comprises history.

Thorough exploration of the bestial leads one to a new appreciation of the human. Perhaps someday an intelligent critic will find subtlety and merit in Miss La Trobe's unforgivable play, though the soul of Virginia Woolf will find no consolation in our approval, in our eagerness to give praise and pardon. The characters about whom she writes are undefined, some would even say unreal; but she has, in *Mrs. Dalloway*, in *Orlando*, in *Flush*, in *Between the Acts*, extended as significantly as any writer of the twentieth century the boundaries of the human character. We know from her diary that at times she thought herself as fuzzy and ill-defined as any of the characters; she worries that her multitude of styles do not cohere, even says at one point, "I'm 20 people" (*A Writer's Diary*, p. 33); yet surely a novelist can well afford to be even more than twenty people, for much of what seems to be inchoateness is simply the twisted form which human sympathy takes in the twentieth century.

One of her most profound inquiries into the nature of literary characterization is found in her paper of 1924, "Mr. Bennett and Mrs. Brown." She confesses that the characters of books are typically derived from idle musing about someone unknown to the novelist whom he sees by chance, for instance in a railroad car; from an old lady sitting across the carriage one can infer an occupation, a past, a family, a situation which necessitates a trip; and this mass of nacreous inference is the raw material of a novel. This situation is borrowed exactly from the early short story, "An Unwritten Novel," and it will appear again in *The Waves*, when Bernard meditates about a man in a railway carriage whom he calls Walter J. Trumble. It is not enough for a novelist, in the standard English fashion, to make Mrs. Brown into a "character," to "bring out her oddities and mannerism; her buttons and wrinkles" (*Essays I*, p. 325), nor is it enough to describe with the unwearying superficial eye of Arnold Bennett her clothes and probable class; the novelist must attend to something deeper, the old lady in herself. "Mrs. Brown is eternal, Mrs. Brown is human nature" (*Essays I*, p. 330):

> You should insist that she is an old lady of unlimited capacity and infinite variety; capable of appearing in any place; wearing any dress; saying anything and doing heaven knows what. But the things she says and the things she does and her eyes and her nose and her speech and her silence have an overwhelming fascination, for she is, of course, the spirit we live by, life itself. (*Essays I*, pp. 336–37)

This is the doctrine of the rigid core of identity, like Mrs. Ramsay's wedge, or, more precisely, the paleolithic hag of *Mrs. Dalloway*; but it is also a firm reminder that the literary artist is dealing with something inviolable and objective which he must respect. The object of his fidelity, however, is not outside himself; it is not strictly the old lady; instead it is his vision of the old lady, about whom he in fact knows nothing. This is Virginia Woolf's solution to a major paradox of modern fiction: on one hand, characterization is a form of reference to the human exterior; on the other hand, there is nothing in the novel which refers to anything but the equable and impalpable personality of the novelist. For Virginia Woolf, stray passersby give her the clues by which she can split off and project various aspects of herself. This is true, she says, even of such a master of typed and quirky characters as Dickens:

> above all some gigantic and dominating figure, so stuffed and swollen with life that he does not exist singly and solitarily, but seems to need for his own realization a host of others, to call into existence the severed parts that complete him. (*Essays I*, p. 193)

But the more of oneself that is farced into any given character, the less sternly outlined and defined that character becomes. At times Mrs. Woolf could find this indefiniteness relaxing; a certain loss of the rigors of identity can cause tranquillity; and once she stated, in her essay "On Being Ill," that self-multiplicity is in fact the highest human joy: heaven.

> Heaven-making must be left to the imagination of the poets. Without their help we can but trifle—imagine Pepys in Heaven, adumbrate little interviews with celebrated people on tufts of thyme, soon fall into gossip about such of our friends as have stayed in Hell, or, worse still, revert again to earth and choose, since there is no harm in choosing, to live over and over, now as man, now as woman, as sea-captain, or court lady, as Emperor or farmer's wife, in splendid cities and on remote moors, at the time of Pericles or Arthur, Charlemagne or George the Fourth—to live and live till we have lived out those embryo lives which attend about us in early youth until 'I' suppressed them. But 'I' shall not, if wishing can alter it, usurp Heaven too, and condemn us, who have played our parts here as William or Alice, to remain William or Alice for ever. Left to ourselves we speculate thus carnally.
> (*Essays IV*, p. 199)

What a pleasure, to be man or woman, knight or country maid; it is the disquieting carnal joy of *Orlando*. It is personality swollen and conglomerated into paradise. Who am I?—the cry comes from the sickbed; from the British Museum; from the undulation of land and sea. I am everybody; I am Virginia Woolf.

F O U R

There is every reason to trust one's impression that Mann's fiction is the kingdom of the tangible. Where else does verbal assertion so convince, the depth of reference so compel? Here all things abide: nourishing food will always be served on thick china; the books are too learned and heavy to be removed from the bookcase; the paternal hand is laid firmly on the questionable child's shoulder; most appointments will be observed punctually, despite the imminent liquidation of the firm. It is useless to suggest that Mann's weightiness is inflexible, useless to point out that his India consists of Germany with stone temples, his Egypt of Germany with palm trees; if Mann is inflexible it is because mountain and plain permit little distortion; if he is monotonous it is an indictment of human life itself. Mann's first desire as an author is to create the feeling of heft, not just in his furniture but in his characters, in the very words that he employs. Before anything else his characters are sturdy handicrafts, as if carved rigorously by a German artisan in some dense and impermeable wood. At the end of his foreword to the English edition of *Joseph and his Brothers*, Mann asks himself whether his immense novel will survive, or whether it will be relegated to the antiquarians; foolish doubt; Mann is perfectly confident that *Joseph* is "good, solid work," informed by human fellow-feeling, durable, immortal. As for his language, Mann has the ability to impart climactic emphasis perhaps beyond any other novelist of his time; when Naphta utters the long-delayed word *terror*, when Huia laughs about the castration of his son, when the Devil tells Leverkühn the six words which best embody hell, the effect on the reader is comparable to that of the boulders of the Lestrygonians. Mann is above all the master of gravity; and because the elephant that supports the world has his feet

198

so firmly planted on the back of the turtle, the reader feels well-oriented, basically secure. But Atlas in this case may not be so trustworthy as he appears; his finest shocks and best jokes obtain not from his amazing strength but from unexpected lightness and imbalance; one suspects that the weight is cunningly established only so that the sudden vertigo may be more intense; and if Lübeck and Munich and Switzerland, all those countries which Mann seems to have raised up in brick single-handedly on the face of literary Europe, were revealed to be the pasteboard and balsa props of an ethical fantasy, if the ponderousness of personality were to flash at an instant into froth and flame, we might suspect that Mann is not only the Hans Sachs of the novel but its major innovator, and that the last works of this long-suffering public man may be the first books of that literature of the future to which, in converging paths, Nabokov, Borges, and perhaps the young American Thomas Pynchon are leading us.

Mann was fond of claiming that the work of his maturity and old age was an organic growth, hidden and sleeping in the work of his youth, just as he attributed almost everything he believed true of Goethe's career to his own; it is, of course, inconceivable that a writer could exist to whom such a statement would not apply, but Mann's insistence suggests that his early work was a conscious source and treasure trove for the remarkable developments of his later years. In the stories written around the turn of the century and in *Buddenbrooks* we become aware of two distinct methods by which Mann creates and organizes characters, two distinct narrative modes: the first is in the tradition of continental realism, redolent of Maupassant and Tolstoy, those parodists of the objective; the second is more fantastic and introspective, owing much to the already extensive *Bildungsroman*. This is the analysis that Mann himself made in the American preface to *Royal Highness*; he speaks of two styles, the naturalistic and the ideational (p. vii). On one hand human character is defined by gesture, facial description, idiosyncrasy; on the other hand character is reticent, without the strict peculiarity of the individual, probing, self-experimental. In the early works Mann had not always successfully learned how to coordinate these two modes, the puppet show, the narrative meat, the plot motion, and the depiction of the naive or indeterminate soul. That Mann eventually did learn how to do this, learn it as well as anyone ever has, goes without saying; but even in his later life his awareness of the difference of these modes and the difficulty of integration remains. For example, in his detailed account of the writing of *Dr. Faustus* Mann points out that from the introduction of Marie Godeau on, the novel becomes "more and more novelistic, that is to say, dramatic" (*Story of a Novel*, p. 206), a story of love, jealousy, intrigue and murder; one assumes that the "novelistic" is opposed to the biographical elements of the earlier parts of the book, the formation of Leverkühn's ambiguous soul, the description of personality. One might say that the "novelistic" is the domain of static characters, while the biographical, the *Bildungsroman*, is the domain of developing characters; this is generally true, but it must not be assumed that Mann's magnificent infants, Hanno Buddenbrook, Tonio Kröger, the *Wunderkind*, the Felix Krull of 1911, are meant to develop toward a state of high contour and individuation, adult stasis. These superb children and their many brothers and cousins, who are perhaps the chief delight of Mann's early fiction, do not harden into quirky and brittle adulthood; their faces will never turn blotched and red; their heads will never nod uncontrollably; their eyes will not goggle nor their lips drool; the reader will never learn to recognize them instantly through some astonishing grimace; and the sad paraphernalia of bodily decay, Mann's chief apparatus of "novelistic" characterization, will never approach their lovely vague features. In the early years, before World War I, Mann is quite careful never to let his prodigies attain much age: Hanno dies, Felix is abandoned, Tonio grows into an enchanted maturity that is little more than a gifted boy's dream of an adulthood as promising and emotive as infancy. Mann's own maturity can be correlated directly to his ability to bring one of the blessed children past puberty; and Mann reaches his sixties before he is able to let one of them, Joseph, attain middle-age. Even so Mann discovers he is reluctant to expose his youthful beauties, whose potentiality so exceeds any possible accomplishment, to the necessary definitions and strictures of human mortality: "I myself confess that I have found it more enjoyable to talk about the charming seventeen-year-old lad or even about the thirty-year-old man than about one hovering round fifty-five" (*Joseph*, p. 1172); and although he could at the very end of his life bring Felix Krull into his deft and incomparable adolescence, the novel was abandoned a second time, and the depiction of the weary Felix who is the ostensible autobiographer was left forever undone.

There are, then, two races of characters, the hard and the soft; the subtle and the crustacean, if it is permissible to use the categories of Protos in Gide's *Lafcadio's Adventures*, a book most curiously related to certain aspects of *Felix Krull*. The hard characters wear badges of identification; when Mann, in his essay on the making of *The Magic Mountain*, speaks of the *leitmotif* "as Tolstoy and Zola use it, or as I used it myself in *Buddenbrooks*, naturalistically and as a means of characterization—so to speak, mechanically" (*Magic Mountain*,

p. 723), he means these distinctive traits, amusing or grotesque, endearing or demonic. Several times a character becomes so·encrusted in these that he becomes, so to speak, trait-bound, automatic, incapable of freeing himself for an instant from spasm, blinking, and shrug, and therefore genuinely self-less, meaningless; such a character is Herr Kesselmeyer in *Buddenbrooks*, the vicious lawyer who bankrupts Herr Grünlich, Tony Buddenbrook's first husband. Kesselmeyer is defined, overdefined, by his "Ah ha!"s, his mobile rodent's-mouth, the peculiar accents of his speech, his alarming laughter, the sinister gaiety of his grimaces; but his vileness is thoroughly undermined, even forgiven, by his helpless automatism; he seems "irresistibly comic" (p. 156), and we feel that any drama of such puppets as he, even if the plot is tragic, must be a comedy. Yet it is not as far as it would appear from such apes as Kesselmeyer to the more important actors of *Buddenbrooks*. Shortly after his introduction Kesselmeyer goes into a fit of laughter when Tony blurts out Grünlich's weak excuse for his financial problems, that Tony is ruining him by her extravagance; Grünlich repeats irritably "She is very luxuriously inclined":

> Tony did not contradict him. She leaned calmly back, her hands in her lap on the velvet ribbons of her frock and her pert upper lip in evidence: 'Yes, I am, I know. I have it from Mamma. All the Krögers are fond of luxury.'
> She would have admitted in the same calm way that she was frivolous, revengeful, or quick-tempered. Her strongly developed family sense was instinctively hostile to conceptions of free will and self-development; it inclined her rather to recognize and accept her own characteristics wholesale, with fatalistic indifference and toleration. She had, unconsciously, the feeling that any trait of hers, no matter of what kind, was a family tradition and therefore worthy of respect. (P. 157)

It is as if the representation of a character as strained and exaggerated as Kesselmeyer persuaded Mann that it was time to introduce a brief explanation of his usual technique. Tony Buddenbrook is a character of substance and charm, the major female character of an extremely long novel; and yet her self-acceptance is a perfect image of the rigid nature with which Mann has imbued her. Even those traits that are implicit rather than explicit in her self-description, her complacency, vanity, and fairness, are invariant from her infancy to her middle age. Hard characters, even the gentlest and most winning, are fully formed, set, in the womb; in no world could Tony Buddenbrook have evaded that fate which she attempted with such seeming decisiveness to evade, her marriage with Grünlich; her imagination was too weak, her sense of possibility and potentiality too impoverished, to allow her the plasticity, even the will to break seriously with her pre-determined self.

One of the attributes of the bourgeoisie, according to Mann, is this belief in the invariance and familial likeness of the child's soul; indeed Tonio Kröger was raised in the same faith as Tony Buddenbrook:

> His thoughts at times would run something like this: "It is true enough that I am what I am and will not and cannot alter: heedless, self-willed, with my mind on things nobody else thinks of. And so it is right they should scold and punish me and not smother things all up with kisses and music. After all, we are not gypsies living in a green wagon; we're respectable people, the family of Consul Kröger." And not seldom he would think: "Why is it I am different, why do I fight everything, why am I at odds with the masters and like a stranger among the other boys? The good scholars, and the solid majority—they don't find the masters funny, they don't write verses, their thoughts are all about things that people do think about and can talk about out loud. How regular and comfortable they must feel, knowing that everybody knows just where they stand! It must be nice! But what is the matter with me, and what will be the end of it all?" (*Stories I*, p. 160)

Tonio too, when young, regards himself as immutable; but instead of Tony Buddenbrook's perfect self-acceptance, dimpled self-content, Tonio rages against the scandalousness of his own identity. It is the envy of the plastic for the rigid; Tonio is radically undefined—he can scarcely formulate himself beyond the divine "I am what I am"—so he yearns for the simple joys of definition, wishes his soul were not so fluid and ambiguous that it leaks out of those stern molds regarded as proper by fathers and the public. His friends know just where they stand; but Tonio is alien, a product of an obscure and hybrid generation, and has no perceptible social role whatsoever. It is illuminating to notice those characters whom he loves. Hans Hansen, the blond boy whom he adores at the age of fourteen, is a character in every way limited and compassed, but not by the rigidities of idiosyncrasy. Idiosyncrasy is a kind of disease, a degeneration of nerve and muscle, a condition of tics and tremor; indeed most characters in Mann's work, most of the hard characters, decay into adulthood. Hans, on the other hand, is ideal; and his ideality strictly defines and limits him. In loving Hans, Tonio falls into that pattern of yearning for a different kind of identity which is near the core of Mann's creative imagination; but Hans represents not only the bourgeois, the natural, the brutal, the indifferent, but also a kind of flesh-and-blood, or genetic, art, an aesthetic image; and when Tonio falls in love with him it is under the aspect of the artist's love for the products of his own imagination. Hans may stand for bourgeois and brute; but he is bourgeois and brute elevated into *type*. The personal reference from Mann's own childhood to this affair is well known, and there is something uncomfortable about Hans that the reader may feel in the story; in later life Mann revealed what the source of this discomfort was:

> What to me were his [Nietzsche's] "blond beast" and his phi-
> losophy of force? Almost an embarrassment. His glorification of
> "life" at the expense of mind—that lyricism which turned out so
> disastrously for German thinking—I could assimilate in only one
> way: as self-criticism. True, the blond beast haunts my own
> youthful work; but it is, on the whole, divested of its bestial
> character, there is not much left of it but the blondness and the
> lack of mind. (*Sketch*, p. 23)

Mann in 1930 perceived Hans not as a foretaste of Hitler, but as a foretaste of Hitler's ideal, Hitler's art, the monumental and vapid face of Nazi sculpture, itself wholly innocent but exciting the most remarkable arousal, the itch of Institoris in *Dr. Faustus*. Mann in his maturity missed no opportunity of drawing his reader's attention to the multitude of typal figures in his novels; but, as he always explained if given time, what interested him was the individual's relation to the archetype, not strictly the archetype itself. Characters can become inhuman, unpleasant, by following individuality to the point of Kesselmeyer, or by following typicality to the point of Hans. Mann invests characters with the illusion of full humanity by keeping them suspended between type and individual; this is one reason why his best characters must remain labile, inchoate, able to accomplish difficult transformations of identity, leaps of redefinition. Idiosyncrasy destroys and typicality famishes, but the great openness of self needed to keep oneself in a state of flux between various identities is itself a shock to the system; the chameleon must change not only the color of his skin but the organs of his body as well, must endure convulsions of self-knowledge with a sensibility already much vexed by the ordinary abrasions of childhood. No wonder that Mann's bright children are no healthier than the plebeians; no wonder that Hanno is carried off by typhoid, Tonio roused to despair by his own iciness, his extrahuman indecisiveness.

This does not mean, however, that Mann's problem children are so like each other as to be indistinguishable. It is true that these bland faces unblemished by the asperities of flesh or the sharpness of bone are not visibly distinct from each other; and it is true that they mostly grew up in the same home by the Baltic sea, are clothed in the same incidents and similar friends. Indeed, while the hard characters are unique and incommensurable, atomized, fallen into division—one could make a catalog of stutterers, or the sallow-faced, or the pimpled, or the red-nosed, but that would prove only the paucity of human ailment, not any kinship of character—the soft characters share a secret brotherhood, almost an equivalence, the sympathy of Proteus the eel for Proteus the lion. And yet there is one major criterion which ranks and separates them. Some are outward and others are inward; some concentrate on the surface, others on the depths. The superficial are adored by parents and community; the profound are troubled, reviled, and envious. Hanno Buddenbrook is the most incompetent and profound of all, and the child to whom Mann felt personally the closest. In his *Story of a Novel*, an account of the writing of *Dr. Faustus*, he confesses that "I never loved a creature of my imagination . . . as I did Adrian. The only exception, perhaps, was Hanno Buddenbrook" (p. 88). This hint of a connection between Adrian Leverkühn, the demonish and syphilitic composer of *Dr. Faustus*, and Hanno Buddenbrook, his mother's darling, is perhaps not obvious; yet they are not such remote figures as they seem. They are, first of all, secretive; they face society with hesitation, embarrassment, and failure; Hanno cannot finish his recital, breaks down into girlish tears, wishes to retreat to the kindness of sickbed; Leverkühn, as he grows out his uncomfortable adolescence, retreats increasingly into a simulacrum of childhood, his parents' old farm translated house for house and dog for dog into a well-insulated and harmless habitation. Hanno too is a composer, and his musical education resembles Leverkühn's; he is taught that Bach was more harmonist than polyphonist, and he experiments with invertible melodies in a surprising foreshadowing of Leverkühn's twelve-tone organization. But, most importantly, the spareness and reticence of the exterior are in such characters accompanied by an astonishing proliferation of the interior; it is in meditation, dream, and vision that they live their lives.

These personalities whose tendency is oriented to the interior require little or no gratification from the outside; Hanno, four-and-a-half years old in the politically troubled year 1865, needs nothing more than "a few pebbles, or a stick of wood with a dandelion for a helmet" (p. 338) to organize his internal world. This is not unusual, but very soon his introversion becomes alarming to his family; he is subject to nocturnal fits, in which he sits up suddenly in bed, "stammering incomprehensibly, and staring with wide-open, strange golden-brown eyes into a world which he, and he alone, could see" (p. 358). In the later part of *Buddenbrooks*, the novel becomes less and less occupied by the "novelistic" stuff of Tony Buddenbrook's vicarious "third marriage" and the decay of the family fortune; instead we have Hanno's privacy, the almost unverbalizable world of pure play and abstract fancy. This world finds affinity with music because it is most comfortable with the immaterial and the free; and Hanno at last succeeds in composing music which satisfies him, a long improvisation, in which a "worthless trifle, this scrap of melody" (p. 580), after tentative and painful beginnings, becomes expressive of shrieks of pain, of stormy processions, of flames, castles, and dragons, of the abyss, of fulfillment, of orgy and exultation, at last dying away into sweetness and weariness. Yet in all of this the tiny theme persists; it is, of course, Hanno himself, translated altogether into music out of sad reality, a weak boy who contains folded up in himself all the pang and ecstasy of mortality. It is similar with Adrian Leverkühn, who, in his Apocalypse oratorio, embodies the emotion of his race, the twentieth century; and the narrator can remark of the music, "That is Adrian Leverkuhn. Utterly" (*Dr. Faustus*, p. 379). Such enormous self-utterances nearly exhaust; in Hanno's case, after the great self-translation of his improvisation, he dies immediately. He has become too adept at the suppression of the external, too expert in the invisible.

The character of Hanno Buddenbrook suggests a major problem in the depiction of personality in Mann's novels. For the characters whom he loves best, upon whom so much of his care and attention rests, self-expression is difficult, a violation of their being, and must be oblique if it can exist at all. The motto of *Buddenbrooks* is a simple one, given formula by Thomas Buddenbrook at the turning point of the novel, at which the story of Hanno begins to be the central narrative:

> Often, the outward and visible material signs and symbols of happiness and success only show themselves when the process of decline has already set in. The outer manifestations take time— like the light of that star up there, which may in reality be already quenched, when it looks to us to be shining its brightest.
> (Pp. 332–33)

This is a plot summary of the novel, repeated in the subtitle; and it is a genetic myth that informs Mann's work from the beginning to the end; and it is an analysis of human personality. No one has taken its wisdom to heart more firmly than newborn Hanno: he lets nothing escape from his concentrated interior, except a few tears; and because his private vitality is not exhausted in display, self-revelation, and worldly accomplishment, he keeps himself inviolate, pure. His father Thomas is a man vitiated by self-expression, his lofty will translated coarsely into house and personal finery. In this novel money symbolizes the inner wealth of soul, the viability of enterprise; when money is spent, personal sanity and integrity are exchanged for physical comfort and ostentation. Hanno's self-expression, his improvisation, is designed for his ears alone; he is a perfect miser of the riches of his fantasy. It is precisely because he keeps himself bottled up that his private utterance is so passionate and complete; the source of his volcanism, the first condition of his art, is repression. As he becomes increasingly involved with phantoms of sound and order his body is asked to perform less and less; the body is not an instrument he chooses to play; and finally he deserts it altogether.

One can appreciate Mann's problems in trying to write novels in which characters reveal themselves only at the expense of their self-destruction. Each novel attempts a different solution to this problem; in *The Magic Mountain*, which is the most cunningly designed of Mann's novels, he uses as the matrix of the work the mind of Hans Castorp, a mind as hugely open and receptive as those of his earlier bright children, an almost characterless medium; and through his sensibility the rest of the characters emerge, billow enormously, flaunt themselves until self-exhaustion causes them to dissipate into mist. Then other characters take their places; when Settembrini and Naphta have so talked themselves out that they are fixed and boring even to themselves, Peeperkorn steps forth as a new center of energy, a counterforce, only to grow big and himself merge into the dissolute natural world. So it is with the other novels too: a point is reached at which the sustaining characters have extinguished themselves in the fury of their self-revelation, and if the novel is to reach its appointed end a new and brilliant, contrasting character must enter the cast. In the preface to *Joseph* Mann admits he had exhausted his stock of female characters by the time of *Joseph the Provider*, and was delighted to discover that he had one after all, Tamar, the "most amazing figure in this whole story" (p. xii), whose ambiguous and vital presence so animates the last novel in the sequence. *Dr. Faustus* is transfigured by the introduction near the end of the divine child, Nepomuk Schneidewein, and *Felix Krull* by the Kuckuck family; and the first two-thirds of *Lotte in Weimar* is an intricate preamble to the greatest theatrical stroke in Mann's work, the sudden immersion of the narrative into the mind of Goethe.

It is with hesitation that Mann experiments with methods of integrating the demands of an external plot—and no one appreciates good rousing stories more than Mann, whether from family history or fairy tales or even, in the case of Rudolf Schwerdtfeger in *Dr. Faustus*, newspaper clippings—with the difficult entrance into self-revelation of those sensitive and restrained characters who are Mann's pampered favorites. What has the story of the decline of the Buddenbrook family and Tony's marital difficulties to do with Hanno's secret joys and public sorrow? For one thing, there is Mann's genetic myth: as the bourgeois spirit exhausts itself in outward glory, it eventually takes to wife a dark Mediterranean artistic woman, and in their offspring, a difficult male child, the spirit now baffled and frustrated in its descent into matter turns instead to the interior, exfoliates into art. In a general way, then, Hanno's private world is conditioned and informed by the events that have preceded his birth; but the narrative structure is far from mythical, and there is much that is anecdotal, homely, though far from extraneous. It is only in retrospect that Hanno seems of central importance; Mann quite rightly said that Thomas Buddenbrook was the hero of the novel; and it is only because in the later novels the characters who are kin to Hanno have swallowed the objective world that one would wish to inquire about the relation between Hanno's mind and the external family that labored for so many decades to produce it. There is a clue that links the method of Mann's later works with the method of *Buddenbrooks*. Young Hanno receives for Christmas, at his own request, a toy theater. It is magical, the realization of his highest dreams. It is almost more beautiful than a full-sized theater; it is ever so much more beautiful than real life. The stage is set for the last act of *Fidelio*, the moment at which the trumpet is about to announce freedom for the democrat Florestan. The episode is not prominent, but it has great resonance in Mann's imagination; in the story "The Dilettante," written just before this section of *Buddenbrooks*, the Dilettante tells how he spent much of his childhood drawing and cutting out little puppet-figures in operatic costumes, conducting whole opera performances in his puppet theater, imitating horns, clarinets, and flutes with his own voice, exhausting himself in these solitary excesses. This scene is a metaphor for the whole story, for the Dilettante's life is a futile attempt to satisfy himself through the motions of his own imagination, to lead a life of exquisite private sensation rather than human society. It is one of many stories that Mann wrote about the calamity of the aesthetic life; the Dilettante is the ordinary man who tries to imitate the life of genius, what Hanno Buddenbrook might have come to if he had had no talent, no viable fantasy. It may be that act 2 of *Fidelio* is a prophetic scene in Hanno's case too, for Hanno does indeed liberate himself from the bourgeois determinism of the Buddenbrook family, though the trumpet tune that announces his freedom is no celebrated fanfare of Beethoven but the "harsh, imperious call" of life (p. 583) that reaches his distant spirit in the crisis of his typhoid fever, the call that he gladly ignores. In the work of Mann's maturity, however, the substance of the novel is what would correspond to Hanno's puppet show; when the great central mind is at last capable of reaching out into society it attains self-expression, not by declension into grimace, shrug, and vocal accent, but by mysteriously ordering all beings around it into the image of its own personality. Even Thomas Buddenbrook understands that this impalpable organization is the chief business of the hero of a novel by Thomas Mann:

> What is success? It is an inner, and indescribable force, resourcefulness, power of vision; a consciousness that I am, by my mere existence, exerting pressure on the movement of life about me. It is my belief in the adaptability of life to my own ends. Fortune and success lie with ourselves. We must hold them firmly—deep within us. For as soon as something begins to slip, to relax, to get tired, *within us,* then everything without us will rebel and struggle to withdraw from our influence. (P. 332)

Personality exerts a mysterious compulsion upon men and events; and we shall see that it is through such magnetism that Mann will tame his external plots, harness them into the secret revelation of the workings of a single mind. Self-expression is self-betrayal only if it descends into matter, into bodily gesture, into verbal confession; as long as the self is tightly sealed, spiritual, it retains control over matter to the point of psychokinesis, and all merely public men cannot choose but obey. It is significant that Hanno's friend little Count Mölln, a literary twin to the musical Hanno, writes a fairy tale

> which went forward in the depths of the earth among glowing metals and mysterious fires, and at the same time in the souls of men: a tale in which the primeval forces of nature and of the soul were interchanged and mingled, transformed and refined. (Pp. 556–57).

Almost every book of Mann's after *Buddenbrooks* is exactly such a tale, an infusion of psychic into external forces, a demonstration of the hidden convergence of event and desire, sequence and will.

I take Hanno as the prime case of the gifted child who is stifled, unable to engineer any accord between the outer world and the world in his head; Hanno is the purest of children, and the most childish. In Hanno's successors there is growing skill in the covert manipulation of the outside; self-expression becomes first competent, then omnipotent. Tonio Kröger begins at approximately the same age at which Hanno leaves off, as if the Buddenbrook family had received a last-minute reprieve by a simple expedient, the metempsychosis of Hanno into one of his cousins, the Krögers. Tonio is nearly as profound and wretched as Hanno at the beginning; he too is a misfit, he too wishes he were a different kind of human being. But Tonio's strength lies in his superior adaptability, his capacity for education. The Hanno sequence of *Buddenbrooks* is, strictly speaking, not a *Bildungsroman* at all; Hanno at the point of death is little more mature than the infant of four years, still embedded in the world of play, an increasingly poor response to the pressures of family, school, and society. Tonio by contrast absorbs into his play all those things that Hanno, out of fear, rejects; so Hanno attenuates into glad death while Tonio gains mastery over a world that, although it is always painful, can at least be a source of useful pain.

The Aesthetic

Why do people become novelists? If we look at the artists and failed artists who are characters in Mann's fiction, it seems that novel writing is an assertion of an order that embraces the palpable disorder of life, the assertion that sorrow and joy are not responses in isolation but something shared, meaningful. The novelist sees a society in which all men perpetually cry out their names, insist on themselves, in an orgy of self-expression; but the novelist knows that their loud self-indication indicates much more than they realize. If all the separate notes of the human are coordinated properly, they form a finished symphony; the idea of individuality is so much delusion, and individuals who emphasize their uniqueness only reinforce idea, type, race, some pole of a timeless antinomy. Yet this observation of hidden pattern in social behavior is nearly indistinguishable from control; the novelist beholds a society behaving as if it were controlled by a secret intelligence, and finally that intelligence becomes confused with his own. It is at this point that novel writing becomes sinister. The novelist wishes to express himself, not in the coarse and exhausting manner of ordinary people, but obliquely, analyzing the factors of his own life through a literary microcosm; the novelist wants to discover within his soul all the amplitude and variety of the human, and to put himself in the position of omnipresent sympathy; yet he cannot keep the realm of his control limited to literature, and therefore becomes responsible for human catastrophe as well as the events of the printed page. The novel began as something palliative, soothing, but it ends in a kind of horror; life cannot help obeying the script. The novelist can find himself burdened with a sophisticated, deflected, yet intense feeling of guilt, like the guilt of Leverkühn in *Dr. Faustus*; or he can find himself the perpetrator of conscious atrocity, like Cipolla in *Mario and the Magician*.

Mann more than most novelists was content to admit that many of his works are autobiographical; he said for so many years that *Tonio Kröger* was the story of his own youth that at the age of sixty-six he at last had to tell a friend that he felt it was no longer proper for him to be addressed as "Herr Tonio Kröger" (*Letters I*, p. 368); and *Tonio Kröger* is the one story of Mann's in which the gifted child makes the transition from weakness of private revery to the budding strength of aesthetic control. In *Tonio* the child's revery is not isolated and involute, as in Hanno Buddenbrook's case; his fantasy is not obsessed with fairy tale or with the incorporeal, but with human desire, those bright matching cathexes Hans and Inge. For Tonio then, the aesthetic is earthly; it walks, idles, and is capable of rebuff; it must be wooed. Hans and Inge are purified shapes in his mind, not because he misunderstands or falsifies them—he is already a master psychologist even at the age of fourteen—but because he invests their every action with glamor, with meaningfulness. If Tonio avoids those forms of disaster to which the aesthetic mode often leads elsewhere, it is because he has made the aesthetic into something empirical, he insists that rapture and bright image be tested against reality. He decides that he will be faithful to Inge as long as he lives, even though she ignores him:

> "Faithfulness," thought Tonio Kröger. "Yes, I will be faithful, I will love thee, Ingeborg, as long as I live!" He said this in the honesty of his intentions. And yet a still small voice whispered misgivings in his ear: after all, he had forgotten Hans Hansen utterly, even though he saw him every day! And the hateful, the pitiable fact was that this still, small, rather spiteful voice was right: time passed and the day came when Tonio Kröger was no longer so unconditionally ready as once he had been to die for the lively Inge, because he felt in himself desires and powers to accomplish in his own way a host of wonderful things in this world. (*Stories I*, p. 171)

This is a healthy defensive mechanism by which fantasy and literature are kept honest; the image is most potent if it is not allowed to become so rigid and light, devoid of substance, that the least wind can carry it off; the image must be fed with blood and the terrestrial. The ideal figures of Hans and Inge—as Mann pointed out in later life, *Tonio* is the first story in which the plot is organized musically, by means of the repetition of idea rather than of naturalistic detail (*Magic Mountain*, p. 728)—are not under Tonio's control in the sense that he can make them gratify his conscious needs; but that is a power that the artist almost never possesses; even Leverkühn in *Dr. Faustus*, whose presence is far more pervasive and controlling than Tonio's, hardly persuades anyone to do what he requests. Tonio yearns for Hans to read *Don Carlos*, aches for Inge to tell him she loves him; and he suffers disappointment after disappointment; yet events nevertheless shape themselves to provide Tonio with a secret gratification. How can an artist really wish that Inge cuddle with him as if he were a character in an insipid story for adolescent girls? How can he desire that Hans violate all the principles of his bourgeois being by trading his book of horse photographs for the plays of Schiller? It is unthinkable. What Tonio, and Adrian Leverkühn, and possibly Thomas Mann himself, desire unconsciously and powerfully is the same: that their lives make a significant story, with a dramatic plot, something that millions can enjoy. Tonio shapes his life in such a way that it will be *readable*; and his presence in the story provides hidden reinforcement to the presence of the actual author, who wills and contrives that his story be governed by suspense, repetition of motif, and order.

One of the most remarkable aspects of Mann's narrative technique is his insistence that his characters understand that they amount to nothing but characters in a novel. A few indications of this can be found even in *Buddenbrooks*: when Tony Buddenbrook says that the traits of her character are determined and invariant, it has a certain disquieting feeling, as if she is a character who has a little too much insight into the tricks her author has employed in her construction; like the X-ray photographs in *The Magic Mountain*, there are certain kinds of insight into oneself that seem to be beyond what is good for us to know. In the short stories it sometimes happens that a minor character will look like "a figure out of Hoffmann" (*Stories I*, p. 85), as in "The Wardrobe"; even in *Tonio* it happens that our hero sees "a comic figure stepped bodily out of a Danish novel" (*Stories I*, p. 203), as everyone Tonio sees becomes assimilated into his novelist's eye. But in the later novels more devastating kinds of awareness take place in the *dramatis personae*. In *Joseph and his Brothers*, for example, Joseph's brothers carry Tony Buddenbrook's self-complacence to almost undreamed-of extremes. Joseph's flaunting of the coat of many colors finally reaches such a point that the brothers take counsel on how to tear down this intolerable fop. Much of their conversation consists of their declarations of identity, as if Mann's epithets and similes for them were touchstones that they had to fondle often in order to remember who they were. "It may be," says Dan, "that I am called snake and adder, forsooth, because I am said to be somewhat malicious" (p. 326). This kind of utterance, in which the character

211

does the narrator's work for him, should be taken as a joke; it is a smiling admission of technical artifice; it is a collection of the debt that the characters owe to the narrator for their definition. In the great rhetorical set pieces of *Joseph*—the enormous conversations of Joseph and Potiphar's wife, of Potiphar's wife and Potiphar, and of Joseph and Pharaoh—the comprehension of the characters of their status as created fictions reaches its culmination. Here is a brief excerpt from the dialogue between Potiphar and his wife, Mut-em-enet, a sustained argument that extends for more than a score of pages; Potiphar, whose emotions about his wife are ambiguous and strong, is trying to conduct a decorous conversation, while his wife is trying slowly to bring around the conversation to the subject of Joseph, whose dismissal she wishes to demand:

> "I should be untruthful," he said at last with a little sigh, "were I to say that your share in our pleasant conversation is conducted with great tact. I made a skilful transition to the more worldly and material things of life, bringing the subject round to Pharaoh and the court. I expected you to return the ball by asking me some question, such as for instance whose ear-lobe Pharaoh tweaked in token of his favour when we went out of the hall of the canopy after the levee; but instead you turned aside into observations about such irritating matters as mines and desert wells, about which, truly, my love, you must certainly understand even less than I."
>
> "You are right," she replied, shaking her head over her blunder. "Forgive me. My eagerness to know whose ear-lobe Pharaoh tweaked today was only too great. I dissembled it by small talk. Pray understand me: I thought to put off the question, feeling that a slow leading up to the important subject is the finest and most important feature of elegant conversation. Only the clumsy blunder in their approach by precipitation, betraying at once the whole content of their minds." (P. 688)

Husband and wife speak in rounded paragraphs, and it is within their rhetorical rules to make analytical commentary upon the form of their conversation, as they struggle to impart elegance and suspense, all novelistic virtue, to the unwieldy material they must utter. They are trying to direct the flow of this rhetorical ceremony, to shape it satisfyingly; they let us in illicitly on Mann's troubles in organizing the chapter, whisper to us Mann's self-congratulation. The reader's ear can often discern how the voices of Mann's characters, especially in important or climatic utterance, betray the timbre of Mann's own voice; his major characters are all conceived fairly simply as self-extensions, masks that are easy to solve.

> I have always lived a very secluded life, and it was certainly not my way of handling people which has won me friends for my person and my work. I can hardly call myself a judge of human nature in the practical sense of the word, and I believe that this is true of many portrayers of humanity whose work shows much psychological insight. In my opinion, these insights spring from self-observation and self-criticism rather than from particular attention to others. (*Letters II*, p. 509).

It is self-observation, the interior, that is the source of the whole multitude of Mann's characters; and when a character indicates, as Felix Krull does to Zouzou, exactly where the paragraph divisions fall in his speech, one is inclined to believe that Mann's description of his technique is accurate.

If the characters in Mann's novels like to pretend that they are characters in a novel, it is also true that some of Mann's characters pretend that they are authors. Tonio Kröger moves through society "grey and unobtrusive among his fellows like an actor without his make-up, who counts for nothing as soon as he stops representing something else" (*Stories I*, p. 173); and soon afterward Tonio tells his confidante Lisabeta the sad story of a great actor who, when he was not playing a role, always fell into a fit of insipidity, "an exaggerated consciousness of his ego" (*Stories I*, p. 178). Tonio sees himself as a creator of characters, a man who, containing all roles within him, has therefore no role whatever in human society; he feels himself shapeless, inchoate, standing "between two worlds," "at home in neither" (*Stories I*, p. 208). Yet this very lack of definition, this excess and overspilling of ego, that allows him to find order everywhere in the tale that is his life, compels him to understand that the luminous personages of his childhood are not haphazard characters, but the embodiment of a myth, the myth of Tonio Kröger; and by that route Hans and Inge lose their existence as distinct individuals, become projections of Tonio's fantasy. His amorousness toward the blue-eyed Nordic type becomes an emblem of the division in his being between the paternal and the maternal strain, the bourgeois and the aesthetic; he understands that Inge's personality is insignificant and commonplace, but the genetic myth demands that he should crave the ordinary. The progress of Hans and Inge through the story is in the direction of rarefaction and myth; Inge is first adored as a real girl, then as an undying image of love, then as the memory of an image of love, and finally as a racial type, so easy and diffuse that an unknown Danish girl whom Tonio sees in a resort can stand for Inge just as well as the original could. At every stage Tonio's control over Inge becomes more acute; it is he who decides her identity, her function, her recurrence in the story of Tonio Kröger; and the satisfaction occurring in the fulfillment of the myth—that art loves nature while nature cannot love art, a myth of tragically incomplete reciprocity— is surely far greater than the satisfaction of Hans' awe, Inge's embrace. *Tonio Kröger* ends in the "whirl of shadows of human figures who beckon to me to weave spells to redeem them" (*Stories I*, p. 209), Tonio's discovery of the plenitude of his internal cosmos, the figures of his fantasy pressing forward to be converted into literature. But what is Tonio about to write? Surely it is *Tonio Kröger*, and those shadows are only Inge and Hans and the other characters. It is at this moment that Mann's childhood is complete. He has converted the characters of his youth into art, and he has converted himself as a converter of character into art, too.

Tonio Kröger is distinguished from all of Mann's stories about artists written in comparative youth by the successfulness of the aesthetic resolution of the plot; in all the works even remotely contemporaneous with it the aesthetic itch is disastrous. I have suggested that the mature artists of Mann's later career, the prodigious builders, poets, composers, and confidence men who occupy his fiction after 1930, are the sons of such rightminded and thoughtful children as Hanno Buddenbrook and Tonio Kröger; but the literary paternity of Joseph, the Goethe of *Lotte in Weimar*, Adrian Leverkühn, and Felix Krull is more complicated than that; for every marvelous child there are a good many freaks, fools, overgrown embryos, and villains who befoul the whole aesthetic mode, and who yet explore the same profound problems as the great artists of Mann's maturity, prefigure their characters with epic distortions. It is true of many artists that they must write a major story in parody before they can write the sober version; T. S. Eliot had to write *Sweeney Agonistes* with its music-hall tropical islands and missionaries before he could tackle the serious plays of redemption and conversion, like *The Family Reunion* and *The Cocktail Party*; similarly Mann could not depict authentic greatness until he had given forth a number of rogues and asses who claim talents they do not possess, who surround themselves with the spurious trappings of creativity, or who employ their abilities to pervert, slander, and mutilate.

It is easy to commiserate with the frustration which is so prevalent in Mann's early letters, his anger over the common verdict over his fiction that it was icy, inhuman, lacking in feeling. Mann occasionally liked to terrify his readers when he was young, but far more characteristic of his early work is a certain overripeness that comes from the difficulty of controlling feeling grown nearly boundless. The author of "Tobias Mindernickel" could reasonably be described as icy: Tobias is described with great precision, a sharply defined puppet that contracts as the story proceeds into a still sharper, still punier configuration. But soft characters abound in these early stories; in "Disillusionment," the first story of Mann's which he wished to preserve, the central character is ageless, indescribable, so indefinite that he is no more than a literary phantom in pursuit of beauty and high sensation, as restless and vague as the hero of Shelley's *Alastor*:

> "Speech, it seems to me, is rich, is extravagantly rich compared with the poverty and limitations of life. Pain has its limits: physical pain in unconsciousness and mental in torpor; it is not different with joy. Our human need for communication has found itself a way to create sounds which lie beyond these limits.
>
> "Is the fault mine? Is it down my spine alone that certain words can run so as to awaken in me intuitions of sensations which do not exist?" (*Stories I*, p. 32)

Here, at the beginning of Mann's canon, the aesthetic mode is the source of human depravity; the character of "Disillusionment" is bedeviled by the fantasies of poets into believing that there exist sensations in excess of what the spine can feel; the embodiment of beauty is too feeble and disfigured to compare with beauty itself. He rebels, beats his fists against the finitude of human emotion; yet he is overcome with a disillusionment so vast that it nearly refutes the principle that causes it. From him we learn the obsessiveness, the mania, that governs the relation between the sensitive man and the beautiful; and from him we learn that irony, critical detachment, self-remoteness is not sufficient to remove the pain of life, but instead is itself a source of pain; but the most important truth we learn here is that self-preoccupation is the first and most basic requisite for the artistic sensibility. Even this distended shadow of a sensitive man is ceaselessly attentive to the sensations of the spine, to the pleasures of his eye; he, who is almost the first character that Mann created, is the first connoisseur of his own body.

The theory of self-preoccupation haunts Mann's early work, in "Disillusionment," "The Dilettante," and of course most of all in the character of Christian Buddenbrook, Tom's obnoxious brother and Hanno's dissolute uncle, a kind of artist of disease. It is in Christian that the narrowness of the boundary between artistic success and artistic failure is the most visible, because many of the traits of his childhood, and some of the traits of his maturity, closely resemble those of Felix Krull, who is perhaps the most successful character Mann ever invented: Christian is an accomplished, even a virtuosic mimic, fascinated by the theater to such an extent that at the age of fourteen he is scandalously enamored of an actress—an experience similar to Felix's encounter with Müller-Rosé; and at one point he does a delightful imitation of a pianist (*Buddenbrooks*, p. 203), despite his inability to play the piano, an exact analogue to Felix's famous violin trick. Mimicry is curiously precious to Mann, and his writings are saturated with it: Christian, Felix, Ingrid in "Disorder and Early Sorrow," Schildknapp in *Dr. Faustus*; Mann describes Chekhov's youthful powers of mimicry with detailed delight; his letters record again and again how Artur Rubinstein captivated through mimicry, how he "laughed till the tears came" (*Letters II*, p. 488) for three hours at Charlie Chaplin's imitations and clowning, as if the population of parties which Mann attended consisted principally of mimics. This primacy can be explained as follows: the mimic is a low analogue of the novelist, related to him as the body is to the mind. We have seen how Tonio Kröger at the end of his story was preparing to project out of himself the whole society which he had assimilated into his fantasy, thus showing how self-preoccupation can exfoliate into social preoccupation, racial preoccupation. The case of the mimic is little different: he studies himself, measures his reflexes, experiments with the timbre of his voice, so minutely that bodily gesture and facial expression can match another's. The humor is not in the caricature but in the exactitude of reproduction; mimetic accuracy, in the case of Felix Krull, is a secret sign of the indivisibility of all that is human, a passage into glory, an authentication of the comic spirit itself.

It is not so in Christian Buddenbrook; his mimicry is a symptom, not of the potency of his identity, not of suppleness under conscious control, but of a will-lessness, a softness of being so great that it cannot help taking the impress of any passing stamp. The self-preoccupation of the artist is a state that is highly questionable even in the best of artists; Mann often perceives it as a falling-off from spontaneous unity of being; and in Christian we see how creaky and sputtering, inert, such self-preoccupation can become. Self-preoccupation always requires a split in one's being between cognition and affection; one's body, one's feelings, one's memories, all become objectified, studied in the detached consciousness with an eye toward the useful potentiality of interior resources. Body and soul to the self-preoccupied man are objects of speculation and play, even to the point of recklessness; both the protagonist of "Disillusionment" and Christian Buddenbrook wonder what would happen if they fell into a gorge, or jumped out the window. No act is unthinkable, no crime too monstrous to the self-preoccupied man; that is one reason why the artist is criminal. He is chiefly interested, whether novelist or mimic, in uncovering possible selves, of demonstrating that what he perceives is not outside the range of his being; *nothing human is alien to me* is the explicit motto of some of Mann's artists, the implicit of all.

However, it is always dangerous to regard the self as raw material. The Dilettante, who originally regards himself as too fine for human intercourse, is eventually driven by his own incompetence to believe himself too base for any fate but isolation; in this case self-experimentation leads to a reversal of the desired fate, although to the self-preoccupied man his own dullness is just as interesting as his sensational refinement, and he can invest even the fact that he is a bat blinking in a cave with a kind of horrified glamor. Even Tonio Kröger does not emerge unscathed from such habits of mind. He feels that the emotional discipline of his artistry has become a mental mechanism from which he cannot escape; and in his compulsive rejection of simple human intimacy he feels sick, sick of himself:

> There is something I call being sick of knowledge, Lisabeta: when it is enough for you to see through a thing in order to be sick to death of it, and not in the least in a forgiving mood. Such was the case of Hamlet the Dane, that typical literary man. He knew what it meant to be called to knowledge without being born to it. To see things clear, if even through your tears, to recognize, notice, observe—and have to put it all down with a smile, at the very moment when hands are clinging, and lips meeting, and the human gaze is blinded with feeling—it is infamous, Lisabeta, it is indecent, outrageous—but what good does it do to be outraged? (*Stories I*, pp. 180–81)

Self-preoccupation almost always has a component of self-revulsion, which is made harder to bear by the fact that the existence of the self-revulsion is a kind of commentary upon itself. The self-preoccupied man does not feel an emotion, he says to himself "I am feeling an emotion"; then he starts to feel emotion—outrage, despair—about his lack of spontaneous emotion, but instead of feeling outrage and despair, he says to himself "I am feeling outrage and despair." We have seen this now in "The Dilettante" and *Tonio Kröger*; and it is through this kind of catch, this mirror-regression into the dim depths of self-devouring cognition, that the devil hopes to entrap Leverkühn in *Dr. Faustus*. Irony in Mann's work can rarely be the disinterested mode of balance and judgment to which it aspires; the ironic consciousness is usually tinged with self-contempt, because irony is thought an inadequate response to a world that requires our love as well as our accurate estimation; and tinged as well with contempt for the world, because the world for all its clamoring and importunity has not yet been quite potent enough to shake us into commitment and self-sacrifice.

In Christian Buddenbrook the ego is too weak to permit such disciplines as irony; the gifts of his self-preoccupation, which seemed so plentiful and promising in his boyhood, his quickness, his mimetic skill, his profound aesthetic emotion at the theater, come to nothing. The infant Felix Krull attains such mastery over his body that he can create fever; his eye is developed to such an extent that the muscles of the iris, usually so brutal and involuntary, obey the commands of his will, dilate and contract on demand. This unearthly control is far beyond Christian Buddenbrook's coarser clay; but even the minor aptitudes of his youth deteriorate as he grows up. Felix translates his body into a direct extension of his will, as swift and luminous as the mind itself; but in Christian's case the will atrophies, and his fascination with his body causes an unfortunate bloating and suppuration of the corporeal. The progress of Christian Buddenbrook is a steady growth of confusion, of falling out of touch, of self-abdication. One of his most telling anecdotes about himself is the story of a London operetta performance (p. 202) in which the curtain went up while he was accidently on the stage, carrying on with one of the actresses; not only has the boundary between theatrical and real life become indistinct in his mind, but he shows a certain passivity that marks many of his tales. After telling this to Tony and Tom he says suddenly:

> "Strange—sometimes I can't swallow. Oh, it's no joke. I find it very serious. It enters my head that perhaps I can't swallow, and then all of a sudden I can't. The food is already swallowed, but the muscles—right here—they simply refuse. It isn't a question of will-power. Or rather, the thing is, I don't dare really will it." (P. 202)

His body has already begun—he is still fairly young—to take control of his existence, with the full compliance of his weakening will; by this deliberate self-relaxation and self-abandonment Christian discovers that his body has a thick, vegetable will of its own, and can thereby be induced to provide fascinating and unsuspected sensation. For hard characters discipline is no important matter, but for soft and potentially fine characters like Christian and Hanno discipline is all-important; in the absence of discipline Christian's body aches from infrared to ultraviolet, in a symphony of interesting pain, grows purulent, effloresces into rheumatism and stench, glorious decay. In Mann's corporeal myth, this seems to be the natural tendency of the human body; it is only through vigilance that we prevent disease. Christian, by surrendering himself to bodily insanity, shows the demonic aspect of the self-preoccupied man: the depths of the self must be disgorged; and it becomes only a measure of the boundlessness of one's own potentiality that such terrifying stuff can be found inside and manifested. As his brother Tom understands perfectly, his fascination with the unspeakable is a form of self-aggrandizement:

> Christian busies himself too much with himself, with what goes on in his own inside. Sometimes he has a regular mania for bringing out the deepest and the prettiest of these experiences—things a reasonable man does not trouble himself about or even want to know about, for the simple reason that he would not like to tell them to anyone else. There is such a lack of modesty in so much communicativeness. You see, Tony, anybody, except Christian, may say that he loves the theatre. But he would say it in a different tone, more *en passant*, more modestly, in short. Christian says it in a tone that says: "Is not my passion for the stage something very marvellous and interesting?" He struggles, he behaves as if he were really wrestling to express something supremely delicate and difficult. (P. 204)

Christian, like all artists, is all too prone to believe that his feelings are interesting to all men precisely because they are his; and this egotism declines quickly enough into a kind of solipsism. In his later days he has a hallucination of a man sitting on a sofa, when no one is there (p. 446), a foreshadowing of the apparition of the devil that Leverkühn meets in *Dr. Faustus*; an odd badge of artistic kinship between such remote figures. At the death of his brother Tom he is alarmed, exactly in the manner of Tonio Kröger, that he cannot cry at the funeral: "His constant preoccupation with his own condition had used him up emotionally and made him insensitive" (*Buddenbrooks*, p. 531). Neither Tonio nor Christian finds spontaneous emotion possible, but there is a difference: Tonio's self-preoccupation is a vehicle toward self-lability, and sympathy, and extension of his being; whereas Christian's methodical extraction of sensation from his body leads to breakdown of body and mind alike, until he sinks exhausted into a puddle, so yielding and inert that nothing can touch it and leave an imprint. He is soon sent off to an institution; but not before informing young Hanno, the nephew with whom he has a strong personal rapport, that he must never become too involved with puppets and the theater (p. 415), a repudiation of the aesthetic which is in effect a repudiation of himself as well.

It is fair to say that Christian Buddenbrook is a child who never grows up, only withers into a senility that increasingly resembles a parody of childhood; and he is Hanno's true uncle in that neither of them can pass into the puberty of the spirit. There are in Mann's fiction a number of other characters whom Mann describes as elderly children: the cuckold Jacoby in "Little Lizzy," the good dwarf Bes in

Joseph in Egypt, and, most of all, Detlev Spinell in *Tristan*. It is easy
to fit the figure of the artist as elderly child into the general genetic
myth by which Mann explains the origin of the artist. The bourgeois
family, as its blood rarefies through its spasms of self-exhaustion,
throws out progeny who are increasingly frail, nervous, incapable of
practical endeavor, either beautiful themselves or masters of beauty.
It matters little whether these effete children are artists or models of
beauty for artists to employ; Spinell explains the glory of Frau
Klöterjahn to her in exactly that same language that serves to account
for Hanno Buddenbrook: "It not infrequently happens that a race
with sober, practical bourgeois tradition will towards the end of its
days flare up in some form of art" (*Stories I*, p. 119). It may well
happen that these "forms of art" may be too delicate to endure the
rigors of human maturity; if they are beautiful women they marry at
peril and are likely to be much weakened by childbirth; if they are
male aesthetes they will be tempted to preserve the habits and
furnishings of childhood, to build like Adrian Leverkühn a cloister or
fortress that is a replica of the paternal house, in which the
gratuitous play of childhood is maintained forever, its fertile loneli-
ness, its questionable irresponsibility. Yet it may be that these elderly
children, though their art is never very good, are nevertheless the
purest examples of the artistic temperament. When Tonio Kröger
tells Lisabeta that we artists are like "unsexed papal singers" (*Stories I*,
p. 177), he is stating a truth consistent with all of Mann's other
pronouncements, yet the simile fits him badly; it is Spinell who is a
castrato, not Tonio. Tonio, by contrast, participates in bouts of
sexual excess, followed by bouts of revulsion against the senses;
Tonio is in every way a mixed creature, a hybrid of the artistic and the
bourgeois; and it is this plenitude of self which is the strength of his
art. The internal cosmos of the great artist must include evil and good,
ugliness and beauty, the dull and the exalted; while the artist who is
oversensitive, intolerant, hyperesthetic, an axolotl, vitiates his art by
excluding all matter that it is not gorgeous, all emotion that cannot
shiver away into ecstasy.

It is in *Tristan*, published in 1902, a year before *Tonio Kröger*, that
Mann first masters the kind of narrative on which he almost holds the
patent, in which a realistic story is informed in every detail by the
phantasms of the central character's single mind. The plot is simple:
the setting is a sanitorium for tuberculosis; an awkward and ludicrous
aesthete, Detlev Spinell, a novelist of sorts, becomes infatuated with
Frau Klöterjahn, an inconsequential young matron of great delicacy
and beauty; Spinell undertakes what could be called an aesthetic
seduction; he has no designs on her body, but wishes to convince her

that her identity is equivalent to the identity he has invented for her in his fantasy, much derivative from Maeterlinck and the *symbolistes*. His power is irresistible; her thoughts become less and less occupied with the proper matters of a businessman's wife, and instead she is increasingly rapt, involuted in the contemplation of her own un-earthly beauty, until she rejects Klöterjahn entirely, happily accepts the awesome and silvery identity of Hérodiade, where passion is quenched by its own excess, love by its own loveliness, or the identity of Mélisande, who with tremulous hope askes Spinell if he could actually see the golden crown he had imagined on her head. The difficulty of writing a story of hypnotism and alienation of affection should not be exaggerated; but *Tristan* is no tale of Svengali and Trilby, or even of artist and victim; Mann's preeminent keenness and subtlety lie in the overt complicity of Frau Klöterjahn in even the most initial phases of Spinell's wooing. Few relationships in fiction horrify by the same formula as that of Spinell and Frau Klöterjahn: the combination of thoughtless, almost offhanded murderousness and suicide with the most affable mutual gratification. It is hard to know which of them derives most pleasure from Frau Klöterjahn's con-sumption, her surrender into the refinement of death; indeed it is hard to know which of them is more artist.

In this story the two major kinds of artists in Mann's early fiction come together, the novelist and the mimic; and it seems safe to say that Frau Klöterjahn is better at mimicry than Spinell is at novel writing. She accentuates all those traits of her character and body that Spinell esteems, the porcelain pallor, the emaciation, the contempt for the mundane, the yearning for the inanimate; her body is neatly responsive to her will, and she creates a fatal disease out of what was originally a light case. It is certain, however, that the impetus for this transformation is not entirely Spinell's. Frau Klöterjahn, one might say, is not banal enough to be identified strictly as a character of Spinell's imagination. He chose her gratuitously to enact a role in an allegory that is central to late nineteenth-century art as Mann under-stood it; but her alarming affinity for the role suggests that she was a character in search of an author. I have spoken before of the relish which the characters in Mann's fiction take in their status as creatures of literary artifice; and the ease with which Frau Klöterjahn lets herself fall into the character which Spinell ascribes to her, her matchless stageworthiness, is a mirror of this secret desire to take part in a fable, to utter resonant and literary words, which affects even the most ordinary personality in Mann's vision of human life. In the later books it is the homage that minor characters pay to acknowledged greatness, this conformation of behavior to the unknown will of the protagonist; but so eager are Mann's characters to discover their fable that even the most decrepit and carious novelist, if his desires are traditional, will be obeyed. Whatever artistic talent Spinell lacks, Frau Klöterjahn is gladly willing to supply. During an early conversation between them, Spinell inquires into her life before her marriage:

> "Yes, I have precious memories of all those years; and especially
> of the garden, our garden, back of the house. It was dreadfully
> wild and overgrown, and shut in by crumbling mossy walls. But
> it was just that gave it such charm. In the middle was a fountain
> with a wide border of sword-lilies. In summer I spent long hours
> there with my friends. We all sat round the fountain on little
> camp-stools—" (*Stories I*, p. 119)

Here is a woman who needs no prompting to envision herself as a romantic heroine; Spinell can but embroider that little narrative with his golden crown and queenly songs. Her version of her mythic childhood and Spinell's coincide essentially even before much of Spinell's imagination has begun; only Klöterjahn hears the recipe for potato pancakes that was the actual content of the fairy-tale court.

The actors must cast about for a long time before they find the right myth. Maeterlinck and Villiers de l'Isle-Adam seemed a good start; but it is the chance discovery of some sheet music from *Tristan und Isolde* that provides the mythic focus and template for which Spinell and Frau Klöterjahn have been searching. It is just what they want; it is true that a story less directly applicable to these lovers could hardly be devised, but the realm of myth does not pertain to one's actual situation but to aspiration, desire, fantasy. The wound that Melot gave to Tristan corresponds to nothing but the cavities of Spinell's teeth—Hanno Buddenbrook's chief flaw consisted of bad teeth also, a general sign of a softness, vulnerability, or incompetence that persists to too great an age—and Isolde's rapture corresponds to little more than Frau Klöterjahn's tubercular fever. It is all ironic reversal and subversion of spirituality, but it is not pointless: the mystic union of Tristan and Isolde, "Thou Isolde, Tristan I, yet no more Tristan, no more Isolde" (*Stories I*, p. 129), is in a peculiar way validated by these gross beings trying to clothe themselves in the finery of archetype, for Spinell and Frau Klöterjahn are in fact united in the mystery of their interdependence, their need to constitute a theater, their ability to impart an identity to each other that is no less comforting because it is sham. In some of Mann's early stories about artists and myth, one feels that the choice of myth is nearly arbitrary; but the arbitrariness of the myth is itself a testimony to the potentiality and adaptability of the human species. We are all offered innumerable patterns through which we may seek to organize and give meaning to our lives; what does it matter that Isolde will be dispatched through hemorrhage of the lung as long as it is a modulation into ecstasy, what does it matter if Tristan be whirled away, tragically defeated by a brutal child with sunlight in his hair?

There is nothing wrong with living one's life aesthetically, in accordance with myth; indeed the point of the *Joseph* novels is that a life without myth is absurd if it is possible at all; if most of Mann's early characters get into trouble by fashioning their lives according to myth, it is either because the myth reveals the intolerable facts of their lives or because they wrongly decide to sacrifice everything for the sake of archetype. The attractiveness of even the most shabby and stupid story to these characters is astonishing. The major precursor of *Tristan* in Mann's canon is "Little Lizzie": a vile and beautiful woman, Amra Jacoby, married to a lawyer so fat, trusting, naive, obsequious and flabby that he could give cuckolds a bad name, conspires with her lover, Alfred Läutner, a young composer, to humiliate her husband for no reason except pure malice. A party is planned for a great many guests in which the guests themselves design the musical entertainments; Läutner and Amra compose a little song and skit for Jacoby, in which he will dress up in an elephantine baby frock and sing the ditty that his wife's lover has written. Jacoby does so, and the shock of the assembled company at the spectacle of his degradation leads to his collapse and death. Just as in *Tristan* an artistic intelligence composes a scenario which has fatal consequences for a second party. It is easy to see the gratification of Frau Klöterjahn in following Spinell—but why does Jacoby agree to make a fool of himself on stage? He is certainly not enthusiastic when the idea is presented to him. Mann has established his passivity at some length, the ease with which Amra can convince him to obey; but one still wishes to inquire further about his reasons for accepting such remarkable humiliation. Again it is the appetite for a myth at work; when a script is put in front of a character, he cannot help reading the lines, no matter what the cost may be. It may seem improper to refer to Läutner's vicious little song, in which Jacoby must pretend he is a *soubrette* and tease called "Little Lizzie," as a myth, but it is in fact a role in which the hidden realities of Jacoby's life are manifested, his masculine incapacity, his infantile blindness, his epicene eagerness to please. The principle that governs Jacoby's conduct is the necessity for self-expression; a character may consciously try to suppress self-knowledge and public knowledge, but there are forces in the psyche that work toward manifestation and social display. Mann's characters fear few things more than public humiliation, but fear does not hinder them from committing public folly, if that folly is a true expression of their being.

There is a kind of healthiness about Jacoby's performance. Mann prided himself that he had developed certain of Freud's principles independently of Freud, and it is surely true that Mann felt from the beginning of his career that the repression of unpleasantness was a canker and a gnawing worm, and that the utterance of hidden horror was the first stage of cure. Thus, in a sense, Jacoby's grisly enactment may be called therapeutic, even though it is fatal; the "Little Lizzie" skit is the proper myth for Jacoby to enact, even if the script is sufficient evidence to damn its two authors. We may tentatively call mythic behavior healthy if it is a vehicle toward self-realization, or if, as in the case of all the major characters in *Joseph*, the myth imbues the man with a sense of his own awesome resonance and depth; it is unhealthy if the myth becomes prescriptive, limiting, confining. We distrust Frau Klöterjahn's identification of herself with Isolde because she is so much more than that; in repudiating her bourgeois husband she repudiates a great deal of her identity; her best solution would have been to embrace both Klöterjahn and Spinell, the gross and the oblique. What disturbs Mann about the unmixed aesthete is that the kind of life he wishes excludes so much of the human; and for Mann the rich is more valuable than the ideal.

Both of Mann's Wagnerian stories, *Tristan* and *The Blood of the Wälsungs*, treat mythic paradigms that have become obsessive, that have come to define a relationship so fully that all that does not pertain to the myth is excluded. In *Tristan*, Spinell knowingly urges Frau Klöterjahn to die so that her nocturnal ecstasy may pass beyond the reach of Klöterjahn and his insipid daylight; in *The Blood of the Wälsungs*, Siegmund and Sieglinde Aarenhold have appointed their lives so rigorously around *Die Walküre* that they have stopped only at the point of planting an ash tree in the floor of their salon. For Spinell and Frau Klöterjahn, the discovery of the music from *Tristan und Isolde* was a sudden inspiration and revelation of their myth; for the Aarenhold twins, *Die Walküre* is the steady work and patient ordeal of their lifetimes, and they have seen to it that the omen of their first names is fulfilled to the smallest detail. *The Blood of the Wälsungs*, preeminently among all of Mann's stories, is pure sexual phantasmagoria; one can scarcely speak of plot and character, human motivation, in this setting where all identity gladly abdicates for the sake of myth. Yet one can inquire into the psychic conditions that produce this incomparable appetite for Wagnerian pattern. The joke of the title is that these Wälsungs are descended from an upstart industrialist Wotan, the lowest possible blood; and these fond twins, with their hand holding, their kissing, their telepathy, are simply another example of Mann's genetic proposition, that the bourgeoisie decays into a meretricious oversensitivity. Sieglinde counts for little in the story, is scarcely characterized except for her black savage eyes; but Siegmund is one of the last of that line of characters that includes Hanno Buddenbrook and Frau Klöterjahn, soft, immature, self-preoccupied. In many ways Siegmund is the weakest and most eviscerate of all; except possibly for his desire to become a painter he puts up no slightest resistance or self-assertion against that sturdy and bewildered tenor, expert swordsman and source of divine conflict, who dominates every corner of his life. He is christened and ordained Siegmund, but the myth is purposive as well as inevitable. What Siegmund Aarenhold desires above all is to sleep with his twin sister, his image and complement; it is no ordinary lust but self-love refined and objectified, the kiss that savors of glass and mercury. But incest is difficult; the polite society that they respect offers disapproval, although to their brother Kunz it seems little more than a joke; and they are true modern children, full of smart talk and sardonic wit, for whom any expression of passion is gauche. The paradigm of *Die Walküre* suggests a way of circumventing these taboos; so Siegmund and Sieglinde set up an exact duplicate of the plot of act 1, interposing imaginary and purely formal obstacles that may be easily overturned. Sieglinde's fiancé Beckerath, who occupies the place of Hunding, is so ineffectual that he can scarcely mime the role; he is no mighty domestic tyrant but craven, anemic, a gull; Sieglinde is engaged to him only so that none of the ordained conditions which result in incest may be lacking. The twins become mythic for magical purposes; if they allow themselves to thin out, become paradigmatic and arid, then the desired incest will be an act of obedience to a well-known script, ritualized, inevitable, without shame. Their sexual intercourse is a breakthrough in that the facade of smart talk and brittle intellectualizing has been cast aside; but it is chiefly a confirmation of the damned, for the twins are now strictly hopeless, and nothing will ever sever that infantile and compulsive embrace, an embrace that shuts out a world that is necessarily less subtly engorged and responsive than itself. Siegmund's identity was never strong, always overwhelmed by the intricate textures of his own furniture:

> The accoutrements of life were so rich and varied, so elaborated, that almost no place at all was left for life itself . . . . he had the books bound in stamped leather and labelled with Siegmund Aarenhold's beautiful bookplate; they stood in rows, weighing down his life like a possession which he did not succeed in subordinating to his personality. (*Stories I*, p. 342)

His personality itself resembles a possession, precious, inert, thing-like; and it is not surprising that it would find in Wagner's fable an exultation and breadth beyond anything in its own experience. In Siegmund's case the search for myth is a search for lost humanity; the archetype cannot usurp one's being unless the archetype has Wagnerian potency and the individual is slack, effete. In such ways as these vacuity attributes to itself a mock substantiality.

The culmination of these stories about the exploration of the aesthetic mind is *Death in Venice*. Here, we believe, is the artist, the gifted child, who has at last outgrown precocity and evaded sterility; here we may at last utter the monumental word at which we have so long hesitated: genius. Yet, compared to the Goethe of *Lotte in Weimar*, or Adrian Leverkühn, Aschenbach is still a tentative and sketchy character, whose wife and child appear and disappear in a sentence, whose childhood is unknown except for the usual parents, the upright decent father and foreign, musical mother; in 1911–12, his *annus mirabilis*, Mann is at last willing to tackle genius, but only genius circumscribed and isolated, a mind of power and distinction seen without social context, in a strange land, Venice, a country which like all places outside Germany is pure fantasy. The succession from gifted child to flagrant genius flows so regularly, from enchanted infant to the dedicated but troubled adolescent to balked and stunted talent to the full exercise of power that one is tempted to believe Mann's coy and oblique claim that his canon existed from the beginning; and the reader can everywhere see Mann holding himself back from attempting too much at once. He admitted in 1915 that he originally intended *Death in Venice* to be "the story of Goethe's last love, the love of the seventy-year-old for that little girl he insisted he wanted to marry, though neither she nor her family would hear of it—an ugly, beautiful, grotesque, stirring story" (*Letters I*, p. 76). But if Aschenbach looks forward to the Goethe of *Lotte in Weimar*, with whom he shares some similarities—Goethe says in his incomparable monologue that the love of the young is callow and sickly compared to "the head-turning flattery paid to lovely adolescence singled out by maturity and greatness" (*Lotte*, p. 218), says too in respect to Winckelmann's proclivities that the androgyne beauty of male adolescence is indeed as charming as that of girls (p. 264), and keeps a bust of Antinous in his salon (p. 294), showing in all matters a large-minded tolerance for homosexuality, an ease that Aschenbach lacks—Aschenbach's traits are much more closely related to those of Mann's earlier characters; and we should not be surprised if we find in Aschenbach, not much changed, the shy agonies of Tonio Kröger, the dubious elevation of

Detlev Spinell, even the fantastic narcissism of Siegmund and Sieglinde.

I believe that between 1897 and 1911 the central problem of Mann's imagination was the struggle to transform plausible narrative, realistic narrative, into psychomachia. In *Death in Venice* he succeeds, succeeds so well that the fiction of the twentieth century can offer no story that surpasses it for formal ease and strict delight. It is pure, though small; if Mann manages to integrate all events into an extraordinary coherent allegory of the workings of an artist's mind, it is no defect that not much happens. The story resembles *Tonio Kröger* in that the protagonist attempts to deal with his beloved as an artist deals with a being he has created; it is like *Tristan* in that the artist ostensibly seeks through human beauty those glories of the spirit that lie beyond the province of the corporeal; it is like *The Blood of the Wälsungs* in that the protagonist is eventually compelled by the force of myth to hanker for the forbidden, the unthinkable embrace. But *Death in Venice* is far more ambitious than these earlier stories because, among other reasons, the mythic base is much broader. It is generally true of Mann's major artist figures—omitting such deformities as Spinell—that while each is a more powerful personality than its predecessor, each is less individual, more generalized. Aschenbach is shorn of parents and history, except for his novels, so that the operations of his soul may seem more generally valid; he has, one might say, overcome his childhood, overcome the need for individuation, specificity itself. What is the myth that lays such brutal hands on this great man? It is nothing of Wagner; one might call it the myth of Socrates and Phaedrus, the old man's half-spiritual, half-sexual yearning for beautiful youth; but that is no definitive formulation, for Tadzio is identified, not only with Phaedrus, but with Narcissus, Hyacinthus, a Phaeacian, Eros, Beauty itself. Tadzio is any myth, all myth; and *Death in Venice*, like *Joseph and his Brothers*, could be described as a myth about the operation of myth. Aschenbach is not so narrow and well-defined a figure that any single story could embody his achievement and disaster; only Art itself is a broad enough rubric, and, like *Tonio Kröger* but to a much greater degree, *Death in Venice* is disquieting because it calls into question no single abuse of art but Art itself.

Art makes an assumption so fundamental that it is hard to isolate, hard to define; yet it is this elusive, lowly assumption that leads to Aschenbach's destruction. The reader gets a glimpse of it in Mann's description of Aschenbach's developing maturity of style, his repudiation of an intellectual or psychological manner of writing in favor of moral discrimination, detachment, a new classicism:

> But ethical resoluteness beyond knowledge, the knowledge that
> corrodes or inhibits moral firmness—does this not in turn signify
> a simplification, a reduction morally of the world to too-limited
> terms, and thus also a strengthened capacity for the forbidden, the
> evil, the morally impossible? And does not form have two aspects?
> Is it not moral and amoral at once—moral in that it is the result
> and expression of discipline, but amoral, and even immoral, in
> that by nature it contains an indifference to morality, is calculated,
> in fact, to make morality bend beneath its proud and
> unencumbered scepter? (*Death in Venice*, tr. by Kenneth Burke,
> p. 17; cf. *Stories II*, p. 16)

This is a strong foreshadowing of the end of the story; just as morality
pushed far enough becomes immoral, so form when pursued to the
exclusion of all else leads to sensuality, formlessness; one of the
mottoes of *Death in Venice* is that the road you follow leads you in the
opposite direction. But the assumption of which I spoke lies in the
ineluctable exclusivity of art, the blind eye that the artist must turn to
all phenomena that fail to establish pattern, that lack the delight of
formal consequence. The *is* and the *ought* cannot be distinguished in
the aesthetic consciousness; when writing a novel one makes sure that
all external incident is under the mind's control; event must be emblem
and shadow, all things transitory are but a simile. The aesthetic man,
like Spinell in *Tristan*, will also tend to see style and type instead of
things in themselves, to look obliquely instead of full face, to perceive
his casual acquaintances as the representative manifestation of a
hidden pattern; that is, to look at life as if it were governed by the
rules of novels. This is the assumption that Aschenbach holds; he
believes that what happens to him is not fortuitous but part of an
ongoing revelation. If the world is truly governed by the rules that
satisfy the human soul, then the red-haired pilgrim-figure he sees in
Munich and the disobedient gondolier are so many outstretched
index fingers guiding his path; the bewigged old fop who teases him
about his mistress prefigures his own artificial youth; and the brutal
and leering trouper who sings the laughing song provides a commentary on his own art. At the end of the novella, just before
Aschenbach's collapse, Mann makes another reference to the theme of
the congruence of the outer world and the human soul:

> He was not feeling well and had to struggle against spells of
> giddiness only half physical in their nature, accompanied by a
> swiftly mounted dread, a sense of futility and hopelessness—but
> whether this referred to himself or to the outer world he could not
> tell. (*Stories II*, p. 69)

The Venice that seemed eerie and distorted, dreamlike, at the beginning of the story, is now indistinguishable from dream; the interiorization is complete. On human terms this seems to signify a dangerous confusion, but on aesthetic terms it is a logical culmination. As Aschenbach beomes deranged, he becomes aesthetically perfected; and no condition is more perilous. As the world and Aschenbach's fantasy converge, it becomes more and more certain that he wills everything that happens to him; as Mann says of Aschenbach's style, "Development is destiny" (*Stories II*, p. 16). Mann always called *Death in Venice* a tragedy; and he spoke much later of *The Magic Mountain* as an enormous satyr-play to *Death in Venice*, suggesting that he regarded *Death in Venice* as analogous to a Greek tragedy; but in Mann's work tragedy consists of destruction that is not only provoked by the hero but purposely created by him, welcomed at every stage, just as Aschenbach with a little gesture of his hand accepts with a ready will whatever might come (*Stories II*, p. 40).

All things in *Death in Venice* answer to Aschenbach's needs, are informed by his clamorous fantasy; but the real locus of his obsession is the figure of Tadzio. Tonio Kröger's experiment in the taming of the image of Hans here flowers into a success beyond expectation, for all the motions of Tadzio's being bear witness to the controlling power of Aschenbach's imagination; Tadzio is so complicit that he and Aschenbach are more than conspirators, consubstantial. Felix Krull in his later incarnation expresses the doctrine that the highest states of human intensity are the glance and the embrace; and the glance is nowhere more crucial than in *Death in Venice*, in which Tadzio and Aschenbach keep each other transfixed, dancing, on the sweet thread of their vision. In the blaze of Tadzio's first apparition Aschenbach seems to see him in the way that Leverkühn will see the even more unworldly Nepomuk Schneidewein, as Ariel in *The Tempest* secretly obedient to his will; Tadzio mimics reverently Aschenbach's tactful unwillingness to enter into personal acquaintance, meets with equal dignity Aschenbach's serious gaze; and, at the very end, when Aschenbach announces in a speech to his imaginary Phaedrus the full grandeur of his own degradation, he dismisses Tadzio with a gesture as solemn as Prospero's: "Remain here; and only when you can no longer see me, then do you depart also" (*Stories II*, p. 69). At a critical juncture in the novella Aschenbach attempts to replace the sculptural metaphors which he customarily employed for Tadzio with an aesthetic metaphor more consonant with his own art:

> The ringlets of honey-coloured hair clung to his temples and neck, the fine down along the upper vertebrae was yellow in the sunlight; the thin envelope of flesh covering the torso betrayed the

delicate outlines of the ribs and the symmetry of the breast-structure. His armpits were still as smooth as a statue's, smooth the glistening hollows behind the knees, where the blue network of veins suggested that the body was formed of some stuff more transparent than mere flesh. What discipline, what precision of thought were expressed by the tense youthful perfection of this form! And yet the pure, strong will which had labored in darkness and succeeded in bringing this godlike work of art to the light of day—was it not known and familiar to him, the artist? Was not the same force at work in himself when he strove in cold fury to liberate from the marble mass of language the slender forms of his art which he saw with the eye of his mind and would body forth to men as the mirror and image of spiritual beauty? (*Stories II*, pp. 43–44)

Aschenbach does not need to observe Tadzio for long before he begins to experiment in an idle manner with the congruence between Tadzio and the beings of his literary imagination; he feels immediately intimate, knowing, when he sees Tadzio's body, as if it were *his* precise hand that modeled the down on his back, that arranged the symmetries of the ribs, the axillar hollows. At the end of *Young Joseph* Jacob tries to manufacture a *golem*, a clay Joseph to replace the one the boar has killed, believing that the force of his grief is sufficient to animate dead earth; in the reverse process Aschenbach strips off Tadzio's transparent flesh, grasps bone and tense sinew that the plastic forces which shaped and strung them may become magically identical to his own. When Aschenbach speaks of liberating slender forms from the marble mass of language he is implicitly comparing himself to Michelangelo, whose famous description of his art he echoes; and Michelangelo is as good a referent as any for Mann's later artist-heroes; in fact Mann says in *The Story of a Novel* (p. 16) that his Moses in *The Tables of the Law* bears the face, not of Michelangelo's Moses but of Michelangelo himself. Aschenbach immediately attempts, with Michelangelesque hubris, to liberate Tadzio into words, to translate Tadzio into a brief enraptured essay on aesthetic theory, which, somewhat like the promises of Tonio at the end of *Tonio Kröger*, constitutes a surrogate *Death in Venice*, a cryptic introduction of the novella into its own text. By writing this page and a half Aschenbach verifies that Tadzio is his own fiction, stakes his claim, allows Tadzio to be perceived through no eyes but his; the essay is Aschenbach's cachet, a sculptor's signature. By forcing us to acknowledge literary artifice Mann directs attention to his own presence, which is more overt in this work than ever before, especially in the playful cross-references between Aschenbach's literary canon and Mann's own.

It has long been noted that Tadzio in the later stages of the novella is not so ideal as Aschenbach perceives him at first sight; and we must assume that his loss of ideality is part of Aschenbach's design, a coherent theme in the myth of *Death in Venice*, the myth of the progress of the artist's image through the temporal world. There is at work here a reciprocal movement, the same principle of motion that one finds in most of Mann's books: the object of art, whose origin is transfinite, is involved increasingly in the turgidity of the corporeal, while the artist himself becomes increasingly aesthetic, out of touch; the artist and his creation switch places. Aschenbach, who felt such an immediate fatherly and proprietary sense when he first saw Tadzio, does nothing to protect his beautiful ward; instead he exerts all his imaginative pressure to drag him to earth, to debase him. At the beginning he takes pleasure in the thought of Tadzio's sickliness and early death; and it is not long before he wishes Tadzio to be Hyacinthus, broken and bleeding from the effort of divine amorousness, as needful of nursing as the dog that Tobias Mindernickel mutilates so that it will love him. Psychologically this expresses the deflection of Aschenbach's sexual appetite from embrace to laceration; but mythically it shows the necessary embedding and immersion of the aesthetic image into human experience. Myth and psychology do not always integrate easily into literature; and when mythmaker and psychologist are the same person, some uneasiness results, as Mann says in his essay of 1910 on Fontane (*Essays*, p. 305). Tadzio in no way deviates from Aschenbach's ordained pattern. Tadzio and Jaschiu kiss, join in adolescent horseplay, as Aschenbach's desires turn sexual; if it is Prospero's will, the sprite must learn to embrace, the spirit chastely enact a worthy sexuality. As in *Dr. Faustus* and everywhere else, the controlling artist must get no personal gratification from the obedience of his puppets; the precondition of such power is abstraction and nonparticipation, and the artist, whether or not he loves, must renounce gratified desire. On the last page of *Death in Venice*, Tadzio is beaten by a cruel Jaschiu, his face smothered in the sand, as the fantastic brutalization of Hyacinthus is at last enacted; and Tadzio, hurt, humanized, nearly abject, spurns humanity and wanders out into the ocean, seeking liberation, as if the Image yearned after the infinity from which it was snatched and raped.

As Tadzio attempts to conform to the wretchedly human, Aschenbach becomes a wizard, casting spells against the human race, manipulating his Venetians, rejoicing in the cholera that his love-sickness has induced, the dissolution of social structure which accords so well with deranged passion. Like the parody aesthete Spinell he is now on the side of death, seeking consummations of superhuman intensity: if the bourgeoisie cannot be dazzled, then let it be destroyed. Aschenbach as Archimage shows the havoc that aesthetic power can accomplish when it becomes frustrated, perverse; when the novelist finds that his deepest will is operating not on the page but on the level of human society, society is in danger; this too is a prefiguration of the apocalyptic parts of *Dr. Faustus.* As *Death in Venice* proceeds, Aschenbach becomes exalted and degraded in equal measure. When he thinks to himself that the secret consolation of platonic love is that the lover is closer to heaven than the beautiful beloved, the way is being prepared for all manner of mysterious elevation and rapture; it is an ironic reversal of Tonio Kröger's celebrated aphorism, "Who loves the most is the inferior." There is a beautiful moment in *Death in Venice* in which Tadzio comes upon Aschenbach unexpectedly and smiles at him:

> With such a smile it might be that Narcissus bent over the mirroring pool, a smile profound, infatuated, lingering, as he put out his arms to the reflection of his own beauty; the lips just slightly pursed, perhaps half-realizing his own folly in trying to kiss the cold lips of his shadow—with a mingling of coquetry and curiosity and a faint unease, enthralling and enthralled. (*Stories II*, p. 50)

Tadzio, who is himself "mirror and image," looks at Aschenbach and sees—himself. Nothing could more clearly indicate Aschenbach's sense that Tadzio and he are twin, intimate, indistinguishable; and it is now that Aschenbach sinks down, without composure, unmanned, and says to the absent Tadzio "I love you." This is the turning point. Previously Aschenbach kept his feelings in check, restrained, unuttered; but in this collapse of discipline he now turns himself into an expressive instrument, self-dramatized, even theatrical. He still has great controlling power, perhaps more than ever, but increasingly he resembles a character in a novel rather than the author of it. He is not afraid of the winks and leers of those who see him now as actor rather than spectator, an old man chasing a boy; and finally he accepts the necessity of self-declaration by allowing a barber to make him up, in the garish semblance of youth. At this point, when he has traded his impassive Mahler's-face for that of a clown, he has become one of his own puppet-characters; he wants to become Tadzio's double in the flesh as well as spirit, so he has allowed himself to become an aesthetic object, a mask. Tadzio and Aschenbach have reversed their initial positions exactly. I believe that it was for this descent of the artist's impalpable power into materiality that Mann criticized *Death in Venice*, in an enigmatic line from his poem of 1919, *Gesang vom Kindchen*: "Look, it turned from a drunken song into a moral fable." Clearly Mann wished that he had stressed the rapturous, intoxicated, hymnlike nature of the novella rather than Aschenbach's ludicrousness; the artist should stay unrevealed, working toward apotheosis without contaminating himself in the humid apparatus of personal expression. Aschenbach should not have said "I love you," weeping, like some character from a morbid psychological novel or a film of Visconti's; he should have stormed the heavens in a ferocity of song, his rage against the sexual denial of beauty turning more beautiful and limpid than Tadzio himself. There is some evidence that Mann would have liked the novella to have proceeded in these paths, but it is for the best that it did not. One might say that Mann fell into the trap which he knew well enough to allow his fictitious Aschenbach to avoid; that is, the assumption that the only kind of beauty worthy of hymning is the celestial stuff of the *Phaedrus*, the beauty that unstrings the eye in its socket with shivery premonition of the divine. What Aschenbach learns—and it agrees with Mann's later philosophy —is that beauty is inadequate unless it includes the whole human; the lover of beauty must not despise what is merely vulnerable and carnal, but must, with reverence and humility, in a soft voice, bespeak his love for the warm, shabby, necessitous things of the senses. Beauty is that which pleases the sight, as the philosophers say; and the smell, and the taste, and the touch as well.

From the study of *Death in Venice* we are in a position to draw a reasonably complete model of Thomas Mann's aesthetic world, valid at least for some years before and after 1912. The style of Aschenbach at his first encounter with Tadzio, the classical, mythological, delicately pointed, elevated style which Mann imitates in certain passages of chapter 4, is valid for roughly half of the aesthetic world; the later style of Aschenbach, with its murmured avowals of love, imaginary conversation, feverish self-abasement, no less exalted than the first, a drunken song and a moral fable in one, expresses the hidden part of the aesthetic. Here then is the composite picture; half of aesthetic reality takes place in the upper air; four horses, whose backs and tails are a continuous line of fire, draw the luminous chariot of the sun, a gilded youth wearing an emblem of a solar disk on his costume; the stars, arranged into pictures, blush and recede; the sky is everywhere decorated with *putti*, whose wings are too small even for this area of reduced gravity, causing them to flap with the charming incompetence of young birds; but nothing here is mere adornment, for this is the kingdom of the mind, and all is type and prefiguration of the motions of the mind, a fantasy grown as sharp and lucid as human reason. But the lower world of the aesthetic is no less beautiful, where steam and fetor graduate the swamp into a foreground in which ferns and aerial roots intersect in filigree, and a background which promises total immersion into mud; where flamingos and herons make coarse, blurred cries which resemble the shouts of the amorous, and sleeping branches seem like the corpses of men; where, in the flatlands, slow, thick flies grown heavy from ordure are scarcely distinguishable from the bees that make black honey. What I have described here as the aesthetic world—using figures drawn for *Death in Venice* and other sources in Mann—is a world in which all that is mixed or tentative has been resolved; all things that tend upward or downward have reached their destination; a world purged of middle ground, human society; a genius' simplification of the world, in which everything has reduced to a metaphor of the self, the heaven of the mind or the hell of the body. Mann may have believed that the latter part of *Death in Venice* was too ironic and psychological, but it is at least as rhapsodic as the classical fantasia of chapter 4; the descriptions of Venice, of cholera, form an anthem to disease, in the highest style; and Aschenbach's great speech to Phaedrus shows that self-contempt is as sweet and heady to him as wine. He laments that aesthetic form cannot maintain itself because it provokes an itch that only the sexual body can scratch; but his lament is so formal and lovely that it scarcely constitutes a renunciation of form. Everything Aschenbach does is beautiful: his dream of the orgy and the phallic god, despite its bloodthirstiness, is based on well-known classical figuration, the snake-cinctured revelers, and passages in it are redolent of Euripides. Near the beginning, when Aschenbach discovers his desire to travel, he has a vision of a fantastic swamp as his ultimate goal:

> He beheld a landscape, a tropical marshland, beneath a reeking sky, steaming, monstrous, rank—a kind of primeval wilderness-world of islands, morasses, and alluvial channels. Hairy palm-trunks rose near and far out of lush brakes of fern, out of bottoms of crass vegetation, fat, swollen, thick with incredible bloom. There were trees, mis-shapen as a dream, that dropped their naked roots straight through the air into the ground or into water that was stagnant and shadowy and glassy-green, where mammoth milk-white blossoms floated, and strange high-shouldered birds with curious bills stood gazing sidewise without sound or stir. Among the knotted joints of a bamboo thicket the eyes of a crouching tiger gleamed—and he felt his heart throb with terror, yet with a longing inexplicable. (*Stories II*, p. 9)

This is the kingdom of the body. The vegetable swelling and the hidden tiger project those desires which Aschenbach had suppressed; and as Aschenbach discloses his interior, manifests his disease, he perceives it always as something terrifying and beautiful. The self-preoccupied man always has a wide gap between the curious, experimental mind—whose play is represented by cerebral myth and self-conscious loftiness—and the pit of the body; Aschenbach is not dissimilar to Christian Buddenbrook in his horrified fascination at his body's potentialities; but this does not mean that the body does not have its own aesthetic, and by no means a humble one. Mann does not discriminate unequivocally between the delight of the artist in the production of objective beauty and the *voluptué*'s pursuit of tactile stimulation; aesthetics comes from the Greek word for feeling, and even though in recent centuries it has been imagined that there exists a kind of feeling more refined, gratuitous, and poetic than ordinary sensation, Mann often insists that aesthetic feeling and ordinary feeling are disturbingly interchangeable. This is why Mann describes the processes of the body with such precise, delicate, formal attention; the body's sensory mechanism is the basis of art. Although the psychological Hermes replaces Dionysus as Mann's favorite god in his later novels, images of ecstatic body, the possessed body, continue strongly in Mann's art from the first scene of *Tales of Jacob*, in which Joseph howls lunacies at the moon, to the last paragraph of *Felix Krull*. Mann clearly was impressed by Nietzsche's analysis in *The Birth of Tragedy* of the interdependence of Apollo and Dionysus; and so Mann's later artists become increasingly involved with carnal matters, Joseph more successfully than Aschenbach, Leverkühn more intensely, more miserably, more intimately than either, Felix Krull more enormously than anyone. Mann is interested in artists who, like Aschenbach or Leverkühn, wish to produce an art that is icy, formal, beyond the dross of humankind; but such art is always partial and unsatisfying, unless it is broken and compelled to feed on sexual blood. Yeats has said that Dionysus is sad; and for Mann, Dionysus is foul, convulsive, incoherent, full of self-loathing, a god who chews his own forearm and toes; but for all that, still divine.

Beauty is not important in Mann's later works; that is, beauty exclusive of human pain, beauty content to gaze at its own loveliness. In Mann's essay of 1930 on Platen, which has remarkable connections with *Death in Venice*—not only because Platen was a homosexual classicist poet who wrote about Venice but also because Aschenbach quotes a line and fulfills a prophecy of his—Mann pronounces his sentence on classical beauty: it is rigid, cerebral; it pertains to death; its alabaster perfection seems faintly ludicrous to the modern sensibility (*Essays*, pp. 261–62). At the end of the essay Mann suggests that Platen, for all his self-abasement to the beautiful, managed to climb partly out of his sensuality into some genuinely masculine, spiritual, decent humanism, exactly Aschenbach's fondest hope; but Mann finds a happy ending for most of his critical essays, and his usual aesthetic philosophy is skeptical of the power of beauty to lead to positive mental states.

At the beginning of Mann's career, beauty was morbid; as he grows older beauty becomes less interesting than that. Mann, whose taste is so catholic, writes seldom about visual art, and when he does he often finds it suspicious. Paintings are too static, unbending, when compared to the dynamic plasticity, the suppleness, of literature and music; and Mann shows tacit consent, almost secret approval, when he describes the desire to mutilate paintings, feelings which overpower two of his early heroes, Hieronymous in "Gladius Dei" and the Savonarola of *Fiorenza*; they have more spiritual and even aesthetic power than mere painters and artisans—Savonarola overmatches even Botticelli, whom he converts. In *The Magic Mountain* the painted form of Hans' grandfather takes over his grandfather's identity (p. 25), becomes an emblem of all old paternal repressive influences in life; like Hans' stiff image of Death in a starched Spanish collar the painting becomes a link to the grave. In such ways as these the overdefined image becomes worthy of that destruction which Savonarola offers. The next stage in the development of the beautiful image is insipidity; beauty is boring, we are told on the first page of *Young Joseph* (p. 261); without sexual charm or the grace of youth it cannot hold our attention. The last stage is rot. Adrian Leverkühn's father tells him that there are butterflies of surpassing beauty whose flavor is so disgusting that no predator will touch them (*Dr. Faustus*, p. 15); and this butterfly is thematically linked to the prostitute who infects Leverkühn. As for theoretical beauty, Leverkühn has pronounced opinions; the word *beauty* he finds offensive and silly (p. 78); the prelude to act 3 of *Die Meistersinger* may be sublime, but he has only contempt for those rhetorical tricks by which the effect of beauty is achieved (p. 133); beauty is a sham which our era no longer finds valid. On the other hand Leverkühn in his full maturity seems to agree with Zeitblom that aesthetics "is at bottom everything" (p. 308), all that pertains to the human. Beauty is a superficial smoothness, a trick, a labored calculation of effect; aesthetics, on the other hand, has broad reference, is in fact that mysterious principle of control which Leverkühn exerts indifferently upon his music or upon the organization of his friends' lives. In the essays at the end of his life, Mann is not afraid in his own person to denounce beauty. When writing on Nietzsche he accuses him of a murderous aestheticism; the aesthete, like Institoris in *Dr. Faustus*, must adore the blond superman who is in moral terms an infantile sadist; the final development of the figure of Mann's aesthete is Hitler. Mann discovers a simple formula for this: Ethics is life, aesthetics death (*Last Essays*, p. 162). Jewish morality has served civilization well; the Greek aesthetes and artists have vanished quickly from civilization. Nothing further can be imagined from the original classicism of Aschenbach; if the aesthetic is itself bourgeois, as Mann says at the end of his essay on Nietzsche (*Last Essays*, p. 176), we have come 180 degrees from the earlier position. The realm of Mann's later fiction is the aesthetic only in the most extended sense we have developed; the aesthetic turned earthy, ambiguous, smelling of sweat and ozone, unresolvable; for, as Mann says in *The Story of a Novel* (p. 144), life is pain, clarification is death.

Gnosticism

To the aesthetic longing in Mann's novels for bodiless heaven and sexual hell there correspond several philosophical structures, the chief of which may be called gnosticism. Mann's gnosticism, expressed in simple form rather late in his life, should not be identified too closely with the polemical and spiteful philosophy of Valentinus which Irenaeus, one of the few church fathers who saw the narrative merits of heresies, was kind enough to record; Mann's gnosticism is a far more tolerant and enlightened version. As set forth memorably in the prelude to *Joseph*, the journey into the historical hell, gnosticism is a super-myth, the myth of the human race simplified out of all measure: in the beginning the human race consisted of one man, Adam Qadmon, a figure of pure light, a denizen of the spiritual kingdom; this man, seeing his reflection in matter—for matter, at the beginning of time, was simple uninflected substance, as bald, inert, and extensive as a mirror—fell in love, and descended into matter; and this descent was the real Fall of Man. Yet even as a resident of matter the first man was unable to accomplish his desire, for he lacked the power to give shape to the images of his imagination; so a beneficent God created the world, and all the forms in the world, in order that the man might revel as he pleased. But God also sent a "second emissary," evidently part of himself and a double of the first man, to rescue the first man from the wallow of matter, for God envisioned at the end of time a return to the primal stasis, spirit and matter at last equally bland and indifferent, equally incontaminate, liberated from form. At this point human suspense enters the myth. The "second emissary" is prey to the same temptations as the first man; he does not like to find himself in the position of Savonarola, destroying the plenitude of the world, against form, on the side of death; so God's projected ending to the scenario is dubious. Clearly Mann has altered the myth by neutralizing the evil of matter; gnostic hatred of the material is transformed into a recognition of the genuine charm and value of the sensual world; God, who is in Mann the most thoughtful and devoted of fathers, is to be commended for allowing the first man his fling into corporality. It must be noted that this is the barest possible type of psychomachia: the human soul, which the first man represents, is tugged by two opposing forces, spirit—the "second emissary"—and nature, each of which is its image, part of itself; and in the soul's struggle for its realization the entire world and all its richness are generated by the plastic force of the simple oppositions. What is important is the reciprocal motion: two naked poles yearning for each other meet and embrace, unite, ramify; but then, when thoroughly mixed together, they yearn again for separation and simplicity. It is the same process which Shridaman and Nanda undergo in *The Transposed Heads*, which Mann expresses in unusually concise and cryptic language:

> The friendship between the two youths was based on the diversity in their I- and my-feelings, those of the one yearning toward those of the other. Incorporation, that is, makes for isolation, isolation for difference; difference makes for comparisons, comparisons give rise to uneasiness, uneasiness to wonderment, wonderment tends to admiration; and finally admiration turns to a yearning for mutual exchange and unity. (*Stories II*, p. 215)

This is the principle which governs composite things; and, since the soul of man is compounded of nature and spirit, it vacillates between an uneasy but productive union of sensibility, and a jangling schizophrenia or uncomfortable prominence of nature or spirit. In no case is the soul at rest; it is involved in an endless process of alternate fusion and fission.

Yet this gnostic model of the soul, though it could not be simpler, is still too prescriptive to be adequate generally to Mann's career. Its inherent instability is illustrated by the alternate termination which Mann gives to it even in the prelude to *Joseph*. Mann professes to be uncertain of the proper textual interpretation which he should give to the description of the role of the "second emissary"; perhaps his old myth means, not that the "second emissary" is a second version of the first man, but that the "emissary" and the first man will become the same in the future; that is, that a final reconciliation of soul and spirit, the sensual and the divine, will at last obtain, and the final stasis will not be a retreat into separate domains but an everlasting miscibility. In this way Mann makes sure that his conception of heaven allows for all possibilities, and either the strictly separate and defined or indivisible incarnation may turn out to be the proper goal of the human. It is the same problem that faced Mann at the end of *Fiorenza* (*Stories I*, p. 319): Lorenzo believes that the poles of the great antinomy are reconcilable, while Savonarola insists that spirit and beauty are twin abysses, spanned by longing, a rainbow, but ultimately distinct and opposed. But the difficulties of the gnostic model are more severe than this ambiguity of ending. The concepts of "nature" and "spirit" are themselves ambiguous, almost specious. It is easily inferred from the prelude to *Joseph* that the natural man is a harmless fellow, possibly a voluptuary but too sluggish to be evil; any number of passages in *Joseph* bear out the basic lack of complication, the untroubledness, of natural man; while the spiritual man is, like Abram, a great moony wanderer, agonized by the divine thorn, infuriated by the divine itch.

However, this attitude is by no means typical of the rest of Mann's canon. One of Mann's farthest-ranging explorations of the theme of nature and spirit apart from *Joseph* is, oddly enough, not a work of fiction at all but a long literary essay, the most ambitious that he ever attempted: the *Goethe and Tolstoy* of 1922. Here he says, lest the structure of his imagination be in doubt, "nature is not spirit; in fact, this antithesis is, I should say, the greatest of all antitheses" (*Essays*, p. 106); and he proceeds to arrange great writers in these simple patterns, Goethe and Tolstoy as creatures of nature, Schiller and Dostoevsky as creatures of spirit. The attributes of natural and spiritual man are nearly the reverse of those of *Joseph*: the children of the spirit here possess "Clarity, harmony of oneself ... in short, peace of mind," while the children of nature are full of "peculiar coldness, ill will, *médisance*, a devil-may-care mood, an inhuman, elfish irresponsibility" (*Essays*, p. 80). Because of shifts like these it is hard to keep the categories useful, just as Hans Castorp in *The Magic Mountain* makes fun of Settembrini and Naphta for the arbitrariness and inconsistency of their dialectical positions; sometimes Mann feels revulsion against the organic, other times he feels acutely the sterility of art and mind, and such feelings determine the meaning of his private categories. What is most significant is the principle of reciprocal motion, independent of the content of the antinomy—yet even this reciprocity, the most generally applicable feature of Mann's gnostic myth, is far from invariant; usually, as in "The Hungry" or *Fiorenza* or *The Transposed Heads*, the characters fit neatly into balanced pairs, each yearning for the other, but often, as in *Tonio Kröger*, the spiritual hero yearns for an uncomplicated healthy nature-figure who prefers someone of his own race, a kind of ontological homosexuality. The urge to form pairs is strongest between unlikes, but is not exclusive to them; and in a large society a given person will feel attractions in several different directions at once, leading to all manner of incomplete pairs, frustrated chains, misalliances, impossible wishes, infidelities. In this way the neat calculus of dialectic veers into unmanageable richness and complexity. Nature versus spirit may be the most important antithesis, but it is not the only one; and one of the lessons of the study of gnostic myth is that all myths falsify, even the simplest and most basic. At the beginning of *The Tales of Jacob* it seems that all the characters chase mythic role and resonance with the eagerness of refugees hunting for passports or birth certificates; but by *Joseph the Provider* Joseph is coolly insistent on an identity independent of myth or type (p. 937). The relation between man and myth is a most complex interaction; the man can never fully satisfy the myth, the myth can never fully define the man. Gnostic myth, though a useful structural tool, is not definitive. Personality must be intelligible but not too intelligible.

No writer of the twentieth century possessed to the degree of Mann the talent of creating from the play of the intellect, from debate and abstract discussion, a medium of human expression as flexible, passionate, and dramatic as the murmurs of lovers or the cries of despairing. Indeed, in Mann's later works, a scream may find expression as a historical treatise on the Inquisition; a declaration of love as an inquiry into the German character; a belch as a brief citation from Goethe. As the apparatus of Mann's sensibility becomes weighty, the narrative drama of his story refines and expands into an intellectual analogue of human event; some have felt this to be a decline in intensity, but I believe that most readers are grateful to discover that intellect is capable of such affect, that the mind has erogenous zones neatly congruent to the body's. I take Mann's work as the greatest refutation of a famous proposition that is perhaps no longer much debated, but which has done mischief in this century: T. S. Eliot's dissociation of sensibility. Mann's intellect is delicately responsive, aggressive, flirtatious; and it is for this reason that a certain arbitrariness, even inconsistency, occurs in his favorite dialectical categories, such as nature and spirit. Mann does not try to pin these definitions down with systematic rigor; instead he wishes these words to be felt as emotion, evocation, expression. Argument in his novels does not exist to convince the reader but to embody a human situation, and words like *nature, spirit, artist, bourgeois, individualism, communism* comprise his vocabulary of love and hate, hesitation, self-reproach, commitment. It is not surprising, then, that nature and spirit, laden with such connotation, should be fluid and fluctuant terms.

Intellectually preeminent among Mann's novels is *The Magic Mountain*. Certain of his later works are more brilliant, notably *Dr. Faustus*, and each of his later novels is associated with a branch of learning: comparative mythology in *Joseph*, the theory of light and color in *Lotte in Weimar*, music in *Dr. Faustus*, linguistics in *The Holy Sinner*, cosmology in *Felix Krull*; but in *The Magic Mountain* the ideological structure is more pointedly expressive of human conflict and concord than in any other of Mann's works. I have spoken above of the manner in which emotional life can be translated into ratiocination, a process which can itself be described dialectically as the upward translation of nature into the spirit; and *The Magic Mountain* explores with great ingenuity every relation between nature and spirit, their separate powers and the enormous tangles that result when they meet. Gnostic myth is a comedy, in which the soul of man proceeds from monotonous chastity to dangerous sexual delight; and, if the second ending is the true one, the soul's experiment leads to a great redemption of the natural world itself. This, broadly, can be seen as the structure of *The Magic Mountain*.

Death in Venice ends with a terrifying descent, the mind's enmiring in the swamp of the body; and it is in the body's muck that we remain as we pass into *The Magic Mountain*. The First World War, which interrupted its composition for many years, seems only to have heightened Mann's preoccupation with the carnal. With its poison gas, the action of which on the lungs bore some resemblance to tuberculosis, its spawn of amputees, its endless trenches of mud, the war must have seemed like a medical dissection, a protracted and infinitely painful analysis of the human body. I know of no novel, except perhaps *Moby Dick*, in which the shape, structure, products, and functions of the body are a matter of such ceaseless fascination; here character is flesh, identity is bone. I suspect there is an implicit organic metaphor which is a partial determinant of the novel's structure: the splitting of the single cell and its development into an articulate organism. Such processes as this interest Hans Castorp greatly in the chapter "Research," in which a searching self-examination is conducted by means of medical textbooks; he discovers that his body consists of an inconceivable number of tiny organisms (p. 277), which in the midst of their separate lives constitute a whole Hans Castorp. This leads to a remarkable illumination: Hans decides that his ego is not so integral as he had thought; his *I* is multiple, manifold, indiscrete. It is unusual that a character, reading about anatomy, would assume that the structure of his body provides the key to the

structure of his psyche, but that is the least of the carnal marvels of
The Magic Mountain. The fact that the body is a congeries of cells
may offer a clue to the relation of the other characters of the novel to
Hans Castorp; because the characters embody the major principles of
Western thought, they become a complex image of Hans Castorp's
extremely ductile personality. Hans is no Tonio Kröger or Hanno
Buddenbrook, but he bears much in common with those magical
children: he comes from a rich family that is declining in vigor, is
himself delicate in physique; he is capable of deep reverence, and
places himself provisionally on the side of feeling and death; he has
moments of insight and even verbal brilliance. His position in Mann's
canon is that of the stunted or too-soft artist; after 1910 Mann was
capable of presenting such a figure with sympathy, despite his
luxuriousness, his calmness, his sloth, his incompetence, his pro-
vinciality. Hans maintains one major trait of the infant prodigy, a
trait which Mann esteems almost above all others: potentiality. When
the good burghers of his town look at him, a young engineering
student, they are conscious that he might become anything, a
conservative drag or a radical, reckless spender; would he become a
member of his grandfather's political party, or a member of the
opposition? "In his blue eyes . . . his fellow citizens read no answer to
their curious questioning. And he probably knew none himself, Hans
Castorp, this still unwritten page" (p. 36). He is a *tabula rasa*, capable
of development in any direction, a single cell uncertain whether it is
lily, elephant, or man; and all whom he meets are anxious to
incorporate their opinions into him, form him according to their
species. Ludovico Settembrini, the Italian humanist, sets out to block
the formation of those traits that do not conform to Settembrini's
character (p. 98); and then, adopting the narrator's figure of the
unwritten page—another disquieting collusion between author and
character—Settembrini tells Hans he is not an unwritten page but a
page full of contradictory writing, the good and bad mixed together
(p. 100), and it is the schoolmaster's task to erase the bad. Hans is not
one of Mann's geniuses, a figure of such aesthetic power that all
characters perform the mysterious charades of his will; but he is the
passive, lazy analogue of such a figure. Hans, with his vague charm
and teasing inchoateness, seems to offer a piece of blank marble for
anyone to carve; he is not an artist, but the raw material for art; yet he
stubbornly retains his sense of potentiality, will not assume that shape
which Settembrini tries to force on him. In this way he incorporates
into his being all those who seek to educate him; his yieldingness is
stronger than anyone's plastic power. It is the inverse of genius, and
nearly as potent; out of sheer sloth he allows the struggling and

contentious characters of the novel to form themselves into his psychomachia.

Hans Castorp has so few opinions or traits, except for his curiosity about the dead, that he is almost characterless; and in the great bath of Hans' neutral personality the other characters grow and develop according to simple dialectical principles. All emblems generate their opposites, seek their twins: Settembrini, insofar as he is an intellectual, a spiritual irritant, leads inevitably to Mme. Chauchat, all exotic flesh, casual and contemptuous, his first great antagonist; insofar as Settembrini embodies enlightened humanism, individualism, he generates his debating-partner Naphta, who is hermit and communist, Manichaean in the old style; together Naphta and Settembrini, who are secretly as close as brothers, mutually reinforcing, sharpening, intellectual kin, require a counterweight, who appears in the figure of Peeperkorn, a character of such earthshaking gravity that Naphta and Settembrini flit away like bats, fall into serious dissension and disease, fight a duel, disappear. The appearance of Peeperkorn completes the great fourfold pattern of the novel; that he and Mme. Chauchat are lovers only reaffirms the neatness of the quadrilateral, the two natural characters linked through sexual tension, opposed to the two spiritual characters perfecting themselves through the stress of argument. What these four characters, even when not explicitly pedagogical, utter and embody is the content of Hans Castorp's mind; that unbiased but discriminating consciousness formulates its problems and resolves them through the four great subsidiary characters. When Hans notices that Naphta and Settembrini defer to Peeperkorn, despite their harangues against him, it is the physical demonstration and confirmation of what Hans had already tentatively decided, that Peeperkorn is superior to them. In the fourfold design, a variety of minor cross-links are hinted at, though there is not space to develop them all even in *The Magic Mountain*; for instance, an incipient relationship between Mme. Chauchat and Naphta, who are certainly greatly opposed as emblems of flesh and spirit, yet who in one scene find they share common radical political views, chat with interest (p. 581). It is known that Mann thought of the structure of *The Magic Mountain* as a series of organized intellectual temptations; he says so in a letter of 1939 (*Letters I*, p. 301), even suggesting the intellectual component of Mme. Chauchat's seduction.

Yet as the fourfold pattern becomes more highly developed, it does not become more stable; the entrance of Peeperkorn, which completes it, also begins its downfall. For one thing, the later characters are more extreme, Naphta so spiritual that he hates the body, loves torture, Peeperkorn so natural that his personal weight makes the whole novel bottom-heavy; such characters cannot easily be reconciled into a single dialectic. For another, each additional character introduces an element of intellectual confusion. What is Settembrini's stand on the physical body? When he talks to Mme. Chauchat, he is against it, urges Hans to a chaste productivity that is not entangled in the senses (p. 249); when he talks to Naphta, he must defend the body against Naphta's desire to flagellate it (p. 454). Hans finds the inconsistencies amusing, but one cannot keep oneself intellectually pure unless there are only two people, two poles; and the fact that two feel the necessity to become four makes any real clarity impossible. This tendency of pairs to breed, create more pairs, this dialectical instability, becomes more significant in Mann's later novels; it is his major elaboration and sophistication of the gnostic myth. In *The Magic Mountain*, the centrifugal stress reaches its climax with the fourth *dramatis persona* of the myth, Peeperkorn; it is only the peculiar genius of Hans that holds these contentious characters into one tense circle, as Mann tells us in a passage describing his introduction of Settembrini, Naphta, and assorted fools to Peeperkorn and Mme. Chauchat:

> Strangeness, tension, even suppressed hostility there was of course enough between them; it is surely rather remarkable that a comparatively insignificant personality could have held them together. That he did so must be laid to a certain shrewd geniality native to him, which found everything fish that came to his net, and not only bound to him people of the most diverse tastes and characters, but exerted enough power to bind them to each other.
> (P. 580)

Soon Hans has compared and decided; he finds Peeperkorn to his liking, is convinced, and at that point he has learned almost all that the magic mountain has to teach him; so the profound phantoms of the dialectic are dismissed, Peeperkorn and Naphta commit suicide, Settembrini goes off to die, and Hans climbs down, back into direct human experience, war.

The sanatorium for the tubercular, the magic mountain, is a little protected world, an experimental world, a kind of playpen; it is, in greatly expanded form, identical to Hanno Buddenbrook's bedroom or Joseph's pit; it is a place of fantasy designed to prepare one for a more dangerous, more public world. Here all is ordered, as in a fairy tale or game, by arbitrary numerical rule; here phantasm proliferates until it approaches the complexity of the real society outside. There is a single, controlling jest that informs the magic mountain, a single spell that isolates and protects it from mixed and perilous reality: all human problems must be treated as organic disease; the body is mankind's great refuge, for in the body we are safe, sanctified, enchanted. In this corporeal asylum there is a comforting impersonality; the doctors treat the patients without rancor or mistrust, as slabs of flesh that have become deranged. The theoretical center of the magic mountain is the psychologist Dr. Krokowski, who explains that love is a physiological disturbance, disease a form of repressed love (p. 128), epilepsy an orgasm of the brain (p. 300), and therefore the highest anxieties and raptures of the human soul become amenable to medical therapy. But of course the primary treatment consists of simple residence; it is the location that cures better than any drug; and the experience of living a wholly bodily life, that state, induced by thermometer and auscultation, of perpetual, watchful coenesthesis, is the means through which the patient will effect his own recovery. In the 1911 *Felix Krull* the infant genius trains his body to impossible feats, willed fever, willed dilation of the eyes, simply by staring in the mirror, by a self-scrutiny so intense that every secret of the body is mastered. The treatment in the sanatorium is governed by similar principles: if the patient can be raised to a strong enough state of self-preoccupation, he can gain enough control over his body to make himself sick or well as he chooses. This hope is not always fulfilled. For many, if not most, patients, this sudden, monstrous consciousness of one's body leads to the same kind of self-destructive fascination that overcame Christian Buddenbrook: one deliberately induces disease in order to experience the full spectrum of feeling. This is what happens to the unpleasant Frau Stöhr, who speaks of the pleasure of coughing, the extreme pleasure of sneezing; and all of the characters are capable of understanding that, although the better ones seek to suppress this unwelcome knowledge. The abandonment of self-restraint is another aspect of the magic mountain's therapeutic philosophy: Dr. Krokowski encourages the amorous toward full self-expression, and Hofrat Behrens, the head physician, speaks of the necessity for the tubercular metabolism to be accelerated into a full flowering if cure is to take place. Yet it is just this sort of loss of control, which leads Mme. Chauchat to slam doors and tempts Hans too into personal carelessness, leaving doors open behind him, not sitting upright at dinner, which seems to brutalize and destroy; when Settembrini warns Hans that the magic mountain is Circe's isle, in which Hans will soon grunt on all fours if he does not abandon it (p. 247), much of the weight of the novel presses behind that warning. Hans, soon after his arrival, complains of meaningless palpitations of the heart, feels that his body has usurped his identity, turning him into a kind of zombie (p. 71); and Settembrini agrees: "An invalid is *all* body.... In most cases he is little better than a carcass" (p. 100). Close observation of the body gives every reason for alarm, and surrender to the body seems a fatal indulgence; it seems that the patient will be rendered fit for human society only in the manner which Behrens describes to Hans' horrified uncle:

> In the first place, your belly bursts. You lie there on your chips and sawdust, and you bloat; the gases swell you up, puff you all out, the way frogs do when bad little boys fill them up with air. You get to be a regular balloon; the skin of your belly can't stand it any more, it bursts. You go pop. You relieve yourself mightily, like Judas Iscariot when he fell from the bough and all his bowels gushed out. And after that you are fit for society again. If you got leave to come back, you could visit your friends without being offensive. You are thoroughly stunk out. (Pp. 438–39)

But if the body's tendency is morbid, it is in the direction of a death that is boundlessly fertile, even exultant. Mann wrote in 1925 that he had, for the first time in literature, made death into a comic figure (*Letters I*, p. 137); and it is at least true that *The Magic Mountain* may be described as a comedy of the body. The body, disease, and even death are purposive, and serve in mysterious ways the goal of human self-realization. Hans was not altogether right when he feared that the palpitations of his heart were meaningless, automatic; he soon discovered that there existed an emotional referent to those spasms, Clavdia Chauchat; his body was more sensitive than his consciousness, premonitory, subtle. Similarly at the end of the novel Hans suspects that his cousin Ziemssen's relapse, so deplorable and deathly, was due to a secret collusion of soul and body (p. 500), as Ziemssen's deepest desire, to be with Marusja, defeated his avowed purpose, to join his regiment; disease is willed, obedient. Attentiveness to the body's desires does in fact lead Hans out of involution to a richer experience of life, his sexual encounter with Mme. Chauchat, which, although an early experience in a brothel is alluded to, is his real loss of virginity.

If *The Magic Mountain* is merely a parody of a *Bildungsroman*, as Mann insisted (*Letters I*, p. 152), a low carnal analogue of spiritual education, it is nevertheless true that most of the apparatus of the spirit still clings awesomely to the initiation rites of the body. The X-ray room, one of Hans' most illuminating adventures, is clearly a version of a temple, in which the darkness, the ghostly light, accord well with the usual paraphernalia of witchery; it even smells of ozone, suggesting a curious parallel to a passage in *Lotte in Weimar* in which the pedant Riemer speaks, in reference to Goethe, of the smell of ozone that accompanies the apparition of a god (p. 74). Surgery too can be a profound ritual of the body; the pneumothorax operation that leaves Hermine Kleefeld capable of making unearthly whistling with her lungs gives to Ferge an insight into the deepest region of the body:

> The pleura, my friends, is not anything that should be felt of; it does not want to be felt of and it ought not to be. It is taboo. It is covered up with flesh and put away once and for all; nobody and nothing ought to come near it. And now he uncovers it and feels all over it. My God, I was sick at my stomach. Horrible, awful; never in my life have I imagined there could be such a sickening feeling, outside hell and its torments. I fainted; I had three fainting-fits one after the other, a green, a brown, and a violet. And there was a stink—the shock went to my sense of smell and I got an awful stench of hydrogen sulphide, the way it must smell in the bad place; with all that I heard myself laughing as I went off—not the way a human being laughs—it was the most indecent, ghastly kind of laughing I ever heard. Because, when they go over your pleura like that, I tell you what it is: it is as though you were being tickled—horribly, disgustingly tickled—that is just what the infernal torment of the pleura-shock is like, and may God keep you from it! (*Magic Mountain*, pp. 310–11)

This passage bears great resemblance to the Devil's celebrated description of hell in *Dr. Faustus*; hell is the inside of the body. Ferge, who is not a worthwhile man, is rendered almost holy because of his profound knowledge of pain; for on the magic mountain intensity and disease are venerated instead of health. Most of Mann's novels arrive at redemption only after a ceremonial descent into the pit, and in *The Magic Mountain* the pit is that fount of wonders, the body.

The joke of the novel, the reduction and embedding of the spirit into the body, where love is an engorgement of tissue, exaltation a fever, produces images of the body that are amazingly complex; the body, so stuffed with spiritual significance, eventually attains a kind of transfiguration. To the practiced eye the skin is spiritually legible; Behrens, who is an amateur painter, produces a picture of Mme. Chauchat in which the skin is remarkably detailed and lifelike. He explains his technique to the admiring Hans by means of an anatomy lesson: the artist should be a surgeon, for one must understand how a woman takes expressive form according to the distribution of fat in her body, how the minute tension of subdermal muscles produces facial expression, self-revelation. Identity is fully incarnate in one's own flesh; the body's depths manifest themselves on the surface; and the experienced observer can learn how to see the body as a transparent medium. Hans in the X-ray room inspects his own hand-skeleton and feels that he is staring into his grave (p. 218); but the grave is the alembic of the soul (p. 511), as Naphta tells Hans much later, and the penetration into the mysteries of the body becomes an allegory of the soul's free self-discovery. As Settembrini knows, monism is an optimistic philosophy; and the adequacy of the body as the soul's vehicle is a strong affirmation of the human. Hans' researches reveal that life is a fever of matter, and matter and the animating spark of spirit are so mixed together, inseparable, that death seems uniform and congruent with life, as joyous. At the end of the "Research" chapter Hans imagines "beasts of the Milky Way, cosmic monsters whose flesh, bone, and brain were built up out of solar systems" (p. 284), and in these beasts we see a corporality magnified into such infinity that it can excel in grandeur the most exalted construction of the spirit.

The spirit's contentedness and amicability with its corporeal vehicles can be discovered in many odd corners of *The Magic Mountain*. Settembrini's humanism, whatever its philosophical inadequacies, accords well with many of the opinions Mann expresses in his essays; and when Naphta derides Settembrini's vision of human progress as "a sophisticated transmogrification of the Church's doctrine" (p. 382), he is absolutely right. Settembrini's Utopia is the transcendent sinlessness of man's original state lowered into terrestrial form (p. 402); when he speaks of ashes as "man's imperishable part" (p. 458), he is uttering a parody of theological doctrine; and his freemasonry has its origins in alchemistic learning that is only a surrogate to the mystery of transubstantiation (p. 512). Yet Naphta's mockery is a secret validation of Settembrini's philosophy, for if such high and awful mysteries can in fact be realized in human society, if society can be made casually, thoughtlessly incarnational, then human dreams and spiritual ambitions can be fulfilled adequately on an earth which has been too long hostile.

Naphta attempts to deride Settembrini by proving that his humanism is merely a tepid and inane version of the Church's orthodoxy, but this line of reasoning can only serve to abolish the purity of their opposition, destroy the clean dialectic that has been so painstakingly constructed. Mann is nowhere subtler than in his treatment of the catastrophe of Naphta and Settembrini, for as the two distinguished intellects descend to increasingly childish and mechanical contradiction, it becomes clear that the grounds of their antagonism are rooted in no respectable opposition but in willful contrariness; they are too insubstantial, too airy, too much *alike* in doctrine and mind to sustain the titanic struggle that they profess. When dialectical poles are made to touch, confined too long in the same quarters, they exhaust themselves, grow petty and jejune, acquire a curiously intimate

quarrelsomeness; it is no accident that Naphta provokes the chal-
lenge, the catastrophe, by a speech on the "contentious unservice-
ability of the great abstract conception" (p. 694), a speech about the
necessary equivocation of all dialectical positions; in this polemic he
shows the main tendency of the novel, for the two debaters must have
a glimpse of that incoherence, the "morally chaotic All" (p. 464) to
which all dialectic yearns. Naphta and Settembrini teach themselves a
lesson that costs everything, the lesson of their own partialness; they
are halves at best, dependent on each other, and their arguments are
superseded by some loftier, more inclusive vision. The reader can
glimpse the relation of the narrator of *The Magic Mountain* to his
characters in a passage like the following:

> "If I might be permitted," Naphta interpolated, "to introduce a
> little logic into the premises, I should state the question thus:
> either Ptolemy and the schoolmen were right, and the world is
> finite in time and space, the deity is transcendent, the antithesis
> between God and man is sustained, and man's being is dual;
> from which it follows that the problem of his soul consists in the
> conflict between the spiritual and the material, to which all social
> problems are entirely secondary—and this is the only sort of
> individualism I can recognize as consistent—or else, on the other
> hand, your Renaissance astronomers hit upon the truth, and the
> cosmos is infinite. Then there exists no suprasensible world, no
> dualism; the Beyond is absorbed into the Here, the antithesis
> between God and nature falls; man ceases to be the theatre of a
> struggle between two hostile principles, and becomes harmonious
> and unitary, the conflict subsists merely between his individual
> and his collective interest; and the will of the State becomes, in
> good pagan wise, the law of morality. Either one thing or the
> other." (P. 399)

Here there is every appearance of a profound philosophical issue, an
issue fit to preoccupy a civilization: either the world is finite and ruled
by God or infinite and secular; what reconciliation could be possible
to this antithesis? But chapter 6, the chapter of Naphta and Settembrini, begins with the narrator's discussion of this matter: he
proves that neither a finite nor an infinite universe can satisfy us (p.
344); the author embraces infinity and finitude in a single strong
grasp, and beside this immense tolerance of ambiguity the arguments
of less comprehensive genius must seem specious and inconclusive.

In *Joseph the Provider* Mann provides a discussion of the Hebrew
sacred words *Urim* and *Thummim*, the basic antithesis of the universe:
Urim means the light, but *Thummim* denotes a mingled condition,
light and darkness mixed (p. 996). Ultimately dialectic is not the

contest of part vs. part; instead the part stands opposed to the whole. When Urim and Thummin, spirit and nature, yes and yes-and-no meet, they do not finally cancel each other out; the end is what Mann calls a dark yes, that muddy, confused, and fecund affirmation, in which the chthonic and the divine are alike redeemed by their relish of a jest, that is the final flavor of many of Mann's novels. If Naphta and Settembrini are disconcertingly inconsistent, if they leave one puzzled about the exact nature of their dispute, they are nevertheless to be forgiven; for in their eagerness to destroy the intellectual clarity that they both prize, they serve to demonstrate the poverty of all that is distinct and orderly, all that pertains to the intellect; for what is not the whole sphere will in the end prove trivial.

The great testimony to human puissance is the magnificent character of Peeperkorn. The power of this alcoholic Dutchman exceeds that of any previous character in Mann's work; as Hans Castorp says, he is what personality ought to be like, personality incarnate. This personal force expresses itself through the body, through his huge appetites, through that sense of a gravity so intense that no head in its presence can remain unbowed. He has the tics and traits of a defined. character, with his great florid face, white hair, and stuttering, halting voice; but for all that he is little individuated. His features are more emblematic than individual, the traditional features of Jupiter; and if he is inarticulate, in contrast to the neat unreal periods of Naphta and Settembrini, it is because he embodies the point-blank incoherence of the physical world. Hans has a great deal of trouble describing him when he first appears; Hans toys with adjectives he considers self-contradictory, "lean" and "robust," falls into confusion; for Peeperkorn is technically indescribable, much too huge to be reduced to verbal formula. What is truest about Peeperkorn is that he is undefinable, blurred; his face looks like a mask because, as Mann explains when discussing Gerhart Hauptmann, the model for Peeperkorn's appearance, "there was a quality of unfinished development to it; it had a greatness that was never completed, never fully articulated, that remained masklike" (*Story of a Novel*, p. 195). This inchoateness manifests itself in many ways: in his instantaneous transformation between opposite states, such as the laborer and the king (*Magic Mountain*, p. 590), the martyr and the reveler; in his mediation between the aesthetic and the human, for he is half idol, half priest; and in his ability to assume the attributes of characters who seem greatly divergent from himself—in one scene Hans is astonished when the tongue-tied Peeperkorn speaks with the plasticity and rhetorical organization of Settembrini. Peeperkorn represents the natural on some almost subhuman level of articulation, a rough block of granite in which any shape, all shapes, are immanent.

Yet in the character of Peeperkorn nature has contracted to a point of such power, such animating and undifferentiated vital energy, that nature becomes almost indistinguishable from spirit. Many of the episodes in which he takes part use figures that are derived from the gnostic descent of spirit into matter, most notably the scene in which he summons the eagle down from the sky to gash open and eat its prey—a scene parallel with an event in Tolstoy's life that Mann tells in his essay *Goethe and Tolstoy* (*Essays*, p. 130). Hans believes that Peeperkorn's preeminence is based on the superabundance of feeling, and Peeperkorn seems to agree; he tells a parable in which the male is asked by Life, a sprawling female, to prove himself sexually, to exert himself to the utmost, and if his feelings are defeated, Life will mock his impotence (p. 566); and Peeperkorn here sets himself against life, against nature, puts himself in the masculine, spiritual, antagonistic role, as befits Jupiter, a deity of the sky. Peeperkorn returns to this parable when making his major theological speech of the novel:

> "Feeling, you understand, is the masculine force that rouses life. Life slumbers. It needs to be roused, to be awakened to a drunken marriage with divine feeling. For feeling, young man, is godlike. Man is godlike, in that he feels. He is the feeling of God. God created him in order to feel through him. Man is nothing but the organ through which God consummates his marriage with roused and intoxicated life. If man fails in feeling, it is blasphemy; it is the surrender of His masculinity, a cosmic catastrophe, an irreconcilable horror—" (P. 603)

We feel that Peeperkorn, despite the fact that alcohol and disease have nearly destroyed his incomparable body, is nearly to be identified with that god whose organs are the human race; when he can sustain the divinity in him all those around him act in unconscious obedience to his will; his strength is divinely undifferentiated, and out of his mouth the thunderbolt strikes. Peeperkorn, like Tolstoy, or the Goethe in *Lotte in Weimar*, demonstrates how nature through the perfection of its being can elevate itself into the spirit, as Hans Castorp expresses it with difficulty when trying to explain the source of Peeperkorn's power:

> It's not the massive shoulders, or the strength of his biceps; not because he could knock us down if he liked. He isn't conscious of his power; if he does take a notion, he can easily be put off it with a couple of civilized words. —So it is not physical. And yet the physical has something to do with it; not in a muscular sense— it's something quite different, mystical; because so soon as the physical has anything to do with it, it becomes mystical, the physical goes over into the spiritual, and the other way on, and

you can't tell them apart, nor can you cleverness and stupidity.
But the result is what we see, the dynamic effect—he puts us in
his pocket. We've only one word for that—personality. (P. 583)

The body is numinous; and all we need know of the spirit can be
discovered in its complicated structures. This is the meaning of Hans'
espousal of Peeperkorn: the things of intellect and spirit have human
value only when developed through the medium of the body; Hans
prefers to disembodied rational discourse Peeperkorn's elemental
intimacy with the waterfalls, the mystery of incarnation. Earlier in the
novel, when Hans Castorp was lost in the snow, he had a dream, of
lissome bodies imperturbable in an arcadian calm; and of a temple
nearby where, in the sanctuary, old hags dismembered and ate an
infant. Hans felt exaltation in the contemplation of this dream, an
allegory of the body's religion, smooth skin on the outside and blood
and horror within; and the body's divinity, even if it expresses itself as
a baby torn apart or the eagle's prey, abides in him during the bayonet
charge, in the mud fields of the real; for squalor and blood are cause
for rejoicing, ample reason to sing little snatches of song.

The Magic Mountain asserts little, remains fleshy and gigantic, but
hidden in it everywhere are clues by which we learn that the
involuntary motions of the body are governed by the secret laws and
aspirations of the spirit; even in this unsparing narrative of the body's
expressive sickness Mann permits himself such paraphernalia of the
spirit as a poltergeist and a ghost from the dead. One of the reasons
why the *Joseph* novels are a logical extension from *The Magic
Mountain* is that Mann desired to increase the machinery of spiritual
intervention beyond what was available to him in the convention of
modern setting; if *The Magic Mountain* is narrated from a point
within the mire of the natural, *Joseph* is narrated more flexibly, from
below and from above, from the camps of the Israelites and from the
eye of God. In a setting of such vertical amplitude there is scope for
every lust of the soul or reflex of the body to gratify itself. Here we
need not depend on hints and guesses to know the presence of the
spirit, for divinity has mobilized halos and spotlights, an army of
angels, so that nothing spiritual shall pass by unnoticed. Here a lowly
man, an outcast and a wanderer, may lift up his eye to the moon, like
the man of Ur, and yearn after the unclouded singleness of the divine;
here a nun, devoted to the gelid worship of the moon, may sacrifice
everything for the sake of a sudden passion for a young Jew, and the
reverent Judah succumb to sexual temptation, dissolve in sexual guilt.
But in addition to this usual seesaw between nature and spirit there is a
spiritual crux that is especially exasperating to the characters: the

composite and rickety structure of personal identity. *The Magic Mountain* is primarily a novel of the body, and of the immense, comprehensive complexity of physiological response; but *Joseph* is primarily a novel of the spirit, a "psychological soul-romance," in which the soul, it will be discovered, has a terrain as various, teeming, and inextricably amorous at the natural world itself.

In *Joseph and his Brothers* the body is rather docile and unilluminating. Little is known of Joseph's personal physiology; his noble tenement of flesh, like those of his father and brothers, is sufficiently exempt from natural process that he ages very slowly, is boyish at the age of thirty-four; Jacob effortlessly attains the age of 106. The most interesting body in the novel is surely that of Potiphar's virginal wife, Mut-em-enet, a high-breasted and lithe physique that enters, as her lust for Joseph increases, an artificial puberty, becomes buxom, big-hipped, overripe. This new witch's-body is a mere corporeal extension of her desire, a sign of the amazing plasticity of the body to the will of the soul. So tame and obedient is this body that it begins to resume its normal contours as soon as the stimulus of Joseph's presence is removed. This bodily will-lessness, this reduction of the body to spiritual metaphor, is common in Mann's later fiction; for instance, the insatiable Sita in *The Transposed Heads*, instead of causing the alteration of her own body, manages to accomplish the almost unthinkable feat of conflating the most sexually pleasing parts of two men's bodies into a single, temporarily perfect lover.

But if the body is relatively unimportant, then spirit and archetype proliferate at such a rate that they can represent the full natural world. The community of men in ancient times, according to Mann, was not a community of individuals; in *Joseph* God created man generic, typal. This is revealed early in *The Tales of Jacob* when Jacob's servant Eliezer speaks as if he were the same Eliezer who was Isaac's servant, and Abraham's servant, as if his memory compassed the furthest beginning of history:

> Joseph listened with a pleasure in no way marred by Eliezer's syntactical idiosyncrasies, and certainly not by the fact that the old man's ego was not quite clearly demarcated, that it opened at the back, as it were, and overflowed into spheres external to his own individuality both in space and in time—embodying in his own experience events which, remembered and related in the clear light of day, ought actually to have been put into the third person. But then, just what do we mean by actually? And is man's ego a thing imprisoned in itself and sternly shut up in its boundaries of flesh and time? Do not many of the elements which make it up belong to a world before it and outside of it? The notion that each

person is himself and can be no other, is that anything more than
a convention, which arbitrarily leaves out of account all the
transitions which bind the individual consciousness to the general?
The conception of individuality belongs after all to the same
category of conceptions as that of unity and entirety, the whole
and the all; and in the days of which I am writing the distinction
between spirit in general and individual spirit possessed not nearly
so much power over the mind as in our world of to-day which we
have left behind us to tell of the other. It is highly significant that
in those days there were no words for conceptions dealing with
personality and individuality, other than such external ones as
confession, religion. (P. 78)

Eliezer's function in Jacob's household is not a contingent convenience
or hired arrangement; it has divine sanctions; the reach of God extends
far down into the minor actions of this world. I will venture the
allegation that, in the whole of *Joseph*, there is not a single character
who is not manifestly typal; Mann has said that the characters in
Joseph are not based on real models—though one must treat such
statements with care—and it is true that the less important a character
is, the more his personality reduces to a subhuman lack of individuation. Joseph's father-in-law, a priest of Atum-Re, is "gentle, benevolent
and blithe of countenance; for thus had every servant of Atum-Re to
be by virtue of his office; and if he was not by nature thus, then by
some necessary disguise he had to become so by second nature"
(p. 1001). Even more trivial than this priest is Potiphar's head gardener,
a man called Red-Belly:

> Bunches of all sorts of herbs hung out of his apron, roots and
> shoots, which he snipped off or dug out as he moved among his
> plants; shears, chisel, and a little saw hung from his waist and
> clanked as he went. He was stout, with a red face screwed up in
> an expression not at all unfriendly; his nose was knobby; his
> mouth, likewise wried, whether in satisfaction or the opposite
> one could not tell, was covered with irregular, unshaven hairs like
> little rootlets; they added to the earthy aspect of Red-Belly's
> blinking, sunburnt face. His short forefinger, brownish-red and
> soil-encrusted, when he held it up to threaten some malingerer,
> looked like nothing so much as a freshly dug beet. (P. 590)

Here is a character who is nothing more than a projection of vegetable
traits, a beet-shaped man as inscrutable as a beet, a being so usurped
into specialization that he is clearly sacred, the creature whom the
God who made beets created in order to keep them well tended. This
is the extreme case of a character who has surrendered to his type; as
we look to more complex characters we see increasing investigation of

the limits of typal behavior, and even some rebellion against this divine generality. For it is in God that all these types are grounded. In *A Sketch of My Life* Mann credits his meditations on Kleist's *Amphitryon*, on which he wrote a fine essay, with stimulating his mind in connection with *Joseph* (*Sketch*, p. 70); and Mann reads the *Amphitryon* as a fable of identity. In the play Mercury, in disguise, attempts to arrange a tryst between Jupiter and Amphitryon's wife; to accomplish this he decides to take the place of Amphitryon's servant Sosias by the remarkable expedient of cudgelling Sosias until he, Sosias, renounces his identity, admits that the name Sosias refers not to Sosias but to Mercury. In this way Mercury reduces Sosias to a state of inconceivable abjection: he is forced to believe that he is no one at all. This may not be entirely a trick, for the granting of identity may indeed be a divine prerogative; later in the play Jupiter disguises himself as Amphitryon and accomplishes his will; and when Amphitryon's wife—now falsely certain that she is speaking to her husband—asks him, in an agony of doubt, who it was who slept with her, he says "It was I." Mann is fascinated by the ambiguity of this "I"; and goes on to remark that Jupiter is he "in whom the all is comprehended and who has taken on himself an identity over which he has command, as over every other he chooses" (*Essays*, p. 221). In *Joseph* too identity bears some resemblance to a military rank, assigned from above, capable of promotion and demotion. The mythic and typal roles to which the various characters are assigned are a source of great security and even exaltation; but the best of them, Jacob and Joseph, cannot easily be content with a sense of self that is so wholly arbitrary and contingent, and choose to experiment with other, headier self-definitions. God more or less allows men to think what they will about who they are; indeed, for all the apparatus of the supernatural, direct divine intervention is rare and always unmiraculous; but at the end all submit gladly to that Presence to whom their names, their persons themselves refer.

Joseph and his Brothers, like most of the works of the last twenty-five years of Mann's life, with the exception of *Dr. Faustus*, may be called a metaphysical farce, for there is nothing more quixotic or hilarious than the attempt to discover some divine reference in the ordinary occupations of life. Mann appreciates the aspirations of these shepherds and servants who are eager to trace the lineaments of Gilgamesh or Osiris in their features; but Mann always keeps hold a burgher's-eye watching the ground, conscious that lunatic exaltation about one's identity always has a certain ridiculous quality; like Don Quixote in Richard Strauss' tone poem, the rider in the clouds, ascending through chromatic gusts in the woodwinds of the upper air, nevertheless remains grounded on his wooden horse, a steady and invariant pedal point. The characters of *Joseph* are capable of effortless slippage into mythic roles; but there is often a certain self-conscious, disingenuous quality that enters into these redefinitions:

> Joseph played with many forms of imitation and artlessly deluding self-metamorphoses, knowing how to make an impression with them and win men to himself, even if temporarily. But just now he was entirely preoccupied with the return of the father-idea and its resurrection in him. He was Jacob the father, a refugee from home, fleeing before fraternal hate, stolen to the kingdom of Laban to escape from the Red One's jealousy of the first-born blessing. This time, to be sure, there was not one Esau but ten, and Laban's present form was quite other than the old one: he was Potiphar. (P. 551)

It requires a good deal of whittling and tugging to reshape Joseph's years with Potiphar into a good semblance of Jacob's years with Rachel's father Laban; and, besides, Joseph's purpose in his toying with archetype is somewhat tendentious, a desire to reinforce his public charm with a teasing resonance. Joseph's experiments with his identity suggest something of the confidence man; when Joseph is called a juggler by the malicious scribe Khamat (p. 858); when Joseph tells Reuben "I and my mother are one" in a tone so modest and solemn that Reuben is shaken to his depths (p. 335); when Joseph steps forward before Mai-Sachme, his prison warden, and says "I am he" with such simplicity that the warden feels that he has heard the formula by which a god discloses himself (p. 803); when Joseph advances from slavery, unbeing, to Pharaoh's right hand by means of his virtuosity with pancakes, lullabies, and dreams; then we see Joseph's kinship with Felix Krull, another brilliant child who mastered the language of enchantment, the width of the ego.

Yet it would be wrong to believe that Joseph's primary purpose in his mythic reidentification is ingratiation or advancement; Mann's farce is far subtler than that. There is some human desperation behind all his avidity for the prehistoric, the divine; the quest for a higher mythic self is in general a quest for self-extension, self-preservation. In the Egyptian half of the novel Mann is everywhere fascinated with the Egyptian preoccupation with death: Potiphar sits contemplating his statue, himself statuelike; the embalming of Jacob is described in great detail, even down to the extrusion of his brains through a straw; and there is a peculiar story about Re, an old king of Egypt before his apotheosis, whose "bones gradually turned to silver, his flesh to gold, and his hair to genuine lapis lazuli, a very beautiful form of senescence, yet attended with all sorts of ailments and pains" (p. 888).

The Egyptian habit of opposing aestheticism against mortality, even to the point of converting the corpse into a beautiful image, is another aspect of the urge which causes Joseph to identify himself with Gilgamesh and Jacob; the narrative art of myth, like the visual arts, offers a refuge against banality, limitation, and death. Jacob in extreme old age loses touch with his real children, becomes rapt in the contemplation of zodiacal correspondences; and when Jacob, a younger patriarch, is informed of the death of Joseph, Jacob rends his garments, laments Joseph according to the "prescribed formulas" used for the lamentation for Tammuz, a useful custom that regulates "our joy and our grief in prescribed channels" (p. 426). We are told that Jacob is "far too individual" to confine himself to formula, but we perceive the utility of myth in such extreme situations: typal behavior is anesthetic, an unconscious discipline by which unbearable pain is deflected, averted. Mankind by itself is too naked, puny, and must wrap itself in fictions to have a good opinion of itself, to keep warm. However, as the story of Re shows, the amelioration of flesh and blood, their improvement into myth or metal, is no guarantee of superior ease; Re is wracked by pain precisely because he has traded his unservicable body for aesthetic heaven. We enter into contract with myth because it offers us strength and impersonal glory; but we only bind ourselves to a different pain, a different weakness. When Potiphar's wife is trying to seduce Joseph, she offers him a festival garment, which he refuses, as he realizes later, with the words that Gilgamesh used to refuse a gift of Ishtar's:

> Such a recognition can have its soothing as well as its disturbing side. A man says to himself: "There it is again!"—with a sense of the solid ground, the shelter afforded by the myth, the reality, or even better, the truth, of what is happening—all of which re-assures him. But at the same time he is startled to find himself playing a part in the feast and representing such and such a myth as it is then being made present—he feels as though he were in a dream. (P. 748)

A certain loss of substantiality is the inevitable result of the attempt to shore up one's identity with mythic reference. This is why the soul entangled in myth grows hopelessly composite and confused, all cognition encrusted with foreknowing. There is a beautiful passage in *Young Joseph,* in which the sullen angel, who is Joseph's unwilling guide, delivers a great obloquy against the corruptibility of the human body, against the dubious and superficial beauty of skin that barely hides the oil, salt, and stench that is the truth of identity; Joseph replies, mildly, that the stranger must stick to carved images, like the divine icons of Tammuz that the mourners worship; but that he must not imagine that his preferences do not also constitute a deception, for the icon is painted to counterfeit a human body mangled by a boar: "So it is: either life is deception, or beauty. Thou canst not find both united in truth" (p. 364). This interdependence, this interexplicability of the human and the aesthetic, also defines the relation between the man and his mythic referent: each is partial, mutually evasive, each deceives by resembling the other. For angels, who are ontologically self-sufficient, this perplexity of being is merely an exasperation; Mann's angels with their homogeneous interior physiology, dislike the dual and impure, although their wrestling matches with men do not produce a clear victor—Mann depicts Jacob's struggle as the doubtful victory of the man, whose hip socket is movable, against the angel with his fixed, utterly immobile joints. Mann's attitude toward angels is a sign of his attitude toward the oversimplified spirit: the personality of angels is inflexible, smug, illiberal, prissy; the complexity of human affairs is clearly preferable, no matter how debilitating that complexity may be. Jacob is particularly overburdened with identity; he is a man so ravenous for mythic resonance that he sees in himself the identities of Isaac, Abraham, Noah, earlier patriarchs, even God; his repertoire of possible selves is large enough that he can take part in no human event that does not fit into a prepared slot.

Mann, in his letters and elsewhere, is anxious that his use of myth in *Joseph* be understood correctly; he usually insists on the equivalence of "myth" and "type." I do not suggest that this does not correspond to Mann's practice, but it is possible to make a brief discrimination between several kinds of myths and types which appear. The simplest of types is the occupational, like the beet-man Red-Belly, or the scribe, or, slightly more complex, the baker and cupbearer; these vocational types are fairly humble, unambitious, sanctified insofar as duty, custom, and the cycles of nature are holy; they can be called mythic only because there must be a patron saint or first, divine practitioner, whom all subsequent practitioners must imitate. For the more intelligent or developed characters, this sort of occupational type is nearly impossible to achieve; there is a passage in *Joseph in Egypt* where Joseph tells his new owner Mont-kaw, Potiphar's overseer, that he does not know any trade; Mont-kaw replies that he, Mont-kaw, is of gentle birth and himself knows no trade, that overseers in general are leaders and not cobblers or potters (p. 605). For the Josephs of the world, identity does not reside in activity but in birth. Another simple type is the representation of a single emotion or moral quality; Potiphar's wife becomes for posterity the symbol of uncontrolled lust, and Joseph consciously acquiesces to the judgment of those future generations that assign to him the role of the chaste man (p. 857). Above these simple types are the mechanisms of self-extension, the purposive compounding of identity. Sometimes Mann seems to suggest that each man has a heavenly *Doppelgänger*, somewhat like the Egyptian *Ka*, an entity that fits neatly into the gnostic legend as the "second emissary" or spiritual twin that descends to rescue the soul enchanted to the forms of matter. Eliezer teaches Young Joseph that earthly events have a "heavenly image and counterpart. In Abram became flesh that which had previously been celestial" (p. 282); and he tells Joseph stories which refer to the heavenly Abram, who builds a brazen city in which the sun never shines, a city of the underworld (p. 291). Israel is the name of the heavenly Jacob; and in the case of Joseph, Mann presents us with a remarkable multiplicity of abstract twins, a pale throng who shadow Joseph's footsteps through the novel. The most modest of these are the images of Joseph that detach themselves in the consciousnesses of the other characters and veer into unreality: Potiphar's wife, who has eyes only for his beauty, not for the scrupulousness of his genuine personality, regards him as one of "Ptah's thoughts made visible" (p. 726); and Jacob, believing Joseph is dead, freezes in his imagination an image of Joseph at the age of seventeen, an image that grows more unripe and morbid as the story proceeds. In other passages it appears that there is a celestial Joseph to match, or overmatch, the celestial Abraham; Joseph has an important dream in which a literary eagle bears him into traditional heaven, where God elevates him above all other created beings, makes him his personal servant, wishes he could exalt Joseph's throne above his own (p. 312); and much later, at the death of Potiphar's overseer, Mont-kaw, Joseph has a moving vision of himself and Mont-kaw, both dead, reenacting the scene of Joseph's purchase from the Midianites, a scene lavish with personal detail even though it takes place in the fields of heaven, the hairs of Mont-kaw's beard still in place, the tear sacs still welling under his eyes, Joseph still caught in his famous youth, the studied banter of haggling verbatim (p. 663), like the painted scenes which are still in place at the Valley of the Nobles near Thebes, in which heavenly daughters tug thorns out of their feet, while heavenly cats steal the fish heaped for the sacrifice of the dead and devour them stealthily under the table, a version of death as memorable and random as life itself. The chapter that forms the preface to *Joseph the Provider*, set in heaven, in which angels try to puzzle out divine motivation while actively lobbying against mankind, does nothing to dispel the belief that Mann conceived heaven as a precinct little altered from the turgidities of earth, although possibly more extreme in its contrasts, a heightening of the human; and so the lack of distinctness of these celestial analogues from their terrestrial counterparts should not startle.

The most highly developed form of myth in *Joseph*, and the last entry in this tabulation, is the sort of myth in which the man has no single counterpart or referent but instead an endless series of ancestors stretching behind him, growing ever more simplified and luminous, extending back into the inanities of the divine. This serial myth is seen most clearly in the open-ended Eliezer:

> He looked through him into an endless perspective of Eliezer-figures, who all said "I" through the mouth of the present manifestation. They sat in the twilight shades of the great tree; but behind Eliezer the sun-drenched air quivered in the heat, and the succession of identities lost itself not in darkness but in light.
> (P. 281)

In every generation the patriarch has a convenient head servant, especially useful as a sexual go-between and as a tutor for the patriarch's young successor; and this figure must bear the name and compound identity of Eliezer. No other kind of mythic structure could so effectively assert a continuum between earth and heaven; identity and memory remain continuous and steadfast from the creation to the present. But this sort of mythic identity, precisely because it asserts so much, is the most rickety of all. There seems to be a tacit agreement in Jacob's household not to examine with overmuch care the limits of Eliezer's memory; and at one point, when Eliezer attempts to console Jacob for the loss of Joseph, Jacob taunts Eliezer, doubts his claim to have been the servant of Abraham. Indeed Mann in his worldly and rationalistic pose suggests that such serial and extensive concepts of myth as the biblical story of the lineage of Abraham, Isaac, and Jacob will disintegrate at the slightest scrutiny: he tells us that not even Joseph could have believed that the man from Ur could have been his father's grandfather; in fact the moon-driven man who founded his race was probably not even from Ur, although the man's father may have been; and Lot of Sodom was doubtlessly not the nephew of the man of Ur but an unrelated proselyte. Myth making is a "dreamy toying with ideas" (p. 8), an unjustified simplification of incidents; an assumption of relationship where none exists; a myth when regarded critically will break down into free articulation, a great dustheap of irrational generation. A man who tries to secure his identity on such a story as this is committing folly: he may desire to impart authority to his will, he may wish to imbue his actions with an artificial magnanimity, but he risks his soul over an abyss of time. The characters of *Joseph* manipulate mythic parallels with varying success; Jacob is, I believe, not notably successful in developing or maintaining a satisfactory identity. His large repertoire of referents suggests a certain unwieldiness and instability to his personality; and he is perhaps too zealous to uncover mythic justification to his ethically questionable actions. Early in *The Tales of Jacob* Esau's son Eliphaz, eager to avenge Esau's loss of the birthright through trickery, overtakes the fleeing Jacob in a camel race; Jacob dismounts and abases himself in the dust, pules, whines for his life. Mann explains that Jacob's dignity was not forever impaired by this operation because he was obliged to survive at all costs: "Not, we must remember, out of common cowardice but because he was consecrated" (p. 87). His archetypal role, the Blessed Son, is ample excuse for the most self-serving and unworthy act; and this is the first of many times in *Joseph* that personal responsibility is evaded by the recourse to myth. It is a sign of Joseph's superior strength that he, when Potiphar's wife attempts to seduce him, feels acutely the tug of mythic parallels which permit this indulgence, even wonders whether this "honeyed satisfaction" (p. 763) might not be the gift of God, but nonetheless refuses to diminish his integrity with that pleasure which archetype allows. Preoccupation with the archetype and surrender to it are indications of personal weakness, as we have seen in *Tristan* and *The Blood of the Wälsungs*; and there is another kind of mythic self-indulgence which Jacob permits himself which is equally severely condemned in Mann's early fiction. Jacob's personality is kin, and not a remote kin, to that of Christian Buddenbrook: he is the self-preoccupied man. Much is made throughout the novel of Jacob's cult of feeling, feeling that inclines "to unrestraint and an enervating cult of itself" (p. 51); this state of tender self-enamouredness has mythic reference, not to Isaac or Abraham or Adam, but to God himself; it is a spontaneous imitation of the "majestic caprice" (p. 51) of the divine, God's uncanny favoritism and arbitrary selection. Identification with myth is an act which usually has the potentiality for self-discipline; any given myth consists of a finite story in which action is delimited and defined; but Jacob's habit of first identifying with all myth, then with God himself, circumvents self-definition entirely; so Jacob disturbingly dissolves, like Christian Buddenbrook, into rapt self-admiration, a state in which tremor, whim, and small affection have divine sanction. At the very end of the novel the trauma of dying shocks Jacob for a moment out of his mythic insanity, and he abjures his feeling, asks to be buried not with Rachel, the wife of his heart, but with official Leah and his ancestors, as is legally more fitting (p. 1177); but for the most part even death is to be for Jacob a farther exploration of radical self-dissolution, of the unreal validity of feeling over immutable fact, as he contemplates his journey to revisit Joseph in the morbid land of Egypt:

> He was about to carry out quite literally what he had dreamed of at the peak of his affliction and feverishly prattled in Eliezer's ear: he was going down to his dead son in the underworld. That was a cosmic procedure; and where the ego opens its borders to the cosmic and loses itself therein, even until its own identity is blurred, can there be any thought of narrowness or isolation? (P. 1140)

And Jacob's embalming, accomplished according to the best Egyptian technology, seems in many ways a perfection of his zodiacal and antihuman tendencies, an extension of himself into the mythic and inanimate.

Joseph's interest in mythicality, by contrast, is limited by a certain utilitarian or pragmatic aspect of his character; the myth must be compelled to serve social purposes. Joseph shamefully takes advantage of mythic language to enforce the awe that his masters feel at the sight of his beauty; but this canniness, in which myth is the tool of human ends, while it may be selfish, is nevertheless healthy, even productive, according to Mann. Joseph, like Jacob, seeks in myth a vehicle for self-extension; but whereas Jacob throws himself into ambiguous night, loses form and self-knowledge in a wilderness of reference, Joseph strives to find broader and broader fields on which his personality can operate; like a crystal in a saturated solution Joseph attempts to magnify his being without self-violation or loss of form. Like Jacob he is confident that God has so ordered affairs that he will triumph, but he lacks the certainty that what he wishes is what ought to occur, that what he feels is immediate and paramount. When besieged by Potiphar's wife he meditates on his chastity and renounces specifically the doctrine that one's desire is automatically divine (p. 750), his father's cult of feeling; indeed he believes that his present predicament is a punishment for his father's intemperate indulgence in feeling. Joseph is capable of postponing immediate gratification for the sake of future satisfaction; Jacob by comparison is immature. Joseph's farsightedness, however, has taken a long time to develop. Up until the time when his brothers took their great revenge, Joseph assumed that all the world wished to do his bidding, that all feeling directed toward him was adoration; this is the reciprocal or feminine form of Jacob's cult of feeling. When Joseph flaunts his coat of many colors, Bilhah, a wife of Jacob who is not fond of Joseph, tells him to show his coat quickly to his brothers, that they may sing hosannas at

him; Joseph misses the sarcasm entirely; and, deaf and blind, proceeds
to his doom:

> Indifference to the inner life of other human beings, ignorance of
> their feelings, display an entirely warped attitude toward real life,
> they give rise to a certain blindness. Since the days of Adam and
> Eve, since the time when one became two, nobody has been able
> to live without wanting to put himself in his neighbour's place and
> explore his situation, even while trying to see it objectively.
> Imagination, the art of divining the emotional life of others—in
> other words, sympathy—is not only commendable inasmuch as
> it breaks down the limitations of the ego; it is always an
> indispensable means of self-preservation. But of these rules Joseph
> knew nothing. His blissful self-confidence was like that of a spoilt
> child; it persuaded him, despite all evidence to the contrary, that
> everyone loved him, even more than themselves, and that there-
> fore he needed to take no thought of them. (P. 324)

For Joseph this kind of blissful self-preoccupation is catastrophic; and
we see that egotism, for all its sweet and specious self-aggrandizement,
is in truth a narrowing, and constriction, a loss of intensity. Joseph's
sojourn in the pit teaches him above all sympathy, a most charitable
sympathy felt for those who have in all probability murdered him.
Instead of evading responsibility he assumes a greater share of it than
circumstances seem to warrant, for he blames only himself for
provoking his brothers to this viciousness; and through such meditations as these he is flexing a new, highly extended concept of himself, a
much more protean, elusive, and powerful self than that he used to
possess, the world's darling, the immobile infant waiting for gifts.
Both before and after the pit the central fact of Joseph's life is his own
charm, that fatality by which all act according to the motions of his
will; but whereas Joseph's charm was once a bludgeon, in the second
half of the novel he insinuates his wires into the delicatest corners of
his subjects' psyches, gains unparalleled intimacy with those whom he
manipulates. Overresponsibility is simply the angelic obverse of
irresponsibility; and indeed Joseph in the pit feels himself attenuated
to ghost, turned into a counterpart and inversion of his former self:

> A strong impression had been made upon Joseph by what Dan
> had said: that they might say what they liked before Joseph, since
> every word they uttered only heightened the impossibility of his
> return home, and that it was good to utter them, since each one
> bound him more firmly to the lower world and made of him more
> and more a ghost before whom one shudders. Joseph saw in such
> words the counterpart and inversion of the role which he had
> played so far in life, that of needing to heed nobody because all

the world loved him more than they did themselves. For it was come to this, that no one heeded him at all! The thought conditioned those undertones and basses of his composition, and the weaker he became, the more did they sonorously predominate over the overtones. (Pp. 388–89)

Throughout the account of Joseph's metamorphosis in the pit, Mann embodies the complexity of Joseph's personality with the figure of symphonic form: Joseph in his upper register weeps, implores deliverance, while other, more profound, more real motions take place in the undertones and ground-basses of his being. The personality that is structured according to the principles of serial myth will necessarily contain these discords, this independence of line. The effect of the sojourn in the pit, however, is to strip off the treble, to uncover and develop the deepest, most divine layer of personality. All coats are removed from Joseph, until he glitters like Tammuz or Osiris in the darkness of the pit; he grasps his godlikeness with such assurance that resurrection is wholly inevitable; indeed so serviceable and exact is mythic identity that the mysterious course of Joseph's exaltation can be plotted on a graph. Accompanying this preternatural self-knowledge is a reintegration of the higher levels of personality, an achievement of a new consonance of identity. Joseph may etherealize into a ghost, but it must not be forgotten that the pit is itself richly organic, a haven of "beetles, wood-lice and other crawling things" (p. 379); in that maternal matrix he grows younger and younger, finally so fetal and inarticulate that his errors of feeling and egotism are undone; he is now ready for serious public exploit, like Grigorss in *The Holy Sinner*, who, having discovered the horror of his birth and marriage, spends seventeen years in abject repentance on a rock in the middle of a lake, shrinks into a Neanderthal, a hedgehog, a horny lump, until at last he is prepared to assume his identity of Pope Gregory the Great. For the gifted hero even his own past action is to some extent plastic, undoable. Joseph arises mute out of his earthy womb; when he is ready to speak, on the first page of *Joseph in Egypt*, he immediately recants his inconsiderate egotism by announcing his new doctrine, the plural universe, in which each man walks around like F. H. Bradley in a complete, self-contained, self-centered version of the universe, a doctrine by which Joseph manages to extend to others some of the prerogatives which he formerly enjoyed alone.

From this moment on, the theme of mythic identity evolves in two directions: on one hand, Joesph becomes increasingly conscious of the ways in which all men unconsciously work toward his personal exaltation, thus reinforcing his character with archetype, his sense of his own divinity; on the other hand, he attributes more and more of his own power to God his friend and protector; as he comes to understand divine power in him he nevertheless dissociates himself from it, becomes less confused and composite. Throughout *Joseph in Egypt* he equally accepts the proposition that the Midianites are the agents of his personal destiny; when the sullen angel chafes against his status as Joseph's tool, Joseph says nothing to comfort him (p. 475); when Mont-kaw cavils at Joseph's purchase Joseph is serene (p. 537); and even the narrator is forced to smile at the Midianites' delusion that they sold Joseph to Mont-kaw for profit (p. 547). Man and event serve Joseph in ignorance; but it must be emphasized again that they do not obey Joseph's superficial and conscious desires, but only that profound will which decrees what is best for Joseph even against his desires. Mont-kaw's death leaves Joseph in perplexed lamentation, for Joseph takes a peculiar and secret responsibility for the death of his boss; Mont-kaw is a good friend, whose life Joseph would have gladly extended, but the overseer's death is the simplest avenue to Joseph's promotion (p. 655). Mont-kaw's death becomes therefore a reflex of divine favoritism, in the most painful manner; and Joseph's new humility, new reliance upon God, is to some extent an effort to keep himself distinct from an insufficiently sensitive and humane ambition. Whereas Joseph in the earlier sections of the novel was eager to expand his powers, to test them against difficult obstacles, in the later sections Joseph develops an odd reticence about himself, a desire to ascribe his good fortune to a fate beyond his control. We are told in *Joseph the Provider* that, while Joseph has many great titles, his actual power is necessarily rather circumscribed (p. 990); and in the climactic unveiling of Joseph to his brothers he is most anxious to make them regard him, not as regent or demigod, but as their ordinary, all-too-human brother, "a farmer and manager" (p. 1116). Joseph is also conscious of the limitations of myth in defining identity: when he presents himself to Pharaoh as a dream-interpreter he warns Pharaoh that his identity is not fully defined by the assertion of his role as prophet:

> For the pattern and the traditional come from the depths which lie beneath and are what binds us, whereas the I is from God and is of the spirit, which is free. But what constitutes civilized life is that the binding and traditional depth shall fulfill itself in the freedom of God which belongs to the I; there is no human civilization without the one and without the other. (P. 937)

To Joseph the most felicitous personality is the best integrated, the one in which choice of identity most exactly corresponds with one's assigned role. Joseph has at this point exhausted the benisons of fluidity, of self-expansion; he is interested at the end of the novel in harmony, in paring down one's free existence to a manageable definition, in an identity which, if it is comparatively small, is at least intimate and secure. Jacob for the most part evolves into falser and falser mythic delusion; his blessings to his children on his deathbed show a mind so befuddled with zodiacal correspondence that he speaks to gentle Benjamin as if he had the personality of a raging lion; but Joseph's self-definition evolves into economy, even austerity, an eschewing of what is galactic and thrilling for the sake of human simplicity, a simplicity that is perhaps exaggerated in one so God-beloved as he.

The rhetoric of grandeur he forswears; yet he is always aware that, whether he is merely farmer or merely Pharaoh's right hand, his position has such an aura of divine sanction that it is not surprising that some confuse him with God. When Joseph's supernatural halo first dazzles Mont-kaw, Mann offers the following explanation: "He, in truth, has given us all our senses for our pleasure; yet reserved to himself their uses as medium and avenue for His larger purposes to play upon our minds" (p. 535). This is close to Peeperkorn's doctrine that mankind is an organ of the divine; and I think it is fair to say that in the later stages of *Joseph* a certain impersonality enters into our conception of the hero. I have tried to show how Joseph's conception of himself alters and establishes itself as the book progresses, but our conception of him may become less vivid instead of more. There is a passage in *Joseph the Provider* in which Joseph dismisses his early self, the "young cock of the walk, full of really vicious vanity" (p. 1051); but surely that peacock is better defined, more endearing, less technically interesting, than the elusive, benevolent, canny, calm, too-knowing, nearly personalityless hero of the later books. He is modest and he espouses the human, but after the pit there is too much of the divine in him. He evolves before the reader's eyes from characterhood, a version of personality perfectly comprehensible to the nineteenth century with its attraction to the more pathetic biblical personages, Cain, Ruth, Job, to a state of such competence and ideality that he is nearly impersonal; and in Mann's later novels this replete blankness, all white or all black, becomes the chief subject of an increasingly elevated art. Character is a state which pertains to fallen man, a state of necessary deformity; but the terrestrial is not always Mann's favorite province. In *Joseph* there are several ways in which all the characters add up to one character, are but the fractured pieces of the divine personality, or the stains, masks, and drawings that sheathe an incandescent deity. Potiphar and Dudu, the keeper of his jewels, for instance, seem together to comprise one person:

Potiphar is grossly fat, tall, spiritual, just, a eunuch, while Dudu is a dwarf, a malicious schemer, highly potent sexually, Potiphar's inverse and complement. We are told in the chapter located in heaven that the action of the novel takes place in "the theatre of God's mind" (p. 849); and the characters take on distinct personality only as they fall away from God into a state of illusory self-will, or to earth itself; no one could illustrate the gnostic fall into the enchantment of matter better than Red Belly the beet-man, who has turned bodily into that thing which he handles and loves. Everywhere in *Joseph* there is encouragement for the belief that private personality is a delusion; during the long, artificial debate between Potiphar and his wife on the fate of Joseph, the disputants embark on a complicated technical point, whether a man's talents are intrinsically his own or an arbitrary gift (p.697); and thus a disturbing possibility is suggested, that a man may call nothing about himself personal or private, may dwindle down to the merest wisp of personality. At the very end of *Joseph* the villainous brothers are encouraged to believe that their villainy was ordained on high as a necessary function in the story; and like Joseph they surrender their identities to God, in effect, yield themselves to that governing consciousness, the playwright and director of the whole tale of *Joseph*.

Yet it would be unwarranted to deduce from this that Mann is in any sense pious or theistic. His God is a creature of jest and nuance, whose presence may be felt everywhere but who is nevertheless difficult to pin down. The excursions of God into the orbit of the human are always dubious and never inexplicable; there are no miracles in Mann's fiction, except possibly for the apparition of Ziemssen in a uniform of the First World War in *The Magic Mountain*; indeed Mann carefully provides rationalistic explanations for biblical miracles, nowhere more tediously than in *The Tables of the Law*, in which every plague on Pharaoh's house, every marvel of Moses in the desert, is outfitted with a mechanism of ordinary causality. Mann's attitude toward divine intervention is expressed well in a sentence which he uses to account for the sudden entry of the chastening image of Jacob into Joseph's mind when Potiphar's wife, having summoned her utmost seductiveness, succeeds in inducing an erection: "This it was which saved him. Or, rather, he saved himself—for I would speak in the light of reason and give credit where it was due, not to any spirit manifestation" (p. 830). God—the single, indivisible God of the Hebrews—came into existence through the imagination of one man, Abraham; and it is clear from the novel that the great compact between Abraham and God is mutually sustaining, a mutual verification of identity. Mann's God exists for the sake of affirming man's importance, giving ethical approval to his deeds; God is the human personality conceived as something exterior to mankind, larger, man's jealousy, curiosity, and desire magnified to that limitlessness to which man aspires. For Joseph and his brothers, God bears Jacob's features; that is not dishonor but a smiling act of reverence. Belief in God, in this novel, is the belief in the objectiveness of one's own personality, the secret universality of the individual will. The knowingness of Joseph arises from the fact that he, understanding himself, can understand all other men, who are but distorted versions of that one overmastering human personality which he perceives so clearly in himself; therefore Joseph, sent a second time to the pit, the prison, is tranquil about his jailer, though the scribe Khamat attempts to terrify him; he knows that his jailer can be no demon but a man much like other men. When Mann says in the prelude and many other places that his theme in the novel is man (p. 33), the general nature of man, the foundations of man (p. 3), he could say with equal justice that his theme is God; for he defines God as man in his most general and abstract form; the archetype of the whole human. The human race can be described by a few simple stories; fathers are jealous of their children and elevate them not according to law but according to preference; brothers are jealous of each other and sometimes commit murder; as for women, their destiny is so oppressed by maternal and sexual instinct, the feminine archetype, that one can hardly speak of them at all. God may be described as the agent on all sides of these simple stories; God is father and son, the doter and the doted-upon, the murderer and the victim.

But if Mann's God is the repository and source of human affection, human identity, the warehouse of myth, that suggests a relation between the narrator and his tale that has been glimpsed before in Mann's earlier work. If God is the theater of the novel, if God is a product of Abraham's imagination, if hero and villain alike draw comfort from surrendering their identities to divine disposition, then God is more than a narrative convenience, nearly the principle of narration itself. As Joseph's piety increases, as he discovers divine motivation everywhere about him, he simultaneously becomes conscious of his life as a divine fiction. In *Joseph in Egypt* he tries to persuade Potiphar's wife to renounce her lust for him by telling her that their story will become an episode in the history and literature of the world, and her name may become blackened by her wicked desires (p. 773); and such talk is itself intoxicating, for she too develops a desire to go down into history, not as the butt of an ethical fable but as a legendary lover (p. 794). As for *Joseph the Provider*, one of the chief motifs of that subnovel is the process of narration itself; as God's will evolves toward a culmination it manifests itself everywhere in the form of little recapitulations, tiny *Josephs* which twirl cunningly about the skirts of the main drama; Joseph tells *The Tales of Jacob* to Pharaoh in an epic singsong that prefigures some of the technical artifice of *The Holy Sinner*, and when Jacob's little granddaughter Serah hears the story of Joseph from the returning brothers she converts it all into a poem. More importantly, however, Joseph becomes obsessed with the idea that his life moves according to a predetermined script, which he needs all the sensitivity and transparency that he possesses to read correctly; if he is too eager, too full of private desire, he may muff his lines, spoil the story. "Great is the writer's art!" he tells his authorial stooge Mai-Sachme, his former prison warden and a timid autobiographer, "But truly I find it greater yet to live in a story; this that we are in is certainly a capital one" (p. 998). And a little later we learn that he conceives the whole scene in which his brothers will recognize him as a divine charade which "must be celebrated and adorned with all sorts of solemn flourishes" (p. 1054) so that it may have emotive effect over five thousand years. In this last phase of the novel Joseph loses all interest in personality; plot is all, character nothing:

> "I don't know, Mai, what sort of man I am. One does not know beforehand how one will behave in one's story; but when the time comes it is clear enough and then a man gets acquainted with himself. I am curious myself to see how I shall act and how talk to them—at this moment I have no idea. That is what makes me tremble so. When I had to stand before Pharaoh I was not a thousandth part so excited. And yet they are my own brothers. But that is just it. Everything is upside-down inside me: it is a perfect muddle of joy and dread and suspense and quite indescribable." (P. 1053)

This indescribable delirium, what Felix Krull would call the "Great Joy," is the delight in attained loss of self-definition, an unbearable sense that one's own numinousness is about to be revealed; it is the actor's effacement of his common self for the sake of a sacramental role. Joseph believes he must at all costs observe dramatic form, delay his unmasking to his brothers until suspense has built up to the limit of what is tolerable to man: "I will not ... burst out headlong with the climax like an inexperienced story-teller" (p. 1055); and in this way Joseph acts as a surrogate narrator, a surrogate God. What is it that Mann's characters desire? They desire to be characters in a novel by Thomas Mann, and they will go to any lengths to please or appease the author. Joseph is full of happy stage fright because he desires to be as charged with dramatic purposiveness as possible; and the other characters are all too zealous in their desire to help the story along to its appointed climax, or to hinder the story's evolution for the sake of suspense. Both Mai-Sachme and Tamar, the Kundry-like woman who seduces Judah in order to be in the lineage of the blessing, fight with every weapon they possess simply to take part in the story; Mann's characters desire to be written about, to preen in verbal attentions; to exist. If there is a discrepancy between psychology and myth, as Mann sometimes affirms, then *Joseph* is a novel of myth, not of psychology; individuation and personality are comparatively insubstantial, and the characters discover their highest mission in the enactment of a tale. Psychology here is a province of the divine, for the workings of the mind are comprehensible, not in the head of any single character, but in that totality which the characters together comprise. The God of *Joseph*, in whose book "this whole story is already written down," is a being himself as composite as man, compounded of godlikeness and fertility, in a state of perpetual declension, downward spin, devolving from the single to the double, from the double to the quadruple, from there on to the full multiplicity of the terrestrial, a God fallen from eternity into sequence and narrative; and if human history is in fact a formal whole, a satisfying story, if this enormous tetralogy of *Joseph* is in fact but "an interpolation in an ‸epos incomparably vaster in scope" (p. 1016), then we may believe that the storyteller's God, a God not dissimilar in facial expression to Thomas Mann, indeed exists and governs; but if those gestures by which mankind indicates its upward striving seem to resemble a malediction against the heavens rather than a prayer, if history is shapeless and intractable, then we may reject the gnostic reconciliation of flesh and spirit, the happy end, even doubt the adequacy of the narrative model to the inconsequential clamor of that troubled world in which Mann wrote the last lines of *Joseph and his Brothers*, on 4 January 1942.

Psychomachia

Embedded in *Joseph and his Brothers*, and cognate to it, is *Lotte in Weimar*, a novel based on an episode in Goethe's life, written during the hiatus that preceded the composition of *Joseph the Provider*; and in some sense it can be regarded as an alternate termination to the *Joseph* sequence, for it is a novel as saturated in mythic pattern, in the convolutions of personality and verbal analogues to personality, as *Joseph the Provider*; and its end is even more ecstatic, more suffused with the rich divinity of the human. The fable is comparatively simple: Charlotte Kestner, née Buff, an ample bourgeois widow of some social standing, decides, late in life, to visit Weimar and the celebrated poet Goethe, whom she knew in youth; and in fact she has attained some vicarious celebrity herself, for she is the model for the Charlotte of Goethe's *Werther*, the novel which resounded throughout Europe. Thus Charlotte is helplessly compound in her being, a lithe maiden with whom Goethe dallied chastely in his twenties, and an old lady whose head nods uncontrollably, juxtaposed in uncomfortable counterpoint. The dramatic substance of Mann's novel consists of Lotte's interior dialogue with that charming fictive creature, Werther's Lotte, of whom all the residents of Weimar are in awe, and also Lotte's investigations into a might-have-been life, in which she married Goethe and not Albert Kestner, a phantom extension of her being, itself a myth. In this way she is simultaneously active and passive, a character in a novel, caught in what could be called an agony of createdness, and yet a mythmaker herself; such breakdown of ordinary distinctions of subject and object comprises the intellectual development of the novel.

Lotte is much burdened by "Lotte," an entity insufficiently distinct, easily confused with the real woman, whose eternal youth and loveliness form a bizarre reproach to her sexagenarian debilitation. Sometimes she indignantly wishes to disclaim "Lotte," repudiate that verbal shadow who seems all too eager to usurp the substance of the living woman:

> That character in the novel did become so real, so living, and so widely celebrated that actually a person could come to me and say that between us two she was the real and more substantial one— the which I was, of course, most seriously concerned to disclaim. But the character in the novel is quite different and distinct from my former self, to say nothing at all of my present one. For instance, anyone can see that my eyes are blue, whereas Werther's Lotte is well known to have black ones. (Pp. 20–21)

But such gestures of independence are desultory and incomplete, for the real Charlotte is secretly enamored of her alter ego, the fiction; the fiction has flattered her unspeakably for forty-four years, has offered her the envy and adulation of a generation and the prospect of immortality. When she triumphantly points to the black eyes of "Lotte," so different from her own, she is giving voice in distorted form to her most private anxiety: that she is *not* the Lotte of *Werther*, that the eyes of one of Goethe's other loves may have infiltrated into the tale, that "Lotte" may be a creature so contaminate with alien reference that she may be unrecognizable. Novelists have a disturbing habit of taking a face from one acquaintance, a gesture from another, a tone of voice from a third, a bit of dialogue from Euripides: "An

271

artist is allowed to compose a Venus from the study of various different beauties" (p. 93). Like Tamar and Mai-Sachme in *Joseph the Provider* Lotte is desperately interested in the longevity and memorability the fiction can impart to her; but, having achieved that to everyone's satisfaction but her own, she cannot be sure that what appears in the book is a faithful enough portrait. Her dilemma shows a crux in the art of the novelist: his characters purport to be individuals, but the individuation of verbal constructs is a matter of convention, trickery, even deceit. Perhaps one may even suggest that, to Mann, as to Lotte, a human being is incomplete without verbal analogue, without novel and autobiography; and yet the man who involves his personality with objective self-description is binding himself to all manner of intrusion and falsification. Lotte, though intelligent, is not an enlightened woman, and her intimacies with "Lotte" are a perpetual embarrassment; through a mild friendship, long terminated, with a young man she has been rendered, without prior consent, ambiguous and compromised; parts of other bodies have been grafted onto her own; the color of her eyes has become unstable. This self-violation is to some extent more profound than any rape; against her will her being has been mingled imperishably with Goethe's other loves, her predecessor Friederike Brion, who dwindled to death out of spurned love, and many successors, living and dead, her unwilling sisters and images. This openness of ego, which she cannot in good conscience repudiate, is most distressing to her: "A single heroine is enough for one episode—but there are many episodes; people say there still are. It is a sort of dance I have joined—" (p. 94). Heroines, like other verbal objects, are never single enough; the object of every love poet is a synthetic Venus, like the *dompna soiseubuda* of Provence. The real woman may be jealous of the manufactured creature in the song, but she knows, too, the secret intoxication of this aesthetic participation, this extension of the physical being into verbal trance and archetype.

Lotte in Weimar, then, is a distant corporeal appendage tacked on to the quick of Goethe's *Werther*, as a tin can clatters behind a dog's tail. *Werther* is the stuff of pure myth, a web of prose grown luminous with its own tactile sensitivity, in which joy is depicted by floods of antemundane light, despair by the shudderings of a mind engaged in the annihilation of its world. The myth of *Werther*—itself a myth of personality, of a hero striving against human finitude—informs every part of *Lotte in Weimar*, though its lineaments are greatly deformed, the old bodies forced to squeeze into the corsets and waistcoats of a departed youth, a departed fashion, or their callow children forced into an insensitive parody, mimicking the gestures of a romantic excess too great for their lesser beings. *Werther*, for Mann's purpose, is a tale about the grandeur of creative desire, and the awful consequences of its frustration; Werther's suicide is only one of the possible forms, however, that the deflection of a poet's desire may take. In the case of the young Goethe, for instance, Lotte's unwillingness to accept his love led, not to self-destruction, but to the writing of *Werther*; and Lotte and Goethe both see the poet's career as a succession of renunciations, a deliberate reluctance to form stable human alliances, an experimentation, a toying with human emotion, almost parasitical. We see here, I believe, what is nearly the key situation in Mann's fiction: an artist discovers that all the people in his acquaintance comport themselves as if they obeyed the artist's profoundest will, his narrative will, even though his conscious desires are everywhere balked, his human happiness circumscribed. *Lotte in Weimar* and *Dr. Faustus* bring this theme, the theme of the artist's psychomachia, to its highest development; the two novels are neatly paired, for the first presents this theme in the stylish guise of the nineteenth-century romantic growth of a single sensibility into an organic, pragmatic, ameliorative social force; while the second presents the theme as something characteristic of the twentieth century although equally romantic, the growth of a single sensibility into the vehicle of universal destruction, the soul's internecine war. The kinship of the Goethe of *Lotte in Weimar* with the protagonist of *Dr. Faustus*, Adrian Leverkühn, the basic intimacy of God and the Devil that is so often asserted in *Joseph* and in *Lotte in Weimar*, can be seen most easily in the black side of Goethe's genius, as shown in *Werther* by the suicide, as shown in his life by his relation with his son August, an unstable, drunken, much diminished replica of his father: Goethe encouraged an unfortunate marriage between his son and the lofty and beautiful Ottilie von Pogwisch—a marriage that takes place just beyond the confines of *Lotte in Weimar*, extends into historical disaster—because of his own infatuation with Ottilie; just as Ottilie permits the engagement to August out of deflected admiration for his father. Thus the insatiable desire that caused so much difficulty in Lotte's life at the time of *Werther* claims its victim in various devious and direct methods in a subsequent generation as well; Mann in his essays marvels several times about how few of Goethe's loves reached sexual consummation, and it seems to be Goethe's nonparticipation, his aesthetic aloofness, that is responsible for the power of his secret, meddling will, which imparts a tragic or a comic shape to the otherwise random stuff of daily life.

The divinity of Goethe, his power to realize enactments of his desires in low analogy to himself, using acquaintance and fiction indifferently as the actors in the theater of his will, is surely one of Mann's most impressive achievements; for if Goethe resembles Leverkühn he also resembles Joseph, and the God of *Joseph*; often the language with which the other characters refer to him has overtones of reverence, prayer, or even theological technicality:

> Indeed, August's sorry passion for Ottilie was but the expression, and the result, of the father's desires. The son loved in her the very type of the father's election; his love was imitative, traditional. It was bond-service, and the breach was revolt, an act of attempted independence. I did not estimate very highly its strength or persistence. (P. 157)

Here Adele Schopenhauer, a close friend of Ottilie's, is attempting to persuade Lotte to intervene in the betrothal of the young couple; and it is clear that she sees August as little more than a blunt instrument of his father's desire. This speech is formally identical to any number of speeches in *Joseph* in which men try to extricate themselves from divine compulsion, the oppression of myth; early in *Lotte in Weimar* the pedant Dr. Riemer, an educated man who assists Goethe, complains of his lot with all the anguish of Joseph's sullen angel, for, in complete contrast to his desire for an independent life of scholarly distinction, he is compelled by the force of Goethe's personality to accept a vicarious and contingent respect from posterity, the bitter honor of self-subordination (p. 52). This recognition, which comes less painfully to some than to others, of one's loss of independent being in the presence of genius, is similar to that other recognition so common in Mann's fiction, the realization of one's own fictiveness; in both cases there is a peculiar sense of satisfaction involved in yielding up one's identity to a superior being. Riemer himself, for all his caviling, admits that everyone in Goethe's presence enjoys "an extraordinary sense of well-being" (p. 48), the usual feeling of those in the presence of a Joseph or a Goethe or a Felix; to involve oneself in the fables of the great gives pleasure, even if the fable offers little but human catastrophe. Adele Schopenhauer, a most wise woman, also offers a theory of intrinsic role, similar to Joseph's theory of the plural universe: she points out that, while August von Goethe was reviled for not joining the army during the Napoleonic wars, her younger brother Arthur, a philosophical and scholarly sort of lad, was never criticized for not flinging himself into the struggle; she infers from this that ethical judgments are not objective but personal, and that what is most satisfying in life "is harmony, is being in tune" (p. 148). There is a sense of rightness, a harmony between man and role, over the gamut of human society; it is exactly this global euphony that is the highest triumph of the controlling intelligence.

Probably Mann's furthest exploration into the inclusive personality, the artist's personality, is the seventh chapter of *Lotte in Weimar*, which is mostly an interior monologue in the mind of Goethe. Here is a personality in which all emotion and all thought are simultaneously viable; here is a mind so drenched with light that the forms of the created world pullulate into indivisibility. It is, I believe, a vision of the divine mind which can bear comparison with any effort in literature. For Goethe the universal service of mankind to the exigencies of his will is a matter scarcely to be remarked, although he does remark in passing that a certain friend of his is "but my instrument and my tool" (p. 234); for Goethe the theme of psychomachia is merely the social analogue of a more general theme, the relation between the whole and the particular. Goethe, both historically and in the novel, was interested in color theory: he rejected the theory of Newton, that white light is compounded out of various complementary darknesses, colors, for the belief in the primacy of the single, undivided white beam; to Goethe the prism itself is merely an opaque object, though much less opaque than most other substances, and the opacity of the prism deforms white light into color. This accords well with Mann's gnostic theme: for it is the touch of the terrestrial that shatters light into the multiple charms of the rainbow. Throughout the chapter this kind of relation informs Goethe's thought, the relation in which the complex features of natural life and the temporal universe suggest a mysterious kinship to some divine singleness, divine simplicity. For instance, he meditates on the cruelty of love, and wonders, "What if sweet love itself were put together out of nothing but sheer horror" (p. 226); and his anatomical researches in which he discovered the human intermaxillary bone through accurate study of animal structures enforce a belief in the recondite indivisibility of the whole animal kingdom. Like Hans Castorp before him and Felix Krull after him, Goethe is deeply fascinated by convergence of the organic and the inorganic, the resemblance of certain small crystals to cell nuclei, the similarity of animal alimentation and reproduction to the accretion of crystals (p. 268); this loss of the universe's major boundary line is Mann's highest verification of the unreality of articulation, the truth of the doctrine that the universe is but an extension of the human mind into space and time.

Yet the width of Goethe's erudition, his Adamic supremacy as the namer and controller of the world (p. 224), should not conceal Goethe's dislike for the partial, for the colorful, for the finite, for the articulate; his loyalty lies with the white light. He is contemptuous of animals and crystals alike, finds something deathly in their blind unconscious growth (p. 269); better to be human, to strive toward self-perfection. But for the most part even the realm of the human is inadequate to Goethe's imagination; his fictions are full of partial, distorted versions of himself, and it is only in the totality, the psychomachia, that his full personality emerges. Riemer pins down this quality when he remarks on the lack of great characters in Goethe's work: "A great character? But what about Eduard, Tasso, Clavigo, what about Wilhelm and Faust, even? When he portrays himself he makes problem characters, weaklings, unstable human beings" (p. 66). Some of this clearly reflects Mann's own beliefs: in his essays he always speaks of Mephistopheles as a splintering-off, a projection of one aspect of Goethe's personality, a psychological antagonist and complement to the character of Faust. Indeed Mann's Goethe can be comprehended only fragment by fragment, never as a complete personality; he is a total oxymoron. Like Peeperkorn, Goethe epitomizes personality, according to Riemer (p. 60); the stamp of his personality, of his fables of renunciation, has been impressed indelibly upon the world (p. 186), yet his personality is elusive, undefinable. He is benevolent, possessed of universal sympathy, but he is cold and annihilating; he subordinates all to his art yet disbelieves in art, mocks its sterility; he even regards himself, paraphrasing a line in his *Iphigenia*, as monster and demigod at once (p. 240). In the account of his birth we see the genetic myth of *Tonio Kröger* pushed to its farthest extent: instead of being the product of the noble union of the two polar temperaments, the bourgeois and the artistic, Goethe is the expression and summation of the whole human race, the furious generations of journeymen, wenches, surveyors, bailiffs, the high and the low, all striving back toward the reconstruction of the single being who contained in head and loins them all (p. 241). What traits can be ascribed to such a personality? All traits; his personality is technically infinite.

The reader should not exaggerate the difficulty of this depiction of sublimity. Like the twelve-tone fugues in the real *Pierrot Lunaire* of Schoenberg, or in the fictitious studies of Adrian Leverkühn, it takes no great genius to speak always in oxymoron, to utter the trait and its antonym in the same breath. I do not mean to minimize Mann's achievement in the Goethe chapter of *Lotte in Weimar*, for it is a difficult critical problem to distinguish the sublime from the mechanical—in both cases expectation is totally gratified; but it can be argued that Mann is more daring in his treatment of Lotte than in his treatment of Goethe. The character of Goethe is a magnificent development of the soft vigorous genius who has been growing in Mann's fiction since Hanno Buddenbrook; but Lotte is a creature comparatively original, for through her character Mann admits how much credit the model deserves for the work of art. The plot of *Lotte in Weimar* is not wholly different from that of *Death in Venice*, but whereas Tadzio remains for nearly the entire story an overbeautiful boy, caught in the enchanted, limiting gaze of Aschenbach, Lotte has been released from the artist's spell for decades, allowed to turn dumpy and mature, to lead her own life. There is perhaps a joke about Tadzio in the seventh chapter of *Lotte in Weimar*; Goethe, meditating on the homosexual idealism of Winckelmann, thinks "Seduction by one's own sex—that might be a revenge, a mocking retribution for the seduction practiced by oneself—Narcissus, for ever deluded by his own image" (p. 264). Tadzio is indeed the image of Aschenbach, his own aesthetic charm embodied for his visual delight; but the heterosexual disparity of Goethe and Lotte permits a more complicated, more indirect relation between artist and model. Tadzio, as we have seen, was pliant, complicit in Aschenbach's idealism; and in the case of Lotte, the artist's model gains a certain dignity beyond that of mere obedience, becomes a collaborator in the myth of *Werther*. Lotte tells us at one point that some of *Werther*'s dialogue is a direct transcription of her innocent prattle, recorded to her chagrin for the amusement of the ages; and one of her purposes in visiting Weimar, although she is not wholly aware of it, is to establish her personal claim on the novel. Indeed the concept of the revisitation, the Beloved's Return, is an unconscious resumption of a myth, a myth of which Goethe is only too aware; in this way Lotte and Goethe, who have already co-written one novel, manage to write another, with Thomas Mann as a benign third party. In *Joseph* there is a good deal of talk about the sanctity of all roles, even villainy, when they exist according to the divine will; in *Lotte in Weimar* the lesson can be observed more easily, for Lotte, the actress, is a genuine coequal with Goethe in the myth.

One of the oddest and most emphatic motifs in the novel, iterated variously by Adele Schopenhauer, August von Goethe, and Lotte herself, is Lotte's secret motherhood of both August and Ottilie (p. 208): of August, because any child of Goethe might well have been her own child, if she had married him, and of Ottilie, because Ottilie's position in respect to August is analogous to Lotte's position in *Werther*, the young woman wooed by a Goethe. This bizarre incest— for in myth the analogically related can be siblings as easily as those related by heredity—shows how "Lotte" has grown old side by side with Lotte, has given birth to phantom children. The responsibility for these myths and mythic offspring is extremely diffuse—Goethe may have written *Werther*, but he could not have done so alone, and the story has quickly developed into something nearly independent of him, capable of its own peculiar self-propagation. In myth all identity blurs into vague collusions and resolutions, unexpected simplifications and reintegrations; one can speak of the central overwhelming mind of Goethe, but Lotte too is involved in mythmaking, strange maternities, along with all the other participants in myth. Goethe, too, thinks of the characters of his fictions as beings independent of himself: he imagines that, if he had died before Schiller, Schiller could possibly have finished *Faust* (p. 212); and Goethe speaks of consigning Schiller's Demetrius to death by his refusal to finish his friend's play (p. 211). Characters, to some extent, create themselves, shape their own stories.

The historical termination of Lotte's visit to Weimar—Lotte went home after a single dinner with Goethe, which evidently did not impress her greatly—displeased Mann, although it was his intention to stay faithful to the historical "downbeat" (*Letters I*, p. 311) until just before he reached the moment of writing it; so he substituted an untruth, a great intellectual flourish, in which a spectral Goethe greets Lotte after the performance of a play in the flickering light of a coach. This deviation from fact, in addition to the historical sublimities, the atmosphere of high myth, caused difficulties in Mann's audience; and he was pestered to account for his behavior. Eventually, in 1947, he wrote a playful, extremely interesting letter in which he emphasized the unreality of the final dialogue: Goethe is given an epithet of Wotan; the coachman behaves as if he does not exist.

> I suspect that she has so deep a longing for a concluding dialogue which will bring matters to some resolution that she simply produces the scene for herself. But even so, it is still not possible to speak of pure unreality. What we have here may be a phantom dialogue, which comes about because the woman's longing meets that of her old friend, a dialogue of phantoms in which Goethe speaks his thoughts, although he is not sitting physically beside her, and which therefore has a higher reality. (*Letters II*, p. 521)

First Mann hints that the scene is a projection out of Lotte's head; then he suggests a less conceivable thing, that the scene is a double projection, a double fantasy, *folie à deux*; but it is consistent with Mann's beliefs on the nature of myth to postulate this curious mutual causality, in which the phantom of Goethe is evoked by the combined yearning of two parties. Indeed the tenor of the whole scene suggests the effacement of human distinctness, the coalescing of single identities into white light. Goethe, at the climax, speaks of the parable of the moth and the flame, a story which indicates the upward metamorphosis of the body into the soul, nature into spirit; indeed Goethe suggests that his flame has turned Lotte's poor body into the immortal myth of *Werther*, and her revisitation, her little joke in which she dressed for Goethe's dinner in the costume in which he had known her forty-four years ago, is a sign and adumbration of that inexhaustible spiritual youth which is the reality of myth. The reducibility of human life to the state of fable prefigures our divinity. Goethe insists, in the same language Joseph uses in order to suggest the resonance of his identity, that he is the flame, he is the candle, he is the butterfly: "metamorphosis is all that is dearest and innermost of thy friend" (p. 330). Lotte and Goethe thus grow indistinct; her whole being is absorbed into that fictiveness which had formerly pertained chiefly to "Lotte," the incomparable virgin of the bread and butter; and Goethe too fuzzes out into the divine welter of his own masks, a Proteus shapeless in the multiplicity of his own shapes (p. 74).

Mann's departure from historical accuracy in this scene attests to the very theme he presents here. History is a prison in which every action is a rejection of a myriad of other potential actions; therefore the renunciation motif, which characterizes Goethe's career, becomes the general emblem of temporal life, as Lotte tells Goethe:

> "I came to see the might-have-been, the possible. Its deficiencies compared to the actual and existing are plain to see. Yet there it is, beside the actual, in the world, whenever we say 'If only' or 'As once it was'. And it is worth our questioning. Do you not find it so, old friend, do not you too sometimes, in all the glory of your actual, question the might-have-been? For your actual, well I know, is the effect of renunciation, and in consequence of impairment and loss; for renunciation and loss lie close together, and all reality and achievement are nothing but the impaired possible. There is something frightful, let me tell you, about the impairment." (P. 329)

Her sojourn in Weimar is an investigation into a potential life, in which she married Goethe; and it is the greatest charm of myth that it accommodates these unrealities with ease. Real biography is always a sad story, full of checked desire, wasted opportunity, a deadly pettiness; it is this search into the forking paths, the phenomenon of overlay, that provides zest. There is a certain smallness, even in Goethe's inconceivable career; Riemer points out, not without satisfaction, that even Goethe's skull is a closed, limited world, as is proved by the repetition of the motif of milk-and-water nursing (p. 63) —an image of thin blue milk, which Goethe employs both in the early *Faust* and in his more recent *Elective Affinities*. One attains the breakthrough from limitation by learning to understand that history and human personality are themselves fictions, phantasmal; real event carries no more weight than imaginary, and all human alienation is illusory. Goethe in the last scene solves the problem of Lotte's jealousy, her desire to be the sole canonical Lotte of *Werther*, to be the Laura with whom Goethe will romp in the Elysian Fields, by telling her that her identity is consubstantial with all his other loves: "Jealous —of whom? Of your sister, nay, your reflection and other you? When the cloud forms and re-forms, is it not still the same cloud?" (p. 329). Heaven, the afterlife, is the simultaneity of all personality; Goethe on the last page imagines himself dead, reveling with his women, his artistic creations, at last understood as comprising part of his own simplified and exultant, androgyne multiplicity; and here Mann carries to a close one of the most persistent of romantic fantasies, that of the dead poet rejoicing with his extensive fictions. As August says of his father earlier, "The universe takes on a human visage, and the ego looks out with eyes of stars" (p. 189). In such ways as these authors hope that their immersion into verbal analogues of the universe and human personality represents a genuine self-extension; but the small voice of Riemer, that insists on the limitation, the delineated contours, of even the widest and most empathic personality, is hard to still entirely. It is clear that Mann knew that he was no bland immensity but a man with his own little traits and tics, his milk-and-water repetitions; in his essay on *The Magic Mountain* he points out that such *leitmotifs* give coherence to an author's work:

> There are authors whose names are associated with a single great work, because they have been able to give themselves complete expression in it. Dante *is the Divina Commedia*, Cervantes *is Don Quixote*. But there are others—and I must count myself among them—whose single works do not possess this complete significance, being only parts of the whole which makes up the author's lifework. And not only his lifework, but actually his life itself, his personality. He strives, that is, to overcome the laws of time and continuity. He tries to produce himself completely in each thing he writes, but only actually does so in the way *The Magic Mountain* does it; I mean by the use of the leitmotiv, the magic formula that works both ways, and links the past with the future, the future with the past. The leitmotiv is the technique employed to preserve the inward unity and abiding presentness of the whole at each moment. (*Magic Mountain*, pp. 717–18)

Here Mann expresses, in a more muted manner, hope of self-perpetuation similar to that which Goethe cries out at the end of *Lotte in Weimar*; his canon will constitute, after his death, a full reflex of his personality. But the conflicting demands of hierarchy and plenitude are vexations indeed, and I will end this discussion of *Lotte in Weimar* with a sentence which offers a transition to the problems of *Dr. Faustus*: order in history is a demonstration of the poverty of reality; order in literature is a demonstration of the poverty of the imagination.

What is wrong with Adrian Leverkühn, the damned composer of *Dr. Faustus*? He has committed, in an indirect way, vile deeds; but his state of criminality precedes the commission of any crime. No childhood trauma has unsettled his unhappy soul; no disappointment in later life has blighted his hopes. He is cold as an adult and he is cold as a child; submarine contempt clings to him from the womb. He despises himself without provocation or cause; his self-hatred is therefore a condition of his being, almost divine, as innate and conspicious as his genius. He is notorious, as a young student, for his inhuman intellectuality; but his intellect more than the rest of his faculties yearns to abolish itself. From the beginning he dislikes puzzles, and his first manifesto as a composer is to rid art of intellectual play. In an extended analysis of the prelude to act 3 of *Die Meistersinger*, one of Wagner's weaker efforts at depicting sensible grievance, Leverkühn reduces Wagner's hair-raising effects, theatrical climaxes, to a collection of dubious tricks and strained grimaces; in the new world to which Leverkühn wishes to lead us, "Art would like to stop being pretence and play, it would like to become knowledge" (p. 181). But if art is purged of grandiose repetitions of theme, insinuating novelties, polyphonic development and homophonic splendor, all the claptrap of Western emoting, there is not much left; and indeed Leverkühn, in the early part of his career, constricts the scope of his work until his chief interest is the terse simplicity of folk song; like Webern, whose music Mann read about while writing the novel (*Story of a Novel*, p. 191), Leverkühn seems headed in the direction of nullity, a few brief scrawls and whorls of music, crescendo, scurry, and silence. The gesture is made; it is not developed, repeated, transformed, or altered in any way; it accomplishes itself, and stops. Thus the intellect, seeking spiritual purity, turns against itself in a massive flow of self-criticism; better to compose flecks of ice than to contaminate onself with the humane and conventional; best to leave the page white. In this we can see, in disastrous parody, the preoccupation of the Goethe of *Lotte in Weimar* with the simplicity of white light; but Leverkühn, who is incomparably the most gnostic, in the old sense, of Mann's characters, truly despises the whole kingdom of the corporeal—he requests that his corpse be thrown onto a pile of horse dung during his latter utterance (p. 499), despises all expression for its inadequacy to what wishes to be expressed. Goethe attained a

281

state which could be called impersonal through his personalization of the created universe, whereas Leverkühn is involved in a serious attempt to depersonalize himself and his art alike by means of subtraction and not inclusion, struggles to perfect his coldness, his alienation. Art, in his early career, is not designed to be self-revelation or expression, but *knowledge*, a disquisition into the spiritual as valid as mathematics or theology; but Adrian's self-effacement extends further than this intellectual inhibition and dismantling of art. The narrator, an interesting intermediary called Serenus Zeitblom, Ph.D., a childhood friend and lifelong worshiper of Leverkühn, reflects at one point that only the neutral is free; that whatever has character is bound, stamped, and determined; and that the character of Adrian Leverkühn has been inevitably shaped and defined by the town of Kaisersaschern, in which both composer and narrator grew up, a medieval town full of ghosts and goety in slightly modern dress (p. 83). Leverkühn, in his struggles to escape from the grip of evil, the demon's tooth, is thus attempting to rid himself of genetic possession, his fate; he must eradicate his own character, exterminate himself. Goethe, too, saw his "mark," his distinguishing stamp, on the poetry that he wrote (*Lotte*, p. 216); but in Leverkühn's case such discoveries are more sinister. When the devil appears to confront Leverkühn, in the most powerful chapter Mann ever wrote, the devil advises Leverkühn to tell himself "Where I am, there is Kaisersaschern" (p. 226); myself am Hell; and from that moment on Leverkühn's self-hatred becomes holy, for to save his soul he must destroy his own identity, grow vegetable and infantile, his mind blasted and his body incompetent.

In all the works and gestures of a creative mind, some sign by which he characterizes himself must appear; and even in such small matters as Leverkühn's library or the pictures on his wall we can see the author's hand, full of stray revelations, little clues concerning the shape of character. Kierkegaard and Kleist are among Leverkühn's favorite authors; during a conversation on German destiny between Leverkühn and Zeitblom Adrian points to a volume of Kleist on his desk:

> "Here too," said he, and twitched the little red marker in the volume of Kleist on the table—"here too it treats of the break-through, in the capital essay on marionettes, and it is called straight out 'the last chapter of the history of the world.' But it is talking only about the aesthetic, charm, free grace, which actually is reserved to the automaton and the god; that is, to the unconscious or an endless consciousness, whereas every reflection lying between nothing and infinity kills grace. The consciousness must, this writer thinks,

have gone through an infinity in order that grace find itself again therein—and Adam must eat a second time from the tree of knowledge in order to fall back into the state of innocence." (P. 308)

That quest for innocence, or a travesty of innocence, dominates much of Adrian's musical efforts; it is, in effect, a radical repudiation of his guiltiness, the guiltiness of being, by trying to undo Western civilization, with its apparatus of convention and technique. But again we see that the tendency is subtraction, and Kleist provides a formula to describe this: the limit of inclusion is God, the limit of subtraction is the automaton. This is the difference, or the similarity, between Goethe and Leverkühn: the former comprehends all phenomena sympathetically, as autonomous self-extension; the latter works toward incomprehension, invisibility, the disintegration of ego and world at once. These two figures are the zenith and the nadir of the artist's impersonality.

Leverkühn's celebrated breakthrough, in which the devil offers him an escape from his obsessive inhibition in return for his soul, is another manifestation of his quest for automatism. The devil uses as his example of difficult creation the figure of Beethoven, struggling over a theme through draft after draft, writing "Meilleur" in no great certitude (p. 237); but the inspiration the devil offers is of a different nature, an inspiration that is rapturous, convulsive, an attack of lightning. This can be considered a breakthrough, but it is also a logical extension of the intellectual self-destruction that had led Leverkühn into miniaturism; although the devil tempts Leverkühn to self-admiration, an exaltation of his ego, what he offers Leverkühn is the abnegation of the intellect, of self-control, a further research into the inhuman. This kind of inspiration has nothing of spirit or divinity about it; it is only the devil's parody of the numen; in fact it is a distillation of the corporeal, something gross, mechanical. On physical terms the devil's inspiration is merely the osmotic infiltration of spirochetes into the brain, an invasion of the spiritual kingdom— exactly that area which Leverkühn most avidly wishes to keep sealed and impregnable—by the fevers and lusts of the lower body; but even more profoundly low is the kind of music to which syphilitic inspiration leads. The devil allows Leverkühn to put into practice the twelve-tone theory which he had discovered before; a purely mechanical sequence of the twelve distinct notes of the octave, in which the structure of a piece of music is governed by rigid transformations and inversions defined in advance. Schoenberg's *Harmonielehre*, which seemed in so many ways outrageous and fascinating, almost licentious, to Mann's sensibility, appears to us now more as a schoolchild's primer than as the manifesto of a new music; and Schoenberg's later insistence on the intellectual rigidity and determinedness of twelve-tone music is known to be poor description of his usual practice, which is as imaginative, unpredictable, and inconsequential as that of the great music of the past; and Leverkühn's later compositions should be heard in the reader's ear, not as a literary variant of Schoenberg's affable music but as intellectual cacophony, brilliant but incomprehensibly bound to strange laws. I cannot say whether Mann believed Schoenberg's later music to be overdetermined, but I am fairly sure that he thought it ugly; he says in a letter to Bruno Walter that his ear is hopelessly romantic, that his eyes overflow at a lovely diminished-seventh chord (*Letters II*, p. 465). Mann was perhaps born in the last generation that would have used the theory of composition in twelve tones as a metaphor for inhumanity.

Automatism extends into every corner of the novel; the inexpressive organ-grinder who churns out twelve-tone music with all the lucid comfort of law finds his habits of mind reflected in the narrator's treatment of much of the plot. One might say that *Dr. Faustus* is governed by a principle of homologous transformation, the mechanical repetition of forms in various experimental contexts; all the criminals in this book are recidivists. This principle is expressed chiefly through parody, and Mann informs us often that parody is Leverkühn's delight, his element, his genius. Much of Leverkühn's work is traditional parody, the self-conscious subversion of a particular form through the exaggeration of its nonfunctional convention and idiosyncrasy: his early symphonic piece *Ocean Lights* is a parody of impressionism; his opera on *Love's Labor's Lost* is a more advanced kind of parody, in which both sides of a philosophical antithesis, culture and nature, are mocked at once (p. 217). Leverkühn's letters, which mimic the erudite and archaic style of the university, suggest another aspect of parody, that it is a means of self-deflection, self-concealment. Parody, then, need affirm nothing; through the automatic revival of exhausted forms a style may be created which is simultaneously intelligent, pointed, and perfectly characterless and undescriptive. Parody is the most accessible mode in which negation can choose to operate, and it is a mode that, in its theory, has been most intriguing to the modern sensibility. One of Borges' earliest typical stories, "Pierre Menard, Author of the *Quixote*," in which Menard's artistic lifework is the painstaking, word-by-word re-creation of a few chapters of *Don Quixote*, not from memory but from a duplicate act of genius, shows that parody in its highest form can become a replication so automatic, so devoid of individual character, that it approaches the condition of xerography. The direction of Leverkühn's researches into parody, however, is slightly different. In his first speech on the subject there is a revealing sentence: "Why does almost everything seem to be its own parody?" (p. 134). This suggests that there exists a kind of parody far more inclusive and devastating than satire or burlesque, a parody independent of any prior model or known convention, a parody that is in essence a universal manner of perception rather than a discrete joke on a single theme: a condition of negation in which each entity in the created world seems to mock itself, to deny the virtue of its own creation. In this way Leverkühn orders the universe according to his own self-rejection, attributes his own sensibility to all things. For Leverkühn in his despair is in fact a parody of himself; when the devil tells him that his twenty-four-year period of ecstasy and abomination, great achievement and the renunciation of love, will be but an exaggeration of his previous life, the devil merely affirms Leverkühn's self-parodic status. At the very end he does escape, incompletely, from parody; but for the rest his efforts to evade his own brand of nihilism, like his violin concerto dedicated to the man he wishes to love, Rudi Schwerdtfeger, in which "the parody of being carried away becomes a passion which is seriously meant" (p. 410), lead to a situation that is ineffectual, embarrassing, void. The automaton dares not pretend to human emotion, venture out of its labyrinth of parody.

In Leverkühn's last two masterpieces, the *Apocalypse* oratorio and the oratorio *Dr. Faustus*, parody is perfected and then abandoned; but the abandonment leads to strict serialism, an even more mechanistic style of composition. In the *Apocalypse* oratorio there are parodies of all music styles from fugue *ad absurdum* to impressionism and jazz, a musical version of Joyce's "Oxen of the Sun"; but what disturbs Zeitblom most is a pair of peculiar transforms. At one point a coloratura soprano, the Whore of Babylon, turns so brilliant that the human voice becomes flutelike, impersonal, while a "muted trumpet suggests a grotesque vox humana" (p. 375), thus accomplishing a transference between the human and the inhuman, a shift in the boundary between man and thing, in the manner of Leverkühn's father's alchemical experiments in which crystals mock the organic growth of cells; again we see that convergence of organic and inorganic form which hints sinisterly that all that we cherish may be explicable as an excrescence of the inhuman, a fever of matter. But still more fascinating to Zeitblom is the musical identity of the concluding section of the first part, a depiction of demons howling and laughing in hell, with the opening chorus of the second part, in which children sing in glassy harmonies, distilled to alien purity, the music of the spheres; every note of the former corresponds rigidly with every note of the latter, a trick which Mann could have borrowed from a number of romantic sources, but most conspicuously from the Faust symphony of Liszt. Zeitblom remarks of this point-for-point transformation of hell into heaven, "That is Adrian Leverkühn. Utterly" (p. 379). It is the automaton, the blind mechanism whereby all that is valuable in the cosmos is reduced to a set of variations on a single banal theme, the virtuosity of the void. In *Joseph* or *Lotte in Weimar* the identicality of heaven and hell is a profound comic mystery, but in *Dr. Faustus* heaven and hell become parodies of each other, mutually undercutting. Leverkühn's mind is so contaminate with its own knowledge that earth, heaven, and hell seem, like Wagner's prelude, a kind of inflated art, the creator's bombast in which the tricks and seams of construction are all too apparent; the theatrical joke in the middle of the *Apocalypse* oratorio is only a parody of that exterior heaven and hell which manifest, to Adrian Leverkühn, the automatism of the divine.

But Leverkühn's experiments with the various sequences of transforms which imitate the mechanism of the universe are only part of a larger set of researches into automatism which take place in the course of the narrative. Mann's use of the personality of an artificial narrator, Serenus Zeitblom, is only one indication of this novel's division into superimposed layers, each of which represents a figured and complex version of a simple underlying design. Mann liked to think of *Dr. Faustus* as a rigidly structured book; he called it in a letter "an extremely tight-knit composition in which, musically speaking, 'no note is free,' and in which all elements are interrelated" (*Letters II*, p. 548). That comparison of the novel to one of Leverkühn's twelve-tone compositions—"no note is free"—is most interesting, and leads us to hunt for predetermined patterns in the actual working-out of the plot, themes which strictly govern the behavior of the characters. Such patterns are not hard to find; everywhere there is the sense of fatality, of controlling intelligence behind the actions of seemingly independent characters. The principle of organization in the novel is, once again, the psychomachia, in which the struggles of the characters are a projection of the conflicts within Leverkühn's mind; but unlike *Joseph* or *Lotte in Weimar* everything comes to the worst possible resolution. Leverkühn, in effect, orchestrates his desires, assigns to some characters passionate *cantabile*, to others heavy, sustained devotion, while a few play, like bassoons, a comic obbligato; the plot of the novel may be conceived as Leverkühn's greatest score. At these levels, however, it is impossible to distinguish Leverkühn from Mann. Narrative jest is ubiquitous; and the simplest of Mann's designs is the Faust legend, not in any stable form, but distorted, shattered into bright fragments:

Helene is not the wife of Leverkühn but of the mild, faithful, complacent Zeitblom; Waltpurgis is no night of orgy but the name of a stable girl; the official tempters who attack Leverkühn, his enigmatic patron Frau von Tolna and the impresario Saul Fitelberg, are among the most benign characters of the novel. So one can see an orchestration of the Faust theme, too, in the analytic manner of Webern's Bach. Mann, in this novel, speaks to us via parody, allusion, and analogue, never about the thing itself; for instance, the rise of nazism is explained only through the intellectual depravity of Kridwiss' circle, never as a political phenomenon; Mann thereby conceals himself completely, like Leverkühn, insists on developing oblique subjects by means of deflected narration. In a letter Mann mentions a critical hypothesis, in passing: "It has also been said that I had bisected myself in the novel, and that the narrator and the hero each embraced a part of me" (*Letters II*, p. 569). It is bad rhetorical form to say that a character is part of an author; but the presumption that *Dr. Faustus* is a charade of identity, a manipulation by an author of fluid and almost indistinguishable figments of his being, is certainly valid.

The narrative intimacy between Zeitblom and Leverkühn—an analogical mirror of the intimacy between Leverkühn and his real narrator, Thomas Mann, who said of Adrian that he loved him best of all characters, except perhaps Hanno Buddenbrook (*Story of a Novel*, p. 88)—reaches to the point of Zeitblom's slavishness; to the old scholar it appears that his life has been given meaning by his relation with Adrian (*Dr. Faustus*, p. 509); he calls himself Adrian's alter ego (p. 448); it is he who approached Marie Godeau, in preliminary fashion, as Adrian's vicarious wooer (p. 426); he feels that he lives on after Adrian's death in Adrian's place, bearing on his sturdier shoulders the horrors of life in the modern age (p. 253). They are twins, Adrian and Serenus, complements, for here the biographer has attained a mystic union with the subject of his art; but those who serve Adrian less eagerly do not serve him less well. Zeitblom may be said to represent Leverkühn's faculty for self-verbalization, and his biography may be seen as a mode of Leverkühn's utterance; in his *Story of a Novel*, on a remarkable page, Mann even asserts that the secret of Leverkühn and Zeitblom is that they are "identical with each other" (p. 90). Compared to this identity, the whole outward plot is a fairly unimportant episode: Adrian, whose *Gesta Romanorum* is a puppet show, deploys his external puppets in tranquillity or in agitation. He keeps a picture of Meyerbeer on his wall, showing the composer surrounded by hovering forms of characters from his operas (p. 195); and in like manner the characters of *Dr. Faustus* hover around him.

In his presence one had always the feeling that all the ideas and points of view made vocal round about him were present in himself; that he, ironically listening, left it to the individual human constitutions to express and represent them. (P. 433)

Leverkühn's relation to the marvelous child Nepomuk Schneidewein is that of Prospero to Ariel, a role he validates by setting the songs of *The Tempest* to music and by dismissing the agonized soul of the dying infant with Prospero's words (p. 479). Some of his favored tools occasionally revolt against their dependent status, as Rudi Schwerdt-feger does by deciding to woo Marie Godeau on his own instead of as the agent of the bashful Leverkühn; but his rebellion only confirms his obedience to his composer, he becomes the secret agent of Leverkühn's murderousness, provokes his own death. We know that this plot line had been in Mann's head for many years; over the decades it had, so to speak, ossified, grown well-known and inevitable; the whole story of Rudi and Clarissa and Inez is as rigid and well-defined as a twelve-tone row. In fact some of the language which describes Clarissa's suicide is found in Mann's account in *A Sketch of my Life* of his sister's suicide, on which the Clarissa subplot is closely based. The law that these subsidiary characters obey is the law of Leverkühn's identity, not of his superficial desire: Leverkühn wishes to be loved, but his being is cold, loveless, the abjurance of love; and the others obey his will by thwarting all his human relation, extinguishing themselves so that he may stand alone. We can call Leverkühn Dr. Faustus because the lines of force that emanate from Leverkühn cause the minor characters to constellate themselves in the pattern of the Faust story, but the major thrust of his vitality works toward the balking of all the attempts of his acquaintances to temper or mitigate his annihilating self-perfection. The doctors who could cure Leverkühn's syphilis disappear; Inez enacts his jealousy by murdering Rudi; and this elimination of the minor characters is carried to its highest degree in the scene of Leverkühn's last confession, in which almost all his acquaintants walk out in horror at the spectacle of his utterance of the myth of his life in its final form, his subtle homicide put on public display, his mythic kinships with his nephew Nepomuk and his syphilitic muse much simplified and personalized in this magnificent act of self-disclosure. At the climax Leverkühn and Zeitblom, the indivisible friends, are alone, with only Frau Schweigestill, Mrs. Silence, on the stage with them, to provide a certain assuring presence of the human norm.

What is the substance of Leverkühn's achievement at the end of the novel? He has managed, in the oratorio *Dr. Faustus*, to state himself in music in a definitive form, just as Goethe's total canon comprises a self-definition; but the same general reversal that has held before in these comparisons can be discovered here too, for the *Dr. Faustus* oratorio, ostensibly an attempt to undo Beethoven's choral finale to the Ninth Symphony, is an act of self-dismantling as well. Here rigidity has conquered all; every bar derives from a single twelve-note phrase, each note of which corresponds to a syllable in the following sentence: "For I die as a good and as a bad Christian." This is Leverkühn's personal *leitmotif*, his signature tune, an oxymoronic, nearly self-canceling phrase, a phrase which becomes the matrix of all that appears in the oratorio. Zeitblom hears in the oratorio another melodic figure as well, *h e a e es*; this is the motif of "hetaera esmeralda," the prostitute who infected Leverkühn; and we remember, though it is not present in the oratorio, that Nepomuk too discovered that his personality had been converted into musical notation, was fascinated by the inky dots in the Ariel songs which represented him. It seems that each person has a tune; and that all tunes are brief episodes in Leverkühn's statement of his own melody. These tricks of note-spelling and verbal reference, which were in fact much practiced by Schoenberg's Viennese colleagues, manage to link Leverkühn's music strongly to the world of words; and there is good reason to suspect that the oratorio *Dr. Faustus* is partially a covert introduction of the novel into the text of the novel itself, a strategy Mann has employed before. We are told that the movements of the oratorio "correspond to the textual units of chapters in a book" (p. 487); and Leverkühn once remarked of an earlier work, "I have ... not wanted to write a sonata but a novel " (p. 456). We have seen in Mann's earlier novels how his characters become aware of their status as characters in a novel; here, the characters become aware that they are the subsidiary themes, the second and third and fourth subjects of an oratorio. In this context Zeitblom's repeated insistence that he is writing no novel but a sober and scrupulous biography (p. 295) becomes slightly presumptuous, a vain attempt to free himself from Mann's verbal confines.

Leverkühn, in the last oratorio and in his confession to his friends, states his theme so conclusively that he can sink into well-earned madness; nevertheless he draws himself in such a manner that it constitutes an erasure of himself as well. Zeitblom says of Leverkühn's later years that he "gave one the feeling that he came from a country where nobody else lived" (p. 411). This sense of alienation beyond all boundaries of human rapport, this nimbus of hell that clings about him, finds an echo in certain descriptions of the divine child, Nepomuk Schneidewein. Nepomuk is "a friendly ambassador from

some other better clime" (p. 462), not yet well adjusted to the local
customs of earth; and, though Leverkühn's exact antithesis, a being of
such charm that the human race pays him its gladdest obeisance,
Nepomuk is nevertheless an analogue, an alternative self, of his
reclusive and gifted uncle. Zeitblom says that Nepomuk's adorers
consoled themselves for his inevitable growth into adulthood with the
consolation of Christian doctrine, that Christ is always a Babe, even
when stretched out on the cross (p. 467); and this mysterious
simultaneity of identity is to some extent represented by the simultaneous appearance of Nepomuk and Leverkühn. Nepomuk is Leverkühn's self-extension, in a fashion much more intimate than that of the
more rigid characters; and Nepomuk's death is the most serious
incident in the general tendency of the latter part of the novel, which is
the withdrawal of Leverkühn's extensions, the elimination of his
psychic arms and legs. I haven spoken of the process of Leverkühn's
contraction; this contraction by the end has reached such an extent
that he is literally inarticulate. Involved in the internecine combat of
Leverkühn's soul, the other characters kill themselves off, or simply
lose agency, fold themselves up into Leverkühn's all-embracing despair. Goethe reaches out to grasp sun and star; Leverkühn cuts
off his fingers. In what to my mind is the most subtle and illuminating
self-criticism Mann ever wrote, he comments on his reasons for not
providing any description of Leverkühn's features:

> I scarcely gave him any appearance, any physical body. My family
> was always wanting me to describe him. If the narrator had to be
> reduced to a mere figment, a kind heart and a hand trembling as
> it held the pen, well and good. But at least I should make his
> hero and mine visible, should give him a physical individuality,
> should make it possible for the reader to picture him. How easily
> that could have been done! And yet how mysteriously forbidden
> it was, how impossible, in a way I had never felt before!
> Impossible in a different sense from the impossibility of Zeitblom's
> describing himself. Here there was a prohibition to be kept—or,
> at any rate, a commandment of maximum restraint. To depict
> Adrian's outer appearance was instantly to threaten him with
> spiritual downfall, to undermine his symbolic dignity, to diminish
> and render banal his representativeness. That was the way it was.
> Only the characters more remote from the center of the book could
> be novelistic figures in the picturesque sense—all the Schild-
> knapps, Schwerdtfegers, Roddes, Schlaginhaufens, etc. But
> not the two protagonists, who had too much to conceal, namely,
> the secret of their being identical with each other. (*Story of a
> Novel*, pp. 89–90)

Mann was reluctant to forfeit Leverkühn's generality by providing him with a face; and archetypically Leverkühn is facelessness itself, loss of individuality, renunciation of the human. *The Story of a Novel*, from which this quotation is taken, is to some extent a digressive sequel to *Dr. Faustus*; and in this later book Zeitblom and Leverkühn have collapsed into a oneness greater than what they attain in the novel, a further development in the general collapse of personality so prominent in the closing chapters.

Dr. *Faustus* is Mann's only lengthy excursion into the problem of the existence of evil. The development of Leverkühn owes some of its oddness to the fact that it is an adaptation of the techniques of the comic novel to the requirements encountered in the depiction of real viciousness; and it is worth a page of discussion on Mann's conception of evil in order to see Mann's reasons for embodying Nazi atrocity in the unatrocious and self-abnegating figure of Adrian Leverkühn. The central document for the purpose is Mann's novella *The Tables of the Law*, written between *Joseph the Provider* and *Dr. Faustus*, conceived to some extent as a reply to nazism and an execration against it. Moses' advice to his tribe in the wilderness suggests a figure of civilization struggling against sheer lumpish and recalcitrant nature: he patiently instructs the rabble not to defecate wherever they lie but to take a scoop and dig latrines; not to sleep haphazardly with daughter or sister, boy or animal; not to eat parasitical and infested meat; in short, his monitions do not go far beyond a basic bourgeois commandment, Wash your hands. When he returns from the mountain with the Ten Commandments, and, what is even more important, an alphabet, the gift of literate expression, he discovers that his charges have reverted in his absence, now worship a golden calf that is not splendid but misshapen and ugly, now defecate freely, masturbate zestfully, sleep indiscriminately with their sisters. Nazism, then, can almost be defined as bodily incontinence. This is a great advance from Mann's earlier parable of nazism, the 1929 *Mario and the Magician*, in which the hypnotist Cipolla uses his irresistible will to force his subjects into committing all sorts of grotesque and unnatural deeds; Aaron by comparison is no sinister mastermind but an ordinary, lax and self-indulgent, relatively innocuous figure. The *Führer* has shrunk from a personage of overwhelming viciousness, a distorted and fallen archangel, to a kind of nonentity; and the crowd of his followers have turned from rebellious, nearly heroic victims to a gang of rowdies, chaotic and uncontrollable, another diminishment in stature. Evil is carelessness, inarticulateness, slurring; it is doing whatever you want to do, spilling your innards on the spot. As such, the evil character becomes a variant of that common type in Mann's fiction, the self-preoccupied man, who is irresponsibly fascinated by his own feelings to the exclusion of human considerateness. In those two or three pages at the center of *Dr. Faustus* in which the devil describes hell, a passage of such astonishing imaginative vigor that Mann reread it whenever he needed to be cheered up by a display of his power, the devil describes the wailing of the damned:

> " 'There shall be wailing and gnashing of teeth.' Good; these are a
> few word-sounds, chosen out of a rather extreme sphere of
> language, yet but weak symbols and without proper reference
> to what 'shall be' there, unrecorded, unreckoned, between thick
> walls. True it is that inside these echoless walls it gets right loud,
> measureless loud, and by much overfilling the ear with screeching
> and beseeching, gurgling and groaning, with yauling and bauling
> and caterwauling, with horrid winding and grinding and racking
> ecstasies of anguish no man can hear his own tune, for that it
> smothers in the general, in the thick-clotted diapason of trills and
> chirps lured from this everlasting dispensation of the unbelievable
> combined with the irresponsible. Nothing forgetting the dismal
> groans of lust mixted therewith; since endless torment, with no
> possible collapse, no swoon to put a period thereto, degenerates
> into shameful pleasure, wherefore such as have some intuitive
> knowledge speak indeed of the 'lusts of hell.' And therewith
> mockage and the extreme of ignominy such as belongs with
> martyrdom; for this bliss of hell is like a deep-voiced pitifull
> jeering and scorne of all the immeasureable anguish; it is accom-
> panied by whinnying laughter and the pointing finger; whence the
> doctrine that the damned have not only torturement but also
> mockery and shame to bear; yea, that hell is to be defined as a
> monstrous combination of suffering and derision, unendurable
> yet to be endured world without end. There will they devour their
> proper tongues for greatness of the agony, yet make no common
> cause on that account, for rather they are full of hatred and scorn
> against each other, and in the midst of their trills and quavers
> hurl at one another the foulest oaths. Yea, the finest and proudest,
> who never let a lewd word pass their lips, are forced to use the
> filthiest of all. A part of their torment and lust of shame standeth
> therein that they must cogitate the extremity of filthiness."
> (Pp. 245–46)

The wailing, shrieking, howling, all that figured anguish—it is an error of the translator to introduce rhymes, for properly all the nouns are distinct—is little more than the rude individualism of Moses' Israelites translated into music, a fit chorus for Leverkühn's ears. Mann has written that this passage would have been "Inconceivable, incidentally, without the psychological experience of Gestapo cellars" (*Story of a Novel*, p. 108); but the line between the tortured and the torturer is here blurred, for in either case they emit their private racket in a careless cacophony. Here language approaches the condition of excrement, for the damned utter filthy words with the fecal relish of those who celebrate around the golden calf. The society of hell, however, has no camaraderie but is instead an endless swarm of mutual derision, a version of hell close to Mann's heart, for the decision to invite public scorn is a crucial one in such diverse characters as Aschenbach and Hans Castorp. What is important about the derision is that wilderness of pointing figures, which illustrates another stage in the debasement of language, as it declines into a state of point-blank, nearly wordless indication. If each person has his private musical theme, as is suggested elsewhere in the novel, then this hell consists of sweating selves, separate selves, persisting in hopelessly unrelated identity beyond death, each insisting on his own noise, so that the totality fuzzes out into a chromatic blur, a vision of hell appropriate to an atonal composer.

Mann remarks in *The Story of a Novel* that the devil is "the secret hero of the book" (p. 91), and it is certainly possible to read the novel as the devil's psychomachia rather than as Leverkühn's. But insofar as the devil and Leverkühn are distinguishable, I would say that this version of hell quoted above pertains very well to the devil but not to Leverkühn; whereas in the oratorio *Dr. Faustus* the hand of Leverkühn supersedes that of the devil. Hell is a place of utter disorder; it is all notes played at once all the time in random chirps and twitters. Leverkühn in the rapture of syphilitic inspiration is the devil's truest servant; but the Leverkühn who contains himself, works toward his own impoverishment and contrition is no emblem of nazism. The Nazi fouls the world with his corrupt will, with the feces of his language and his brutality; indeed nazism tends toward disgusting hugeness, dissipation, wide contamination, as Mann points out in his fine late essay on Nietzsche when he describes Nietzsche's intellectual legacy to nazism: "romantic passion; the drive to eternal expansion of the self into space, without any fixed object; will which is free because it has no goal and aspires to the infinite" (*Last Essays*, p. 175). This is almost the kind of language which Mann uses to describe Goethe, but without, of course, the aimlessness, the lack of discipline. Certainly there are ways in which Leverkühn too participates in this sort of development: through insufficient restraint of his jealousy and other lower urges he causes Rudi's death; but for the most part his love of finely tuned control, his self-abomination, his self-destruction, all represent tendencies which can be used toward his salvation. His annihilation at the end of the book seems to represent salvation achieved at the expense of everything, and his *Dr. Faustus* oratorio, though it reflects the devil's automatism in all its members, is nevertheless the antithesis of the hellish smear of random voices: it is expressive. Mann makes much of the fact that the oratorio, while its melodic lines are wholly determined, nevertheless allows the apparatus of rhetorical expression unparalleled scope, with its long sighs, its suspensions, it falling cadences. Here musical art becomes identical to the art of literary declamation. Its choruses are expressive of a single sensibility, Leverkühn's sensibility, or Mann's, the faceless sensibility of the human race, lamenting in canon for its thoughtless holocaust; and to oppose the bloated pettinesses and orotundities of hell Mann and his Leverkühn offer *Dr. Faustus*, a fabulous coordination.

Schopenhauer

The intuition of Thomas Mann, and of many other writers who are contemporary with him, the increasing doubt over the validity of the individual, the suspicion that the apparent multiplicity of the human race is only a deceit, has philosophical sanction from a number of sources in the nineteenth century; chief among these is Arthur Schopenhauer. Mann's debt to the celebrated pessimist is clear in his essay of 1938, "Schopenhauer"; and it is not the least of Mann's achievements that he, a century after the first appearance of *The World as Will and Idea*, has created a body of work in which the depiction of human identity is accomplished according to the precepts of Schopenhauer's philosophy; and I believe that Mann is the first writer to have done so, although D. H. Lawrence's theory of allotropic characterization—Lawrence read Schopenhauer aloud to Jessie Chambers—bears strong resemblance to Schopenhauer's Will. To Schopenhauer, as Mann perceives him, the great bulk of society consists of naive egoists, ordinary people who believe that their private desires are more important or serious than the desires of others (*Essays*, p. 389), who see the universe as a "ballet," a spectacle for their benefit. The fictional counterpart of this egoism is the traditional character in the traditional novel; and, more specifically, it is the attitude of Mann's selfish or self-preoccupied characters, his various Christian Buddenbrooks. The enlightened man of Schopenhauer, however, perceives that the line of demarcation between himself and anyone else is illusory; each man, each being in the created universe, is a stage in the disintegration of the One, what Schopenhauer calls the Will. The Will is no Plotinian tranquil unity of being but a raging flux, desperately articulating itself into the reaches of time and space:

> Will becoming world according to the *principium individuationis*,
> and being dispersed into a multiplicity of parts, forgets its original
> unity and, although in all its divisions it remains essentially one,
> it becomes will a million times divided against itself. Thus it strives
> against itself, seeking its own well-being in each of the millions of
> its manifestations, its place in the sun at the expense of another,
> yes, at the expense of all others, and so constantly sets its teeth
> in its own flesh, like that dweller in Tartarus who avidly
> devoured his own members. (*Essays*, p. 381)

The expression of this emblem, the dweller in Tartarus who eats his
own limbs, the slayer who forgets that he plunges the knife into his
own flesh, may be seen as the central problem of Mann's work. How
can the novel, in which all depends on the psychological dignity of the
individual, be adapted to present this terrifying singleness of agency,
this technical unanimity? Can the true protagonist of a novel be made
into something inhuman, incompetent, Schopenhauer's Will?

There are nearly as many strategies used to attack this problem as
there are novels of Mann. What is arguably the climax of *Buddenbrooks* occurs when Thomas Buddenbrook, ordinarily no lover of
literature or philosophy, chances upon Schopenhauer's chapter on
death, an encounter of such seminal nature that Mann refers to it with
renewed awe forty years later in his essay on Schopenhauer. Individuality is "poor, grey, inadequate, wearisome" (*Buddenbrooks*, p.
506); death is a great broadening of identity: "I shall be in all those
who have ever, do ever, or ever shall say 'I'—*especially, however, in
all those who say it most fully, potently, and gladly!*" (p. 507).
However, the revelation fades, leaving Thomas Buddenbrook more or
less in the same confusion as before. A reputable critic has alleged that
Buddenbrooks is Mann's most Schopenhauerian novel (Thomas A.
Riley, in Thomas Mann, *Der letzte Buddenbrook* [Boston: D. C.
Heath and Co., 1965], p. viii); I would venture to say instead that,
from the standpoint of characterization, it is his least. Thomas'
rapture does little to mitigate the general fixity and quirkiness of the
characters; individuality may be gray and wearisome, but individuals
they mostly remain. In the teens and the 1920s, Mann's vision of the
Will begins to assume the form of a fable; and in *The Magic Mountain*
the Will stirs, rumbles, lifts up its head out of some Jurassic sea.
Mann claimed that Schopenhauer derived his concept of Will from
Kant's *Ding an sich*, the supersensible reality which lies beyond the
mind's conception, that concrete base to which all perception refers;
and so the Will becomes identified with Mann's nature forces, with the
cold elementality of Goethe that challenges the kingdom of the spirit.

In *The Magic Mountain* the heavings of the Will manifest themselves in bodily force, in disease. When Hans Castorp is alarmed by palpitations of his heart that have no psychological referent, palpitations which suggest that his body is taking control, turning automaton; when he learns to think of life as a fever of matter; when Peeperkorn communes in solemn unanimity with a waterfall; then we see great assertions of the Will, transpersonal, serpentine, overwhelming the intellectual claims of individuation. In general the continuing potency of the body in Mann's imagination is a Schopenhauerian phenomenon: his unforgettable description of Schiller's burial in "On Schiller" suggests the brooding and immutable power of earth; and there is a moving passage in *The Story of a Novel* in which Mann, in great pain while recovering from a lung operation, imagines that the body when cut into suffers even in the haze of anesthesia, that the body in its lowest levels may feel pain even after death, in its own dissolution (p. 175). Nothing could show better Mann's faith in the persistence and omnipotence of the Will: the turmoil of flesh, the ceaseless raving of all that is corporeal, will not be stifled by death.

What I have called the gnostic myth of *Joseph*, that endlessly ramifying dichotomy of nature and spirit, Will and Idea, has, as one of its bases, the philosophy of Schopenhauer, with a few revisions and supplements; and the myth of *Joseph* is nearly adequate for the rest of Mann's career. Gnosticism and Plato and Schopenhauer all meet in the following sentence from "Schopenhauer":

> Plato's already slightly ascetic and pessimistic devaluation of the senses by the soul, wherein alone reside all salvation and truth— here it is most grimly reasserted and reinforced; in two thousand years it has received an imprint of suffering and complaint foreign to the early Occidental: the actual world is the product of an arch-sinful, arch-stupid act of will, which never should have taken place; and if it has never become completely and formallly a hell, that is because the will's will to live has not been vehement enough. (*Essays*, p. 383)

The God of *Joseph*, although benign and not a representation of nature, nevertheless extends himself into the roles of his terrestrial actors in that manner in which Schopenhauer's Will evolves into murderous multiplicities; and in the compoundedness of the deity we see something of that primal cell from which the universe develops. The creation of the world in *Joseph* may not be "an arch-sinful, arch-stupid act of will," but its wisdom is highly questionable, and sometimes questioned. Also, in *Joseph* Mann begins to perfect that form of mythic expression which seems most adequate to Schopenhauerian philosophy. It is difficult to use or sustain a plot if one cannot distinguish the active from the passive, the female from the male; if all existence tends toward complex and androgyne homogeneity. Some authors, like Nabokov and Borges, have attempted to create peculiar reflexive fables to abolish the distinctions between individual characters; Mann's method of dissolving identity, though simpler, is no less effective. Mann employs a well-known story, like the Joseph legend, but he makes sure that his principal character plays both hero and villain, actor and acted-upon. Therefore Joseph, anticipating Felix Krull, is a waiter in the house of Potiphar who metamorphoses into the master; the son turns effortlessly into the father, Joseph in one half-turn of the wheel of myth recapitulates the adventures of Jacob. On still higher levels of myth, we know that Zeus or Typhon castrates his father Cronos or Osiris and usurps the throne; but Mann informs us that this mythic act exists in perpetual revolution, that Osiris had originally castrated *his* father to obtain the throne, and that Typhon the usurper, once seated, himself awaits a son, who is already sharpening his knife (pp. 125–26). Through this law of rotation of role any given story may be made to fit the requirements of Schopenhauerian myth, in which the actor and the acted-upon are identical.

If the benignity of the God of *Joseph* seems improper in the context of Schopenhauer, then *Dr. Faustus* provides a more typical setting. An equation can be made with some security: Leverkühn's genius, the principle of impalpable control in the novel, is the Will of Schopenhauer. As in *The Magic Mountain*, the Will manifests itself as an upheaval of physical disease; and its ramifications lead to mortal combat, a duel or a murder, world war. In *The Magic Mountain*, however, there is some fertility in all this muddiness, whereas in *Dr. Faustus* the Will is bent on its own annihilation. Both ends can be derived from Schopenhauer, for it is true that, while the Will wills its own proliferation, it is so predatory and confused, so deluded by individuation, that it engages itself in perpetual self-destruction. Schopenhauer's one hope is that the Will, in its lust for objectification, will so extend itself, so coagulate, that it approaches that state of self-liberation which he calls Idea, the state of abstract self-representation. In the world of *Dr. Faustus* an Idea would be a genuine inspiration, like the one with which Beethoven wrestles in the devil's chapter; but the inspirations of Leverkühn are seizures as blind and irresistible as the Will itself, and his music is therefore as inflexible and automatic as those genetic, Darwinian mechanisms that control the evolution of species. Twelve-tone music is but an artistic realization of the genetic code. Yet this rigidity nevertheless has the aspect of chaos, as

Zeitblom warns Leverkühn during his first explanation of his new music system (p. 194); and likewise the rigidity of the plot has its fluid, dreamlike aspects. Mann liked to call the novel a montage, in which bits and pieces of the life of Tchaikovsky, of Nietzsche, of Schoenberg, of his own sister, of personal friends, were cut out and glued together; the place of each detail is determined, but the whole is chimerical. If one searches out the referents whom Mann has employed in creating the character of Leverkühn, it is clear that Leverkühn is monstrous. Mann conceived the world of *Dr. Faustus* as a fictive world alternate or parallel to our own, in which "the euphoric musician has been made so much Nietzsche's substitute that the original is no longer permitted a separate existence" (*Story of a Novel*, p. 32); and it takes all Mann's verbal cleverness to conceal the stitches, the broad lacerations, which remain on Nietzsche's corpse after this daring revivification and transmogrification into Adrian Leverkühn. This technique accords well with a Schopenhauerian vision of identity: one character may indeed be a conflation, an inspissation, of diverse and unrelated personalities.

Yet it is a remarkable feature of Mann's career that after all this orthodox despair he was nevertheless able to imagine what Schopenhauer could not conceive, the redemption of the Will. At the end of the Schopenhauer essay Mann says, in effect, that Schopenhauer was wrong: the only solution to the Will's dominance is *not* chastity and the mortification of desire; it is not necessary to keep Will and Idea so strictly separated, for their union, "sensuality spiritualized . . . spirit informed and made creative by sex" (*Essays*, p. 406), can be benign, bountiful. an artist's reconciliation. Chastity was never a viable solution to Mann; indeed, in his novella *The Transposed Heads*, written at about the same time as "Schopenhauer," there is a humorous Hindu ascetic who represents, I believe, a direct parody of Schopenhauerian chastity. *The Transposed Heads* also illustrates the final direction that Schopenhauerian myth did take in Mann's imagination, for it is a metaphysical tale, a story of fabulous and incoherent identity: the two central characters, entangled in the bonds of common lust for a woman, swap heads by means of a miracle; but this interchange, which seemed to clarify everything by putting the most desirable head on the most desirable torso, instead leads to atrophy and hypertrophy, partial atavism and incomplete hybrids, a great perplexity of body and soul. However, this miscibility of identity is comic, and by the path of comedy the Will is channeled into humanly acceptable form. The characters of *The Transposed Heads* do not enjoy their monstrousness, but they discover that this messiness of being has its compensations: if Shridaman-Nanda becomes jealous of sexual activity between Nanda-Shridaman and his, their, wife, he can at least reflect that part of himself is enjoying her in absentia. These comic complications and compensations, in which any moral event has pain and pleasure mixed in equal doses, are an easy extension of Schopenhauer's doctrines concerning the inseparability of all living beings; even the *urobolus*, the universal snake that eats its own tail, may become a comic emblem if it discovers that its flesh has good flavor. It is typical of Mann's metaphysical vein that he becomes more sexual, one might say earthier, at the same time; the dark forces in the viscera and organs of the earth, the Will, once purified, can permit a freer speech on libidinous themes.

In the books written after *Dr. Faustus*, Mann's fables become increasingly tangled, increasingly naughty. Occasionally he writes of a spirit, like that of Schiller, so lofty that it escapes altogether from the orbit of the terrestrial; but for the most part the spirit is firmly embedded in earthly soil, and it directs with steady guidance the fractious Will. In an essay of 1936 on Freud, Mann equates Schopenhauer's Will with the Freudian id, Schopenhauer's Idea with the ego; and he employs, from Freud, an interesting metaphor for their interaction:

> As for the ego itself, its situation is pathetic, well-nigh alarming. It is an alert, prominent, and enlightened little part of the id— much as Europe is a small and lively province of the greater Asia. The ego is that part of the id which became modified by contact with the outer world; equipped for the reception and preservation of stimuli; comparable to the integument with which any piece of living matter surrounds itself. (*Essays*, p. 417)

The Will, by a natural, organic process, thickens inevitably into a formal husk, a functional shape. This assumes that the Will, far from Schopenhauer's random self-dispersal, is governed teleologically, has it own spiritual and felicitous vigor. In the years following the end of World War II Mann develops a new confidence in the body, in the body's determination of its goals. During the era of Hitler, Mann perceived the human body as an organism in perpetual disintegration, feces, putrefaction, sexual stench. Now the Will imparts to his fables significant shape rather than spasmodic repetition; and putrefaction is itself made holy. In *The Black Swan* Rosalie, walking in the woods, comes across a pile of excrement mixed with a greatly decayed animal, a nauseous musk, an emblem for her own body and its sexually stimulating cancer (*Stories II*, p. 357); and the novella ends with her autumnal acceptance of death and the black fecundity of her dying body. The Will may be dissolute, may be fatal; but it brings certain enhancements, and therefore is forgiven.

The atmospheric contrast between *Dr. Faustus* and Mann's later works cannot be better seen than in *The Holy Sinner*, for the plot of this novel is found, in abbreviated form, in one of Leverkühn's *Gesta Romanorum*, in which the agonies of Pope Gregory the Great, who married his mother by accident, himself the offspring of incestuous parents, are turned into an erotic farce, a puppet show. For Leverkühn this plot represents an occasion for a display of wit, a wit given point by his contempt for the convolutions of sexual desire. In *The Holy Sinner*, however, the erotic farce turns into the theater of the divine; and incest becomes a metaphor of identity, a genetic token of human fraternity. Incest always fascinated Mann: the sinister incest of *The Blood of the Wälsungs* is a kind of degeneration, an escape to the fastness of the womb; the incest of Huia and Tuia in *Joseph in Egypt* is similarly retrogressive, an embrace which insulates the couple from the clangorous world. Huia and Tuia may be vile, but they find themselves metaphysically interesting; their state is akin to that of the prehistoric, presexual world, "the swamps and the black river mud, where the mother-stuff breweth and giveth itself to its own embrace and fructifieth in the darkness" (p. 579). Incest, then, can be a strategy to heal the great fissure in the human race, the split between male and female; incest pertains to unsundered mud, protoplasm, spontaneous generation, a condition of divine homogeneity. There is a letter in which Mann acknowledges his debt to the philosopher of matriarchy,. Johann Jacob Bachofen, with respect to the primal mud of Huia and Tuia; and in the same sentence in which he mentions Bachofen he also mentions Schopenhauer (*Letters II*, p. 490). Indeed this parodic mud accords well with Schopenhauer's Will, in a condition antecedent to any objectification; and it becomes clear in *The Holy Sinner* that incest can be a magical act performed in order to affirm the egglike oneness of human society, in which outrageous scramblings of social relations prefigure the absorption and simplification of identity which will occur in heaven. After death the veil of individuation will drop away; and mother, brother, and son will all revert to that singleness for which the sexual embrace is a sacrament. One of the jokes of the novel is that the clerical narrator and his tangled subjects all deplore, sometimes in great anguish, this multiple incestuousness; but the ongoing sanctity of it all is established unequivocally at the end: "We thought to offer God an entertainment" (p. 225). *The Holy Sinner*, like *Joseph*, is a divine play, for what is playful is divine. Gregory and his mother sigh with relief at the thought that Gregory is never to sleep with their daughters, an act which would propagate this great knot of incest to yet another generation, to yet greater abolition of social structure; they are Christians, and rejoice, with the medievalism of Naptha, that the world and its lusts are finite. Yet the limitations of these inclusive creatures, infatuated with the undifferentiatedness of the ovum, are by no means great; and the paradise to which Gregory looks forward, the paradise in which he will meet his dead father and uncle Wiligis (p. 226), in which the narrator will meet the reader (p. 228), is clearly infinite, for all men are brothers in Adam, guilty of incest, down through the farthest extension of the human race.

But it is in the promiscuity of Felix Krull that Mann's Schopenhauerian myth reaches its culmination. The ease, the continuity, of Mann's addition to his 1911 story has been stressed in recent years, but one must understand as well the radical departure of Mann's last novel from its early source. We know from Mann's letters that the writing of this most vivacious of novels was a weary chore, so dubious that he regretted, for the sake of his literary reputation, that he had not died after writing *Dr. Faustus*; and indeed the looseness of the plot, the casual outrageousness of Felix's personality, may have convinced its author that the novel showed a decline of his powers. The development of Felix's character in the early fragment *Felix Krull* is organized with extreme care: his first talent is that of a mimic, the charming little charlatan who gives recitals with greased bow and silent violin; then he becomes a model for his godfather, the artist Schimmelpreester, a creative model who can so animate his costumes that he appears to be an authentic bullfighter (p. 19), an authentic dandy, a medieval Florentine, a vast extension of his repertoire of gesture; from this stage he enters the world of the theater, the artifice of operetta; at last he makes use of what he has learned from the stage, converts everyday life into his private theater, becomes a confidence man, steals candy and makes love. The artifice that had been unusual, sealed off from normal life, becomes quotidian. It is all an orderly self-invention, a mastery over one's body which leads to widening circles of influence over human affairs. If Mann had not decided to interrupt its composition for *Death in Venice*, *Felix Krull* would not have been so extraordinary as it is in its present form: one can guess that the confidence man would have made some spectacular thefts, lived in lubricious splendor, and finally become arrested and imprisoned. A certain principle of moderation can be seen in the early story: after his loss of virginity he espouses cool sexual discipline, warns the reader that the sexual overuse of one's body exhausts the spirit and diminishes charm

(p. 46). The middle-aged Felix who narrates the story is somewhat exhausted; and perhaps his catastrophe would have been due to overindulgence, loss of discipline.

Yet something in the story dissuaded Mann from continuing it; and something made him wish to resume it. As we have seen, Mann hesitated for decades over the matter of allowing a child prodigy to turn adult; 1911 was clearly too early, and he may have not wished to sully Felix's adolescent beauty with the responsibilities of a haggard adulthood. As for Mann's resumption in late life, that is easily understood, for *Felix Krull* is the perfect vehicle, even in its 1911 form, for a tale about the expansion of identity, the comprehension of space and time into a single inarticulate skull. Felix attempts in the early story to describe an unnamable delight which he intuited since early childhood, tentatively labels "The Great Joy," felt acutely in his embraces with the maid Genovefa, his first mistress; it is not a purely physical rapture, we are told, but something spiritual, infantile, dreamlike (p. 46). It is noteworthy that Felix's chief pleasure in sexuality is not in his own orgasm, but in Genovefa's; and it is this necessity for mutual response that gives a clue into what Mann meant by "The Great Joy." It is the mutual vibration of actor and audience; it is the abolition of structural divisions, the loss of individuality; it is Schopenhauer's passage into revelation.

In the sections of the novel written late in his life, Mann's powers of invention are devoted wholly to the creation of incidents which demonstrate Felix's capacity for self-inclusion, self-extension. Nothing could be more different from the taut plot-form of *Dr. Faustus*; Felix wanders to Frankfurt, to Paris, to Lisbon, idle, vagrant, yet curiously purposive, an amoeba gathering matter into itself. Like Leverkühn he is solitary; he wishes to form no intimacy of friendship with the flunkies and noblemen whom he attracts, the Stankos and Strathbogies; but, unlike Leverkühn, all men love him. What Felix dislikes in the other characters of the novel is their overdefinition, their limitation to a single role; after he evades the draft board by counterfeit epilepsy he imagines to himself how enjoyable a soldier's life would be, with its fancy uniforms and elegant parades, but he has second thoughts:

> For although martial severity, self-discipline, and danger have been the conspicuous characteristics of my strange life, its primary prerequisite and basis has been freedom, a necessity completely irreconcilable with any kind of commitment to a grossly factual situation. Accordingly, if I lived *like* a soldier, it would have been a silly misapprehension to believe that I should therefore live *as* a soldier; yes, if it is permissible to describe and define intellectually

an emotional treasure as noble as freedom, then it may be said that to live like a soldier but not as a soldier, figuratively but not literally, to be allowed in short to live symbolically, spells true freedom. (P. 101)

Felix will not be a soldier, no more than he can really play the violin, really draw, really speak foreign languages: but inspired counterfeiting does not hinder one's identity, unlike real achievement. Felix's roles are entirely flexible, symbolic, literary; a kind of titivation; and the plot of the novel, if such a slender premise can be called a plot, consists in the replacement of all the other characters, with their gross delusions of individuation, with Felix Krull, labile, agile, eager, dressed in another of his endless repertoires of costumes, of identities.

There is no talk in the later portions in the novel of Felix's exhaustibility, his mortality; the figure of the narrator, wearied by prison, becomes less and less in evidence; as Mann grows toward his death Felix becomes increasingly ideal. One of Mann's first acts in his addition to the short story was to remove Felix's heredity: in the story Felix is the true son of his father, an obese and lively fraud who makes undrinkable *Sekt* dressed in pretty bottles; a true Mann father, a father who liquidates his firm; a suicide; but in the later chapters these premonitions of hereditary disaster are swept away in a scene where Felix gazes at the portraits of his ancestors and sees his features in none of them. Goethe by contrast summed up all the traits of his ancestors; here the genetic myth reduces to zero. Felix is at once the end point and provenance of phylogeny, self-created, self-responsible, the rawest egg. Yet if his bodily form is amazingly malleable, Protean, it is only because he is made of the highest, most tractable and transparent flesh, what he calls "finer clay." Here the body is perfected, made spiritual and responsive, a stuff that can be modeled to any shape, with the greatest possible elegance of surface; a marquis and a lapdog are both within the range of its mimicry. Felix in the Lisbon museum sees a diorama depicting various scenes from Neanderthal life; he feels a certain sympathy with the aspirations of the caveman, the crudest clay, toward sun and spirit; and indeed the study of anatomy makes him understand the secret identity of the tapir's foreleg, the seal's flipper, with the arm of a woman. In the later stages of the novel, when Felix notices a beautiful woman's arm, he thinks of its anatomical referents in the lower species; in this manner the thrill of touch extends indefinitely from man to animal, from animal into the inorganic, a seamless vivacity, and Felix can trace inside the labyrinth of his own body the whole progress of form through time, the one inconceivable Will.

The erasing of Felix's ordinary heredity, the supplanting of it by this cosmology, is only one of a number of changes which Mann had to make to increase the plasticity of his hero of 1911. In the main intrigue of the novel, Felix's switching of roles with the Marquis de Venosta, in which the Marquis wishes Felix to discharge his noble responsibility of world travel in return for allowing him to assume Felix's Bohemian and careless life, Felix discovers that to pretend the role of marquis effectively he must banish from his soul all memories of his now invalid past: "It gave me a strange feeling of faulty memory, of emptiness of memory rather" (p. 252). Thus Mann undoes the Felix of 1911, evacuates him of childhood and identity, annuls him for the sake of that condition of divine plenitude which will be his fate. This deliberate blurring of self takes place on the train to Lisbon; and the next moment he feels Professor Kuckuck, the starry-eyed paleontologist who introduces him to "The Great Joy," in the newer, more powerful form in which Mann conceived it in the 1950s: it is what Freud called the oceanic feeling, that infusion of the infinite on the human spine for which orgasm is a weak metaphor. Kuckuck tells him of the indivisibility of man and animal, cell and crystal, stone and star; tells him of atomic theory, of the electrical insubstantiality of the earth and of all created things. All things resolve into froth and dreams, the stuff of the mind's free play; and so Felix begins to understand that he is the player, he is the dreamer. His real childhood, the incidents of his adolescence, are by this point wholly evaporated; and in this manner the process of narration itself becomes lax and open, no longer limited by the usual finitude of event. What happens to Felix is unimportant, is not even valid; here the genre of the novel becomes light-fingered, a nocturne.

There is an emblem for this dreamy consubstantiality of our race that occurs early in the new section of the novel: the Double. Felix, adolescent and impoverished in Frankfurt, looks up from a cold street to an open balcony of a great hotel: he sees a brother and sister, possibly twins, of indistinct or mixed race—like the Portuguese whom he encounters later—"Pretty as pictures" (p. 76), and indeed behaving as if their existence were more pictorial than actual, for they wear light, rich evening dress despite the snow and the cold, only pretend to shiver, as if caught forever in some operetta in which all is judged by the grace of gesture; they withdraw, and Felix never sees them again. But this image profoundly moves him, for he sees in them an emblem "of primal indivisibility and indeterminateness" (p. 77), the egg of Aristophanes in *The Symposium* antecedent to its painful partition into sexual duality. What takes the place of plot in *Felix Krull* is the irresistible formation of pairs, for Felix's self-extension proceeds through systematic confusion, the habitual inability of his eye to see anything in isolation, as an individual. Felix himself is a radical and overwhelming force who destroys the conceptual categories of the other characters; his boss at the Hotel St. James and Albany in Paris, M. Stürzli, is embarrassed by his nascent homosexual longing for Felix; indeed Felix is sufficiently Protean that he answers to the unique sexual ideal of every character, enjoys this replication of himself in the countless mirrors of everyone who beholds him. Sexual desire thus becomes an ideal metaphor for the Will, for nature is sexually One: men desire men, women desire men, men desire women, men desire their mothers—as the sophisticated Diane Houpflé points out, claiming that all love is perverse (p. 172); there is even an anecdote about a Great Dane's unfortunate desire for a lapdog. Each created being is spurred on by the uniform itch; and so the novel evolves into an orgy of relatedness. Felix and the Marquis de Venosta switch identities; now the real marquis has a mistress called Zaza, and the first girl Felix meets in his disguise is called Zouzou. They are opposites, Zaza and Zouzou, the former a *soubrette* and flirt, the latter the chaste daughter of Kuckuck, the Lisbon scientist; but the nonsense-identity of their names, along with an aptitude for the role of mistress, makes them into a pair, makes them related, finally indistinguishable. Felix cannot keep their names straight; he discovers that the marquis' bad, blurred drawing of Zaza can easily be adapted, with the addition of a few curls, into a representation of Zouzou. Of such superficiality, we may assume, are the differences between one individual and another. But if this is not sufficiently confusing, there is the case of Dona Maria, Zouzou's mother, whose relationship to her daughter is also that of double-but-dissimilar; Felix's sexual desire is fastened firmly on both of them, but reciprocally, sometimes preferring the daughter's prettiness, other times the mother's austere beauty; but what is unusual is that he treats them as if they were one person, for he stares at the mother while complimenting the daughter, and vice versa. At the end of the novel such doubles are proliferating at amazing speed; a bullfighter enters the text for a moment, and it seems that in the unwritten sequel to the novel he will form some sort of pair-relation with Felix; the characters, however, have almost become too interconnected to permit further narrative, too unstable, too likely to change shape, and it is not surprising that this mad novel must stop prematurely, with Felix swept away in a whirlwind of Dona Maria's embrace, the ocean, the incoherent cries of the mind's dissolution, the dissolution of the novel.

I have suggested that the intellectual basis of these convulsions of fantasy is the philosophy of Schopenhauer; and there is a long dialogue between Felix and the pious Zouzou, the substance of which is the clash between Schopenhauer and Christianity. One of the odd corollaries of writing a novel about the Will is that the theme does not permit much obstruction or suspense; and *Felix Krull*, above any other novel of Mann's, is a work in which the protagonist does not meet with much resistance. Such resistance as Felix does meet with is of a single, well-defined nature; his antagonists try to *see through* him. So Health Councillor Düsing, when Felix as a boy creates a real fever in order to avoid school, tries by means of winks and crude suggestion to persuade Felix to admit tacitly that it is all part of the game of truancy—to admit that his deception is in fact a deception, not a higher truth; and Zouzou's tactic for denying Felix's sexual potency is also an examination of Felix's interior, a repudiation of what lies beneath that glittery surface. Her position is that mankind is aboriginally vile: that sexual congress exposes those bodily profundities that should be kept hidden at all times, and involves a loss of self-respect, even a loss of identity, to the point of cannibalism; and she has a little nursery rhyme to describe the condition of the human body:

> However fair and smooth the skin,
> Stench and corruption lie within. (P. 350)

This is the Christian model for the body: each man has a deceptive exterior enclosing his own private filth, a bag of corruption; lust is shameless self-exposure; Zouzou has a vivid sense of how the deep blood beats close to the surface of lips engorged by sexual desire (p. 350). This Christian model is identical to that of Schopenhauer's unenlightened man, fixed in his follies of human privacy and egoism, sealed from his neighbor by the impermeable membrane of his skin. To Zouzou's celibacy Felix opposes, in the most heroic form Mann ever devised, a great vision, Schopenhauer's lamentation turned into a hymn: yes, for the most part each natural being seems separate, recoils from the touch of its neighbor; but there is an ongoing miracle whereby the body's haughty sense of its self-containedness vanishes in a spasm of extensive and selfless sympathy; the skin's boundary is annulled, body touches body with heightening delight, charity so infuses us that we touch the beggar's lice-ridden hair with joy. The superficial is here raised to its highest pretension, for to Felix all the world is one, each being an elegant inflection of a single surface. Here is Mann's highest prayer: that the Will will discipline itself with such buoyancy and conviction that it will voluntarily leave off its raving and turn to gratulation; that the Will will reveal itself at last as a miracle, universal sympathy. This is impersonality at its farthest range, at its most benign. I think that few will doubt that Mann's own aspirations are here expressed in Felix's apocalypse; the unique choice of the narrative form, autobiography, reinforces one's impression of Mann's personal closeness with Felix; and the novel is more than usually replete with references from Mann's life, of which the episode of the call to military service is the most celebrated example. In a diary that Mann kept during the composition of *Dr. Faustus* he notes, in respect to a number of minor acquaintances, "All sheer personalities! I think I am none, I personally will be as little remembered as Proust" (*Story of a Novel*, p. 154). No one would take that as a modest remark; it suggests that his sense of his personal amplitude was equal to that of Leverkühn or Felix Krull. Thomas Mann died two decades ago, and impersonality is a state very credible to the dead; in death Mann has come increasingly to resemble the protagonists of his later novels, even though an author does not manage to survive in his books.

F I V E

Epilogue

The novels of Mann, and Lawrence and Woolf, and Joyce and Proust and Beckett and the rest, are tedious; but their tedium is sacred to us. These novelists devoted their great ingenuity to the solution of certain technical problems without, perhaps, any clear knowledge of the general utility of their work; but they have succeeded in providing us with models of personality of unprecedented amplitude and subtlety. No verbal analogue of personality, even if it reaches to a thousand pages, can claim without presumptuousness to be faithful to any real personality; yet in that endless struggle to frame, analyze, and sublimate personality much that is valuable occurs. I doubt that anyone would confess that the motions of his mind resemble those of a character in any novel; and if I were asked which were a better representation of the actual patterns of human thought, the interior monologues of Jane Austen's Emma or of Joyce's Stephen Dedalus, I would guess the former. But the modern novel, despite its impudent concentration on vast and solitary minds, has bequeathed to us something we may need, the knowledge that other minds exist that have the range of our own. That is, the modern novel, despite its solipsism, its impersonality, has granted to us a society and a community.

From the diary of Virginia Woolf we have good insight into how one of these novelists created character. She looked at a stranger; she made up an episode, a life history, the sole determinants of which were the costume and body and location and putative class of the alien. I take this story as a metaphor for the way in which all of us greet our fellow men. We conceive acquaintance and friend alike as idle or extensive fictions; most of what we believe, even about the simplest incidents in the life of father or lover, is doubtless untrue. What do we say to a friend whose wife has died? We do not tell anecdotes from her life; the charm of her gestures, her eloquence, her beauty, all the particulars of her being are alike unmentionable; we turn to well-known expressions of condolence in a situation in which all parties agree that condolence is impossible. It is the specific that falsifies, not the general; the last thing we wish to do is to introduce our myths of the dead into that warm bereavement, inarticulate life. We know that we conceive others wrongly, so it is no loss in dignity that we conceive others according to the most elaborate fictions we know; and for many of us, those fictions have been influenced by the sophisticated work of Virginia Woolf and Lawrence and Mann.

Without literature we would be sociologists and fools. Our vision of mankind would be limited to a catalog of behavioral traits, and with the coldest eye we would renounce any knowledge of the mind that anatomy could not offer, renounce the kinship between others and ourselves. Whenever we feel that we perceive something profound about a companion, some immensity of conception or emotion, we are only projecting feelings that we feel about ourselves onto him. To the extent that we admire another, we taint him with our own egoism. Through this process the modern novel has evolved into a condition in which it is wholly bound, in every ramification of character, to the central ego of its author; but there is no harm in that. The discovery in others of minds analogous to our own is the means by which human sympathy is advanced; and to that extent one might say that the authors whom we cherish are, in spite of themselves, in spite of their critics, humanitarians. We need to find the overweening ego expressed in words, for novels become formulas by which we extend our imaginations about our acquaintances. My mother's inner meditation may be as rich as Clarissa Dalloway's; the boy chasing a ball on the beach may not be inferior to Stephen Dedalus; you may be capable of the intellectual dalliance of Rupert Birkin, or of me, who, to your perception, am equally fictitious. Therefore the novel of the twentieth century, for all its asperities and abominations, can be the vehicle of what we least suspected, what prose can scarcely tell, what might lie all around us if mutual imagination but guessed, the eye embraced, human love.

Works Cited

Auden, W. H. *The Dyer's Hand*. New York: Random House, 1962.

Bell, Quentin. *Virginia Woolf: A Biography*. New York: Harcourt Brace Jovanovich, 1972.

Eliot, T. S. *Selected Essays*. New York: Harcourt Brace and World, 1960.

Forster, E. M. *Two Cheers for Democracy*. New York: Harvest, 1951.

Gide, André. *Les caves du Vatican*. Editions Gallimard. 1922.

LAWRENCE, D. H.

Aaron's Rod. New York: Viking Compass, 1961.

Apocalypse. New York: Viking Compass, 1960.

Collected Letters of D. H. Lawrence. 2 vols. New York: Viking Press, 1962.

Complete Poems of D. H. Lawrence. New York: Viking Compass, 1971.

Complete Short Stories of D. H. Lawrence. 3 vols. New York: Viking Compass, 1961.

Kangaroo. New York: Viking Compass, 1960.

Lady Chatterley's Lover. New York: Evergreen Black Cat/Grove Press, 1962.

The Lost Girl. New York: Viking Compass, 1968.

Phoenix. New York: Viking Press, 1968.

Phoenix II. New York: Viking Press, 1970.

The Plumed Serpent. New York: Vintage, 1954.

Psychoanalysis and the Unconscious & Fantasia of the Unconscious. New York: Viking Compass, 1960.

The Rainbow. New York: Viking Compass, 1961.

St. Mawr & The Man Who Died. New York: Vintage, 1953.

Sons and Lovers. New York: Viking Compass, 1958.

The Trespasser. Harmondsworth, England: Penguin Books, 1960.

The Virgin and the Gipsy. New York: Bantam Books, 1968.

The White Peacock. Harmondsworth, England: Penguin Books, 1950.

Women in Love. New York: Modern Library, 1950.

Mann, Thomas

Buddenbrooks. Harmondsworth, England: Penguin Books, 1957.
Confessions of Felix Krull, Confidence Man. New York: Vintage, 1969.
Death in Venice. Translated by Kenneth Burke. New York: Modern Library
   College Edition, 1970.
Dr. Faustus. New York: Modern Library, 1966.
Essays of Three Decades. New York: Alfred A. Knopf, 1948.
The Holy Sinner. Harmondsworth, England: Penguin Books, 1961.
Joseph and his Brothers. London: Secker & Warburg, 1970.
Last Essays. New York: Alfred A. Knopf, 1966.
The Letters of Thomas Mann. 2 vols. London: Secker & Warburg, 1970.
Lotte in Weimar. Harmondsworth, England: Penguin Books, 1968.
The Magic Mountain. New York: Modern Library College Edition, 1955.
Royal Highness. New York: Alfred A. Knopf, 1965.
A Sketch of my Life. New York: Alfred A. Knopf, 1960.
Stories of a Lifetime. 2 vols. London: Secker & Warburg, 1961.
The Story of a Novel. New York: Alfred A. Knopf, 1961.

Moore, G. E. *Principia Ethica*. Cambridge: Cambridge University Press,
   1959.
Wilde, Oscar. *The Artist as Critic*. Edited by Richard Ellmann. New York:
   Vintage, 1970.

Woolf, Virginia

Between the Acts. New York: Harvest, 1969.
Collected Essays. 4 vols. New York: Harcourt Brace and World, 1967.
Flush. New York: Harbrace Paperback, 1961.
A Haunted House and Other Short Stories. New York: Harvest, 1949.
Jacob's Room & The Waves. New York; Harvest, 1950, 1959.
Mrs. Dalloway. New York: Harvest, 1953.
Night and Day. New York: Harvest, 1948.
Orlando. New York: Harvest, 1956.
To the Lighthouse. New York: Harvest, 1955.
The Voyage Out. New York: Harvest, 1948.
A Writer's Diary. New York: Harcourt Brace, 1954.
The Years. New York: Harvest, 1965.

Yeats, W. B. *Explorations*. New York: Macmillan Publishing Co., 1962.

Index